# GLOBAL APPETITES

*Global Appetites* explores how industrial agriculture and countercultural food movements shape ideas of U.S. hegemony in the century since the First World War. Allison Carruth's study centers on the "literature of food" – a body of work that comprises literary realism, late modernism, and magical realism along with culinary writing, food memoir, and advertising. Through analysis of texts ranging from Willa Cather's novel *O Pioneers!* (1913) to Novella Carpenter's nonfiction work *Farm City* (2009), Carruth argues for the centrality of what she terms American food power to the history of globalization and examines its ramifications for regional cultures and ecosystems. Lively and accessible, this interdisciplinary study will appeal to scholars of American literature and culture as well as those working in the fields of food studies, agriculture history, science and technology studies, and the environmental humanities.

ALLISON CARRUTH is Assistant Professor of English at the University of California, Los Angeles, where she is affiliated with the Center for the Study of Women, Institute for Society and Genetics, and Institute of the Environment and Sustainability. Her research focuses on contemporary American literature and new media, the environmental humanities, food studies, and science and technology studies. She received her PhD from Stanford University.

# GLOBAL APPETITES

*American Power and the Literature of Food*

ALLISON CARRUTH

*University of California, Los Angeles*

CAMBRIDGE UNIVERSITY PRESS
Cambridge, New York, Melbourne, Madrid, Cape Town,
Singapore, São Paulo, Delhi, Mexico City

Cambridge University Press
32 Avenue of the Americas, New York, NY 10013-2473, USA

www.cambridge.org
Information on this title: www.cambridge.org/9781107032828

© Allison Carruth 2013

This publication is in copyright. Subject to statutory exception
and to the provisions of relevant collective licensing agreements,
no reproduction of any part may take place without the written
permission of Cambridge University Press.

First published 2013

Printed in the United States of America

*A catalog record for this publication is available from the British Library.*

*Library of Congress Cataloging in Publication Data*
Carruth, Allison.
Global appetites : American power and the literature of food / Allison Carruth,
University of California, Los Angeles.
    pages  cm
Includes bibliographical references and index.
ISBN 978-1-107-03282-8
1. Agriculture in literature.   2. Food in literature.
3. American literature – 20th century – History and criticism.
4. American literature – Women authors – History and criticism.
5. Cather, Willa, 1873–1947 – Criticism and interpretation.   6. Morrison, Toni. Tar baby.
7. Ozeki, Ruth L. – Criticism and interpretation.   8. Food writing – United States.
9. Agricultural industries – United States.   10. Globalization.   I. Title.
        PS228.A52C37   2013
        810.9$'$3564–dc23          2012031891

ISBN 978-1-107-03282-8 Hardback

Cambridge University Press has no responsibility for the persistence or
accuracy of URLs for external or third-party Internet Web sites referred to
in this publication and does not guarantee that any content on such
Web sites is, or will remain, accurate or appropriate.

*To Barron Bixler*

*For the words in this book and the many meals that inspired them*

# Contents

| | | |
|---|---|---|
| *List of Figures* | | *page* viii |
| *Acknowledgments* | | xi |
| 1 | Introduction: The Power of Food | 1 |
| 2 | Rural Modernity: Willa Cather and the Rise of Agribusiness | 19 |
| 3 | "Luxury Feeding" and War Rations: Food Writing at Midcentury | 49 |
| 4 | Supermarkets and Exotic Foods: Toni Morrison's "Chocolate Eater" | 90 |
| 5 | Postindustrial Pastoral: Ruth Ozeki and the New Muckrakers | 117 |
| 6 | The Locavore Memoir: Food Writing in the Age of Information | 154 |
| *Notes* | | 169 |
| *Bibliography* | | 213 |
| *Index* | | 235 |

# List of Figures

1  "Still Life #30." 1963. Museum of Modern Art, Counter Space: Design and the Modern Kitchen Exhibition. © Estate of Tom Wesselmann / Licensed by VAGA, New York. Reprinted with the permission of VAGA and Art Resource. *page* 3
2  "Electrified Farm." 1939–1940. New York World's Fair Exhibition. Courtesy of the New York Public Library, Manuscript and Archives Division. 3
3  "Feed Mill, California 2008." © Barron Bixler. Reprinted with the permission of the artist. 13
4  "Your Country Calls: Enlist – Plow – Buy Bonds." Circa 1917–1918. World War I recruitment poster created by Lloyd Meyers and published by Hamilton Press. Reprinted with the permission of the World War Posters Collection (Mss 36), Literary Manuscripts Collection, University of Minnesota Libraries, Minneapolis. 36
5  "Save Waste Fats for Explosives." 1943. World War II food rationing poster created by Henry Koerner and the Office of War Information and published by the U.S. Government Printing Office. Courtesy of the Hennepin County Library, Kittelson World War II Collection. 57
6  "Rationing Means a Fair Share for All of Us." 1943. World War II food rationing poster created by the Office of Price Administration and published by the U.S. Government Printing Office. Courtesy of the Hennepin County Library, Kittelson World War II Collection. 63
7  Photograph of Hershey Ration D Bar and Tropical Chocolate Bar. Circa 1942–1944. Courtesy of the Hershey Community Archives, Hershey, PA. 74

| | | |
|---|---|---|
| 8 | "Nestlé's Swiss Milk – Richest in Cream." Théophile Alexandre Steinlen, 1894. Reprinted with the permission of the Mary Evans Picture Library. | 110 |
| 9 | "Battery Cage." © 1990 Sue Coe. Reprinted with the permission of Galerie St. Etienne, New York. | 125 |
| 10 | "Milking Parlor, California 2007." © Barron Bixler. Reprinted with the permission of the artist. | 130 |
| 11 | "Feed Lot." © 1991 Sue Coe. Reprinted with the permission of Galerie St. Etienne, New York. | 133 |
| 12 | "Veal Skinner." © 1991 Sue Coe. Reprinted with the permission of Galerie St. Etienne, New York. | 134 |

# *Acknowledgments*

I cannot imagine *Global Appetites* without Barron Bixler, who saw a scholar in me a decade ago and has, ever since, supported my work and enriched my life. My gratitude to him runs deep. In addition to the time he devoted to reading drafts and weighing in on ideas, his photographs of the San Joaquin Valley and Northeast Brazil transformed how I see the massive interventions of industrial agriculture as well as more intimate acts of farming, fishing, and breaking bread. Those images inspire the pages that follow. *To you, B, I dedicate this book with love.*

I have benefited over the years from extraordinary mentors and colleagues. I owe my greatest debt to Ramón Saldívar, who, as my dissertation director, guided the development of this project at every turn. My admiration of him as a scholar, teacher, and leader is difficult to convey. Other faculty members at Stanford were generous with their time and ideas. I thank Gavin Jones and Andrea Lunsford for pushing me to conceptualize the power of food for literary studies, Ursula Heise for blazing a trail in the environmental humanities, and Sianne Ngai for helping me to think in new ways about the pastoral. In 2012, I was fortunate to join the faculty at UCLA, where I brought this project to a close. I am grateful to Ali Behdad, Elizabeth DeLoughrey, Carrie Hyde, Rachel Lee, Marissa López, Kathleen McHugh, Michael North, Felicity Nussbaum, Mark Seltzer, and Robert Watson for their warm welcome and intellectual camaraderie. I thank the UCLA English Department and Office of Faculty Diversity and Development for providing generous research funds, and I thank my research assistant Brendan O'Kelly and indexer Helene Ferranti for their careful work while the book was in production.

A year in residence at UC Santa Barbara as the Arnhold Postdoctoral Fellow provided the initial opportunity to develop the book manuscript while working with a marvelous group of faculty that included David Cleveland, Bishnupriya Ghosh, Stephanie LeMenager, Alan Liu, Rita Raley, Russell Samolsky, Daniela Soleri, and William Warner. Colleagues and graduate students at the University of Oregon helped me to hone the book's argument. Thanks especially to Lara Bovilsky, Alan Dickman, Margaret Hallock, Kate Mondloch, Paul Peppis, Carol Stabile, Courtney Thorsson, David Vázquez, Molly Westling, and Harry Wonham. I would also like to thank Darra Goldstein for her judicious responses to the manuscript and for her friendship. The opportunity to serve as the Associate Director of the Program in Science, Technology, and Society at Stanford from 2011–12 was fortuitous. I owe a great deal to Fred Turner and Colleen McCallion for making the year productive and inspiring.

At Cambridge University Press, I am indebted to Ray Ryan, Louis Gulino, Marielle Poss, and Cherline Daniel as well as to my anonymous readers, who all improved the book in incalculable ways. The book further benefited from feedback at the American Comparative Literature Association, Modernist Studies Association, Modern Language Association, and Willa Cather International Seminar as well as from a dissertation fellowship made possible by the Mellon Foundation. I also acknowledge the University of Oregon for a Summer Research Award and Junior Professorship Development Grant, the Wayne Morse Center for Law and Politics for a Resident Scholar award, and the UCLA Friends of English for generous funding to support image permissions. Thank you to Martin Schapiro for his work on the cover design, which originally came from Greenpeace and an anonymous designer. I thank the following individuals and organizations for permission to reprint images: Sue Coe and Galerie St. Etienne, the Estate of Tom Wesselmann, Hennepin County Library, Hershey Community Archives, the Mary Evans Picture Library, the New York Public Library, University of Minnesota Libraries, and, once more, Barron Bixler.

The years spent in graduate school and as a new professor were made more joyful thanks to family and friends. For the countless hours spent sharing meals while talking about our work, I thank Yanoula Athanassakis, Denise Boulangé, Benedetta Faedi, Harris Feinsod, Michael Hoyer, Ruth Kaplan, and Ju Yon Kim. I am profoundly appreciative of Claire Bowen, Laura Crescimano, Heather Houser, and Amy Tigner for being there through thick and thin in addition to being cherished collaborators. To all of the Carruths, Bixlers, Evans, Emrys, Hilkers, and Skeens in my life, I am grateful to each of you for making my sense of family big-hearted indeed. To Penney Carruth and Pat and Harold Hilker, I thank you for loving me as your own and for providing oases in which to write. And to my granny Polly and, in memoriam, my grandparents, I express my gratitude for teaching me the art of storytelling. I can only begin to acknowledge all my mother, Patricia Carruth, and my father, Dennis Carruth, have done for me. They have buoyed me through times of self-doubt, celebrated every milestone along the way, and taught me to make work a labor of love. *For this, and so much more, I thank you.*

Finally, I offer thanks to the farmers and farmworkers who bring food to San Francisco, Santa Barbara, Eugene, and Los Angeles as well as to the many chefs around the world who confer to food both a poetry and a politics.

CHAPTER 1

# Introduction: The Power of Food

> It is to serve the farmers of this great open country that teeming cities have arisen, great stretches of navigation have been opened, a mighty network of railways has been constructed, a fast increasing mileage of highways has been laid out, and modern inventions have stretched their lines of communication among all the various communities and into nearly every home. Agriculture holds a position in this country that it was never before able to secure anywhere else on earth.... [I]n America, the farm has long since ceased to be associated with a mode of life that could be called rustic. It has become a great industrial enterprise.
> Calvin Coolidge, Address to Farm Bureau Federation (1925)[1]

> [T]oday in cosmopolitan Dublin, you can choose to eat an Indian curry, a Mexican burrito, or an Irish breakfast. With an increasingly global food trade a single meal can originate from ten locations across the planet.... In eagerness to minimize the distance our food travels, and connect flavours to places, we may risk over-simplifying the complex systems that comprise our food systems. But, whether one grows local or eats global, food will always be inextricably linked to place; and places are in constant flux.
> Center for Genomic Gastronomy,
> *Edible: The Taste of Things to Come* (2012)[2]

In 1925, Calvin Coolidge looked out on an audience of farmers and policy-makers and effectively broke with the agrarian rhetoric of his predecessors. If Thomas Jefferson imagined the United States to be a nation of yeoman farmers, Coolidge called 150 years later for a rural workforce savvy in "management," "intricate machinery," and "marketing."[3] Even as the president announced the arrival of industrial agriculture, his rhetoric anticipated a postindustrial era in which farming would be just one among many "enterprises" constituting the human food chain – what the *Harvard Business Review* would call in 1956 "agribusiness."[4] The speech captures a new dimension of the American national imaginary, I contend, according to which food and agriculture propel, rather than offer a retreat, from modernity. A concept of *the food system* thus takes hold in American culture, calling into question what is currently an intellectual separation of agricultural history from food studies.[5] At World's Fairs that took place from the 1930s through the 1960s, the systemic connections between the nation's farms and kitchens were evident in exhibits about the future of food, which were also very much about the U.S. appetite for international power. These futuristic displays presented a cornucopian nation whose agricultural surpluses and scientific innovations combined to generate a global utopia of edible goods. The Fairs gave symbolic expression to a material reality: the nation's agricultural economy, in Warren Belasco's words, "had reached its geographical limits," and the power Coolidge correlated in 1925 to food production would now require not (or at least not only) territorial expansion but new technologies and new markets.[6]

At the same time, a neo-Malthusian streak haunted the American vision of a global food frontier. Plans for futuristic farms and kitchens foresaw a world in which the reduction of farmland and the growth of the human population would make technological fixes vital to manufacturing experiences of culinary abundance out of a handful of staple crops. In the 1960s, the decade in which the Fairs came to an end, American Pop Art painter Tom Wesselmann exposed the rhetoric of American abundance as a fallacy in his "Still Life #30," a garish painting of a kitchen teeming with food (Figure 1). The apparent cornucopia in the still life is, in fact, a monoculture of consumer brands, while the repetition of packaged meat, bland starches, and canned goods undercuts the colorful kitchen scene and the verdant townscape beyond its open window. Notwithstanding a smattering of vegetables and a bright red apple (whose singularity suggests the post-Edenic character of the Cold War food supply), "Still Life #30" offers a mosaic of culinary monotony. The "Electrified Farm," which appeared at the 1939 New York World's Fair, suggests that the conceptual origins of Wesselmann's homogenous yet overflowing kitchen lie in earlier designs for standardized and productive farms (Figure 2).[7] Today, we may not find the push-button farms that engineers forecasted in the thirties, but we can find farmers who spend their time, as novelist Ruth Ozeki pictures a character in *All Over Creation* (2003), "at a computer, sweating at it, trying to input data and generate readouts and maps."[8] So, too, can we witness a global market for biofuels that require more energy to produce and distribute than the energy they provide.[9] In line with Coolidge's claim that the "network" of railroads, highways, and communication lines served above all to support the industrialization of food production, future-oriented designs like the "Electrified Farm" predicted a time when power would be all too literal as an organizing concept for the modern food system.

## Introduction: The Power of Food

1 "Still Life #30." 1963. Museum of Modern Art, Counter Space: Design and the Modern Kitchen Exhibition. © Estate of Tom Wesselmann / Licensed by VAGA, New York. Reprinted with the permission of VAGA and Art Resource.

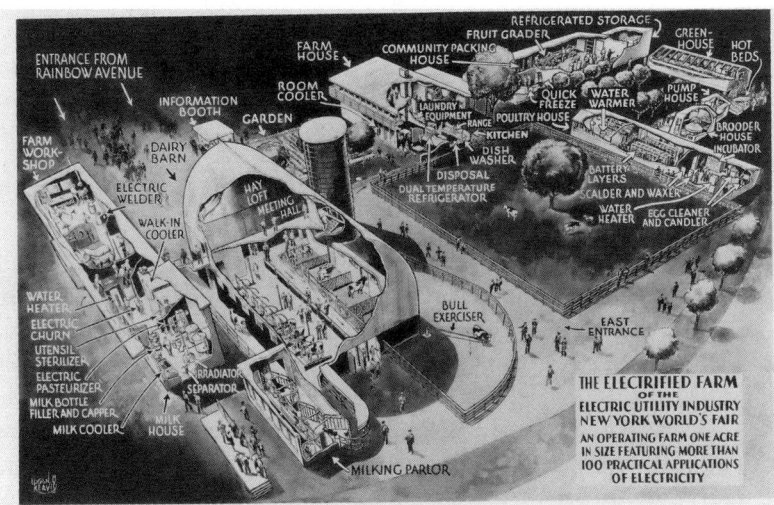

2 "Electrified Farm." 1939–1940. New York World's Fair Exhibition. Courtesy of the New York Public Library, Manuscript and Archives Division.

Since the moment when Coolidge addressed the Farm Bureau, the political and economic power that has accrued to those who control the world food supply has turned out to be an indicator of global power writ large, and the hegemony of the United States has had a great deal to do with food ever since. Today, what I term *U.S. food power* is both global in scope and subject to manifold forms of opposition: it drives the international adoption of genetically modified seeds (GMOs), but fuels anti-GMO movements and seed-saver organizations; it inspires the post-9/11 revival of "victory gardens" as instruments of national food security, but spurs community supported agriculture (CSA) as a means to make food systems ecologically and socially sustainable; and it enables the global reach of American food brands, but energizes alternative dietary practices. The United States is, moreover, not the world's sole food power. Nearly a century since Coolidge delivered his speech, the "great industrial enterprise" has taken root in China, Brazil, Mexico, Australia, India, France, and elsewhere, while transnational social movements have mobilized to contest that enterprise. Put simply, food has become a political mobilizer and cultural buzzword. In the United States, the number of protests, activist groups, conferences, books, films, art installations, and websites devoted to food and food politics grows by the year. This popular discourse attests that food both participates in "complex systems," from regional watersheds to international markets, and circulates in multivalent cultural forms, from traditional genres like almanacs and cookbooks to new media like blogs and bioart experiments. To invoke Roland Barthes, the "polysemia" of food in contemporary society – as in the multiple social and, I would hasten to add, ecological structures it shapes – is a constitutive feature of modernity.[10]

The reasons for the proliferation of food movements and food media during the last decade are numerous. Perhaps most importantly, environmental groups have publicized scientific findings that industrial agriculture is a major contributor to climate change at the same time that volatility in rice, wheat, and corn prices have highlighted a troubling paradox of the modern food system: despite tremendous gains in the productivity of agriculture, nearly one billion people are hungry.[11] The 2012 exhibition *Edible: A Taste of Things to Come* illustrates another paradox of the modern food system, one that inspires this book: the richness of cultural responses to the system's perceived failings. Organized by the playful art collective known as the Center for Genomic Gastronomy, the exhibition assembled artists, activists, cooks, scientists, and hobbyists to imagine possible futures of food. With installations like "Disaster Pharming" and "Vegan Ortolan," the exhibition showcased the outer reaches of molecular gastronomy and agricultural genetics alongside more familiar "countercuisines"[12] such as vegetarianism and raw food. In positing these futures, the exhibition was highly critical of the status quo. The *Edible* catalog concludes with two infographics: one showing disinvestments in small farmers and increases in obesity rates and another charting the decline of agricultural diversity under the industrialized food regime (in which wheat, rice, milk, potatoes, sugar, and corn have displaced the thousands of edible plants long cultivated around the world).[13] Paired with this lament about the present, however, is a celebration of the culinary cosmopolitanism that the present affords. De-centering the United States, and indeed the nation state, as the locus of food power, the *Edible* curators suggest that the global circulation of foodstuffs and food cultures allows the individual eater to act as a world citizen.

Although *Global Appetites* makes the case for the cultural significance of the modern food system and the power of a nation like the United States within it, U.S. food power in the period since the First World War certainly has historical precedents. Coolidge acknowledged in 1925 that the farm had "*long* . . . ceased to be associated with a mode of life that could be called rustic." Broadening his point, we can identify in European empires and in the colonial United States the twin impulses to expand the geographic scale of food distribution and transform the technological apparatus of agriculture. We also can trace back to the ancient world the very forms of cosmopolitan consumption that the *Edible* exhibition identifies as uniquely modern and urban. Food historian Massimo Montanari observes that the "social expansion of globalization" should not lead us to "forget its ancient origins as a cultural model."[14] At the same time, Montanari contrasts the "infinite local variations" that once defined international cuisines with the current "tendency toward uniformity of consumer goods" that multinational corporations have effectively promoted.[15] It is my contention that literature provides a powerful medium through which to chart both the historical continuities and cultural ruptures that inform late modern appetites for world cuisines and national aspirations for global food power.

Moving from the First World War to the post-9/11 era, *Global Appetites* argues for the centrality of food to accounts of globalization and U.S. hegemony that pervade the literature of this period. Across genres, literature is a vehicle attuned to the modern food system due to the capacity of imaginative texts to shuttle between social and interpersonal registers and between symbolic and embodied expressions of power. Just as importantly, literature has a facility with shifting from macroscopic to intimate scales of representation that can provide an incisive lens on the interactions between local places and global markets that are so central to how communities and corporations produce, exchange, and make use of food in the modern period. While wide-ranging in its primary materials, the book zeroes in on one question: What forms does the writing of food take in the age of American agribusiness? This question proves pertinent to a wide array of texts, from cookbooks that challenge the products and ideologies of fast food to novels that depict the modernity of rural communities. The literature of food that this book maps includes not just culinary writing and agrarian narrative, but also experimental poetry, postmodern fiction, government propaganda, advertising, memoirs, and manifestos. This body of literature takes shape after the First World War, when industrial agriculture really took off in the United States, and gains momentum during the Cold War, a period in which U.S. corporations began to market food brands and packaged foods internationally. Engaging with these historical shifts, writers elucidate and at times challenge what Henry Luce called in 1941 "The American Century."[16] For Luce, the exceptional history of the United States underwrites a national imperative to lead the world in the twentieth century toward the arguably competing goals of "free enterprise" and political "freedom and justice."[17] From Willa Cather to Toni Morrison, the writers whom I discuss in the pages that follow articulate this sense of American exceptionalism, yet often through a negative form that defines the United States as the main origin of imperialist and unjust practices attending the globalization of food.

One could argue that the literary history this book traces reaches back at least to the turn of the century, when writers such as Upton Sinclair and Frank Norris begin to investigate the rise of industrial agriculture and the corporate ownership of food infrastructure. Hsuan Hsu reminds American Studies scholars that 1898 is a particularly pivotal year for the history of U.S. power as a moment when the Spanish-American War crystallized the nation's imperial aspirations and actions.[18] Although writers like Sinclair make cameo appearances in *Global Appetites* and although I concur with Hsu's historical argument, I show that it is not until the First World War that a discourse of food power pervades both politics and literature, just as it is then that the methods of industrial agriculture and the products of U.S. food companies pervade the world system.[19] Investigating a set of writers who tackle these historical developments, the book contributes to cultural theories of globalization. Since the 1980s, globalization has come to describe a set of institutions, ideologies, and practices that advance modes of border-crossing connectivity – what sociologist Anthony Giddens terms the "disembedding" of communities from local contexts.[20] While the term *globalization* offers a kind of clarity in connoting free trade, mass media, and consumer culture, scholars have employed it in often sharply divergent analyses. As Ursula K. Heise observes in *Sense of Place, Sense of Planet*, some theorists "see globalization principally as an economic process and as the most recent form of capitalist expansion, whereas others emphasize its political and cultural dimensions, or characterize it as a heterogeneous and uneven process whose various components ... do not unfold according to the same logic and at the same pace," an insightful gloss of a field that includes the work of Arjun Appadurai, Ulrich Beck, Daniel Bell, David Harvey, Fredric Jameson, Saskia Sassen, and others.[21] The now omnipresent concept of globalization in the social sciences and humanities serves, furthermore, to encapsulate a host of social conditions associated with the contemporary period as well as to synthesize the overlapping historical designations of late modernity (Beck), late capitalism (Harvey), postmodernism (Jameson), postindustrialism (Bell), and postcolonialism (Appadurai and Sassen).

Shifting the lens of globalization inquiry to food, I have come to question a central premise within this body of theory: the idea that globalization separates spaces of production and consumption, intensifying the process Karl Marx termed "commodity fetishism" and giving rise to decolonial modes of resistance to late capitalism (or what Harvey labels the "new imperialism").[22] *Global Appetites* addresses decolonial movements that resist economic globalization, such as those calling for food justice and seed sovereignty. So too does the book credit those late capitalist ideologies – from free trade to global branding – that depend on the geographic and psychic distance between people and that profit from our enchantment with things. Indeed, we see commodity fetishism at work nowhere more clearly than with food. Outside a small if growing subculture, most consumers in the contemporary United States shop weekly at supermarkets, where the labor conditions and environmental consequences of the produce are as hidden as those of the brand-name packages overflowing from the center aisles. If global commodities like a can of Coke and the Big Mac exemplify Marx's theory, one's indulgence in a fair-trade-certified bar of chocolate is surely no less an instance of commodity fetishism than the hurried purchase of a fast food meal. However, despite how robustly the modern food system reinforces the idea that globalization is the apotheosis of capitalism, there is a countervailing pattern to apprehend. Globalization, as this book concludes, also provides the imaginative frameworks and material structures for the contemporary movement to re-localize food and reconnect producers and consumers. This contention speaks not only to globalization studies but also to environmental criticism, and especially to recent work that has questioned the centrality of place-based politics and localism in North

American environmentalism.[23] From Cather's novel *O Pioneers!* (1913) to Novella Carpenter's memoir *Farm City* (2009), the primary materials I examine span a century to provide a new account of globalization that emerges out of an environmental sensibility at once local and global in its coordinates. Imaginatively reconnecting farmers and eaters – cities and countrysides – the literature of food shows us that the endgame of globalization may not be the free market that the United States has underwritten for decades and backed with its military. Rather, it opens up the possibility that the outcome of globalization may be a postcapitalist system defined by interchanges between regional communities and the global networks that not only fulfill appetites for exotic foods but also circulate the knowledge and resources that advance alternative food movements, from organic agriculture to urban farming.

This thesis informs my analytical methodology, which expands the parameters of food writing beyond taste, the table, and cuisine. I depart from what has been a tendency in the humanities to treat as separate objects of analysis, on the one hand, culinary practices and gastronomical rhetoric and, on the other, agricultural production and agrarian discourse. This intervention informs the predominance of women writers in the book, which emerges out of my finding that the distinction observed between writing about eating and writing about farming is gendered as much as it is formal. Scholars of the American pastoral and agrarian traditions have emphasized male writers, from Frank Norris to Wendell Berry, particularly when their interest is in how rural literature treats the sweeping forces of industrialization and U.S. expansionism. Although Cather is among the exceptions to this pattern, in focusing on her importance to American regionalism, critics tend to diminish her attention to matters national and global in scope. With respect to culinary literature, critics have defined that rhetorical mode primarily around the spaces of the kitchen and the table, thus bracketing it from the wider food system. Rethinking the divide between agriculture and cuisine in literary and cultural studies, I examine a group of women writers whose texts mix formal modes to depict the entanglements of growing, procuring, and consuming food and the interdependencies of food culture and agriculture under globalization.

Food studies scholars such as Warren Belasco, Amy Bentley, Denise Gigante, Harvey Levenstein, and Doris Witt have shown just how significant dietary habits and culinary regimes are to cultural histories of race, class, and gender.[24] This scholarship revitalizes structuralist theories of cuisine that

Barthes, Mary Douglas, and Claude Lévi-Strauss formulated in the sixties, while also asserting the value of historicist approaches to the study of food.[25] That early cohort of structuralist thinkers argued for the social significance of eating by defining food as a system of communication with the capacity to create meaning beyond its "material reality."[26] In turn, their semiotic analyses provided the intellectual foundation for foodways[27] to become a subject first in anthropology and cultural geography and, more recently, in the humanities. As Jennifer Fleissner notes, the turn to food in the humanities has focused since the late nineties on reexamining an established philosophical distinction between "aesthetic and gustatory taste," a distinction Barthes called into question in his seminal comparison of French and American cuisines.[28] At the same time, the work of Terry Gifford, Leo Marx, Raymond Williams, and others has made rural culture and agricultural industry important subjects for literary history.[29] These scholars demonstrate how multivalent the pastoral tradition is by comparing ideas of rural landscapes that draw on idyllic poetry to realist narratives of farm life that activate the georgic and almanac traditions. The arc and argument of this book are indebted to both of these trajectories within literary and cultural studies. *Global Appetites* departs from prior scholarship, however, in showing that the history of modernity centers in no small measure on *the interactions* between places of food production and experiences of food consumption. The book thus recontextualizes Berry's assertion in "The Pleasures of Eating" that "eating is an agricultural act" by intervening in the localism that his assertion has inspired in sustainable agriculture and related environmental movements.[30] In the period that *Global Appetites* covers, the term *food* signifies a chain of activities that travels all the way from planting a seed to relishing a square of chocolate and from farms near and far to one's evening meal.

In the twentieth and twenty-first centuries, the literature of food breaks from two genres that map onto the scholarly gap I am identifying between studies of the culinary and studies of the agricultural: namely, gastronomical primers focusing on taste and fine dining and pastoral narratives about the relative simplicity of rural life. Although both genres remain active, as we will see, new cultural templates emerge alongside them to articulate how the social structures and experiential realities of food most change with the rise of factory farms and branded foods. My aim is to define these templates and situate them within the social, technological, and environmental histories of food in the context of agribusiness and in the related context of globalization. Chapter 2 elaborates on this keyword of agribusiness through a reconsideration of Cather's Nebraska novels *O Pioneers!*, *My Ántonia* (1918), and *One of Ours* (1922). Central to these novels is a story of rural modernity: a sense of agrarian communities as new sites for industrial infrastructure and consumer culture that Coolidge lauded in 1925. Although her fiction conveys ambivalence about the modernity of rural life, Cather disturbs the myth of the United States as a nation of small-holding pioneers by chronicling the importance of modern farms and farmhouses to the nation's expansionism in the first decades of the twentieth century. The "great industrial enterprise" of food became even more interwoven with U.S. global power during the Second World War, as evident in propaganda that made the productivity of farms and efficiency of kitchens vital to the Allied war effort and to U.S. economic growth. By 1945, the United States had become the world's largest food exporter.[31] Challenging the imperialist character of wartime and postwar food rhetoric, writers on both sides of the Atlantic lay bare what they saw as a growing rather than diminishing stratification of the world's edible resources. These mid-century writers politicize modernism by juxtaposing rhetorical assertions of American abundance to lived experiences of hunger within and outside the United States. Chapter 3 develops this argument through discussions of the experimental lyrics of Lorine Niedecker, the unconventional culinary writings of M. F. K. Fisher and Elizabeth David, and the absurdist theater of Samuel Beckett (an arguable outlier in this group of writers, but one who makes poignantly visible not only mid-century famine, through the existential sparseness of his stage and the meager rations of his tramps Vladimir and Estragon, but also the power of those – like Pozzo and Godot – who control agricultural land).

The second half of the book turns to contemporary novelists and journalists whose accounts of globalization in the late twentieth and early twenty-first centuries revolve around agricultural corporations and cosmopolitan consumers as well as countercultural food practices that aspire to disrupt American agribusiness. Chapter 4 focuses on Morrison's 1981 novel *Tar Baby*, which is set on a fictionalized Caribbean island that Philadelphia candy executive Valerian Street develops into an enclave of vacation estates. A novel that speaks to the environmental justice movement, *Tar Baby* links bodily desires for exotic foods – chocolate and other delicacies – to the historical forces that give rise to the supermarket and its promise of plenty. Extending the mid-century dialectic of "luxury feeding"[32] and physical hunger, the novel offers a searing critique of free trade that moves from the hemispheric impact of U.S. food companies on the agriculture of island states to everyday acts of food indulgence and food resistance. The chapter has a distinct position in the arc of *Global Appetites*, as it breaks from the focus on the interconnections of world war and American agribusiness that centrally informs the first half of the book and that returns in Chapter 5. The role of *Tar Baby* in the book is to move us geographically beyond the United States to refract through a hemispheric lens the image of the world food system as a new frontier for U.S. farmers, corporations, and consumers. In this sense, the chapter builds out my transnational framework for U.S. food power while deepening the book's historical arc. Published during the period when neoliberal ideologies of free trade were coming to the foreground of U.S. foreign policy, Morrison's novel de-centers the United States not just by homing in on the Caribbean but also by showing that the spectral origins of U.S. food power lie in colonial histories of empire, botanical prospecting, and slavery.

Turning from chocolate to meat and from the Caribbean to the Pacific Rim, Chapter 5 puts Ozeki's satirical novels *My Year of Meats* (1998) and *All Over Creation* in the context of recent muckraking exposés of the American factory farm. Although the meat industry garnered scant attention in the decades after Upton Sinclair published *The Jungle* (1906), this inattention turned to alarm at century's end as environmental groups publicized the brutal working conditions and animal abuses of confined feedlots along with their ecological impacts as a major contributor (via methane pollution) to climate change. The chapter concentrates on *My Year of Meats*, which critics have read as a feminist narrative in which cosmopolitan bonds among women provide an antidote to late capitalism. While critics have focused on parsing Ozeki's political allegiances to third-wave feminism and to slow food, I reframe the analysis of her novels around their formal strategies of pastiche and satire. Through these formal methods, Ozeki illuminates contemporary conflicts between postindustrial agriculture and localist food movements. Similar to *Tar Baby*, *My Year of Meats* extends the geography of the industrialized food system and its postindustrial developments beyond the transatlantic horizons of Chapters 2 and 3. Her narrative of the U.S.-Japan meat trade, in particular, is a story that takes the reader back to the postwar occupation of Japan to satirize the rhetoric of an American meat-and-grain diet, which presented that diet as an engine of both bodily and national power during the Cold War.

As for the book's principles of selection, two additional points merit explanation. First, I exclude two writers whom readers may expect to encounter: John Steinbeck and Jane Smiley. Although these quintessential novelists of American farm work and rural culture address the industrialization of agriculture, neither Steinbeck in the first half of the twentieth century nor Smiley in the contemporary period takes up the dialectic of farming and eating or the global horizons of the U.S. food system – the twin concerns that animate *Global Appetites*. Even though I have chosen not to give these writers prominence, the book does offer a launching point for a reexamination of American regionalism. Second, while my focus is on U.S. literature, each chapter develops a transnational context for the topic at hand. This approach follows from my claim that the literature of food coheres in the twentieth and twenty-first centuries around conflicts as well as synergies among the local, the national, and the global. Chapter 4 thus situates an analysis of the cosmopolitan food tastes and neocolonial food politics that inflect *Tar Baby* in relationship to Columbus's *Voyages*, on the one hand, and Édouard Glissant's postcolonial writings, on the other. That said, Chapter 3 is the only place where I treat at length writers from outside the United States; there, discussions of Beckett and David show how a creeping U.S. hegemony structures mid-century representations of food power on either side of the Atlantic.[33]

The idea for this book originated with my observation that pastoral tropes have come to structure much of the contemporary discourse surrounding American agribusiness. The persistence of pastoral sensibilities in the information age extends out from the marketing campaigns of companies such as Foster Farms, Chipotle, and Horizon organic milk to, on the one hand, apologies for GMOs and, on the other, polemics for farmers' markets and whole foods. This pastoral turn has a specific flavor, however. Although in some instances contemporary food rhetoric features idyllic images of shepherds and meadows, more often it reaches back to a classical georgic tradition that sees food as melding the natural, the cultural, and the technological. This georgic streak today pops up in cultural forms as divergent as molecular gastronomy cuisine, avant-garde bioart, and the agribusiness exposés of writers such as Jonathan Safran Foer and Eric Schlosser.[34]

In contrast to this recent renaissance of georgic notions of food, the first half of "The American Century" tended to the modernist veneration of industrialized agriculture that we see in Coolidge's 1925 speech. This vision of an engineered food system severed, thru technical fixes, from the unpredictability of natural ecosystems and the diversity of culinary traditions redoubled during the Cold War. In 1968, USAID Administrator William Gaud coined the now notorious moniker of the Green Revolution, a term that categorized the multiple industries constituting agribusiness – from seed companies and pesticide manufacturers to food science labs and packaged food makers – as participants in a humanitarian project to solve world famine. In line with the Nobel Prize winning scientist Norman Borlaug, Gaud suggested that the same compounds that had gone into chemical weapons (DDT most infamously) were migrating from combat zones to fields of grain, where they would serve the common good. The Green

Revolution failed to realize this political promise for its critics, who instead saw its end result as a global trade in pesticides, fertilizers, and seeds that produced skyrocketing farmer debt and eroded regional food traditions.[35] The amalgamation of weapons production and agribusiness began during the First World War, when chemical gas and barbed wire simultaneously structured the trenches of Europe and the industrializing farms of the American Midwest. The tacit alliance between war and food accelerated in the fifties and sixties, when corporations began marketing chemical inputs to farmers as part of the Green Revolution while supplying the Department of Defense with weapons such as Agent Orange. In our own historical moment, we can witness this militarization of the food system in the physical infrastructure that has developed to support American agribusiness for nearly a century. A 2008 photograph of a California feed mill showing an intricate series of pipes and silos, brings powerfully to mind – in the mill's scale and complexity – what Dwight D. Eisenhower termed in 1961 the "military-industrial complex" (Figure 3).[36] To quote food journalist Michael Pollan, agribusiness has aimed throughout the twentieth century and into the twenty-first to put the national "war machine to peacetime purposes."[37]

The multinational corporation Monsanto provides a window onto the important cultural shift that occurred between the Cold War and the early twenty-first century – the transition from the modernist exaltation to the

3 "Feed Mill, California 2008." © Barron Bixler. Reprinted with the permission of the artist.

georgic redefinition of agribusiness.[38] Founded in 1901, Monsanto got its start manufacturing saccharin and caffeine, growing rapidly during the century into nearly every realm of commercial chemistry. By the start of the Cold War, Monsanto had outpaced its identity as a "Chemical Works" and rebranded itself a life science research firm, adding to its product portfolio hybrid seeds, synthetic pesticides, and, beginning in 1982, the first commercial GMOs.[39] In mid-century advertisements for household plastics, Monsanto extolled the synthetic quality of Green Revolution technologies and advanced the idea that technology would transform not just farms but everyday spaces of eating. One *Saturday Evening Post* advertisement features a family of four standing in their living room, where an assembly line of red, yellow, and green plastics is laid out before them.[40] With the tagline "for happier picnicking days," the ad suggests that consumers have no need of open space or fresh food but instead can take pleasure in the convenience of disposable plastics.

In the 1960s, while Monsanto was crafting a national brand identity as a company that brought dazzling technologies to both farms and kitchens, the biologist Rachel Carson became one of Monsanto's first public critics. Her famous exposé *Silent Spring* (1962) interweaves scientific data with pastoral and apocalyptic narrative to document the pernicious effects of agribusiness, describing the net impact of DDT and other chemical compounds as a worldwide alteration of the human food chain and the ecosystems supporting it.[41] Monsanto evidently perceived *Silent Spring* as a pressing public relations threat, a perception that prompted the company to publish a 1962 parody of Carson's opening chapter in an internal newsletter. Entitled "A Desolate Year," the parody rejoins *Silent Spring* with a story of apocalyptic blight caused not by pesticides but by pests.[42] Although Carson's environmental activism and Monsanto's business model could not have been more opposed, both drew on a similar logic according to which the modern food system culminates in a fully industrialized and technologically amended system. In the case of *Silent Spring*, this *telos* inspires not colorful images of agricultural and alimentary bounty but dystopian anxieties about environmental and somatic crises. Carson, to this point, connects her frequent trope of pesticides-as-weapons to a sense that the suburban American home has joined forces with the chemically fueled farm. Alluding to Monsanto's kitchen plastics and home gardening chemicals, Carson takes U.S. consumer culture to task for "the use of poisons in the kitchen," "the fad of gardening by poisons," and the presence of pesticide-laden foods on supermarket shelves.[43]

As of 2009, Monsanto stood among the most profitable companies in the world, with revenues representing one-fourth of the global agrochemical industry, one-tenth of the commercial seed industry, and an estimated 90 percent of the GMO market – a monopoly that led the U.S. Justice Department to launch an antitrust investigation.[44] During the last fifty years, the rhetoric that supports Monsanto's power has moved from the modernist valuation of synthetic technologies to a quasi-pastoral image of transgenic seeds. This observation resonates with Belasco's analysis of "recombinant culture" – a conceptual framework for prototyping food technologies that combine nostalgia with novelty. This framework comes to the fore, he shows, in the 1990s and 2000s.[45] Exploiting the current appeal of products that recombine the pastoral (or artisanal) and the postindustrial (or high-tech), Monsanto spins a vision of GMOs that downplays both the company's R&D investments and the environmental risks some of their biotechnologies may pose, and it does so by presenting GMOs as an extension of, rather than a radical break from, ancient constructions of agriculture.

Through its "Imagine™" rebranding effort (launched in 2003), Monsanto draws explicitly on georgic motifs to articulate a green vision of its technologies. The logo that accompanies the "Imagine™" tagline features the company's name adjacent to an evergreen-colored vine, perhaps one of the most archetypal of images in georgic literature dating back to Virgil's *Georgics*. Monsanto's visual mark advances an ethic of corporate environmental responsibility and depicts the continuity of the organic world and agricultural biotechnology. However, the press kit announcing the new brand identity also endorses Monsanto's technical virtuosity: "The new Monsanto tagline, Imagine, emphasizes the 'ag' in Imagine and reflects the company's strategic focus on investing in and developing new agronomic tools. Monsanto is committed to researching new agronomic systems that are more environmentally sustainable and that will deliver value across the agricultural chain."[46] In advertisements that the company has run since launching "Imagine," Monsanto continues to leverage georgic ideas of agriculture as a careful balance of nature and *techne*. Consider, for example, a recent print marketing campaign that ran in *The New Yorker* and *New Republic* for Monsanto's most successful GMOs: Roundup Ready soy and *Bt* corn.[47] Directed at consumers anxious about the rise of a technology that remains unlabeled and hence invisible, the advertisement intimates that Monsanto's patented seed technologies are safe to eaters by suggesting GMOs synchronize with ecological cycles even as their engineered traits serve to "squeeze more food" from the environment.[48]

The pastoral mode – whether in its idyllic or georgic form – has perhaps always worked to mask the environmental, somatic, and social consequences of the technological interventions that have long characterized agriculture. In the contemporary period, however, the gap between rhetoric and praxis undergoes a categorical shift. Although farmers have for millennia altered plant and animal genetics, the arrival of transgenic crops represents a major change in the technologies of food production and, by extension, in the stories we tell about food. Monsanto's planned release of the so-called terminator gene, for example, would prevent farmers from saving seeds for future plantings, an ancient and economical practice.[49] Signaling a threat to seed saving, this spectral technology has prompted legal battles over the authority of corporations to predetermine how communities grow and harvest food. Monsanto has vacillated in press releases about the fate of the terminator gene, which has only exacerbated concerns over the ecological risks and social injustices it embodies for opponents. As long as Monsanto officially withholds the technology, scientists are unable to test its effects and, hence, are unable to quell dystopian accounts of the terminator gene that have gone viral. Environmental activists meanwhile have alleged that Monsanto has incorporated the gene covertly into existing transgenic seeds. Conflicts such as the one over the terminator gene are, I argue, about narrative flows of information and misinformation as well as material flows of food and food technologies. In an elegant critique of GMOs, Anne-Lise François highlights the literariness of both agribusiness and countercultural food movements. She defines Monsanto's vision for GMOs, as I do, to be a teleological one that culminates in a "genetically engineered bioculture" wherein corporations determine which genetic traits and even which species will persist in the future.[50] Her analysis suggests, however, that the story of food in biotechnical times is "ongoing and unfinished" and, hence, invites counter-narratives.

From the advertising campaigns of Monsanto to the jeremiads of anti-GMO activists, contemporary food discourse reanimates long-standing pastoral narratives. However, in this discourse we can also recognize an emergent narrative of the information-intensive and networked structure of food in the twenty-first century. Positing the network society as the most apt descriptor of globalization, Manuel Castells speculates that the "informational, global economy" organizes around "command and control centers able to coordinate, innovate, and manage the intertwined activities of networks of firms."[51] For Castells, those who manage information are "at the core of all economic processes."[52] *Global Appetites* demonstrates that these information and communication networks are also at the core of the food system. During the industrial revolution, American literature oriented around what Leo Marx termed "the machine in the garden": a pastoral trope through which writers could acknowledge "unprecedented" appearances of technologies like the railroad and the telegraph in rural places.[53] For writers like Nathaniel Hawthorne, however, technology interrupts the rural scene without completely altering the cognitive difference between the city and the country. In the postindustrial era of networks, the boundary between the lab and the field all but disappears and the rural landscape is as likely to host a server farm as a field of grain. As a result, the recourse to pastoral tropes, even georgic ones, rings increasingly hollow. Contemporary representations of the food system thus reorient around a double recognition that the rural no longer provides a retreat from technological and economic networks and that the future of food production may move from the farms of the countryside to the vertical greenhouses and biotech labs of the city. I term this recognition the "postindustrial pastoral."[54]

One strain of the postindustrial pastoral concerns the global networks of people, places, and things found in the supermarket – an idea Morrison's *Tar Baby* as well as Allen Ginsberg's iconic poem "A Supermarket in California" explore. In his blockbuster book *The Omnivore's Dilemma* (2006), Pollan coins the term "supermarket pastoral" but restricts its use to organic food marketing: the "grocery store poems" that, contra Ginsberg's surreal description of the imported foods and immigrant communities populating a Berkeley supermarket at night, tap into consumer nostalgia for quaint dairies in Wisconsin and verdant fields in Iowa.[55] The supermarket pastoral is not limited to a sentimental and commercial mode, however. Consider the kitchen of Oedipa Maas in Thomas Pynchon's novella *The Crying of Lot 49* (1965):

Oedipa had been named also to execute the will in a codicil dated a year ago. She tried to think back to whether anything unusual had happened around then. Through the rest of the afternoon, through her trip to the market in downtown Kinneret-Among-The-Pines to buy ricotta and listen to the Muzak ...; then through the sunned gathering of her marjoram and sweet basil from the herb garden, reading of book reviews in the latest *Scientific American*, into the layering of a lasagna, garlicking of a bread, tearing up of romaine leaves, eventually, oven on, into the mixing of the twilight's whiskey sours against the arrival of her husband, Wendell ('Mucho') Maas from work, she wondered, wondered.[56]

In its lyrical key, the scene invokes an elegiac sense of a lost georgic landscape: the citrus farms of Southern California eclipsed by master-planned communities. In its postindustrial key, however, Pynchon spoofs the fantasy of integrating bucolic landscapes into the logic of suburban convenience and the metropolitan infrastructure of freeways, mass media, and strip malls. Oedipa's herb garden is strictly décor, in other words, garnish for food bought at the gleaming "Kinneret-Among-The-Pines" supermarket and a visual accompaniment to the easy-listening tunes piped in to her suburban world.

*Global Appetites* concludes with a genre of contemporary nonfiction that seeks to integrate pastoral ideas of rural life into a polemic for local food. Yet this polemic – and practice – of revitalizing local food systems is partly made possible by the very networks of information, technology, and trade that its authors seem to discredit (but that a postmodern novelist like Pynchon would likely say are impossible to escape). I call this genre the "locavore memoir," adapting the term that has come to signify the 100-mile-radius and kindred diets in the United States. An early adopter of this popular form, ethnobotanist Gary Paul Nabhan documents in *Coming Home to Eat* (2002) a fifteen-month commitment to grow, forage, barter, and otherwise consume only foods native to the Sonoran Desert region where he lives. He contextualizes this experiment as a protest of free trade institutions and American agribusiness.[57] In the more recent *Farm City*, Carpenter – a self-proclaimed urban farmer living in inner-city Oakland – documents her own decision to feed herself "exclusively off of [her] urban farm" for a single, and tortuously coffee-free, month.[58] On its surface, the locavore memoir advocates a radical extraction of the individual eater from the global food system. However, even as these writers give voice to just such a cultural practice, their language of eating locally and knowing where one's food comes from has made its way into fast food menus and national farm policy debates. Furthermore, locavores like Nabhan and Carpenter depend on seed and livestock networks and also participate in political coalitions that are global in scope and networked in structure. To this point, it is difficult to imagine how a "greenhorn" like Carpenter could have turned a vacant lot into an urban farm, complete with chickens and two pigs, in a time before computing technologies and online communities. By the close of the century this book examines, globalization makes available modes of production and tools of interconnection that no longer serve only agribusiness. The literature of food no doubt continues to spotlight the detrimental consequences of globalization and the culpability of the United States in advancing the "great industrial enterprise" Coolidge eagerly described nearly ninety years ago. At the same time, twenty-first-century writers and their activist compatriots are today re-positioning food practices that resist the globalization of agribusiness within networks of people, places, technologies, and appetites that are themselves global in nature.

CHAPTER 2

*Rural Modernity: Willa Cather and the Rise of Agribusiness*

For the title of her 1913 novel, Willa Cather borrowed from Walt Whitman's "Pioneers, O Pioneers," a poem about North American homesteaders that correlates agricultural settlement on the frontier with military conquest.[1] Published three years after the 1862 Homestead Act, the poem proceeds as an ode to those pioneer farmers whose geographic migrations and acts of sod-breaking help to guarantee the territorial expansion of the United States.[2] The speaker depicts the pioneers as an elite, "sinewy" (7) race of men and women who expand the nation's borders through agricultural interventions: clearing "primeval forests" and tilling "virgin soil" (25–27). Whitman takes up the discourse of Manifest Destiny (the "Western movement" in his terms) as the poem transposes the role of the U.S. military onto the pioneers, who figure as soldiers fighting with "pistols [and] sharp-edged axes" (3, 58). The symbolism of the poem conflates environmental, cultural, and imperial forms of nation building by depicting the settlement of the prairie grassland as a militarized project. Cather's allusion to "Pioneers, O Pioneers" thus frames her narrative of late-nineteenth-century Nebraska within the history of U.S. expansionism. The allusion also complicates an organizing conceit of *O Pioneers!*: the idea that pioneer-farmers like the Bergsons labor largely separate from the violence of war and the speed of industrial life. After the onset of the First World War, this conceit becomes even more difficult to sustain in telling stories of rural America, partly because the United States enlisted farmers as soldiers during the conflict at the same time that the Department of Agriculture marshaled farmland to provide food to allies. Putting pressure on the American pastoral tradition that no doubt had shaped and would continue to shape her body of fiction, Cather's postwar novels *My Ántonia* (1918) and *One of Ours* (1922) delve into these ways that rural farmland became the "great industrial enterprise" that President Coolidge deemed American agriculture to be in 1925.[3]

*Pastoral* in this chapter signifies not the strict genre of shepherds' dialogues but a wider aesthetic and political vision of rural life that, to cite Raymond Williams, conveys nostalgia for an ever-receding past but also ambivalence about the cultural divisions between the county and the city.[4] Reaching back to Thomas Jefferson's image of the yeoman farmer in *Notes on the State of Virginia*, the American pastoral has long been of two minds about the technological, economic, and geopolitical involvements of rural society – opposing impulses that map onto Leo Marx's terms of simple and complex pastoral.[5] If the former holds fast to the idyllic, the rustic, and the small-scale in imagining rural America to be an oasis from both industry and war, the latter draws on georgic rhetoric to document quotidian and often technology-driven practices of food production.[6] It is in the space between the idyllic and georgic modes that Cather develops her narratives of Nebraska. By the end of the First World War, national discourses of food and farming cultivated a view that rural society was not a barrier to but a vehicle of global commerce and consumerism. This vision stems from the emergence of rural modernity[7]: a confluence of war-related technologies, industrial protocols, and cultural practices that transforms food-producing communities into crucial sites for U.S. economic and geopolitical expansion and, moreover, gives rise to new narratives of rural life. Although ambivalent about the modernity of rural society, Cather keys into the industrialization of agriculture to disrupt the idea of the United States as a country comprising family farms and homesteaders. Her fiction articulates, this chapter argues, the development of national and global food systems that yoke farming to the spheres of engineering, finance, consumer culture, and, finally, world war.

In the main, readers have interpreted Cather's most canonical novels as romantic stories of the American Midwest that mythologize the pioneer and obfuscate the forced removals of Native Americans.[8] Mike Fischer and Louise Westling, for example, argue that Cather's fiction neglects the history of forced displacement of Native Americans from the plains even as she confronts head-on masculinist ideas of homesteading.[9] Although I concur with the assessment that Cather papers over the ongoing land claims of and injustices against Native American tribes, this chapter shows that her fiction is less romantic about pioneer communities than we might think. Narratives of farmer debt in *O Pioneers!*, the railroad in *My Ántonia*, and wartime food production in *One of Ours* reposition the pioneer-farmer as an agent of industrial capitalism; and they do so by co-locating technologies of food production and modern war.[10] These novels develop a transnational story of Nebraska that employs georgic tropes to trace the arrival of global capitalism in the agricultural, rather than urban, United States. Focusing on *One of Ours*, I argue that Cather's postwar fiction chronicles a shift in the global dimensions of American food production and food culture: the transition of family farming into industrial agriculture. Although a prior generation of writers that includes Frank Norris and Upton Sinclair pinpoint the beginnings of "Big Ag" in the late nineteenth and early twentieth centuries, their Progressive Era narratives tend to allegorize food production as a touchstone for other economic and political matters (corporate monopolies in Norris's 1901 *The Octopus* and urban labor conditions in Sinclair's 1906 *The Jungle*).[11] In contrast, Cather's sharp focus on farms and farmland makes her fiction an important early account of the transformation of agriculture into what would be termed in the 1950s *agribusiness*.[12]

### THE CAPITALIZED FARM

Throughout the interwar period, Cather repeatedly argued against the novel of social protest. Her famous 1922 essay "The Novel Démeublé," for example, critiques muckraking novelists who depicted the consequences of industrialization in urban working-class communities for, in Cather's view, making the novel a commodity. "If the novel is a form of imaginative art," she reasons, "it cannot be at the same time a vivid and brilliant form of journalism."[13] The essay first appeared in *The New Republic*, whose readers would have been familiar with the exposés of Sinclair, Jacob Riis, Lincoln Steffens, and Ida Tarbell.[14] Although Cather worked from 1906 to 1912 as an editor at *McClure's* (the magazine that published Tarbell's *History of the Standard Oil Company*), she evidently came to believe that fiction should be decoupled from political reportage.[15] In a 1936 apology for the aesthetic function of novels, Cather continues this critique by denouncing fellow novelists who agitated, via their fiction, for progressive social reforms and Marxist economic theory. The art of fiction, she writes, requires "not so much freedom from restriction, as freedom from the intrusion of foreign matter," a phrase that calls to mind xenophobic discourses and policies of the time.[16] The essay goes on to discount the particular aims of socialist novels, asserting, "industrial life has to work out its own problems."[17] Cather here positions the novel within high culture, a project, Mark McGurl shows in *The Novel Art*, that modernist writers from Henry James to William Faulkner shared with Cather in aligning mass media with industrialization while elevating the novel to the status of an art form.[18] In contrast to someone like Sinclair, Cather seems to untether the social role of the novel from issues of poverty, industrialism, and corporate corruption. While she concedes that the early-twentieth-century writer depends for income on economic systems of marketing and consumerism, her nonfiction advances the notion that the artistic integrity of a novelist is at odds with sustained concern for the cultural and economic structures that "industrial life" produces.

Cather conveys in these essays a skepticism about the marriage of fiction and investigative journalism. Critics accordingly have suggested that her novels eschew most of the political debates that defined both the Progressive Era and the interwar period – with the crucial exception of debates over the New Woman and women in the workforce (including the agricultural workforce). The outcome of this critical take on Cather has been to define her as a regional novelist who shuns the histories of U.S. empire and industrial capitalism even as she interrogates gendered identities and experiments with narrative depictions of lesbianism and asexuality.[19] Michael North correlates Cather's claim that 1922 marked a "definitive end" for her generation to her self-styled "antimodernism," while also illuminating points of connection between her conceptions of gender and those within the work of high modernists like Gertrude Stein.[20] Cather's career as a journalist and editor puts her within the new managerial class of urban professionals and producers of creative work, a group, McGurl shows, that came to eclipse the American leisure class during the first decades of the twentieth century.[21] This class included editors, marketers, lawyers, accountants, and corporate executives, a social field in which the modern novelist occupied the double position of working professional and creative producer. In her nonfiction, Cather responds to this sociological development and its implications for the history of the novel by aligning, if unintentionally, with high modernists like James. Put differently, she distances her work as novelist from the industrial economy and aligns it instead with a service economy in which mental work is the "primary producer of value."[22]

Although fruitful discoveries about Cather's aesthetic and social commitments have emerged from biographical criticism as well as archival research into her letters and essays, authors are rarely the most consistent explicators of their own work. Contra her nonfiction and occasional writings, Cather squarely addresses the problems of "industrial life" by way of her narrative of how industrialization and modernization unfold in rural contexts. This narrative first takes shape in *O Pioneers!*, whose female protagonist, Alexandra Bergson, represents the first generation of agricultural businesspeople – farm owners who consolidate holdings, make capital investments, assume debt, and interface with commodity markets. If this description makes Cather's iconic pioneer sound more like an early-twenty-first-century investment banker, the parallel is apt. William Conlogue, who sees Alexandra's decision to implement industrial agriculture as her means to achieve economic and social independence, suggests that Cather drew from the "New Agriculture" of the 1870s and 1880s, a period in which large wheat farms adopted industrial principles of scale, speed, and productivity.[23] In a book-length study of "Bad Lands pastoralism," Matthew Cella counters that this historicist interpretation of Alexandra does not sufficiently credit Cather's environmental imagination of the plains, according to which farming can coexist with a transcendental relationship to uncultivated land.[24] For Cella, Alexandra is a farmer-cum-artist who balances material and spiritual attitudes toward the land she farms ("the Divide") and who obtains economic success as a reward for her intimacy with the grassland ecosystem.[25] Such intimacy hinges, however, on a claim of Alexandra's indigeneity that forecloses Sioux land claims while glossing over her ties beyond the prairie of Nebraska to modern technologies and markets. The competing readings of her character – as archetypal pioneer and path-breaking woman farm owner – demonstrate that the political investments of Cather's fiction resist categorization by recalibrating gendered divisions of food labor while oscillating between critical and laudatory depictions of American farming.

When *O Pioneers!* opens in the final two decades of the nineteenth century, the Bergson farm is under water financially, a situation that finds an echo in the sickly state of Alexandra's father. From his deathbed, Bergson bequeaths the farm to his daughter rather than to one of his three sons and thereby causes social upheaval within the fictional world of the novel. This bequest reverses English legal codes and literary conventions according to which estates go to male relatives in families of daughters, making the novel an implicit provocation to the conventional marriage plot. Cather's story highlights the strictures on married women's property rights in both England and the United States while also exploring the relative liberties of unmarried women under the Homestead Act to possess land and title.[26] The second section of *O Pioneers!* ("Neighboring Fields") begins sixteen years later at a moment when Alexandra's incredible success has fueled resentment on the part of her brothers Lou and Oscar. Now the largest landowner on the Divide, she rejects her brothers' attempts to control either her marital status (she remains single until the novel's close, when she decides for her own purposes to wed Carl Linstrum) or her farming methods. A demonstrably modern farmer, Alexandra tracks grain prices and reads about the latest trends in agricultural science and economics. The word "account" and its derivatives recur dozens of times in *O Pioneers!*, a pattern that encapsulates Alexandra's financial and business acumen as well as her difference from others on the Divide who spend their time outdoors or in kitchens rather than behind a desk. The most striking reference to this difference occurs in Part Four ("The White Mulberry Tree"), which ends tragically with the murder of Alexandra's brother Emil and his lover Marie when Marie's husband discovers the couple in the orchard and shoots them. As Pearl James explains, orchards frequently signify idyllic space in Cather's fiction, and the violent acts that occur within them tend to represent, in James's terms, "an encroaching modernity."[27] The financial books and accounting principles to which Alexandra dedicates herself are emblems of modernity and particularly the economic procedures of industrial capitalism; but they are not only negative and threatening in their consequences. On the one hand, her "accounts" keep Alexandra indoors and separate her from her immediate community; on the other, her fiscal activities go hand in hand with a life of invention, innovation, and independence. If farmland seems to function in Cather's fiction as either an Edenic bulwark against or a victim of the machine age, for Alexandra, the modernization of agriculture is a conduit for economic and social autonomy. At another point in the novel, Alexandra is hard at work settling her "account-books" while others are "amusing themselves at the fair" (149). Her brothers interrupt this work to dissuade their sister from continuing her relationship with Carl and to bully her into making them partners in the farm. In response, she palpably shuts her brothers out of the farm's management: closing her "account-book firmly" and asserting that she "can't take advice on such a matter" (150). Just as she claims that her relationship is no one's "business" but her own, so too she implies that the business of farming is her dominion. Alexandra thus redefines her original position as heir to a family farm. She has become, instead, the President and CEO of an agricultural company.

Whether Cather would have lamented or celebrated this transition, *O Pioneers!* shows its inevitability in turn-of-the-century rural America while also insisting on the role of individual ingenuity and "acumen" in reshaping the nature of farming. Alexandra succeeds because of her initiative in learning new techniques and her capacity to integrate regional agriculture into a global food system. Cultural geographer Susanne Freidberg shows that turn-of-the-century technological developments – from refrigerated train cars to home iceboxes – laid the groundwork for food producers to ship their goods across the country and around the world.[28] However, prevailing consumer expectations about the seasonal cycles of farming, which had encouraged home gardening and food preservation, persisted for decades, and it was not until the midcentury that the supermarket ushered in new habits of food procurement for the majority of American households. *O Pioneers!* shows that farmers like Alexandra were early adopters of the technologies and systems needed to make global, year-round food markets possible, particularly for staple crops like corn and wheat that would increasingly be milled, refined, and processed into an abundance of consumer products. Of course, all is not rosy in Cather's narrative of large-scale agriculture. Lou and Oscar Bergson struggle to make a living on their plots, while the youngest family member, Emil, rejects farming entirely. Emil's friend Amédée also flounders where Alexandra thrives. Becoming overburdened with the costs of "new machinery" and the narrow margins on his wheat crop, Amédée amasses three thousand dollars of debt and ends up with a burst appendix that ultimately kills him (218). His death sets up an analogy between the physical health (or illness) of individual bodies and one's economic prosperity (or indebtedness) within a modernizing rural America. The social landscape of farming in the early days of industrial agriculture is, in other words, a highly uneven one.

The feminist stakes of *O Pioneers!* inhere in Cather's decision to put Alexandra at the top of this increasingly hierarchical world. In stark contrast to her compatriots, she deftly manages the debts that farming now seems to require. Early on, for example, she convinces Oscar and Lou to cosign on a bank loan that will pay for new equipment and ease the need, in her words, "to grub for every dollar" (68). The loan is one among many that Alexandra acquires to finance the modernization and expansion of the farm, but at no point does debt drive her to the brink of bankruptcy or illness as it does for others in the novel. Alexandra is an exceptional figure, then, for whom the shift to industrial agriculture brings income and autonomy, and her exceptionalism reverberates in today's divide between profitable agricultural corporations and family farms of all sizes that, even with public subsidies, often require "off-farm" income sources to stay in operation.[29] Alexandra stands out in *O Pioneers!* as a woman farm owner who embraces and turns to good effect mechanization, debt financing, and the wider logics of modernity that have shaped the rural United States since the late nineteenth century.

Many readers nonetheless experience *O Pioneers!* as a romantic story of the pioneer, an impression that continues to animate pastoral notions of American farmland. Both *O Pioneers!* and the subsequent *My Ántonia* no doubt evince nostalgia for U.S. homesteading and small-scale agriculture. Running through these novels is a romance with the yeoman farmer that Jefferson popularized with the publication of *Notes on the State of Virginia*. In that canonical eighteenth-century text, Jefferson positions

American farming directly and insistently against European industrialism and mercantilism: "Those who labour in the earth," he writes, "are the chosen people of God, if ever he had a chosen people, whose breasts he has made his peculiar deposit for substantial and genuine virtue."[30] It is this anti-modernization rhetoric that Cather sounds in much of her fiction and that her heroine Ántonia Shimerda comes to embody within the canon of American literature. To generate nostalgia for these pioneer farmers, Cather locates both *O Pioneers!* and *My Ántonia* in the past, at the end of the prior century. However, as I have been arguing, her fiction also intimates that any idyllic vision of the nation's farms and farmers can only be a historical chimera in the first decades of the twentieth century. As her pithy 1923 essay "Nebraska: The End of a Cycle" makes explicit, many farms had come to depend on and take their cues from the constitutive features of industrial capitalism: corporate ownership, commodity culture, and technological innovation.[31] The essay depicts the first wave of homesteaders to Nebraska as a generation who worked the land and produced tangible goods; in contrast, Cather claims, their twentieth-century descendants had become consumers of machinery and things rather than producers of food and cultivators of land. Here, she offers a vision of the capitalized farm: a model of food production whereby abstract financial instruments of credit, debt, and exchange make possible dramatic alterations of the material world of farms by underwriting both acquisition of new technologies and experimentation with new methods. This vision is one that Cather's fiction variously champions and contests in telling the story of how rural America entered an era of commodity markets and industrial farming.

### CATHER'S NEBRASKA AND THE AMERICAN PASTORAL

If Alexandra Bergson exemplifies the social and material gains that come from modernizing agriculture, Cather's postwar fiction expresses far more ambivalence about the model of mechanizing and managing food cultivation. *My Ántonia* opens in the early 1880s with recently orphaned Jim Burden traveling by train from his family's farm in Virginia to his grandparents' homestead near Black Hawk, Nebraska. Arguably the most read and taught of Cather's novels, *My Ántonia* is styled as a memoir that the adult Jim sends to a childhood friend after the two meet coincidentally on a train ride from New York to Black Hawk. The friend – an avatar for Cather – is a professional writer who agrees to turn Jim's rough notes into a publishable narrative of Nebraska and the homesteaders who made it a national center of grain production. Spanning two decades (and hence ending at the beginning of the twentieth century), the novel chronicles Jim's youth and early adulthood as well as his friendship with Eastern European immigrant Ántonia Shimerda, whose character first appeared in Cather's short story "The Bohemian Girl."[32] The first two sections of *My Ántonia* address Jim's early years in Nebraska, culminating in his grandparents' decision to sell their farm and move to town. In leaving behind the work of farming to attend first secondary school and then the state's flagship university, Jim enters the urban middle-class. Akin to Cather, he ultimately leaves Nebraska altogether for the northeastern cities of Boston and New York, where he pursues a career in corporate law that exemplifies the new managerial and professional class McGurl describes.[33]

As with *O Pioneers!*, critics have shown how *My Ántonia* draws on pastoral tropes in structuring Jim's first-person narrative to parallel the seasonal cycles of planting, harvesting, feasting, and dormancy.[34] The immigrant pioneers who migrate to Nebraska inspire in Jim a sentimental vision of food production that his academic study of Virgil's *Georgics* informs. This vision takes the form of "pastoral intellection," to cite a term from *The Novel Art*: a rhetorical mode of interweaving depictions of rustic (or "simple") people with reflections on complex social structures, such as the hierarchy in *My Ántonia* that separates middle-class Anglo-American farmers who own property from Eastern European immigrants who lease their land and equipment.[35] For his part, Jim suggests that he offers an erudite perspective on the story of Nebraska by creating distance between his identity and that of the immigrants he befriends. In recollecting his arrival in Black Hawk as a child, for instance, he describes his grandparents' hired hand Otto Fuchs (6–7). Jim first associates Otto with the cowboys of Jesse James adventure stories; as an adult, Jim reinterprets him to be an archetype of the loyal, uneducated ranch hand who "had given [the family] things that cannot be bought in any market in the world" (140). This sentiment suggests that the immigrant men and women whom the Burdens hire embody preindustrial forms of labor and loyalty that safeguard rural communities against an industrializing and city-centered economy, an attitude that delineates a class division between "hired hands" and landowners. Jim similarly demarcates the social status of Ántonia's family when they decide to bury their father, who commits suicide, at the southwest corner of their homestead out of what Jim terms a "dim superstition" about the afterlife. This loaded observation contributes to a kind of elegy on industrialization as Jim mourns the machines and market forces that would someday "plou[gh] under" the wild grasses surrounding the Shimerda plot and the father's burial site along with them (114).

The elegiac mode is ironic, however, in that Jim's work for the railways implicates him as an adult in the push to consolidate American farms around markets for corn and wheat. Lamenting a future of commodity agriculture that has already arrived when he writes his memoir, Jim seals the Shimerdas off into what Williams terms the "enameled" image of unchanging rural people and places that is a staple of pastoral literature.[36] As Jim extols Otto Fuchs and the Shimerdas, moreover, he cements a cultural divide between his own social position and that of immigrant homesteaders – decoupling the latter from the processes of industrialization. Jim's pastoral sense of Nebraska's past thus effaces histories of U.S. expansionism and industrialization that were well underway during his childhood. Although Jim alludes repeatedly to Virgil's *Georgics*, Fischer argues persuasively that the history of the "American pioneer has more in common with the brutal imperialism recorded in the *Aeneid*" than with the treatment of farming and husbandry in the *Georgics*.[37] Cather's childhood town of Red Cloud, on which she based Black Hawk, takes its name from a Sioux chief under whose leadership the Sioux fought to regain lands guaranteed by the 1851 Laramie Treaty. This violent conflict with the U.S. military ended, Fisher explains, with a defeat of Custer's troops in 1876.[38] Cather draws on her hometown as a blueprint for the setting of *My Ántonia* but then jettisons Red Cloud for the name of the earlier Sioux chief Black Hawk. She thus sets in the past what were ongoing conflicts between Native American and U.S. territorial claims, all the while that her protagonist styles himself a native of Nebraska. *O Pioneers!* enacts a similar substitution of white pioneers for native Sioux, as when Carl Lustrum informs Alexandra Bergson that she "belong[s] to the land" of the Divide because she farms it (272). Such a premise emerges from the U.S. ideology of agricultural settlement and nativism that was prominent in the 1910s and 1920s.[39] In Cather's 1925 novel *The Professor's House*, the brilliant young scientist Tom Outland gives voice to this same nativist rhetoric when he finds Anasazi artifacts on a Southwestern mesa and interprets them as relics of a dead civilization.[40] His pseudo-archaeological journal of the Anasazi site and his effort to place the artifacts in a museum of natural history relegates Native American culture to prehistory, as Walter Benn Michaels observes.[41] Akin to Outland's relationship to the mesa, Alexandra and Jim both fashion themselves into original settlers of the Nebraska prairie. The mystical attachment to place that Cella identifies in such novels emerges out of this nativism.

As Alexandra begins to transform the arable environment of the Divide into an expanse of what we would now term *monoculture* farmland, she imagines that "her heart [is] hiding down there, somewhere, with the quail and the plover and all the little wild things that crooned or buzzed in the sun" (69). This sense of dwelling among wild creatures serves to authorize Alexandra's economic relationship to Nebraska: her project of developing the prairie into a space of efficient and profitable food production. Jim, by comparison, preserves the memory of Nebraska as an uncultivated environment that he felt he knew intimately as a child. In the first section of *My Ántonia*, he recalls his initial response to the land surrounding Black Hawk and his grandmother's vegetable garden:

Perhaps the glide of long railway travel was still with me, for more than anything else I felt motion in the landscape; in the fresh, easy-blowing morning wind, and in the earth itself, as if the shaggy grass were a sort of loose hide, and underneath it herds of wild buffalo were galloping, galloping . . .
 Alone, I should never have found the garden – except, perhaps, for the big yellow pumpkins that lay about unprotected by their withering vines – and I felt very little interest in it when I got there. I wanted to walk straight on through the red grass and over the edge of the world, which could not be very far away. The light air about me told me that the world ended here: only the ground and sun and sky were left, and if one went a little farther there would be only sun and sky, and one would float off into them, like the tawny hawks which sailed over our heads marking slow shadows on the grass. (15–16)

Entirely alone, Jim takes pleasure in the undomesticated flora and fauna (those red grasses and "tawny hawks") while finding the garden's tidy structure dull by comparison. Unlike Alexandra, who aspires to order the "shaggy grasses," Jim feels awe for the prairie and has no proclivity for farming. He has, that is, an urbanite "interest" in the tall grasses and an attendant insensibility toward the work of food production, especially as compared either to Alexandra or to Ántonia. That he leaves Nebraska to pursue first classics and then law allows him to fix the prairie at a point just before agricultural settlement and domestication (processes that lead to the near extinction of wild buffalo) were forgone conclusions.

In their portraits of the prairie at the moment of its metamorphosis into a breadbasket, *O Pioneers!* and *My Ántonia* reach back to St. John de Crèvecoeur's pastoral text *Letters from an American Farmer* (1782), the fictional epistolary account of a French aristocrat who purchases a New York farm after fleeing the French–Indian wars in Canada. Although Crèvecoeur was an emissary to Europe for Presidents Washington and Jefferson and a member of the American Philosophical Society, the persona he crafts in the letters is not that of an intellectual and diplomat but of a plainspoken farmer. The *Letters* characterize such early colonial farmers as yeomen: "a race of cultivators" for whom the vast frontier "open[s] her broad lap."[42] Resonant with Whitman's poem, this sexualized vision of agriculture as the harvesting of nature's bounty draws on ancient and early modern idyllic literature in which shepherds are poet-stewards of the natural world who live apart from, or at times are victims of, imperial violence. This pervasive trope, Williams shows, obscures "[t]he actual men and women who rear the animals and drive them to the house and kill them and prepare them for meat; ... who plant and manure and prune and harvest the fruit trees: these are not present; their work is all done for them by a natural order."[43] This rhetorical fallacy, which influences the early American writings of political figures like Crèvecoeur and Jefferson, persists in the work of modern novelists like Cather and contemporary nature writers such as Wendell Berry, who argues in *The Unsettling of America* (1977) that open land can be served by farming as well as by conservation, provided that the work of producing food is done by small family farmers whose ethic "dissolves the boundaries [dividing] people from the land."[44] Although I am positioning Jim's narrative within this pastoral tradition of situating white homesteaders in an extra-economic relationship to the environment, Cather's Nebraska novels also develop a countervailing story to the Arcadian imagination of rural America by reframing the yeoman farmer as a farm manager who transforms grasslands into fields of wheat. The nativism that we see throughout her fiction suggests that the strains within Cather's work that align with transcendentalism (and anticipate deep ecology) rely on an ahistorical view of Nebraska's past. However, even as the novels strip the history of the American West of imperial violence, they also prove vanguard in describing the origins and projecting the future of agribusiness.

Although this narrative line is most evident in Alexandra Bergson's story, it also emerges through the adult life of Jim Burden. Despite his childhood identification with the Nebraska plains and immigrant pioneers, Jim pursues a profession that facilitates the national and international distribution of food. His legal work for one of the major railways is done, in other words, on behalf of a transportation network that connects Nebraska's farms to the Eastern Seaboard and beyond. In opening the novel twenty years prior to the launch of this legal career, Cather creates dramatic irony between Jim's childhood memories of Nebraska as a place of prairies and smallholdings (those 160-acre plots granted by the Homestead Act) and the rise of commodity farms that the railways promote. Jim's ideas about Nebraska, which gained statehood in 1867, belies when industrial agriculture first emerged in the American Midwest. As Conlogue traces, thousand-acre wheat farms (or "bonanzas") coexisted with small plots in the late 1800s.

While drought conditions in the 1890s discouraged, for a time, further expansion of bonanzas and while family-owned farms remained the order of the day through the first half of the twentieth century, a vision of an industrialized and capitalist food system had taken "firm root in the national consciousness" by the moment when young Jim Burden moves west.[45] Contrary to the picture in Jim's mind about the Nebraska of his childhood, American agriculture was already effecting a major technological intervention in the grassland and high desert ecosystems that stretched from west of the Ohio River basin to the coast of California.[46] It is this intervention that *O Pioneers!* and *One of Ours* announce.

By way of Jim's nostalgia, *My Ántonia* no doubt helps to solidify a national myth of the frontier as Arcadia and of the people who cultivate it as yeoman farmers. But Jim's eastward migration to work for the Burlington Railroad Corporation destabilizes this mythology by signaling emergent interdependencies of agriculture and transportation and of rural and urban economies. In drafting the novel, Westling explains, Cather initially made Jim general counsel to an oil and mining interest before she finally made him a lawyer for the railroads.[47] The successive drafts of *My Ántonia* thus position Jim in service of the infrastructure and natural resource exploration that laid the groundwork for U.S. expansionism within and beyond North America. In addition to his material involvement with agricultural infrastructure, Jim is in awe of the machinery of agriculture. In perhaps the novel's most iconic scene, Jim, who is preparing to leave for college, observes a plow on the horizon after an afternoon picnic with Ántonia and other "country girls": "On some upland farm, a plough had been left standing in the field. The sun was sinking just behind it. Magnified across the distance by the horizontal light, it stood out against the sun, was exactly contained within the circle of the disc; the handles, the tongue, the share – black against the molten red. There it was, heroic in size, a picture writing on the sun" (237). Although this image no doubt conveys anxiety about the horizons of agriculture and the scale of its impact, it also interprets the "magnified" plow as "heroic in size" – a machine whose origins are in the early modern period but whose ever-changing structure marks both a fundamental attribute of agriculture (as itself a technology) and specific agricultural technologies yet to come. Jim's "enameled" vision of early Nebraska is hence a fractured one, and his memoir points to synergies between the nation's breadbasket and its centers of manufacturing and commerce. As I argue about *One of Ours*, these synergies only deepen between the time in which *My Ántonia* is set and the time of its publication at the end of the First World War.

## WORLD WAR AND THE RUPTURED IDYLL

Cather's Pulitzer Prize winning novel *One of Ours* (1922) revolves around Nebraska farmer-soldier Claude Wheeler. In contrast to his father and brother, who typify a new class of agricultural businessmen, Claude admires what he sees as the bucolic lives of his mother, his family's domestic servant Mahailey, and the provincial women of France whom he encounters while fighting in Europe. The sentiments Claude attaches to women's work form a gendered structure of feeling that echoes male characters in *My Ántonia* and *O Pioneers!*, and especially Jim's desire for Ántonia to maintain a close connection to the soil as an earth mother figure.[48] Although all three novels give voice to earth mother myths, characters like Alexandra and Enid Royce (Claude's schoolmate and eventual wife) disturb the perception that women sustain human relationships to the natural world and to the manual work of tending crops and preparing food. Westling contends about Alexandra that her tools of agriculture in fact work to control "Nature's rhythms."[49] Patricia Carden similarly argues that characters like Jim are foils to Cather's ideas about women and land. "While frontier mythology provides the motivating energy and critical focus of ... these 'novels of the soil,'" Carden writes, "Cather's frontier stories restage the romancing of the wilderness – that paradigmatic activity of the self-made man – by situating women in his place."[50] As compared to the two earlier novels, *One of Ours* interrupts violently its protagonist's sentiments as the sense of pastoral refuge Claude finds in the farmhouses of Lovely Creek and the villages of wartime France unravels. Exploring the traumatic dimensions of rural modernity, *One of Ours* tells the story of how the industrialization of American agriculture develops alongside and out of a war that is far more technological – far more modern – than Cather's protagonist acknowledges. To conceptualize American agriculture as a fully industrial enterprise, with the imperative of increasing food productivity through technological interventions, the First World War was instrumental. For it is the war, I argue, that expanded the global horizons of American farms and created new links between military and agricultural technologies.

This argument builds on the scholarship of Richard C. Harris, Janis Stout, and Steven Trout, who have contested the framing of *One of Ours* as a jingoistic and sentimental novel.[51] On the novel's publication, reviewers who included Ernest Hemingway, H. L. Mencken, and Sinclair Lewis faulted *One of Ours* for an inauthentic and naïve depiction of the Great War. This account suggested that women writers were inherently unfit to write war memorials.[52] In a 2010 analysis of how the letters of G. P. Cather written from the trenches shaped the novel, Harris observes that Cather's decision to draw on the life and death of her cousin and other soldiers like him "involved creating a character that necessarily would be romantically and heroically inclined."[53] He goes on to note, however, that Claude's romanticism does not diminish the irony with which Cather crafts the entwined plots of Lovely Creek and the Western Front. Put differently, the tone of *One of Ours* is that of ironic distance between the narrator and Claude (whose name invokes both his own Francophilia and his earthy yet dull temperament).[54] Despite this reassessment of the novel, critics still tend to interpret the narrative through Claude's perspective on the war, a tendency that the 1991 Vintage edition dust jacket endorses: "Claude is an idealist without an ideal to cling to. It is only when he enters the First World War that [he] finds what he has been searching for all his life. In *One of Ours*, Willa Cather explores the destiny of a grandchild of the pioneers, a young Nebraskan whose yearnings impel him toward a frontier bloodier and more distant than the one that vanished before his birth."[55] The 1991 blurb posits that *One of Ours* is the story of a country boy transformed into a war hero, an interpretation that likely contributed to Cather receiving the Pulitzer Prize in 1923. This description of Claude as idealistic in enlisting to fight on a "frontier bloodier and more distant" than the Nebraska of his and Jim Burden's imaginations is certainly not without merit. Claude's flight from Lovely Creek for the trenches stems from his angst over what Frederick Jackson Turner described as the closing of the frontier – a view of American exceptionalism that prompts Claude to set his sights beyond the borders of the United States and, however naïvely, outside modernity.[56] For how else could Claude's fantasy of finding adventure on the battlefields of the First World War be deemed, to quote from the Vintage jacket, a "peculiarly American fairy tale"?

In line with a generation of young soldiers, Claude first learns of the war in the pages of a local newspaper while building a house on his family's land and preparing to marry his pious neighbor Enid. Mary Ryder explains that it was precisely the widespread presence of the war in mass media that made the First World War "total" in nature, providing more civilians knowledge of each battle than in any prior international conflict.[57] Newspapers, along with war posters and booster organizations, served to recruit young men from rural areas and to rally the support of those too young to enlist by promoting the heroic fantasy that Claude finds seductive and that, in turn, underlies the brutal irony of the war's lived realities and literary memorials. Both in his romance of the war and in his exposure to propaganda, Claude symbolizes the war's rural youth.[58] Amid reports of rising food prices and expanding farm incomes brought into the Wheeler house through the "dozen or more" newspapers to which Nat Wheeler subscribes, Claude learns that Allied Forces attacked the German army on the Marne to prevent the fall of Paris, a battle that resulted in more than one million casualties (8).[59] Unaware of this historical fact, Claude views Paris and the Marne as names on a map – abstract spaces that slot into his impression of a picturesque Europe: "He knew he was not the only farmer boy who wished himself tonight beside the Marne. The fact that the river had a pronounceable name, with a hard Western 'r' standing like a keystone in the middle of it, somehow gave one's imagination a firmer hold on the situation" (142). Although soldiers and civilians across the Western Front were living with and dying from the war's violence, Claude decides to join this "wall of flesh and blood that rose and melted and rose again" because of newswires and world maps (142).

This abstract sense of Europe and its battlefronts speaks to what literary historian Paul Fussell terms the "utter unthinkableness" of the war's conditions.[60] In his impulse to smooth over the brutalities of total war, Claude is archetypal. Before the United States declared war in 1917, the American media downplayed the technologies that were devastating the cities and fields where combat occurred. In Book Two of *One of Ours*, Cather alludes to this feature of American journalism at the time. As Claude sits "down before an armchair full of newspapers" in the Wheeler study, the narrator reports that "he could make nothing reasonable out of the smeary telegrams in big type on the front page of the Omaha *World Herald*" (133). Those "smeary telegrams" convey very little to Claude about technologies of violence or about the effects of that violence on real places and persons: "The German army was entering Luxembourg; he didn't know where Luxembourg was, whether it was a city or a country; he seemed to have some vague idea that it was a palace!" (133). This scene pivots on a situational irony that plays up Claude's naiveté of geography and geopolitics, a "smeary" and "vague" sensibility that the national press exacerbates rather than corrects. The odd exclamation mark at the end of Claude's riff on Luxembourg highlights his credulity that the Western Front offers a space of adventure rather than combat. Such an image fails to apprehend the realities of the trenches. In his seminal study, Fussell observes this same disjuncture between how British soldiers anticipated the war and how they experienced trench warfare, arguing that this profound contradiction made irony the dominant mode for memorials and narratives of the war (and, we could add, for the century that followed in its wake).[61]

In the United States, due to the nation's late entry into the war, it was possible to sustain the story of military adventure for young men much longer than in Europe. In *One of Ours*, the syndicated newspaper coverage of the war perpetuated this notion. To cite a *New York Times* headline on the eve of the U.S. war declaration in April 1917, the press reported that President Wilson had called for a "new army of 500,000 men" to join "Germany's foes."[62] The *Times* piece quotes heavily from Wilson's speech to Congress that week, during which the president framed the war as an epic conflict by announcing that the United States had determined to join an "irrepressible conflict between the autocrat and the people" and had done so to make the world "safe for democracy."[63] The president's rhetoric and the *Times* reporting of it provide not a sense of the war from the ground (in contrast to the embedded reportage of the late twentieth and early twenty-first centuries) but a sweeping, aerial vantage on the trenches of Europe. This point of view emphasizes abstract ideas of democracy, heroic service, and a new frontier while diverting national concern from the war's bombs, planes, and guns. Given such a discourse, we can speculate that many young men did, as Claude does in *One of Ours*, think of joining the Western Front as the stuff of fantasy.

The military's formal recruitment campaign of 1917 targeted young men from farming communities to join the armed services. Through posters, pamphlets, and local events – all of which Claude Wheeler encounters before becoming a lieutenant – government propaganda appealed to this population's ideas about the American frontier as well as practical knowledge of agriculture. One such poster with the tagline "Come across and help us!" suggests that Europe's embattled people – encapsulated in the figure of a young French woman – are in urgent need of masculine aid. Another, circulated in the first months after the U.S. declaration, urges young men to "enlist, plow, or buy bonds" (Figure 4). Modernist in design, the poster appeals to two audiences simultaneously by encouraging urban professionals to buy bonds while entreating rural young men either to produce food surpluses or to redeploy their skills in the military. All three routes to patriotic service are coded masculine. This visual campaign divides the nation into those who can finance the war, those who can feed the Allied nations, and those who can fight in the trenches, the last of these groups envisioned as young rural men. At the same time, it imagines that the old instruments of both agriculture and war (the shovel and rifle shown in the poster) are being folded into the technologies of industry (embodied in the cog that overshadows these other tools). Although the Great War disrupted food production across all of its geographic fronts, U.S. propaganda presented Europe as offering a new site of opportunity for the American farmer. The war itself comes off in this portrait as non-technological – a

4 "Your Country Calls: Enlist – Plow – Buy Bonds." Circa 1917–1918. World War I recruitment poster created by Lloyd Meyers and published by Hamilton Press. Reprinted with the permission of the World War Posters Collection (Mss 36), Literary Manuscripts Collection, University of Minnesota Libraries, Minneapolis.

conflict won through the heroic deeds of men who adapt their knowledge of tilling soil and harvesting food to win the peace. The narrative of *One of Ours* breaks with this portrait by showing that the war was a catalyst for modernizing agriculture.

Pearl James demonstrates that the nation's war propaganda was highly contradictory. Although posters like this one tapped into traditional gender roles in rallying men to the Western Front, a concomitant series of posters sponsored by the Salvation Army and American Motor Corps featured women in nontraditional roles within the war economy, roles that resonated with the New Woman.[64] As a woman who assumes many such roles, Enid courts social stigma in Lovely Creek with her scientific approach to cooking and husbandry and ultimately prompts Claude to enlist when she leaves Nebraska to work outside the domestic sphere by joining her sister's missionary project in China. She embodies, James contends, the "dangerous modernity" that war posters voiced when they presented women donning masculine uniforms and performing work other than the feminized labors of nursing, cooking, and sewing. Against these expressions of modernity, Claude sees the war as signifying "an ironically antiquated, antimodern crusade."[65] James defines modernity too narrowly as the combination of machine labor and scientific domestic economy, but she is right to point out Enid's status in the novel as a symbol for the negative consequences of modernization. What makes Enid a character of modernity, and of rural modernity in particular, is not only her adoption of particular technologies and techniques but also her self-distancing from the obligations of place, generation, and sex. In approaching housework as an efficient manager of time and resources and in leaving her husband and her place of origin for China, she highlights two of the central facets of modernity that sociologist Anthony Giddens identifies: a "trust in abstract systems" and the "disembedding ... of social relations from local contexts of interaction."[66]

Whether advancing traditional or unconventional notions of gender, the U.S. poster campaign consistently masked the modernity of the war itself and, in particular, the technologies that were altering both combat and agriculture. Those technologies were, above all, the barbed wire in the trenches and on monoculture farms and private ranches; the gas engines in tanks and tractors; and the chemical gases harnessed as weapons and fertilizers. Read against the military's picture of young American men trading in their plows for rifles, *One of Ours* provides a narrative of the war and its mobilization of rural communities that begins in the summer of 1913 and ends shortly after the Armistice of 1918. The long deferral of the war in this war novel, which forestalls Claude's experience of combat until the fifth and final book, replicates structurally the late entry of the United States into the war. It is precisely this belatedness that makes possible a pastoral vision of Europe in the minds of young soldiers-to-be like Claude. When Claude finally departs for the Western Front aboard the U.S. ship *Anchises*, he anticipates "going over" with an odd keenness (218). Cast in pastoral terms, the Atlantic before him is "a dream. Nothing but green meadows, soft grey water, a floating haze of mist a little rosy from the sinking sun" (218). Even when Claude's company reaches the trenches in France, they seem to skirt the war's periphery – a progression that allows the young lieutenant to hold fast to his idea that the war will provide a refuge from the rush toward modernity at home. While the omniscient narrator observes France to be a "shattered country," Claude sees, instead, gardens and rustic villages (339). In retreat from the societal changes that Enid along with agricultural businessmen like his father and his brother Bayliss embody, Cather's protagonist experiences the Western Front as an oasis from the new economic and technological imperatives of farming (339).

Claude revels in what Fussell identifies as a form of pastoral innocence that European writers often conveyed during the summer before the war began. "Out of the world of summer, 1914," Fussell argues, "marched a unique generation. It believed in Progress and Art and in no way doubted the benignity even of technology. The word *machine* was not yet invariably coupled with the word *gun*."[67] For Claude, who repeatedly criticizes the encroachments of machine technologies and market pressures in rural life, the Western Front affords, absurdly from our vantage point, the innocence that Fussell connects to prewar British culture. Even after Claude experiences machine gun assaults and witnesses up close dead and maimed soldiers in the trenches, his images of the war and of Europe do not waver, refracted as they are through the lens of idyllic landscape poetry and art. During a march from the French coast to the frontlines, Claude imagines his troop to be moving "[d]eeper and deeper into flowery France!" (274). He succumbs in this scene to a lyric mode reminiscent of Hesiod's Golden Age.[68] Although barbed wire fences and bombed-out valleys surround him, Claude perceives everywhere about him "[f]ields of wheat, fields of oats, fields of rye; all the low hills and rolling uplands clad with harvest. And everywhere, in the grass, in the yellowing grain, along the roadbed, the poppies spilling and streaming" (274). His vision of "flowery France" acts as a *pastoral recourse*, a term Fussell employs to explain a device that permeated poems and diary entries penned from the British trenches during the first year of the war. Pastoral recourse works to convey wartime violence and loss via sharp contrasts to fecund landscapes that promise to protect the soldier-writer: such "[p]astoral reference, whether to literature or to actual rural localities and objects is a way of invoking a code to hint by antithesis at the indescribable; at the same time, it is a comfort in itself, like rum, a deep dugout, or a woolly vest."[69] The recourse to pastoral motifs in Claude's accounts of the war occurs often: maps of Lovely Creek drawn in the trenches, references to the ornamental gardens and flowering trees of French villages, and allusions to idyllic literature. These evocations function, however, more to index Claude's idea of Europe than to make sense of the war's calamities.

Although the novel's contravening description of ruin and carnage follows on the heels of his internal monologues, Claude persists in glossing over the "soldiers and sailors of all nations" with their heavy artillery and automatic weapons (268). When his company passes through a destroyed French village, Claude only briefly acknowledges the rubble: "There was nothing picturesque about this, as there was in the war pictures one saw at home. A cyclone or a fire might have done just as good a job . . . . mounds of burned brick and broken stone, heaps of rusty, twisted iron, splintered beams and rafters, stagnant pools, cellar holes full of muddy water" (307). Despite this acknowledgment of war rubble and human death tolls, the choice of metaphor here – the comparison of rubble to the impact of a natural disaster – rips the war out of its historical moment and the technologies that made it so destructive. Claude recuperates, moreover, his original impressions of France. Approaching a Red Cross project in this same village, he describes not the slow rebuilding of a leveled town but a quasi-magical restoration of an orchard: "The gravel walks were clean and shining. A wall of very old boxwoods stood green against a row of dead Lombardy poplars. Along the shattered side of the main building, a pear tree, trained on wires like a vine, still flourished, – full of little red pears" (309). Out of sync with the chronotope of rubble that defines the First World War, Cather's young American soldier thus conjures up an Arcadian garden.

The novel interjects Claude's images of Europe, however, with strident evocations of war: a row of dead poplars, the shattered side of a building, and the wires forming the trenches. These eruptions of an omniscient point of view provide a depiction of the Great War that rebuts Claude's. A lengthy description of Claude and his co-lieutenant David Gerhardt upon their return to the frontlines after a one-week leave testifies to this tonal gap. The passage intimates that as Allied troops are making incursions into the German trench lines during the fall of 1918, Claude is effectively on holiday (340).[70] Yet, Cather balances Claude's evident isolation from major battles with graphic depictions of combat. A gifted violinist and expatriate, Gerhardt enlists in the military because his musical career became both untenable and senseless to him. He rejoins Claude's belief that the war offers a meaningful alternative to the Wheeler family's business plan of launching a major ranching operation in the American West. At the end of their weeklong leave, Claude suggests that the war affords him an exciting escape from this venture. In response, Gerhardt remarks bluntly, "You'll admit it's a costly way of providing adventure for the young" (339). The word choice is significant here in that Gerhardt gauges, as Claude does not, the war's many "costs" – from tremendous loss of life and devastation of infrastructure to the stark financial costs. This pointed comment on the consequences of the First World War is mostly lost on Claude, who thinks to himself, "[n]o battlefield or shattered country he had seen was as ugly as this world would be if men like his brother Bayliss controlled it altogether" (339). Gerhardt's remark lingers, however, inviting the reader to see material and symbolic connections between the trenches of the First World War and the latest frontiers of American agriculture – connections that Claude misses despite how much the Wheelers benefit from them.

The form of the novel further undermines Claude's point of view by foregrounding the technological character of trench warfare. While Claude describes his first battle as "simply . . . done," the narrator describes the same battlefield as a "dead, nerveless countryside" where the bodies of dead men, rather than fields of grain, blanket the ground (294). When Claude is later hit by shellfire, the narrator's language becomes even more graphic:

[H]e went on having continuous sensations. The first, was that of being blown to pieces; of swelling to an enormous size under intolerable pressure, and then bursting. Next he felt himself shrink and tingle, like a frost-bitten body thawing out. Then he swelled again, and burst. This was repeated, he didn't know how often. He soon realized that he was lying under a great weight of earth; – his body not his head. He felt rain falling on his face. His left hand was free, and still attached to his arm. He moved it cautiously to his face. He seemed to be bleeding from the nose and ears. Now he began to wonder where he was hurt; he felt as if he were full of shell splinters. (322)

In this scene, we witness not just a lone hero wounded. Seventeen other Company B soldiers die during this battle, and the only survivor aside from Claude is the company doctor, who is grotesquely maimed. The narrator relays the doctor's injuries in visceral detail: his "groin and abdomen were torn on the left side. The wound, and the stretcher on which he lay, supported a mass of dark coagulated blood that looked like a great cow's liver" (323). This animalization of the doctor's body creates a haunting image of injury that calls to mind the Wheeler ranching operation, debunking Claude's idea that Europe supplies an agrarian escape from the developments at home that he so loathes. One could argue that the image of a cow's body is readily available from everyday experiences of husbandry and is, hence, a stock reference. However, that the image is expressly about animal slaughter makes the metaphor a register of the modern disassembly line that Sinclair documents in *The Jungle*. In the comparison of a cow split open and a ripped-open human body, Cather draws a line from the Fordist slaughterhouse (and the wider application of an efficiency regime to food production) to the mechanization of warfare. The scene details, in particular, German tactics by which mobile companies armed with machine guns and light artillery would capture Allied trenches, resulting in very high injury rates and casualties. Although Claude's narrative seems to skirt the margins of such offensives, Company B's journey in fact follows the final trajectory of the war: they travel from Rouen in Western France northeast along the Seine and Somme Rivers through Arras into the Argonne, and Claude's death in the trenches at the end of Book Five likely occurs south of Ypres, which was the site of final combat on the Western Front before the 1918 Armistice. Both the graphic treatment of combat and geographic details like these provide a texture of historical realism in *One of Ours* that counters Claude's romanticization of and obliviousness to the cataclysmic violence of the First World War.

### GEORGIC MEETS AGRIBUSINESS

Early in the novel, Cather foreshadows the violence of the trenches via the details of how Claude spends the summer of 1914. The summer begins matter-of-factly, with Claude courting Enid to ease his melancholy at having given up university studies in Lincoln to manage the farm while his father and brother launch their cattle operation in Colorado. This banal plot situation mutates quickly into a gritty scene of violence, when Claude experiences an accident in the fields. A neighbor, Leonard Dawson, narrates the pivotal scene at length to fellow farmer Ernest Havel:

'Oh, it's nothing very bad, I guess, but he got his face scratched up in the wire quite a little. It was the queerest thing I ever saw. He was out with the team of mules and a heavy plough, working the road in that deep cut between their place and mine. The gasoline motor-truck came along, making more noise than usual, maybe. But those mules know a motor truck, and what they did was pure cussedness. They began to rear and plunge in that deep cut. I was working my corn over in the field and shouted to the gasoline man to stop, but he didn't hear me. Claude jumped for the critters' heads and got 'em by the bit, but by that time he was all tangled up in the lines. Those damned mules lifted him off his feet and started to run. Down the draw and up the bank and across the fields they went, with that big plough-blade jumping three or four feet in the air every clip. I was sure it would cut one of the mules open, or go clean through Claude. It would have got him, too, if he hadn't kept his hold on the bits. They carried him right along, swinging in the air, and finally ran him into the barb-wire fence and cut his face and neck up.' (115)

Although Leonard describes the accident as "nothing very bad," the character of Claude's wounds suggests otherwise in that his injuries require most of the summer to heal under Enid's care. The accident proves to be an object lesson in the risks of technological innovation. Just before Leonard recounts the event, Ernest is out "cultivating his bright, glistening young cornfield one summer morning" while recalling a childhood memory of his father preparing his own fields with an ox-drawn plow (114). The memory is an instance of the idyllic melding of agriculture into natural cycles and ecosystems. In it, Ernest fuses the green meadows and babbling creek of the prairie with the rows of grain that his parents cultivated as, to his mind, nature's stewards: his "mother walked barefoot beside the oxen and led them; his father walked behind, guiding the plough" (114). Leonard arrives on the scene in a car, whose engine noise breaks up this daydream and underscores the engine that breaks in on Claude's day of fieldwork. Against both his and Ernest's aspirations for farming to be a natural enterprise, the objects that populate this scene encapsulate a continuum of agricultural technologies from the medieval "heavy plough" to the modern "motor-truck" and "barb-wire fence." This accumulation of technologies turns Claude's accident into a microcosm of the transition from agrarian farming to industrial agriculture. Moreover, his injury connects to the many war wounds we later read about in *One of Ours* in that similar forms of technology rip open the bodies of soldiers fighting both for the Allied and for the Axis nations. As the narrative of Claude's prewar accident powerfully conveys, *One of Ours* marks the appearance in the American food system of those technologies that are simultaneously transforming warfare.

Claude laments such transformations, above all, because of the machines that have entered the Wheeler home. To his mind, the mechanization of the farmhouse has become a burden on rather than an aid to the family, a process that portends an era of rural consumerism rather than agrarian work. Spurning the washing machine, milk separator, mechanical dishwasher, and oil stove that his brother Ralph has introduced into the kitchen, Claude celebrates the traditional domestic labor of his mother and Mahailey along with his own handiwork: "Machines, [he] decided, could not make pleasure, whatever else they could do" (38). While Ralph acts as the farm's "chief mechanic," bringing "ingenious machine[s]" to Lovely Creek, and while Bayliss acts as the budding entrepreneur whose "business acumen" with agricultural implements rewards him with considerable monetary success, Claude identifies with his mother's self-proclaimed "old-fashioned" ways and frustration with gadgetry (9, 17–19). Against the simplicity of the carpenter's bench where he spends his spare time, Claude finds the mechanical objects in Ralph's adjacent workshop – which include electric batteries and a stereopticon – unnerving. These "mysterious objects [standing] about him in the grey twilight" herald categorically new systems of work that value productivity and efficiency over craft and tradition (19).

Much to Claude's vexation, Enid adopts the model of a mechanized home in ways that seems to contribute to the couple's lack of sexual intimacy. North's account of *One of Ours* demonstrates that the novel incited hostile reviews from Hemingway and others not because it depicted the war unfaithfully but rather because it described – in Claude's attraction to "flowery France" and Enid's affinities with industrial work – a profound "redefinition of gender: a redistribution of human qualities in which even a battlefield might witness behavior that is conventionally feminine."[71] He argues, however, that the novel is somewhat conventional in its orientation to gender with its evident indictment of Enid for her chaste and cold hearth (a point Susan Meyer echoes).[72] If we turn our attention to Enid's food-centered activities, the novel's indictment is less clearly about the New Woman and more strikingly about the emergence of industrialized food systems, a claim that complements Andrew Jewell's argument that scenes of cooking and eating in *My Ántonia* highlight Cather's general "anti-Americanization" politics and particular concern that the standardization of dietary practices in the United States would erode the diversity and artistry of regional cultures.[73] Enid's reading in the science of unfertilized eggs leads her to raise chickens without a rooster, and her adoption of refrigeration technology allows her to store canned salmon, boiled eggs, and rice pudding in the icebox – all of which results in cold, pre-made suppers for Claude and raised eyebrows from the neighbors. While Mrs. Wheeler's kitchen orbits around the corn-cob-fired stove, Enid's kitchen "glitter[s] with new paint, spotless linoleum, and blue-and-white cooking vessels" (165). Her domestic work reflects the new science of home economics that Warren Belasco and Harvey Levenstein describe as the New Nutrition, a Progressive Era paradigm that defined cooking to be a scientific activity through which women could achieve an ideal balance of the properties of different food groups.[74]

In contrast to Enid's kitchen, the novel begins with a scene that combines Claude's attachment to daily food preparation rituals (when he encounters Mahailey in the early morning stoking the kitchen fire with corn cobs) and his pastoral view of Nebraska (as he looks out over the "broad, smiling face" of the prairie) (3–4). The use of corn to stoke a traditional hearth merits comment: although the corn cobs signal Mahailey's maternal care for the Wheelers, throughout Cather's fiction, corn – as with wheat – replaces the prairie to become a cornerstone of monoculture farming and commodity food production. In light of his aversion to the mechanization and gigantism of modern agriculture and his affinity for cooking and carpentry, Claude's accident takes on additional significance. As the "motor-truck" intrudes on a moment of mule-powered fieldwork – a quintessential example of what Marx calls the "interrupted idyll" – Claude is initiated into the industrial world he spurns.[75] The opening of the novel prefigures this initiation when Claude pleads to take the family's Ford to the county fair, a moment that contradicts his oft-repeated refrain about the problems with machines in suggesting that he finds some modern conveniences appealing. His twin pursuits of a traditional agrarian life and the life of the mind are made possible, moreover, by the fact that his father is "a rich farmer" who could purchase "a new thrasher or a new automobile" without a second thought (11). Claude is, in other words, implicated in the technologies that are integrating a community like Lovely Creek into the industrial economy and transforming agriculture into agribusiness.

The *Oxford English Dictionary* dates the first use of the term *agribusiness* to 1956, when the *Harvard Business School Bulletin* coined it to "define the many diverse enterprises which produce, process, and distribute farm products or provide supporting services."[76] Historians similarly locate the rise of agribusiness in the decades after the Second World War, when corporations commercialized synthetic pesticides and developed a global market for hybrid and then genetically modified seeds.[77] *One of Ours* points to an earlier moment of origin for these developments in the barbed-wire fences and gas engines of the First World War and in the agricultural industries of the wartime United States. While James and others note that Claude thinks enlisting will be his escape from modernization, the novel directs us to the intricate connections of the war and early agribusiness. As combat at places like the Marne and the Somme devastated foreign farmlands, the United States began providing food aid to Allied nations.[78] These programs expanded the U.S. export economy and, in turn, encouraged American farmers to expand their horizons to global food markets. Put differently, food relief opened new geographic markets to large farmers, like the Wheelers, who experienced prodigious harvests at the time.[79] Rural America was crucial to the war in two ways, then: as a source of soldiers and food surpluses. Moreover, businesses like the farm implements company that Bayliss expands over the course of *One of Ours* as well as the commodity markets that Nat Wheeler follows closely in the financial pages of the Omaha *World Herald* became as vital as the industrial farm itself in ensuring a consolidated and coordinated system for exporting American foodstuffs around the globe. As I discuss in Chapter 3, prodigious American harvests during the Second World War combined with European famine conditions to expand the nation's export economy. Taken together, the two periods of world war solidified industrialized agriculture and agribusiness as central to the global reach of the United States.

That Cather's friend Dorothy Canfield Fisher worked for a food relief program in France suggests that Cather would have been aware of the wartime expansion of U.S. agriculture and the opportunities within the war economy for industrializing farms that could produce commodity crops like corn and wheat for international export.[80] Cather's sense of food as an important part of the period's geopolitical and economic upheaval comes most clearly to light in *One of Ours* when the Wheeler family experiences record yields of wheat and oats in 1914. In response to this news, Nat Wheeler defines the war as an economic boon to his grain and cattle operations, remarking on the eve of Archduke Ferdinand's murder, "I see this war scare in Europe has hit the market. Wheat's taken a jump. They're paying eighty-eight cents in Chicago" (132). Claude detests this aspiration for the family farm to function like a corporation with a management team who follows the daily tickers of the Chicago Board of Trade in order to determine what to plant and when to harvest. This distaste leads him to lambaste (rather than welcome) the industrial age of agriculture. That staple foods "could be grown anywhere in the world," he reasons, makes farmers into consumers who accumulate "manufactured articles of poor quality; showy furniture that went to pieces, carpets and draperies that faded, clothes that made a handsome man look like a clown ... machinery [that also] went to pieces" (84–85). This critique speaks across a century to those farmers, chefs, and activists who are working in the early twenty-first century to structure alternative systems to the dispersion of food through supermarkets and global restaurant chains by advocating for community supported agriculture (CSA). Of course, Claude's perspective is not the narrator's, and his wistfulness remains a target of irony. Nonetheless, within the world of the novel, his views have the most resonance with contemporary food movements in the United States and Europe. This resonance demonstrates not so much the prescient character of Cather's 1922 novel with respect to contemporary food politics as a long cultural history for twenty-first-century movements like slow food.

Claude's desire for a family farm whose economic center is the local community rather than world market and whose cultural center is the kitchen rather than farm supply store gives way, tragically in the terms of the novel, to his father and brothers' anticipation of agribusiness. Even as the First World War drew idealistic young men like Claude away from family farms to become soldiers, farms like the Wheelers were expanding their scope to become massive operations capable of distributing food overseas, thanks in no small measure to new shipping routes as well as to the railways that Jim Burden counsels in *My Ántonia*. To harvest the surpluses such farms were producing and to meet the international demand for food aid, the U.S. Department of Agriculture (USDA) and War Food Administration (WFA) encouraged urban workers to emigrate from the city to the country to support the work of planting and harvesting, even as the military was recruiting men from rural towns to serve in combat. Throughout the 1910s, the government also promoted new technologies – such as the Model F tractor and synthetic nitrate fertilizer – as the means to increase agricultural output in the food-producing centers of the Corn Belt, the Central Valley of California, and the Mississippi Delta.[81] War posters promoting agricultural productivity, on the one hand, and household food conservation, on the other, suggest that the government viewed the American food system as analogous to European trenches within the Allied war effort. The slogans of these posters, which include "From home-grown seed, victory" and "Food is ammunition," present agriculture as a martial yet industrial enterprise and equate food to weaponry. The propaganda dovetails with the narrative of *One of Ours*, then, in yoking rural communities to a growing, if not yet named, military-industrial complex. Although the government's metaphor of food as ammunition might seem grotesque, it is actually in line with how technologies, like nitrogen gas, have been repurposed from military to non-military uses throughout the last century. The material substrate of the novel – its farm implements, kitchen gadgets, barbed-wire fences, and motorized vehicles – makes visible the particular interactions between trench warfare, the war economy, and the industrialization of food.

While Cather's novels employ pastoral conventions to romanticize the pioneer and, hence, partly to offset any social critique of modern agriculture, *One of Ours* in the end conveys more anxiety than romance about the evolution of the twentieth-century food system. Rather than idyllic, the prevailing rhetorical mode of *One of Ours* is georgic in representing agriculture in a time of war. Just as Virgil's *Georgics* provides "practical knowledge" of Roman agriculture in wartime, Cather structures the five books of *One of Ours* to apprehend the lived, on-the-ground work as well as the political and economic stakes of agricultural places.[82] The novel's final section supplants any lingering bucolic images of either Lovely Creek or the Western Front with a disturbing reference to the war's aftermath. When Claude's battalion at one point takes the German-occupied town of Beaufort, Cather details a scene of shattering violence. The episode portrays three deaths – those of a French girl, a German sniper, and Claude's fellow soldier Willy Katz – all of which occur in a surrealist mode. The first is that of the child, whose life ends in an eruption of noise and blood: "A second crack, – the little girl who stood beside Hicks, eating chocolate, threw out her hands, ran a few steps, and fell, blood and brains oozing out in her yellow hair" (346). This description of a small child shot in the head lays bare the dissolution of the line between combatants and civilians, and it does so by juxtaposing civilian death with an everyday act of eating. That bar of chocolate – a cipher for peacetime culture (although, as Chapter 4 shows, a cipher, too, of colonialism and neo-imperial trade) – hangs in the air, showing the violence of automatic weapons via the stark contrast of the sensorial pleasures of sweets. On the heels of the girl's death, Claude attacks the German sniper while a fellow sergeant shoots the same man "through the temples" (346–48). The vengeful nature of this second shooting attempts to compensate for the girl's death but succeeds only in underlining the escalating violence that the weaponry and scale of the Great War fueled, a point affirmed when Willy Katz gets "a bullet in his brain, through one of his blue eyes" (348).

In the final episode of *One of Ours*, Mrs. Wheeler reflects on her son's good fortune to die in battle with his ideals intact, a fate that spares him, she imagines, from the "horrible suffering" that disillusioned and injured soldiers experienced during the postwar period (370). The novel, at first glance, domesticates its narrative of war through this concluding scene, in which Mrs. Wheeler and Mahailey stand in the kitchen and mourn a single soldier's death. However, Cather once again interrupts such idyllic strains with a scathing comment on the legacy of the war years by alluding to the high rate of veteran suicides in rural communities (an eerie prefiguring of PTSD and suicide among veterans of the Vietnam, Iraq, and Afghanistan wars). This allusion illuminates the dynamic relationship between total war and industrial agriculture that structures *One of Ours*. In particular, Cather suggests that the economic upside of the First World War for farmers who had the means to integrate their land into an industrializing and globalizing food system was not universally felt, as the war also left many rural soldiers on the margins of the "New Agriculture" and its importance to U.S. prosperity. In the early twenty-first-century, one nonprofit organization is addressing the persistence of this problem in launching an incubator for rural veterans of the Iraq and Afghanistan wars to provide them with training in sustainable – rather than industrialized – agriculture.[83]

*One of Ours* demonstrates that the structure Eisenhower would name, in 1961, the military-industrial complex had its first articulations in the literature of farming communities at the end of the First World War.[84] More pointedly, Nat Wheeler's view of the war as a boon for wheat prices suggests that large farmers engaged in forms of speculation and war profiteering. As compared to earlier forms of war waged for natural resources and arable land, however, such profiting off the First World War depends on the financial centers and commodity markets that the poster "Enlist – Plow – Buy Bonds" depicts. Cather's fiction thus marks the beginnings of a literary form I term the *postindustrial pastoral*, which is a focus of Chapter 5. Cutting across conventional generic distinctions, the postindustrial pastoral retains the aspiration to retreat from the city, the market, and the battlefield and to discover places that exceed the reaches of industrial life; but it simultaneously questions the relevance of idyllic tropes to the lived experience of rural modernity and industrialized agriculture. Evident both in the work of contemporary writers grappling with the horizons of food in the information age and in a writer like Cather working at the height of industrialization, the postindustrial pastoral makes visible not only the mechanization and streamlining of food production (its industrialization, that is) but also the simultaneous emergence of service industries (a hallmark of postindustrialism). As evident in Alexandra's accounting system and the Wheelers' multiple ventures, the rise of agribusiness makes farming just one among many enterprises structuring the modern food system. The array of writers stretching from Cather in the early twentieth century to Ruth Ozeki in the early twenty-first illustrates that a dialectic of food cultivation and agricultural industry is central to the wider history of modernity. Attentive to how the technologies of war and the business of food mutually constitute each other, *One of Ours* traces, in the final analysis, the effects of world war and world markets on places perceived as refuges from the global.

CHAPTER 3

# "*Luxury Feeding*" *and War Rations: Food Writing at Midcentury*

> We all eat food; and whatever sacrifices we may have to make to take care of the needs of our fighting men, the American people will continue, throughout the war, to be better fed than any other nation on earth.
> Elmer Davis, Director of the Office of War Information (1942)[1]

> Apples are high –
> that shows they're scarce,
> still the stores always seem to have plenty.
> Can't get a price
> The farmers say –
> I guess it's because there'r too many [sic]
> Lorine Niedecker, "New Goose" Manuscript (1945)[2]

In a 1942 radio address, war information director Elmer Davis made clear that routine acts of procuring and preparing food were matters of national security during the Second World War, a period when rationing programs defined the daily lives of many, even as the United States had a thriving agricultural economy. Alice McLean characterizes the national food imaginary at this time as consonant with the war effort: the United States, she writes, "adopted the notion of the home front as a war front and meals as munitions to arm the family body against enemy ideology."[3] Lorine Niedecker's mid-century poetry highlights the contradictions within this wartime rhetoric of food – contradictions of sacrifice and prosperity and scarcity and plenty that "Apples are high" highlights. Niedecker returned in these poems to what she had termed in 1935 "the undigestible phrase" of an economy that expanded national wealth even as many people lived with hunger.[4] While propaganda advanced rationing as an egalitarian means to support the Allied armies, writers on either side of the Atlantic made visible the socioeconomic divisions that structured who had access to good food and who did not. However, mid-century literature was far from univocal in responding to the politics of food during and after the war. Edna St. Vincent

Millay, for example, wrote on behalf of the War Information Office with her radio play *The Murder of Lidice* (1942), while several poems from her volume *Make Bright the Arrow* (1940) represent fascism as a threat to U.S. food security and compare American citizens who eat well to soldiers preparing for battle.[5] From Millay's militarized portrayal of eating to George Orwell's 1946 political allegory *Animal Farm* (which locates the totalitarian cooptation of socialist politics in a barnyard), writing about food became a mode through which to voice – and often to contest – the propaganda that aligned national power with productive farms and well-fed citizens.[6] In this same period, culinary writers such as M. F. K. Fisher and Elizabeth David published unconventional cookbooks showing home cooks how to prepare gourmet meals out of scarce resources and even black market ingredients, works that adapt modernist modes of irony, fragmentation, and allusiveness to the cookbook form. Considered together, Niedecker and Fisher articulate the particular pressures on women to comply with national rationing programs while illuminating the class politics of eating well – or what Orwell dubbed "luxury feeding."[7] By contrast, David shows that writing about food during the period of *postwar* rationing in England could be a strategy of political escapism. All of these writers, I argue, contribute to a late modernist project – in Fredric Jameson's and Ty Miller's terms – of addressing mid-century economics and politics through aesthetic experimentation and, more pointedly, of providing literary nourishment to readers in a time of austerity.[8]

Throughout the Second World War, government propaganda showcased white middle-class housewives and their kitchens as a tactic for asserting national solidarity. Against this image, writers contrasted a mid-century culture of gourmandize with a crisis of malnourishment within and outside the United States.[9] Informing this literature of food is a felt anxiety about what President Eisenhower would name the military-industrial complex in 1961. While the U.S. Department of Agriculture (USDA) and War Food Administration (WFA) promoted agricultural productivity and patriotic acts of food procurement and consumption, late modernist writers like Niedecker explored the capacities of experimental writing to expose the nation's competing ideological investments in commodity agriculture and food rationing. Making a case for the politicization of food in mid-century literature, this chapter investigates the conceptual interplay of fine dining, hunger, and what Fisher calls "creative economy" across four texts: Niedecker's *New Goose* (1946), Fisher's *How to Cook a Wolf* (1942), David's *A Book of Mediterranean Food* (1950), and, by way of a coda, Samuel Beckett's *Waiting for Godot* (1953).[10] By including discussions of writers from outside the U.S. literary canon (David and Beckett), the chapter examines the wartime politics of food from the perspective of European writers who show its importance to a creeping U.S. hegemony.[11]

### PRODUCTIVITY AND POVERTY ON THE HOMEFRONT: LORINE NIEDECKER

Lorine Niedecker wrote dozens of poems about the Second World War. In her published volumes *New Goose* (1946) and *For Paul and Other Poems* (1950–51), as well as unpublished manuscripts that span the thirties and forties, the Objectivist poet created a radio ticker of voices speaking about fascism, total war, and nuclear weapons. "To war they kept / us going," opens a 1936 poem, likely about the Spanish Civil War, while "Bombings," a short poem about bomb shelters in London during the blitz, is the eerie title of the second entry in *New Goose*.[12] These poems depart noticeably from the modes of testimony and elegy that mark much war poetry, as the reader encounters violent images ("Nazi wildmen / wearing women" or "Atomic split / shows one element / Jew") in the singsong meter of nursery rhymes and the humdrum rhythms of news, propaganda, and colloquial speech.[13] Among the most striking instances of this provocative juxtaposition is a two-stanza poem that apes the language of war strategy and applied science: "The number of Britons killed / by German bombs equals / the number of lakes in Wisconsin."[14] Lest we rest easy on the evidently simple equation of dead British soldiers and Wisconsin lakes, however, the second stanza concludes with a grisly image of the German army's own casualties: "But more German corpses / in Stalingrad's ruins / than its stones."[15]

In these war poems, Niedecker draws on a wide array of poetic resources – from radio programs and overheard conversations to the avant-garde practices of surrealism and Objectivism. By the early 1940s, Objectivism represented what Rachel Blau DuPlessis and Peter Quartermain term a "non-symbolist, post-imagist poetics" that privileged sustained attention to "the particular historical moment in which [poetry] is written."[16] Niedecker remained interested throughout her career in Objectivist principles of materiality, sincerity, and collectivity, as Louis Zukofsky had articulated them in a 1931 special issue of *Poetry*. She departed from Zukofsky, however, in interpreting Objectivism to demand a practice of drawing "intensities of interior feeling" out of both the material world and folk culture.[17] Several critics have argued that her poetry offers a cosmopolitan view of the folk culture she knew most intimately: the community of Black Hawk Island and the nearby dairy town of Fort Atkinson, Wisconsin, where Niedecker lived most of her life. In his contribution to the 2008 collection *Radical Vernacular*, Michael Davidson shows that Niedecker's work on the Wisconsin edition of the Federal Writers' Project *American Guide Series* connected her to "an atmosphere of Left activism."[18] This atmosphere informed the development of a "critical regionalism" in her poetry – a sense of place that repositions "non-metropolitan spaces within the orbit of capitalist production worldwide."[19] Ruth Jennison echoes Davidson, arguing that Niedecker redefines the "'folksy countryside'": "Niedecker's alembic of avant-gardes from both the American and the Continental urban cores flows forth from a transatlantic Wisconsin, a periphery of our interior stitched into, and pitched against, a world-system that will require the countryside for its domination, and destruction."[20] One of many mid-century writers who articulate, however variously, what Jahan Ramazani terms "transnational poetics," Niedecker writes as a regional poet who has a global perspective on her locale and its international import.[21]

This worldly view of the American "interior" is perhaps nowhere more evident in Niedecker's work than in those poems that address mid-century entanglements of war and food. Both *New Goose* and *For Paul and Other Poems* describe the rural United States in the context of a war at once distant and proximate in its consequences, a war that disrupts everyday life in agricultural communities on both sides of the Atlantic. The much discussed poem "In the great snowfall before the bomb" develops these threads as it moves from an evocation of the post-atomic era to a scene of wartime Fort Atkinson and the print shop where Niedecker worked as a copyeditor for *Hoard's Dairyman* from 1944 to 1950[22]:

> In the great snowfall before the bomb
> colored yule tree lights
> windows, the only glow for contemplation
> along this road
>
> I worked the print shop
> right down among em
> the folk from whom all poetry flows
> and dreadfully much else.
>
> I was Blondie
> I carried my bundles of hog feeder price lists
> down by Larry the Lug,
> I'd never get anywhere
> because I'd never had suction,
> pull, you know, favor, drag,
> well-oiled protection.

> I heard their rehashed radio barbs –
> more barbarous among hirelings
> as higher-ups grow more corrupt.
> But what vitality! The women hold jobs –
> clean house, cook, raise children, bowl
> and go to church.
>
> What would they say if they knew
> I sit for two months on six lines
> of poetry?[23]

Completed in 1950, the poem opens on a road Niedecker presumably traveled from her home on Black Hawk Island to the print shop in Fort Atkinson, setting that journey on a snowy day in early December. The first stanza inflects the Romantic trope of a contemplative walk through a woodsy landscape – a trope evocative of Robert Frost's "Stopping by Woods on a Snowy Evening" – with the spectral figure of "the bomb." The second stanza swerves away from both the figure of a solitary poet in the woods and the hauntingly quiet aftermath of nuclear bombs to introduce the workaday language of "the folk" and hustle and bustle of a print shop. Davidson observes that the two historical moments framing the poem are "the pre- or inner-war era ... and the period of postwar nuclear paranoia," echoing other critics who highlight the "uneasy" relationship of the poet-speaker to the other print shop workers.[24] Peter Middleton and Elizabeth Willis concur that the poem reveals Niedecker's oscillation "between immersion and alienation from [her] local community," to cite Middleton.[25] However, though her poetic process involved collecting ephemera, gossip, and family histories, Niedecker's relationship to "the folk" of Fort Atkinson was ultimately that of coworker rather than ethnographer.[26] "In the great snowfall before the bomb" shows the critical distance as well as quotidian intimacy she cultivated with respect to this community – a community that the poem's speaker refuses to romanticize precisely because of her direct knowledge of its workaday life and its entanglements with the world beyond the town. If Frost's poem is a touchstone for pastoral notions of rural America, Niedecker upsets her reader's associations of agricultural life with stillness and simplicity to offer a complex picture of rural work, folk culture, and poetic craft.

Central to this constellation is the background noise of the Second World War. Through her allusion to the atomic bombings of Hiroshima and Nagasaki, the poem moves out from the Great Lakes region to the atomic fallout over Japan. As Jenny Penberthy explains, Niedecker wrote poems throughout the 1930s and 1940s that positioned Wisconsin in relation to international geopolitics: poems about "the Depression, the growth of fascism, the Spanish Civil War, the Vichy government in France, the American involvement in World War II, [and] the atomic bomb."[27] Willis further observes that the "most frequently recurring nouns" in these poems are *war* and *work*, keywords resonant with Niedecker's poetic process of "including private commentaries on the public matters of governance, art, war, and labor politics."[28] Extending into the midcentury Willa Cather's narrative of rural modernity and wartime agricultural economics (discussed in the prior chapter), her poetry explores how the U.S. war machine permeates rural working-class communities located far from the frontlines.

"In the great snowfall before the bomb" embodies the frenetic pace of manual and domestic work, and its cadence conveys the wartime productivity demanded of citizens generally, and agricultural communities particularly. Poetry occupies a cultural field outside that productivity, which the speaker terms the "dreadfully much else," even as the poem sits somewhere between, on the one hand, the efficient machinery and masculine cronyism of the print room and, on the other, the domestic labor expected of working women. In contrast to the speaker's scant "six lines of poetry," *Hoard's Dairyman* (with its "bundles of hog feeder price lists") signifies a bustling economy fueled in part by the food industries and commodity markets on which *Hoard's* reported. By 1939, the trade magazine had an international circulation of 330,000 subscribers. Throughout the period in which Niedecker worked as a copyeditor, the publication promoted technological innovations – ranging from milking machines to antibiotics – promising to boost the dairy industry's yields.[29] The importance of this industry to Niedecker's sense of place is well established. Willis explains that the area around Fort Atkinson was the national center of dairy production and, at its mid-century apex, boasted eighty-four creameries. Although Niedecker juxtaposes the slow burn of poetic production with high-yield dairies and high-volume printing presses, Willis shows that the condensery became Niedecker's symbol for her own process of writing "concentrated poems intended for long-term consumption."[30] While the condensery may represent an economy of conservation and preservation, the pages of *Hoard's Dairyman* advance an economy of mass production that Niedecker associates with the scale and technologies of modern warfare.

"In the great snowfall before the bomb" lambastes, moreover, the impetus to mechanization and consumerism that guides daily life in rural Wisconsin. Niedecker employs the diction of corporate nepotism as well as military industries like aerospace in enumerating the social forces driving print room workers to climb the ranks from "barbarous hirelings" to "corrupt higher-ups": "suction, pull, ... favor, drag, ... well-oiled protection," in the poem's terms.[31] The correspondences between world war and rural work deepen with a reference in the fifth stanza to "radio barbs," which calls to mind the jingoistic news programs and propagandistic speeches saturating the airwaves at the time. Literary historians may hear in the term "radio barbs" the vitriol of Ezra Pound's pro-fascist addresses on Rome Radio. However, although Niedecker would have been well aware of Pound's 1946 trial and the subsequent controversy over his receipt of the Bollingen Prize, his Objectivist contemporaries would not have heard his live broadcasts.[32] The "radio barbs" of "In the great snowfall before the bomb" more pointedly refer to a domestic culture of jingoistic news programming and government propaganda. Indeed, radio stations served in this period as outlets for propaganda from across the political spectrum in both Allied and Axis nations. As we will see, the U.S. Office of War Information (OWI) utilized radio programming along with posters and pamphlets to propagate the idea that Allied nations would win the war not only through military power, weapons technology, and heavy manufacturing but also through the yields of American agriculture and the labor of rural communities. Government-funded nutritionists, Warren Belasco notes, put forward at this moment a "scientific consensus recommend[ing] unprecedented proportions of red meat as 'a fighting food,'" thus building on what Harvey Levenstein terms the interwar Newer Nutrition paradigm that sought to shape the American diet around principles of fuel and efficiency as well as the emerging science of vitamins.[33] In tandem with scientific nutrition rhetoric, advertisers promoted processed foods as bodily fuel for the American war effort. Broadcast over the airwaves and published in magazines, these advertisements often employed racial epithets that no doubt acted as political "barbs" against the Axis nations. A national campaign for canned grapefruit juice, for example, had the racist tagline, "Just ask a Jap what it feels like to be up against men who are fortified with 'Victory Vitamin C,'" while radio announcements for branded foods like Velveeta Cheese and Planters Peanuts promised "to pack working power into the lunch box sandwiches" and offer "energy-giving fats and oils."[34] In *Radio Goes to War*, Gerd Horten summarizes these various tactics, arguing that advertisers consolidated brand identities in the forties with the notion that nearly any consumable product "could enhance America's fighting power and help win the war."[35] Tracey Deutsch also examines this marketing tactic in her feminist history of grocery stores, explaining that the nutrition paradigm of the Second World War was an "instrumentalist one," instructing women to make "plentiful, protein-rich, filling, and nutritionally balanced meals" for their families.[36] To this point, the hawkish claims for a meat-and-potatoes diet did not typically extend to women, who, government officials and nutritionists suggested, "could make do with protein substitutes" such as bread and other cereals.[37] That advertisers teamed up with government agencies to make the consumption of packaged foods a patriotic act indicates that the war became a profit center for American agribusiness and its growing array of food companies. This profitability is kindred, moreover, to the situation in the First World War when, as with Cather's emblematic figures of agricultural industry in *One of Ours*, large wheat farms and cattle ranches expanded their markets through overseas food shortages.

Having worked on radio plays and radio programming for the Madison station WHA in 1942, Niedecker would have had firsthand exposure to food propaganda and advertising. The medium of radio appealed to the poet, who experienced it as a way to "engage with multiple ... locations and events while situated in one place."[38] "In the great snowfall before the bomb" illustrates, however, that radio was also a "barbed" medium whose messages of national unity and power put pressure on poor rural communities to support the war economy through manual labor and consumer behavior. The poem's final lines – with the provocative image of working-class women who "hold jobs – / clean house, cook, raise children, bowl / and go to church" – invoke food rationing discourses that defined the duty of women simultaneously to conserve food and nourish their families. In contrast to this kinetic imperative, Niedecker's representation of poetry as a still and slow-moving practice contests the civic obligation for women to work industriously both at home and in factories. Radio speeches and war posters often centered on the kitchen, as a 1943 poster entreating women to "save waste fats for explosives" graphically reveals with its image of a white woman's hand pouring a pan of bacon grease into a cluster of exploding bombs (Figure 5). Although the U.S. rationing program aimed in part to conserve food for overseas military and civilian populations, the program also helped to collect food waste, such as animal fats and tin cans, for the production of weapons and supplies. Such campaigns thus aligned a woman's efficient management of her kitchen with the productivity of both U.S. agriculture and the war plant.

Rejoining the rhetoric of shared sacrifice, Niedecker's war poems foreground realities of poverty and hunger in the nation's agricultural communities and especially for women in those communities. Contra

"Luxury Feeding" and War Rations: Food Writing at Midcentury 57

**Save waste fats for explosives**

**TAKE THEM TO YOUR MEAT DEALER**

5 "Save Waste Fats for Explosives." 1943. World War II food rationing poster created by Henry Koerner and the Office of War Information and published by the U.S. Government Printing Office. Courtesy of the Hennepin County Library, Kittelson World War II Collection.

*Hoard's Dairyman*, for example, her poems' working women seem focused on getting on with day-to-day life rather than fueling the engines of either industry or war. Elizabeth Savage, in analyzing how Niedecker draws on cultural discourses of femininity and whiteness, makes the case that her poems trace both the burdens on young women to "define and improve themselves through purchase" and the sexist and racist undercurrents in mid-century advertisements that championed consumer goods as instruments of strength.[39] This marketing discourse, as with government propaganda, depicted women to be a de facto army of middle-class, white housewives. If propaganda and advertising together worked to present the middle-class female consumer as the model citizen and war booster, Niedecker's war poetry represents social inequality and poverty as they affect rural women. A poem from the unpublished "New Goose" manuscript proceeds as an apostrophe to the local grocer: "What's today, Friday? Thursday! Oh, nothing till tomorrow."[40] Another poem, completed in 1945, similarly quips that daily life in "destitute" rural towns is one of "Nothing nourishing, / common dealtout food."[41] Such neologisms pervade Niedecker's poems about the wartime food supply and the politics of rationing – odd-sounding terms that seem chosen to work against the clichéd language of food propaganda and advertising in the period. In *New Goose*, Niedecker's critique of this propaganda is most evident in a poem that singles out the "government men" who control local food production during the war. Even as these bureaucratic figures instruct farmers, "Don't plant wheat, / we've got too much," the speaker zeroes in on the persistence of hunger in rural, food-producing communities:

> Our crop comes up thru change of season
> to be stored for what good reason
>
> way off and here we need it – Eat
> who can, who can't – Don't grow wheat
>
> or corn but quack-grass-bread!
> Such things they plant around my head.[42]

A poignant antiwar poem, this lyric exposes the U.S. war economy as oxymoronic in generating both food surpluses and famine conditions. The poem's singsong rhythm invites readers to think of the OWI's wartime slogans and, by extension, to respond with skepticism to the strictures "government men" place on who can and who cannot eat. The premise of rationing food – storing it up for "way off" battlefronts – comes under fire in the poem, whose speaker implicitly compares that premise to a "quack" idea. Niedecker does not confine her depiction of wartime hunger to Wisconsin. In other *New Goose* poems, she lays bare the extent of hunger in Europe: "a story about the war," as one poem begins, that divides the political elite from civilians who are "too hungry to flatter."[43] Taken together, these poems expose the impoverishment of rural workers, who suffer from a lack of adequate nourishment even as their labor ironically produces food for the nation and the world.

Niedecker thus employs experimental poetics in the service of demarcating the food politics of the Second World War, a project that gives voice to conditions of hunger and that debunks propagandistic images of a nation unified through, on the one hand, productivity and consumerism and, on the other, rationing. Niedecker here puts a distinctive spin on the practice of Objectivist poetry, which situates the material world and commodity culture in its "full cultural and historical signification."[44] Her work of the forties and early fifties explores, in arguable contrast to her Objectivist peers, the "full cultural and historical" significance of wartime factory work and agricultural production for rural communities like those of Fort Atkinson, radiating outward from that locale to show the international scope and effects of food rationing.

## FOOD RATIONS IN A NATION OF PLENTY

As Niedecker's poetry makes both visible and audible, the Second World War was an era of contradictions with respect to American food politics. Government mandates to conserve coexisted with a drive to mechanize and expand the throughput of agriculture, while broadcast media, from radio announcements to war posters, effaced socioeconomic disparities in imagining the nation as unified through its rationed and yet, by comparison to other nations, plentiful diet. American farmers realized gains in productivity and real incomes throughout the forties despite a labor shortage, an agricultural boom that followed on the heels of a long recession in farm prices.[45] By 1945, the United States had solidified its position as "the world's food superpower" by becoming what the then Secretary of Agriculture termed "the greatest agricultural production plant on earth."[46] An alliance between war and agriculture in turn shaped how the United States imagined its place in the mid-century world. Historian Ron Kroese explicates this alliance in his analysis of DDT, which the United States used to delouse soldiers during the war. By 1944, advertisements appeared in farm magazines announcing that these same chemicals would be "coming home" to help farmers control pests.[47] In propaganda, moreover, both farming and eating appeared as vital forms of civic service. The USDA instructed farmers, for example, to "view their farms as factories," while the OWI and Office of Price Administration (OPA) enlisted consumers to apprehend their compliance with rationing and their participation in programs such as food waste conservation and victory gardening as patriotic duties essential to an Allied victory.[48] In contrast to stringent austerity regimes in Europe and Asia, rationing in the United States was more a matter of principle than practice for the American middle and upper classes. John Kenneth Galbraith, the war's first director of the OPA, admitted as much in a poignant remark that unsettles the national narrative of shared sacrifice: "Never in the long history of human combat have so many talked so much about sacrifice with so little deprivation as in the United States in World War II."[49]

The interwar breadlines and unemployment rates of the Great Depression arguably haunt claims that American citizens were comparatively well fed during the war. In his study of New Deal modernism, Michael Szalay demonstrates that the Depression fostered not only new forms of centralized economic planning but also a new political missive to ensure citizens had the means and the will to buy up the ever-expanding output of consumer industries, which certainly included the modernizing industries of farming and processed foods.[50] In response to the purported twin problems of overproduction and underconsumption, the New Deal aimed to ameliorate "conditions of modern life in a rapidly evolving capitalist society" so as to keep the economy going strong.[51] As Franklin D. Roosevelt proclaimed in a 1935 Congressional address, the state's newly conceived role was to "provide the means of mitigating" the risks to economic growth and national GDP that poverty had come to represent.[52] OWI Director Elmer Davis tapped into this New Deal framework when he delivered his 1942 radio address to explain a new points-based rationing program that the government launched as part of the wider "Victory Program."[53] Overseen by Agriculture Secretary Claude Wickard and administered by the OPA, the points program served to ration a wide array of goods while affording consumers greater flexibility in purchasing food.[54] The agencies tasked with administering the points system spurred consumers to do their part, while working behind the scenes with supermarkets to "hold down prices, keep records, and observe the often arcane requirements of federal regulations"; one of the central aims of these negotiations, moreover, was to "impose policy on women customers."[55]

Through broadcasts like Davis's, the OWI distinguished the relative prosperity of American citizens from the impoverishment of people living under fascist regimes. The 1942 radio speech thus concludes by figuring the United States as the perennial land of plenty.[56] After stressing the scarcity of food resources in Europe, Davis goes on to contrast methods of wartime food distribution in the United States and Germany:

Food is a weapon in all wars, but in this one more than usual. The enemy has used it as a weapon, negatively – looting the conquered people of their food supply, and giving back to them just enough to keep them alive – indeed not always even that much; hoping to break their spirit. . . . We are using our food supply as a weapon, positively; so distributing it that the American army and navy, and the American people, will be well nourished; yes, and so that the armies of our allies will be kept strong.[57]

The speech refers to the Nazis' coordinated programs of land seizures and food rationing in occupied countries. In contrast to these tactics, Davis claims, the United States administers an egalitarian system by "using [its] food supply as a weapon, positively" to nourish the armies that will defeat Germany while nourishing Americans especially well. Davis implies that rationing in the United States does not infringe on the liberties of citizens to consume because it proceeds democratically and, hence, does not jeopardize the national imaginary of abundance that stretches back to the colonial period.

The speech relies on the notion that the national body is made up of individuals who consume alike, which gained traction in the period and which Niedecker's *New Goose* poems satirize. In his famous 1941 "Four Freedoms" speech, Roosevelt set the tone for this discourse. Expounding on the freedom from want that democracy ensures, the president promised that an Allied victory would secure the food supply for "every nation."[58] Ramón Saldívar clarifies the chauvinist ideology underlying both Roosevelt's speech and Norman Rockwell's covers for the *Saturday Evening Post* that translated the Four Freedoms into visual scenes: "what is at stake in Roosevelt's momentous pronouncement of a world order built on the groundwork of the Four Freedoms is nothing less than a renewed commitment to an ideal vision of a unified American nation working to effect that brave new world order under the pressure of 'modern [American] social conditions.'"[59] Comparing Rockwell's covers to Carlos Bulosan's accompanying essays in the *Saturday Evening Post*, Saldívar suggests just how fragile the national idiom of prosperity was when the United States went to war. "Against Norman Rockwell's painting of a family Thanksgiving gathering celebrated to overindulgence at a time when people worldwide were dying of starvation," he writes, Bulosan stressed that poor communities and people of color profoundly lacked material security, including the security of having access to food.[60]

While the equation of democracy and abundance informed the government's rationing propaganda throughout the war, the OWI acknowledged in internal documents that food insecurity, rather than freedom from want, defined many communities. If Davis presents rationing in the radio address as an egalitarian system immune to "hoarders," a confidential OWI memo released to radio stations, also from 1942, characterizes the likelihood of hoarding as high and labels "bootlegger[s] of rationed goods" traitors.[61] In direct opposition to the public broadcast, the memo warns, "*We live no longer in a 'land of plenty.'* ... If we are to have ships, planes, guns and tanks.... then we must skimp on sugar, gasoline, metals, rubber and other commodities that once made this the 'land of plenty'..... Rationing is solemn proof that you can't eat your cake and have it too."[62] To suppress the potential for social upheaval, the confidential memo instructs radio producers to reinforce the government's official rhetoric that rationing is an organized and democratic system for sharing limited resources.

These disjunctions between public and private discourses underscore how politically fraught the food system was during the war. From 1942 through 1945, the government contracted an organization known as the Artists for Victory to produce war posters, a group that included commercial illustrators along with surrealist painters such as Austrian expatriate Henry Koerner and architects such as Edward Steese and Ralph Thomas Walker.[63] In 1942, the Museum of Modern Art (MOMA) recognized the artistic significance of these war poster designers by organizing a national exhibition.[64] Many of the artists who designed posters either for the MOMA's juried exhibition or on an ongoing basis as part of the Artists for Victory employed the cosmopolitan styles of modernism to advance the government's nationalist idiom. One of the most omnipresent of the OWI posters from this program, for example, uses a modular, geometrical structure to convey the government's chief tagline for rationing: "produce and conserve, share and play fair" (Figure 6). This modernist style works to mask politicized consumer behaviors by depicting the housewife tasked with ration compliance in a high-culture aesthetic mode. As part of this highly gendered campaign, the government entreated women to ensure the orderly distribution of food by taking the "Home Front Pledge," which, Amy Bentley explains, millions of women did either from their kitchens while listening to radio broadcasts or in public by attending rallies.[65] As with other forms of rationing propaganda, the Pledge worked against a concurrent drive to employ women in the workforce, which increased the percentage of women working outside the home from 27 to 37 percent between 1940 and 1945.[66] If Rosie the Riveter called on women to be industrious workers, the OWI posters and pledges cast an air of the modern over the unpaid work of procuring food in accordance with wartime rations.[67]

"Luxury Feeding" and War Rations: Food Writing at Midcentury 63

6 "Rationing Means a Fair Share for All of Us." 1943. World War II food rationing poster created by the Office of Price Administration and published by the U.S. Government Printing Office. Courtesy of the Hennepin County Library, Kittelson World War II Collection.

Spokespeople like Davis and campaigns like the Pledge put forward the white housewife to symbolize a universal good citizen who moderated grocery store purchases even as she prepared a plentiful diet for her family. At the same time, another line within rationing propaganda undercut this image by pitting hoarders against those middle-class consumers who planned menus carefully and refused to procure food from the black market. These contradictory strains within the government's rationing discourse beg the question of why the United States enforced rationing at all, if the nation's food supply was robust as compared to the rest of the world. The answer may have the flavor of conspiracy theory, but, nonetheless, proves apt from the vantage point of postwar history. In short, competing programs of food rationing and agricultural productivity suggest that the government's control over what women cooked at home enabled an expansion of food exports such that, by 1945, the United States furnished one-tenth of the world food supply.[68] Put differently, it was in this period that food rationing and food aid together provided a foundation for U.S. foreign trade, which, during the Cold War, fueled the consolidation of agriculture and growth of food corporations. However, as Niedecker shows her readers, wartime discourses clashed with the realities of food insecurity for communities like that of Fort Atkinson. Even as the economy grew throughout the forties, those realities troubled ideas of American progress.[69] To quell allegations of food insecurity and thus to maintain images of shared sacrifice and national prosperity, the government sought to convince every citizen that he or she had plenty of food to eat.

### GASTRONOMY IN A TIME OF WAR: M. F. K. FISHER

One might imagine that rationing in the United States and Europe would have inhibited conspicuous displays of food consumption, and yet, throughout the war, upper-class consumers patronized gourmet restaurants in New York, London, and Paris. In the case of Europe, those restaurants often doubled as bomb shelters for their diners and thus elicited derision from social commentators who chafed at the special protection afforded elite civilians.[70] Orwell published just such a send-up of London gourmands in the New York based *Partisan Review*: "At long last, and against much opposition in high places, the Ministry of Food is about to cut down 'luxury feeding' by limiting the sum of money that can be spent on a meal in a hotel or restaurant. Already, before the law is even passed, ways of evading it have been thought out, and these are discussed almost undisguisedly in the newspapers."[71] With his moniker of "luxury feeding," Orwell satirizes the mid-century culture of gourmandize. Historian James Hinton notes that fine dining "was an issue which triggered anger across the social and political spectrum,"[72] and Orwell accordingly depicts the gastronomical practice as a quasi-illegal act of gluttony that flouts food conservation efforts. That Orwell published this column in *Partisan Review*, a little magazine first published in 1934 that addressed left-wing intellectuals in New York, suggests he may also have had in mind the dining habits of Americans and the relative culinary extravagances they enjoyed. A thriving restaurant industry emerged in New York during the war. Chefs who had arrived in the United States for the 1939 World's Fair in Flushing, Queens (such as restaurateur Henri Soulé) stayed on as refugees after the German invasion of Poland and opened French restaurants or joined the staffs of established hotel dining rooms.[73] A group of food critics that included Craig Claiborne at the *New York Times* and Lucius Beebe at *Gourmet* (a magazine founded in 1941) made these restaurants famous to a growing clientele of American gourmands.[74] Orwell's reframing of fine dining as "luxury feeding" exposes a rift between wartime austerity and gastronomy. Wallace Stevens offers a telling illustration of the latter.[75] A food lover, Stevens famously begins the "It Must Give Pleasure" section of his long poem "Notes Toward a Supreme Fiction" (published the same year as Orwell's "London Letter") with a sensorial wonderland of lobster with mango chutney and Meursault wine.[76] This amalgamation of French and Indian cuisines bespeaks the marriage between cosmopolitan tastes and imperial trade routes that made "luxury feeding" possible during the war.

Against the entwined backdrops of transatlantic gastronomy and government rationing, the voice of California food writer M. F. K. Fisher emerged to juxtapose practices of eating well with wartime conditions of hunger, scarcity, and "making do." In the preface to her English translation of the nineteenth-century treatise *The Physiology of Taste: Or, Meditations on Transcendental Gastronomy*, Fisher comments on Brillat-Savarin's aphorism, "the destiny of nations depends on how they nourish themselves."[77] Comparing the famines of the mid-nineteenth and mid-twentieth centuries, her commentary invokes the severe food shortages and seizures in England as well as occupied France. Fisher thus censures devotees of French gastronomy, suggesting that military control of the food supply – in addition to culinary taste and agricultural plenitude – underlies the capacity of gourmands to eat well in times of war. This ambivalence about fine dining comes into focus in *The Gastronomical Me*, her food-centered memoir published in 1943 that dwells on the years just before the war began, when Fisher lived with her second husband Dillwyn Parrish (or "Chexbres") in a restored house outside Geneva.[78] Fisher organizes the book around memories of cooking and eating that unfold on the page as a kind of alimentary stream-of-consciousness. Two chapter headings recur in the text: the sections entitled "Measure of My Powers" (eleven in total) narrate unconventional home cooking projects; while those entitled "Sea Change" (five in total) trace the twelve transatlantic trips Fisher took between Europe and America over the course of just a few years.[79]

The penultimate chapter concerns the final trip to Geneva that Fisher and Parrish made before the war broke out and compelled them to return to California. In describing meals the couple consumed during this 1939 journey across Europe, the chapter alludes to the early movements of the Axis and Allied armies. The memoir's conclusion, which begins with an allusion to Parrish's 1941 suicide at the couple's Bareacres home in California, ends with references to the first year of American combat (202).[80] Detailing her numerous migrations in this period, Fisher refers often in *The Gastronomical Me* to the political events that culminated in the Second World War. About a 1938 voyage to California, she comments dryly, "[a]lmost everyone aboard was fleeing":

> There were a few Dutch-American business men [sic], and a few stiff racial snobs who ate and sat and gambled apart. The rest were Jews. Most of them had gone from Austria to Holland. Then, as things grew worse, they had finally managed to leave Holland for America. They were doctors, many of them, wondering how they could pass state examinations after thirty or forty years of practicing and sometimes months of cruel stagnation in labor camps.
>
> In First Class they walked quietly up and down with little dictionaries, or stood, not speaking to anyone, watching the swift gray waters. (181)

This recollection breaks noticeably from the conventions of food memoir, a genre in which writers tend to depict culinary experiences as markers of cosmopolitan identity and cultural capital. In contrast, Fisher turns from remembering gourmet meals to calling up histories of exclusion and violence that shadow the gourmand.

In the account of her prewar journey to the United States, she moves from the ship's dinner menus (which differ radically for first- and third-class travelers) to the passengers who are fleeing Europe to escape violence and genocide. Fisher positions herself apart from this divide between first-class passengers and Jewish survivors of the pogroms, and yet also undermines the ease with which her fellow passengers (and Anglo-American readers) might enjoy a fine meal (182). According to Susan Derwin, Fisher's writings employ food as a "metaphoric language" to convey symbolic, rather than just physical, hunger, a claim that McLean echoes in emphasizing tropes of psychological and emotional appetite.[81] Such interpretations underestimate the centrality of bodily hunger and the material politics of food to texts like *The Gastronomical Me*, which shuttles between what Pierre Bourdieu defines as the "taste of luxury" and the "taste of necessity."[82] In *Distinction*, Bourdieu catalogues the many ways in which food is both a "nourishing substance [that] sustains the body" and a medium for distinguishing a person's "social position."[83] Although Fisher appreciates culinary extravagance (though in unconventional forms) and travels in a circle of fellow food lovers, her cookbooks and food memoirs integrate personal acts of eating with geopolitical circumstances that surround and often unsettle those experiences. In her food writing from the 1940s, those circumstances are, above all, the traumas of the Second World War. In interrupting descriptions of memorable meals (a stock-in-trade of food memoir) with invocations of food-and-land seizures and ethnic pogroms, Fisher closes the gap between cookbooks and culinary narratives, on the one hand, and political exposé and polemic, on the other.

Throughout the later chapters of *The Gastronomical Me*, Fisher makes several rhetorical leaps from reminiscing about food to worrying about war. One such moment describes a train trip that she and Dillwyn took in June 1939 from Switzerland to Milan, in which she initially dwells on the "old-fashioned" restaurant car. This chapter opens with memories of earlier meals on the same train line that were tailored to the couple's tastes for Asti Spumanti, radish trays, and a main course of meat with "lentils or beans cooked with herbs" and a "fine honest garden salad" (199–201). During the 1939 voyage, however, the appearance of a political prisoner walking through the restaurant car handcuffed to two Italian officers disrupts this elaborate culinary ritual. Fisher associates the disruption with the presence of three young German men who are on board the train. These Italian and German figures stand in for the emerging Axis bloc, a political apparition that undoes the couple's breezy sense of cross-border travel and cosmopolitan dining. After hearing the sound of shattering glass, Fisher learns that a failed escape through a train window led the prisoner to commit suicide on the windowpane shards. As she narrates this chain of events received secondhand from a waiter, her tone grows dispassionate: "Before that summer such a thing would have shocked us, so that our faces would be paler and our eyes wider, but now we only looked up at the old waiter. He nodded, and his own eyes got very hot and dried all the tears. 'Political prisoner,' he said, flicking the table, and his face was more bitter than usual" (204). This resigned response to a violent turn of events dovetails with Fisher's looming personal tragedy (Dillwyn's illness and eventual suicide), but in the context of 1939, it also signals the inevitability of war in Europe. Through tone as much as content, Fisher indicates that an impending world war will make her own practice of eating out an act of indulgence, at best, and of unconscionable elitism, at worst: "There in the train, hurrying across the ripe fields, feeling the tranced waiting of the people everywhere, we knew for a few minutes that we had not escaped. We knew no knife of glass, no distillate of hatred, could keep the pain of war outside. I felt illimitably old, there in the train, knowing that escape was not peace, ever" (209).

## AMERICAN PLENTY, WAR DEPRIVATION, AND FISHER'S "CREATIVE ECONOMY"

Eating doubles in Fisher's writing as a gastronomical escape from and politicized encounter with the war. This pattern is especially salient in *How to Cook a Wolf*, the 1942 cookbook that provides a template for culinary experimentation in the rationed American kitchen but also emerges out of Fisher's firsthand exposure to food shortages in Europe at the war's outset.[84] Although Max Rudin calls the book a work of "culinary modernism," it is better described as an intervention in both food writing and high modernism in that Fisher combines modernist techniques of nonlinear narrative, montage, and irony with journalistic commentary on U.S. consumer culture.[85] *How to Cook a Wolf* can be understood, more precisely, as a late modernist cookbook that alters the social coordinates of both French gastronomy and high modernism. Most cookbooks published in the United States and England during this period – from *250 Ways to Save Sugar* to *Thrifty Cooking for Wartime* – targeted housewives by compiling thrifty meal plans rooted in the new science of vitamins and the points-based rationing system.[86] *How to Cook a Wolf*, in stark contrast, intersperses recipes that are nonformulaic with essayistic musings on the respective ideologies informing government rations and gourmet cuisine.[87] The strangeness of *How to Cook a Wolf* qua cookbook led one *New York Times* reviewer to dismiss it as an incoherent work that could hardly serve the alimentary needs of "adults working in factories or fields."[88] Despite the eccentricities and extravagances of many of the recipes, McLean describes the text as Fisher's most practical cookbook: "Although Fisher defiantly condemns ... popular domestic cookbooks, *How to Cook a Wolf*, more so than any of Fisher's other works, tempers the aesthetic pleasures of gastronomy with a practicality derived from nineteenth-century domestic manuals."[89] In the biography *An Extravagant Hunger*, Anne Zimmerman concurs with McLean, defining *How to Cook a Wolf* as a "revolutionary book" that breaks with the prescriptive and routinized character of recipes found in mid-century women's magazines, cookbooks, and domestic science manuals.[90]

Throughout *How to Cook a Wolf*, Fisher employs her catchphrase "the wolf at the door" to symbolize the traumas of the Second World War, from bombs to hunger. Against this image, Fisher cites early on Ralph Waldo Emerson's claim that "a creative economy is the fuel of magnificence" (10). In the context of a 1942 cookbook offering not step-by-step cooking instruction but a satire of standardized diets and government rations, the Emerson epigraph proves central to the project of *How to Cook a Wolf*. For the "magnificence" Fisher means is the unruly individualism (if also the cultural and material capital) to cook creatively in a time of scarce resources and fuel shortages. Against the government's edict for citizens to share alike, Fisher calls on her female readers to cook imaginatively and to eat selfishly: "Now, when the hideous necessity of the war machine takes steel and cotton and humanity, our own private personal secret mechanism must be stronger, for selfish comfort as well as for the good of the ideals we believe we believe in" (3–4). This call inverts the government's alimentary rhetoric, which, as we have seen, correlated the civic obligations of women with the domestic work of shopping for, preparing, and conserving food. By way of a quick wit resonant with Niedecker's war poems, *How to Cook a Wolf* ties rationing to fear mongering: "Since this country went to war, a great deal has been done to prepare us for emergencies (a polite word for bombings, invasions, and many other ugly things)" (184). Such strident reflections participate in war propaganda while reframing its ideology. Fisher stirs the fear of invasion in her reader while suggesting that many middle-class and upper-class consumers live more acutely in fear of economic disruptions than of the war itself.

Following her wry reflection on the shifting meanings of emergency in wartime, Fisher turns to a practical problem confronting home cooks during the war: fuel restrictions. To cook with scarce oil and gas, Fisher offers her readers the evidently banal advice to invest in small electric grills and keep their kitchens well ventilated: "The people in England have found that electricity usually stays on longer than gas in an actual bombing, so most well-equipped private shelters have little electric grills in them, or at least toasters and hot plates. Now would be a good time to get out the old chafing dish, if you have not already done it" (186). Although this admonishment sensationalizes the potential for an invasion, Fisher's ironic tone foregrounds the relative insularity of most American kitchens and of the United States writ large. The chapter concludes by framing the act of eating gourmet foods under globally uneven conditions of warfare as at once indulgent and subversive. "With a small cautious grin," Fisher reformulates the OWI and WFA's calls to shop and eat with the Allied armies always in mind by inviting her readers to dispense with their ration books and instead procure "as many fresh things" as possible (190). The recipes that *How to Cook a Wolf* comprises bear out this invitation to protest austerity measures by undermining not only government ration programs but also haute cuisine. While state-sanctioned menus encouraged housewives to cook in line with the points system and while posh urban restaurants showcased a cuisine based on rare and often rarified ingredients, *How to Cook a Wolf* advances a model of cooking resonant with Claude Lévi-Strauss's notion of bricolage: a method of assembling meaning out of "a collection of oddments left over from human endeavors."[91] Fisher advocates a kindred method of assembling imaginative and meaningful meals out of whatever one has on hand, whether canned stocks and fresh herbs or cheap cuts of offal and foraged mushrooms. Given the political pressures on home cooks to support the war effort through their behaviors at grocery stores and in kitchens, Fisher's model of improvisation, which urges the home cook to evade the U.S. food bureaucracy, is a nonconformist one that makes resistance to the nationalist and standardized diet a form of political protest.

The recipes and short essays of *How to Cook a Wolf* encourage the reader to be "lavish" with whatever foods she or he can obtain. Although this term seems to speak only to affluent home cooks, Fisher repeatedly promotes a mode of "dressing up" affordable ingredients (8). Although she provides little pragmatic advice for procuring hard-to-come-by ingredients such as truffles and duck confit, her menus have a modular structure, akin to modernist architecture, that offers readers a template for adapting and varying recipes according to their budget. In developing this "creative economy," Fisher recommends an enormous range of cooking techniques. Her chapter "How to Distribute your Virtue," for example, assumes the form of a montage: an almost incoherent primer that combines the traditional and the modern, the technological and the rudimentary, and the time-intensive and the laborsaving. One section on fuel conservation strategies updates the "primitive" technique of steaming food in a hay-packed box, which Fisher outlines as a viable alternative to the modern convenience of a pressure cooker (45, 49). Social historian Joy Parr shows that kitchen technologies like the pressure cooker emerged precisely at the intersection of wartime economics and modernist design during a period when consumer goods companies aggressively marketed machines as emblems of the "capitalized kitchen."[92] This vision extended to Europe, where the famous Frankfurt kitchen inspired a 1944 British Ministry of Works project to construct 156,000 prefab houses in anticipation of postwar housing shortages. One English architect connected to the project described the streamlined and technologically augmented kitchen that featured in each prefab house as "a machine for the preparation of meals."[93] By the war's end, the Western kitchen had become "a complex, technological artifact" – a trend on display during the 1959 "kitchen debate" between Vice President Nixon and Soviet Premier Khrushchev at the American national exhibition in Moscow.[94] The debate included a photo-op with exhibition guide Lois Epstein, who showed the two Cold War leaders how women might use the many machines powering the now famous General Electric demonstration kitchen. Despite how hastily the United States assembled a team to construct the Moscow exhibition, the impact of the kitchen was lasting: "According to American boosters, from then on, technology was to be measured in terms of consumer goods rather than [only] space and nuclear technologies."[95]

As Belasco observes of the numerous futuristic kitchens that made appearances at World's Fairs, kitchen gadgetry and processed foods promised women "emancipation" from the drudgery of cooking.[96] In opposition to this premise, Fisher joins Niedecker in questioning whether the push to make domestic spaces as productive and efficient as industrial ones would indeed be liberatory. When Fisher includes the hay-packed box in her own ideal kitchen, then, she undercuts the increasingly widespread vision of the capitalized kitchen. Fisher moves on from this denunciation of kitchen efficiency (reminiscent of the skepticism about kitchen gadgets in *One of Ours*) to a reflection on the importance of fresh vegetables for wartime cookery. Joan Reardon contends that such moments in *How to Cook a Wolf* highlight Fisher's rejection of prepackaged foods and anticipate the locavore movement of the 2000s.[97] However, we should be wary of seeing prolepses of contemporary food movements in mid-century food writing, however evident they may seem in Fisher's case. *How to Cook a Wolf* shows us that an alternative to "the capitalized kitchen" emerged in the United States decades before the slow food and locavore movements (which I discuss in Chapters 5 and 6) called for a revival of traditional cookery and a revitalization of regional agricultures. In Fisher's case, the alternative imagined to the high-tech kitchen is one that promotes – but also fetishizes – vernacular cooking methods. Elsewhere in *How to Cook a Wolf*, Fisher observes that garden-fresh produce might offer an antidote both to ration cards and to kitchen technologies by allowing the home cook to "play" with food. The 1951 addendum to this section suggests, moreover, that the accompanying recipe for a salad of chilled blanched vegetables is an affront to the meat-and-potatoes diet that U.S. food agencies promoted. The recipe enacts a kind of culinary modernism in, once again, offering up a modular and improvisational style of cooking that squares off against the regimen of "three square meals" a day. One might ask, though, how a "fresh salad" of a "dozen tiny vegetables" can be anything but willfully escapist in the face of world war and genocide? In response to this nagging question, which haunts *How to Cook a Wolf*, Fisher imagines such forms of food-play as her blanched salad to be small acts of cultural rebellion that, in aggregate, undermine the nation's paradoxical ideology of American plenty and sacrifice.

For most readers, Fisher admits, mid-century cookbooks offer nothing more than "good escape-reading material in direct ration to the possibility of following [recipes] in [their] small kitchens and hurried hours" (29). The pun on ration is significant, suggesting that consumers are reading gourmet cookbooks either for practical advice or aesthetic escape in "direct ration" to their incomes. Fisher here makes visible the social chasm between communities who can and communities who cannot afford to cook without regard for food's material costs. Jessamyn Neuhaus reasons that *How to Cook a Wolf* thus critiques the "over-indulgence" of the mid century.[98] To expand on this observation, I would argue that the book does not simply catalogue "half-forgotten luxuries and half-remembered delicate impossible dishes" but rather delves into the rise of American consumer culture (*HW* 191). More pointedly, *How to Cook a Wolf* echoes Niedecker's *New Goose* poems in making inequity and lack cruxes of the mid-century politics of food. The constraints Fisher imposes on her implied reader – to cook creatively with limited ingredients – dovetails, too, with the avant-garde projects of John Cage and the Oulipo group of writers.[99] Just when her readers might lose themselves in "delectable" recipes or gastronomical narratives, Fisher asserts how *little* they have to work with at this historical moment. To prevent her American readers from concluding *How to Cook a Wolf* sated with the flavors of shrimp paté and "Fruits aux Sept Liqueurs," Fisher reminds them that they are at war: "It is plain that a great many of the things in the following recipes are impossible to find, now. That immediately puts the whole chapter in the same class as Samarkand and Xanadu and the *terrase* of the Café de la Paix. It is perhaps just as well; for a time there are other things than anchovies that must be far from actuality" (192). In moving the idea of food scarcity from everyday staples – sugar, flour, butter, and so on – to ingredients that are far from necessary (anchovies, in this case), Fisher juxtaposes the sacrifice of gourmet foods to the actualities of forced starvation and political imprisonment.

Although "lively and amusing" in tone, as Fisher herself acknowledges, the cookbook refuses the gourmand's inclination to "close [her] eyes to the headlines and [her] ears to the sirens and the threatenings of high explosives, and read instead the sweet nostalgic measures of these recipes, impossible yet fond" (192). In the 1951 additions to this same passage, Fisher puts a finer point on her earlier suggestion that food writing need not be a quaint or quietist act but a form of "therapy known to any prisoner of war or woe"; "some of the world's most delectable cookbooks have been written," she goes so far to suggest, "in concentration camps and cell-blocks" (192). The reference to concentration camps may bring to mind, if only by contrast, a pivotal scene in Primo Levi's memoir of Auschwitz when Levi and another prisoner walk the grounds to bring food covertly to their workgroup while recollecting daily food rituals in their French villages.[100] By referring to concentration camps in the abstract, Fisher shakes the reader out of any passive reading of the adjacent recipes for French dishes, but she also reveals her own, and many of her fellow citizens', slow-dawning awareness (or willful ignorance) of the Holocaust. Moments such as this one powerfully illustrate the competing stakes of *How to Cook a Wolf*: a text that is part experimental cookbook, part "escape reading material," and part war protest.

Fisher interleaves these commentaries on war and famine with anecdotes about the U.S. consumer economy. The meals she recommends to her readers in the event of catastrophe, for example, conjure up the burgeoning processed food industry that expanded during the war years as consumer product companies marketed inexpensive alternatives to rationed meats, sweets, and dairy products. Neuhaus catalogues recipes from this period that endorsed these new convenience foods but helped home cooks to disguise them as refined (the most famous example of this tactic being the now much-maligned Jell-O mold).[101] Astute to this trend, Fisher observes that processed foods aid cooking through a "chicanery" that makes meals out of items like canned mushroom soup and Spam (188). Dismissive of the affordability and expediency of processed foods, she maintains that national – and increasingly global – brands such as Hormel, Kraft, and Kellogg market food suitable only for the war's emergency conditions: "The damnable things are fixes; they admit it on the labels ... *simulated* Romano, Cheddar *type*, and so on.... But they perform a special function, I think, in making people feel hungry" (189, emphasis in original). Prepared and synthetic foods will nourish her readers, Fisher reasons, only insofar as the Hershey Ration D and Tropical Chocolate bars will secure the basic survival of Allied soldiers (Figure 7) (188–89).[102]

If soldiers and occupied populations survive on emergency rations, Fisher further reasons that famine conditions outside the United States perversely benefit the U.S. food economy that companies like Kraft and Hershey come to embody. Most strikingly, *How to Cook a Wolf* suggests that the rationing of food to support the military parallels the rise of fast food, for, in both cases, the logics of scalability and convenience are at work. While hunger

7 Photograph of Hershey Ration D Bar and Tropical Chocolate Bar. Circa 1942–1944. Courtesy of the Hershey Community Archives, Hershey, PA.

defined the war years for most people around the world, too much food, Fisher's cookbook relays, typified American consumer culture in the forties. One of the longest sections in the book – "How to Carve the Wolf" – laments that Americans continued to consume relatively large quantities of meat despite government restrictions. As Levenstein explains, those restrictions began in 1942 with a voluntary "Share the Meat" campaign that morphed into a two-and-a-half-pound weekly ration: more than two times England's meat ration and approximately ten times that of most other European nations.[103] Niedecker makes these discrepancies between U.S. and European rations the subject of a 1945 poem, a pithy dramatic monologue about "the story" of a Vichy official who chastises hungry French citizens to "eat your beef-ounce from a doll's platter / you'll think it's a roast wrapped in butter."[104] Through a shift from the mundane to the surreal[105], the poem makes drastic meat shortages outside the United States a foil for American consumption patterns.[106] To contextualize Niedecker's and Fisher's wary portraits of the ideal of American abundance, consider the "hoarding frenzy" that ensued in 1943 when the U.S. government offered consumers advance notice of new and stricter meat rations. The public demand for meat was so high at this moment that the announcement provoked riots and looting: in Cleveland, 50,000 people assembled to demand meat from grocers, while in New York City, 2,000 butchers marched on the wholesale meat district.[107] After the war ended, American meat consumption only increased, and the skyrocketing demand for grain to feed livestock compromised the Truman administration's promise to ship wheat to Europe, Asia, and Africa during the postwar famine of 1946–48.[108]

One passage in *How to Cook a Wolf* connects these consumer appetites for meat to the nation's military-industrial complex as it expanded during and immediately after the war. Fisher here undercuts her earlier commentary on the challenges that meat rationing poses to home chefs by making a comedic allusion to the "zub zub zub" of the media hype surrounding *planned* shortages. For Fisher, this media buzz encouraged the overproduction and overconsumption of meat:

> There are several *more or less* logical reasons why meat grows scarce in wartime: soldiers need it, there are fewer cattle, zub zub zub. It is unfortunate that so many human beings depend on eating some form of animal flesh every day for strength. Many of them do it because their bodies, weakened or diseased, demand it. Others simply have the habit. Habit or necessity, it becomes a truly worrisome expense in wartime, so that money spent for meat must be used to buy as much nourishment as possible, even at the risk of a certain monotony. (87, emphasis mine)

The use of the phrase "more or less" is worth pausing on, for it interrogates the government's claim that rations functioned to curtail future shortages. In fact, some of the food conserved through rationing in the United States went neither to overseas food supplies nor to agricultural reserves but, rather, to weapons production (as was the case with the animal fat and cooking oil that the "Save waste fats for explosives" poster enlists viewers to conserve). The expressed reasons for rationing do not square with the nation's expanding agricultural output, which made consumer runs on meat possible in the first place when rumors of future shortages circulated. Fisher's phrase "zub zub zub" mimics those media outlets that inflamed public fears and prompted food riots, but it also signals the industrialization of agriculture in general and of meat in particular. Akin to the staccato cadence in Niedecker's 1950 poem of the *Hoard's Dairyman* (and its "hog feeder price lists"), this refrain in *How to Cook a Wolf* crystallizes the velocity and technical infrastructure of food production in the United States. If we strain our ear, we can hear – behind the "zub zub zub" of newspaper presses and radio broadcasts drumming up food scares – the disassembly lines of the American feedlot, slaughterhouse, and meatpacking plant (a topic Chapter 5 takes up in examining contemporary narratives and exposés of industrialized meat).

Although *How to Cook a Wolf*, with its unconventional recipes and polemical commentaries, dovetails with Niedecker's lyrics, Fisher also at points glosses over the class politics of cooking and eating. Hunger is at once material and symbolic for Fisher, who claims, "since we must eat to live, we might as well do it with both grace and gusto.... one of the most dignified ways we are capable of, to assert and then reassert our dignity in the face of poverty and war's fears and pains, is to nourish ourselves with all possible skills, delicacy, and ever-increasing enjoyment" (199–200). The meaning of hunger slips here from a condition of extreme malnourishment to a state of emotional want, which Fisher implies aesthetic experience can sate. Fisher later describes the decline of regional cuisines in the United States as just such a form of deprivation: "Why ... are we so ungastronomic as a nation? Why do we permit and even condone the feeble packaged bread that our men try to keep strong on!" (163). She goes on to argue that due to the loss of regional food traditions American cuisine has become "expensively repetitive: we eat what and how and when our parents ate, without thought of natural hungers" (164). *How to Cook a Wolf* acknowledges, then, that hunger is a lived and embodied experience with socioeconomic causes and consequences, and yet the cookbook also transmutes hunger into a symbol of the cultural losses that stem from inartistic modes of cooking.

Fisher ultimately balances her reflections on symbolic hungers for culinary experience with her politicized commentaries on unequal food access, which *How to Cook a Wolf*, like Niedecker's poetry, identifies as one outcome of the Second World War. We might understand the accumulation of "hopelessly extravagant recipes" in *How to Cook a Wolf* as a modernist collage that functions to question the gourmand's demand for foods from around the globe (xi). Fisher is quick to qualify one such recipe – a soufflé requiring no less than "16 eggs!" – by writing that such instances of decadence are intended to parody the gourmet's unreflexive and "automatic extravagance" (61). Addressing the rift separating gourmet cuisine from other forms of cooking and eating during the war, Fisher takes to task the national institutions that presented the war's food shortages as equitably felt. As a corrective to the social pressure toward conformity and the denial of economic inequities that haunt rationing rhetoric, Fisher entreats her readers to "cast off their habits":

One of the saving graces of the less-monied people of the world has always been, theoretically, that they were forced to eat more unadulterated, less dishonest food than the rich-bitches. It begins to look as if that were a lie. In our furious efforts to prove that all men are created equal we encourage our radios, our movies, above all our weekly and monthly magazines, to set up a fantastic ideal in the minds of family cooks, so that everywhere earnest eager women are whipping themselves and their budgets to the bone to provide three 'balanced' meals a day for their men and children. (5)

This passage refers to the "balanced" diet that the WFA and its nutritionists advocated throughout the 1940s. The WFA aimed to standardize American dietary habits according to the Newer Nutrition (and thus to elide regional and ethnic differences) while also conserving the nation's agricultural surpluses for export. *How to Cook a Wolf* reveals that this regime failed to resolve the material structures within and outside the United States that perpetuate malnourishment. In line with Niedecker's poetry, the cookbook raises a perhaps unanswerable question: where does all of the food that American agribusiness produces, to the point of surplus, go? Historians of industrial agriculture suggest that the answer lies partly in how concentrated the food system became in this period around a handful of durable commodity crops that could be transformed into the "value-added" goods of animal feed and processed foods, at the same time that the overall diversity of food cultivation around the world narrowed.[109]

These developments, Fisher implies, produce consumable commodities but a dearth of actual food. Her chapter "How to Pray for Peace," to this point, characterizes the potato as the principal food of impoverished and displaced victims of the war: "It is easy to think of potatoes, and fortunately for men who do not have much money it is easy to think of them with a certain safety. Potatoes are one of the last things to disappear, in times of war, which is probably why they should not be forgotten in times of peace" (121). Fisher alludes here not only to the Irish potato famine between 1845 and 1852 but also to the food shortages in Europe during the Second World War, reminding her readers that scarcity and deprivation are highly contingent experiences. An unorthodox cookbook, *How to Cook a Wolf* demonstrates that evidently innocuous food prescriptions to share alike and to eat a balanced diet conceal the fallout of a globalizing food system. Against U.S. campaigns for food conservation and "unadulterated" national cooking, Fisher parodies the wartime appetites of affluent gourmands even as she celebrates creative cooking. Her 1942 cookbook is thus an important text for both late modernism and food writing. Critics have been quick to classify Fisher's writings as modernist because of their stylistic attributes. Yet Fisher does not simply apply modernist style to food writing but also routes modernism through the mid-century politics of cooking and eating. Both *The Gastronomical Me* and *How to Cook a Wolf* suggest that modernist forms of montage are especially apt to articulating the period's contradictory ideologies of scarcity and surplus alongside lived experiences of famine and "luxury feeding." Through her modernist redefinition of the cookbook and culinary redefinition of modernism, Fisher reveals a nation's growing appetites for industrialized food and the bodily as well as economic power that food promises.

## AUSTERITY AND THE TRANSATLANTIC POLITICS OF FOOD

While the United States lifted rations after 1945, the postwar Labour government expanded the wartime rationing program – a controversial scheme that contributed substantially to the Party's 1951 defeat.[110] As signaled by the trope of dry, dark rationed bread in Orwell's dystopian novel *Nineteen Eighty-Four* (1945), the continuance of rationing incited fears that the austerity of wartime food controls would never end.[111] In his 2005 book on the postwar period, the late historian Tony Judt evokes W. H. Auden's 1947 poem "The Age of Anxiety" to characterize the situation in England at the time: "everything was rationed, restricted, controlled. . . . This was the age of austerity."[112] The chief markers of this postwar economic crisis were, moreover, the state-issued ration card and long food queue, which featured prominently in President Truman's 1946 appeal for the American people to conserve domestic grain and reduce meat consumption in order to support food aid. Despite such appeals, however, voluntary rationing proved largely unsuccessful in the United States, and it would not be until the Marshall Plan that a coordinated international food relief program would take shape.[113] Daily consumption patterns on either side of the Atlantic meanwhile grew increasingly disparate. Between the beginning and end of the war, for example, meat consumption declined by 19 percent in the United Kingdom but increased by 8.9 percent in the United States.[114] To take up a concluding observation of *How to Cook a Wolf*, although the United States claimed that the nation's citizens made tremendous food sacrifices during the Second World War, those sacrifices appear relatively scant when placed in a transnational context.

Although the British government depicted food shortages as universally felt, working-class citizens experienced shortages the most acutely. In a 1941 letter to *Partisan Review*, Orwell foregrounds precisely this inequity: "[although] there is no real food shortage, the lack of concentrated foods (meat, bacon, cheese and eggs) causes serious underfeeding among heavy labourers, such as miners, who have to eat their midday meal away from home."[115] In response to such allegations, British propaganda stressed the need for all citizens not simply to share alike, as in the United States, but to suffer on behalf of the war effort. Austerity, rather than conservation, thus characterized rationing discourse in England, making basic food access the chief concern for most demographic groups and particularly for working-class communities. As early as 1941, a majority of Londoners viewed government food restrictions to be more menacing than air raids.[116] Furthermore, rationing signified a sacrifice made not only to win the Allied war but also to secure the British Empire in the sense that famine conditions led England to rely heavily on food imports from both the United States and its colonies. Judt and other historians have shown that the catastrophic Bengali famine of 1943 stemmed in large part from the amount of food Bengal had been compelled to export to England.[117] The pride that some citizens expressed about wartime austerity measures – or that the Ministries of Food and Finance expressed on their behalf – demonstrates how vital food control was to British imperialism.

The continuation of austerity measures after the war provides the historical backdrop for a continental analogue to Fisher's 1942 cookbook: Elizabeth David's 1950 *Book of Mediterranean Food*. Although John Burnett shows that the first signs of de-rationing in the late 1940s sparked a small wave of gourmet food writing, David's book was nonetheless an outlier in the postwar publishing landscape.[118] Almost every press responded to her book proposal with incredulity, arguing that no one in Europe had enough food to cook complete meals much less to cook gourmet cuisine. Although John Lehmann at Penguin New Writing decided to publish *A Book of Mediterranean Food* (retaining even its more "outlandish" recipes), when the press printed a paperback version in 1954, David's text was, with the exception of Bee Nilson's *The ABC of Cookery*, the only paperback cookery book on the market.[119] Out of step with the prevailing food discourses of postwar England, *A Book of Mediterranean Food* functioned for David as an elegy for the gastronomical wasteland ("the awful, dreary foods of rationing") that she saw on returning to London in 1947 after spending the war years abroad.[120] This disappointing homecoming provoked David to make "the most out of rationed ingredients, ignoring the powdered and dehydrated foods to which the British had become conditioned" and "scour[ing] SoHo" in search of such ingredients as "lemons, olive oil, [and] bootleg butter."[121] In David's case, then, austerity fueled a desire for difficult-to-come-by foods and an aspiration to cook extravagantly with them.

Composed in London between 1947 and 1950, *A Book of Mediterranean Food* grew out of the peculiar forms of war travel and paramilitary service afforded to intellectuals during the war. Following an inverse trajectory to Fisher's, David migrated farther and farther south between 1939 and 1947 – from Marseille and Antibes to Athens, Corsica, and the Greek Island of Syros to Alexandria, Cairo, and, finally New Delhi. Although the original intent of her sojourn was personal (a combination of gastro-tourism and romance), the extended holiday turned into war-related civil service. David worked for the British Ministry of War Transportation in Alexandria, where she befriended the modernist writer Lawrence Durrell; she then served as a researcher for the British Ministry of Information in Cairo; and in New Delhi, shortly after the war ended, she joined her husband for his administrative appointment under the British Commander-in-Chief.[122] The literary outcome of these peregrinations, *A Book of Mediterranean Food* establishes a transnational gastronomy. In the preface to each of the book's four editions, David contrasts the monotonous diet of postwar England with the vibrant cuisines of North Africa and India that she enjoyed throughout the war. She writes her culinary memoir of the Second World War, in other words, by assembling recipes that are "no more than exotic memories" in the rationed homes of postwar London (*MF* 4). For McLean, *A Book of Mediterranean Food* functions to "reliv[e] emotional and material plenitude in a time of scarcity."[123] Not surprisingly given this aim, the book expresses nostalgia for the Mediterranean region and a desire to reproduce the cuisines David consumed while serving as an imperial attaché. In "those icy, hungry weeks" of 1947 London, when severe winter storms exacerbated food shortages, David "took refuge from reality in writing down memories of the food [she] had cooked and eaten during [her] Mediterranean years" (5).

She constructs a microcosm of Mediterranean food, moreover, that decenters French provincial cooking in favor of Greek, Turkish, Moroccan, Italian, and Spanish cuisines. In relationship to the British Empire and to David's civil service within that empire, the cookbook draws a faulty map of the mid-century world and its geopolitics. David's cross-cultural guide to Mediterranean food (her category for cuisines that cut across Southern Europe and North Africa) implicitly diverts attention away from the configuration of the British Commonwealth and the rise of decolonial movements. David serves forth the foods of Italy and Morocco rather than of Egypt and India, the colonial locales where she concluded her wartime service. In his seminal essay "Modernism and Imperialism," Jameson describes such cultural narratives and cognitive maps that came to define the British Empire over the twentieth century. "In Colonialism," he writes, "a significant structural segment of the economic system as a whole is now located elsewhere, beyond the metropolis, outside the daily life and existential experience of the home country, in colonies over the water whose own life experience and life world … remain unknown and unimaginable for the subjects of the imperial power, whatever social class they may belong to."[124] Taking *Howards End* as his tutor text, Jameson argues that empires with capitalist economies like England's must posit a geographic totality in which a citizens of the nation-state and colonial subjects are intimately linked as consumers and producers of the same goods and yet utterly segregated in terms of political identity. The capitalist empire thus evolves into a social body that can never be fully mapped or apprehended. In response to this cognitive dissonance, Jameson argues, modernism adopts mapping as a formal procedure – an always incomplete project of accounting for the geopolitics of empire in the age of global capitalism.[125]

This procedure is arguably at work in *A Book of Mediterranean Food*, but more to augment than to contest the British empire. From her vantage point in postwar London, David maps the Mediterranean region through a culturally and geographically eclectic assemblage of recipes. It is this culinary map – or microcosm – that obscures the contested boundaries of the British Empire and underwrites David's identity as a cosmopolitan food traveler and cookbook author. In the notes to one recipe, David writes, "[t]he octopus sounds alarming to those who have not travelled in the Mediterranean; it is in fact an excellent dish when properly prepared, rich and with a reminiscence of lobster" (67). In the section that follows this sensual description and the more practical advice of how to source good substitutes for octopus in postwar London, we are reminded that, while recipes can migrate around the world, the borders of nation and empire are less fungible. Thus does David describe her adaptation of the recipe for Gigot a la Provençale: "A recipe from an old French cookery book which I have left in its original French; as the author rather severely remarks, this dish is supportable only to those who are accustomed to the cooking of the Midi" (76). In lieu of cuisines from the colonies where she lived during the war, David creates a kind of museum to the specialty foods and cooking implements of a Mediterranean cuisine that exists outside of both imperialism and world war. Although *A Book of Mediterranean Food* begins as a protest of rationing, its "rich" Mediterranean cookery ultimately eschews the bodily experiences of and political reasons for mid-century austerity. In contrast to Fisher's development of a politically engaged (if also whimsical) gastronomy and Niedecker's searing poetics of hunger in the land of plenty, David's cookbook preserves a fuzzy picture of the empire that England maintains in no small measure through both national austerity and imperial food trade.

### CODA: STAGING FOOD'S POWER IN *WAITING FOR GODOT*

In the second act of *Waiting for Godot*, upon the entrance of Pozzo and Lucky, it becomes clear that Vladimir alone can remember the prior day, whose temporal relation to the present is indeterminate. While Vladimir insists on recalling the particularities of the past, Pozzo and Estragon ramble on about time in the abstract and then deny that they have ever met one another. Responding to these nonsequiturs, Vladimir reflects that tomorrow will take the same form as today:

> Was I sleeping, while the others suffered? Am I sleeping now? To-morrow, when I wake, or think I do, what shall I say of to-day? That with Estragon my friend, at this place, until the fall of night, I waited for Godot? That Pozzo passed, with his carrier, and that he spoke to us? Probably. But in all that what truth will there be? (*Estragon, having struggled with his boots in vain, is dozing off again. Vladimir looks at him.*) He'll know nothing. He'll tell me about the blows he received and I'll give him a carrot. (*Pause.*) Astride of a grave and a difficult birth. Down in the hole, lingeringly, the grave-digger puts on the forceps. We have time to grow old. The air is full of our cries. (*He listens.*) But habit is a great deadener.[126]

Lois Gordon interprets such impasses as central to *Godot*'s existential "paradox of survival."[127] In the absence of both verifiable facts about the past and the will to act in the present, Gordon argues, Beckett's characters proceed through the force of habit.[128] Jameson rearticulates this argument about the forms of stasis and repetition that structure the play when he claims that *Waiting for Godot* exemplifies a pattern in late modernist literature of eliding history. For Jameson, the play excludes referential content that would point to the Second World War or to the contemporaneous decline of the British Empire. Beckett organizes the play around the "incomplete sentence," Jameson writes, "a kind of aphasia in which the syntactic conclusion, known in advance, does not have to be given."[129] Stammering begets silence in the world of *Godot*, so this argument goes. Referring to Lucky's largely silent part, Jameson defines the play as a drama that stymies not just logical dialogue and willed action but also our comprehension of the play's significance with respect to mid-century history.

Although compelling, these accounts give short shrift to the material texture of *Waiting for Godot* in neglecting the play's physical environment: the live performance with its lone tree, many props, fallow country setting, and, finally, five actors who play the parts of Vladimir, Estragon, Lucky,

## "Luxury Feeding" and War Rations: Food Writing at Midcentury 83

Pozzo, and "the boy." Attending to those material artifacts in the text and on the stage, we can reframe *Waiting for Godot* as a drama in which the scarcity of objects and the sparseness of emotions testify not to a generalized existential feeling but to concrete outcomes of the Second World War. Joseph Roach begins to unravel the relationship of the play to history by arguing for the spectral presence of the Irish famine in the treatment of hunger.[130] Composed during Beckett's so-called siege of literary activity in Paris, *Waiting for Godot* also explores the ironies of the food economy in the critical years of 1946–48, when both England and France continued to ration food. According to the play's dramatic situation, the absurdity of life after the Second World War inheres in experiences of hunger and rationing – in the most quotidian senses of these terms.

Vladimir's monologue quoted previously demonstrates that however much *Waiting for Godot* expresses existential uncertainty about what happened yesterday and what will happen tomorrow, it does so with a keen sense of the present. As elsewhere in the play, stage directions undercut Vladimir's philosophical ruminations in foregrounding Estragon's struggles for physical comfort and bodily nourishment. While the audience listens to Vladimir ruminate, it also watches Estragon fuss. To Vladimir's rhetorical question, "in all that what truth will there be?," the stage directions respond: "*Estragon, having struggled with his boots in vain, is dozing off again. Vladimir looks at him.*" The cue to action invites the audience to look with Vladimir at Estragon – specifically, at his tattered, ill-fitting, and stinking boots – rather than to pursue further the muddled problem of relativity. Vladimir picks up his train of thought with the grandiose assertion that tomorrow when Estragon wakes, "He'll know nothing," an assertion that the opening of Act II has already affirmed. However, philosophical statement gives way once again to a darkly comedic focus on the body when Vladimir enumerates the pain that will befall Gogo: "He'll tell me about the blows he received and I'll give him a carrot" [sic] (104). The choreographed pause that follows this line is significant, requiring us to pause on the most banal of props in the play – a carrot – before considering Didi's proclamation on the human condition (104). The exchange of food and blows in this scene literalizes the proverb of "the carrot and the stick," which refers to a farmer's practice of prodding donkeys to move forward by either dangling carrots or brandishing sticks. This dead metaphor comes to life when Vladimir dangles a carrot before Estragon, and the chilling joke of this scene is to make Beckett's tramps into working animals that are at the mercy of others for fulfilling their basic food needs.

Vladimir concludes the monologue with an aphorism: "habit is a great deadener." However, the recursive actions that propel the play unfold, especially in the case of Estragon, as if for the first time; nor do these recursions deaden the physical pain, emotional anguish, and fear the couple experiences. "The air is full of our cries," Vladimir says, and then pauses again (105). The two pauses formally link two evidently opposing forces in the play: Estragon's physical appetite for carrots and the harrowing "cries" that fill the air. Those cries belong at once to the characters before us, who shout out in pain repeatedly during both real fights and mock battles, and to the shades of the Second World War, whose bodies seem to fill the landscape behind Beckett's spare country road. The proximity of Vladimir's pauses define the drama of *Waiting for Godot*, for they correlate the bodily hunger of Estragon with the play's allusions to the dead of the Second World War and the social hierarchies that the war years redoubled.

Jameson and Gordon both acknowledge the presence of such historical referents in the play: for Jameson, those referents inform an "allegorical schema" staging the "British Empire [cast as Pozzo] in relationship to its colonies in general and Ireland in particular [cast as Lucky]"; while for Gordon, they bring onto stage the legacy of the Holocaust.[131] However, these insights take the form of asides about anomalous moments of historical signification. Regardless of Beckett's intent for or retrospective assessment of *Waiting for Godot*, the play's references to the Second World War are at once spare and pervasive.[132] Without provocation, Vladimir at one point looks out at the mound of dirt on stage behind them and asks Estragon, "where are all these corpses from?" (71). Interrupting one of his many confounding philosophical discourses, he thus draws Estragon's attention to the presence of dead bodies in the rural territory they inhabit. Anticipating the "cries" that later fill the air on stage, Vladimir "cries out," "A charnel-house! A charnel-house!" (71). Vladimir here alludes to, without naming directly, the Holocaust. Moreover, his own visceral screams undercut earlier abstractions and aver that we cannot think our way out of the horrors of the Second World War, just as this scene suggests that the burden of thought is not the greatest misery of all. The drama of the play arguably inheres these poignant, if scant, evocations of the Second World War and, especially, of the starvation of Jewish prisoners in the concentration camps. In the ruined landscape of *Waiting for Godot* – which, despite the flowering of the lone tree between Acts I and II, shows little sign of arable soil – a social order persists that is at once totalitarian and capitalistic, even as the play creates a negative space outside of the modern state and market. This claim takes its cue from Theodor Adorno's account of Beckett as at once an abstract and realist artist. "Despite their *austerity*," Adorno argues, Beckett's plays "in no way fully renounce costumes and sets: The servant Clov [of *Endgame*] ... wears the laughably outmoded costume of a traveling Englishman; and the sandhill of *Happy Days* bears similarity to geological formations of the American West."[133] From these examples, Adorno defines a politics of abstraction in modern aesthetics, observing that the Theater of the Absurd, like abstract painting, "sympathizes, as from across the abyss of ages, with the superfluous vagrant who will not completely acquiesce to fixed property and settled civilization."[134]

Although the landscape of *Waiting for Godot* is carefully stripped of obvious references to time or place, Beckett provides a cipher for the geographic setting in a memory Vladimir has of the Rhône Valley and the fieldwork he once did there with Estragon. In Act II, we learn that Vladimir remembers harvesting grapes in the Rhône region. The reference calls up the years Beckett spent serving the French Resistance and living in the southwest provincial town of Roussillon. For his part, Estragon remembers almost nothing about the couple's shared history of agricultural labor, while Vladimir forecloses on the memory almost as soon as he recalls it: "There's no good harking back on that" (67). The brief allusion to the Rhône begs the question, however, of how the time and place on stage compare to a past life of rural work.[135] Beyond its fallow and macabre characteristics, the landscape Beckett's tramps describe in dialogue (as opposed to the minimalist one called for in the stage directions) is socially stratified. The reasons that Vladimir and Estragon are waiting for Godot emerge early in Act I, when, after flirting with the possibility of hanging themselves, they decide they should at least wait to hear Godot's "offer." Beckett's use of a term drawn from the financial sphere works analogously to Lorine Niedecker's trope of the "suction and pull" required to succeed in the wartime economy of the American Midwest. In the play, the characters' reasons for waiting are economic as well as existential in that Godot's hoped-for arrival promises to improve their status in what is a nearly impossible-to-apprehend social order. As in Niedecker's poem, the language that Vladimir and Estragon employ when deliberating whether to stay or to go is colloquial, the speech of office workers rather than tramps:

ESTRAGON. Don't let's do anything. It's safer.
VLADIMIR. Let's wait and see what he says.
ESTRAGON. Who?
VLADIMIR. Godot.
ESTRAGON. Good idea.
VLADIMIR. Let's wait till we know exactly how we stand.
ESTRAGON. On the other hand it might be better to strike the iron before it freezes.
VLADIMIR. I'm curious to hear what he has to offer. Then we'll take it or leave it. (13)

The two speculate that Godot will likely consult his agents and bank accounts before responding to their "vague supplication." The humor in this exchange – the comedic progression from contemplating suicide to musing over Godot's financial assets – apes mid-century discourses of political negotiation and economic reconstruction.

This parody recurs when Estragon attempts, in Act II, to extract money from the helpless and now-blind Pozzo. In response to Pozzo's proposal of one hundred francs, Estragon cries out, "It's not enough," to which Vladimir humorously retorts, "I wouldn't go so far as that" (92). We learn here that the two are economically beholden to Pozzo, whose private land surrounds both them and the road.[136] Against the banter on matters financial, the play thus enacts the material power both Godot and Pozzo hold over Didi, Gogo, and Lucky. Answering Estragon's inquiry as to where they stand in this world, Vladimir speculates, "on our hands and knees" (14–15). The figure of speech leads Estragon to wonder if they have "no rights any more," an evidently naïve comment that prompts Vladimir's stifled laughter (laughter being "prohibited" now) (15). As the play's final discourse suggests, Vladimir and Estragon are powerless to move physically because of their material and political dispossession (107). The particular vulnerability that the tramps experience with respect to food and hunger highlights this impoverishment, which bluntly contrasts with the lifestyle of Pozzo and, we imagine, Godot. In one of many embraces, Gogo recoils from Didi, exclaiming that the latter stinks of garlic. In response to this absurd rejection, Didi replies, "it's for the kidneys" (15). The retort provokes laughter, and in that laughter we sense the tragic irony of the exchange. For a man who cannot even furnish a carrot is unlikely to have any meat to sustain himself other than the most inexpensive cuts of offal, a point that recalls Fisher's satire in *How to Cook a Wolf* of middle-class distaste for such things as kidneys.

One of the most poignant expressions of Didi's powerlessness is his utter lack of food, which prevents him from fulfilling his companion's basic needs and constant cravings. On the heels of their first extended conversation about Godot, Estragon "violently" exclaims to Didi, "I'm hungry!," an exclamation that leads to the play's initial dialogue on food (15). By concretizing the poverty of the play's (anti)heroes, the dialogue would surely have reminded Beckett's audiences in Paris and London of the food shortages that had only intensified after the war. Although Pozzo later dines on a rich lunch of chicken and wine, Vladimir can only offer to Estragon one carrot and a handful of turnips, the latter of which he tries to pass off as carrots:

VLADIMIR. Do you want a carrot?
ESTRAGON. Is that all there is?
VLADIMIR. I might have some turnips.
ESTRAGON. Give me a carrot. (*Vladimir rummages in his pockets, takes out a turnip and gives it to Estragon who takes a bite out of it. Angrily.*) It's a turnip.
VLADIMIR. Oh pardon! I could have sworn it was a carrot. (*He rummages again in his pockets, finds nothing but turnips.*) All that's turnips. (*He rummages.*) You must have eaten the last. (*He rummages.*) Wait, I have it. (*He brings out a carrot and gives it to Estragon.*) There dear fellow. (*Estragon wipes the carrot on his sleeve and begins to eat it.*) Make it last, that's the end of them. (16)

In this scene, the act of eating – much like Estragon's fussing with his boots – interrupts, defers, and makes comical Vladimir's hermeneutic inquiries. The keyword in the stage directions is "rummage," an action central to Beckett's subsequent plays *Endgame* (1958) and *Happy Days* (1962).[137] In those absurdist dramas, where characters rummage through trash bins and ash heaps for food scraps and other objects, the act of rummaging is an arguable touchstone for the absurdity of modern consumer culture. If Fisher's bricoleur cook assembles odds-and-ends to prepare inventive meals, Beckett's rummagers struggle to make meaning – much less a decent meal – out of cultural remains. As characters rummage, moreover, Beckett calls up the national canteens and dumpsters of food scraps that populated European cities during the era of food rationing. Condemned to the cheapest and most plentiful output of European agriculture in the 1940s – root vegetables – Estragon subsists on a barebones diet of "free" (as in un-rationed) food. Didi warns Gogo that the proffered carrot will be the "end of them," affording the vegetable a special status that encodes the threat of eventual starvation. These scraps of food may disappear altogether, Didi suggests, a warning that the second act delivers on when Vladimir attempts to pass off a blackened radish as a carrot in order to quell Estragon's ever-present hunger. This same motif recurs in *Endgame* when Nagg repeatedly demands a sugar-plum from Clov only to receive "Spratt's medium" (an Irish brand of dog biscuit).[138]

Immediately following the exchange of dried-out vegetables between Didi and Gogo, Pozzo comes on stage for the first time with Lucky, who is carrying a burdensome load comprised of a stool, a heavy bag, a great coat, and a picnic basket (18). The picnic basket's contents include chicken and wine, foods that would have been clear indicators of "luxury feeding" (to cite Orwell's phrase) at the time Beckett wrote and first directed *Waiting for Godot* in Paris. In the context of postwar Europe, Pozzo's affluence is signaled clearly, as one imagines that the chicken and wine have come either from his land or from the black market. At the same time, the play reduces the economy among these characters to the point that the sole traces of a capitalist market seem to be the circulation of food and the persistence of hunger. The dissimilarity between Estragon's lone vegetable and Pozzo's gourmet meal emblematizes class disparity in the period, as evident when Pozzo flaunts both his social power and culinary glut:

[W]ith your permission, I propose to dally with you a moment, before I venture any further. Basket! (*Lucky advances, gives the basket, goes back to his place.*) The fresh air stimulates the jaded appetite. (*He opens the basket, takes out a piece of chicken and a bottle of wine.*) Basket! (*Lucky advances, picks up the basket and goes back to his place.*) Further! (*Lucky takes a step back*). He stinks. Happy days! (*He drinks from the bottle, puts it down and begins to eat. Silence.*) (22)

While Pozzo gobbles up his picnic, he discards the cleaned chicken bones as refuse on to the road. Much to Vladimir's chagrin, Estragon is emboldened to beg for the scraps. Pozzo tells Estragon to ask Lucky – "the carrier" – who has a first right of refusal. Confronted with Lucky's characteristic silence, Pozzo concedes the bones to Estragon, who "*makes a dart at the bones, picks them up and begins to gnaw them*" (25). While Pozzo dines on chicken and wine at his leisure, then, Estragon scarfs down scraps. This sequence dramatizes Estragon's vast hunger, a hunger that induces him to gnaw on the bones left over from a meal that would have been hard to come by in postwar Europe. These scenes of eating and going hungry thus shape Beckett's existential play. In turn, *Waiting for Godot* discloses just how dire food shortages and famine conditions were for those who, like Didi and Gogo, had no money, no work, and no social power.

Through tropes of bodily famine and luxury eating, the late modernist texts I have examined take up the wartime and postwar politics of food as well as the growing food power of the United States at midcentury. From Niedecker's *New Goose* through Beckett's *Waiting for Godot*, writers illuminate how control over the food supply – whether on the geopolitical scale of government rations or the interpersonal scale of a single meal – determined wider structures of power and disempowerment. These texts also demonstrate that the uneven progress of capitalism was very much on the minds of experimental writers during and after the Second World War, when the United States expanded its international status as a superpower. This historical transition depends crucially on the productivity and industry of the American food system at mid century, a view that *Waiting for Godot* drives home when the capitalistic "offer" Estragon and Vladimir await from

Godot dovetails with the "scraps" of food that Estragon begs from Pozzo. In relation to the twin discourses of food rationing and fine dining that Fisher identifies as markers of American consumerism and that Niedecker figures as a governmental smokescreen for rural famine, *Waiting for Godot* imagines hunger to be the war's ultimate legacy. A foil to Niedecker's and Fisher's satires of rationing, David's *Book of Mediterranean Food* aims to preserve rather than critique the culture of gourmandize. By comparison, *Waiting for Godot* makes the chasm between good food and abject hunger a constitutive feature of the postwar era. A conceptual divide between austerity and "luxury feeding" thus emerges in late modernist texts, one that locates the consequences of world war in both the geopolitics of and lived relationships to the food supply.

Capitalizing on its postwar food power, the United States went on during the Cold War to promote a "Green Revolution" in synthetic fertilizers, high-yield seeds, and chemical pesticides (agricultural technologies adapted from chemical weapons technologies). The Green Revolution exported the nation's wartime vision of agricultural productivity and commodity food production to the global South and especially to India. While contemporary critics tend to locate the origins of industrial agriculture in the Green Revolution, we have seen that it was during both world wars that the United States established an ideological and material foundation for becoming the "greatest agricultural production plant on earth" and for, in turn, globalizing the American food system.[139] In the years between the German invasion of Poland and the first decade of the Cold War, American plenty and European austerity became signifiers of a sea change in the global food chain: a sea change by which the United States became an agricultural superpower.

CHAPTER 4

# *Supermarkets and Exotic Foods: Toni Morrison's "Chocolate Eater"*

In 2000, the United Nations announced the Millennium Development Goals (MDG), a set of eight priorities intended to guide international policy and foreign aid. Among them is the aspiration to "eradicate extreme hunger and poverty" by 2025: a goal that aims to cut in half the number of people living on less than $1 a day and on fewer than the minimum calories that the Food and Agriculture Organizatiaon (FAO) sets as a benchmark for adequate nourishment.[1] Even if this target were met, 600 million people would continue to be undernourished – a stark reality made starker by the fact that world hunger increased rather than declined in the first decade of the twenty-first century. As recent FAO reports on food security[2] show, the regions hardest hit by the 2006–08 food price shocks were those that rely heavily on agricultural imports: Africa, the Middle East, and small island nations, above all.[3] Although the United Nations correlates this condition of heightened food *insecurity* to climate change,[4] the movement for food justice addresses the environmental and socioeconomic dimensions of hunger and advocates for community access to agriculture.[5] Published nearly thirty years before the early twenty-first-century food crisis, Toni Morrison's fourth novel, *Tar Baby* (1981), speaks to the food justice movement by imagining that the transnational routes through which food travels in the late modern period are coextensive with those of the colonial era. A narrative that entwines hunger, consumerism, and tourist development, *Tar Baby* responds to and contests the global circulation of staple commodities and food brands. At the same time, the novel explores the economic and ecological forms of exploitation as well as cross-cultural communities that a global food market has long animated in the Americas.

This multivalent story of food is integral to the setting of *Tar Baby*. Unique in the Nobel Prize-winning novelist's body of work, *Tar Baby* moves across national and linguistic borders.[6] Although sections take place in New York, Philadelphia, and Florida, the novel's geographical axis pivots from the United States and France to the fictionalized Francophone islands of Dominique and Isle des Chevaliers, with the Caribbean as a nexus. Named for legendary escaped slaves, Isle des Chevaliers is, at the time *Tar Baby* opens, an expatriate community that the real estate investment activities of retired candy executive Valerian Street underwrite. The island is a palimpsest of present-day tourism, migration, and food trade, on the one hand, and the *longue durée* of colonialism, on the other.[7] In short, *Tar Baby* crafts a narrative of Isle des Chevaliers reaching from the French and English sugar plantations and the Atlantic slave trade to twentieth-century food and alcohol corporations, whose investments in the Caribbean were aided by U.S. foreign policy. The novel concretizes this expansive historical arc in the sugarcane and cocoa plants on Isle des Chevaliers as well as Street Brothers Candy Company, which Valerian sells to a "candy giant" in order to make his retirement on Isle des Chevaliers possible.[8]

Critics have framed the novel's geographical contours in terms of a conflict between cosmopolitan and black nationalist forms of identity that inflects the tumultuous romance of the worldly character Jadine, who dreams of owning a clothing store in New York or Paris, and the itinerant Son, who longs to return to his rural hometown of Eloe, Florida. Yogita Goyal offers a compelling formulation of this conflict, arguing, "the novel urgently asks the question, what does diaspora mean? Can racial unity offer a clear alternative to Western oppression? Can a unified black diasporic identity counter the modernity that alienates and fragments?"[9] In response to such questions, Linda Krumholz and Andrew Warnes both examine the significance of food to *Tar Baby*. Krumholz observes that the novel, which "burst[s] with references to food," employs acts of eating to demarcate social relationships: "Morrison tells us who eats what, where, and with whom, who prepares the food, and in the case of sugar, its source in the fields and factories."[10] In *Hunger Overcome?*, Warnes similarly highlights the importance of scenes of eating to the fictional world of *Tar Baby*. Comparing the novel to the 1967 film *Guess Who's Coming to Dinner*, Warnes claims that *Tar Baby* reveals how dependent expatriate desires for imported foods are on nonwhite labor while also lauding African Caribbean practices of foraging, backyard gardening, and soul food cooking.[11] This chapter builds on these accounts of *Tar Baby* by shifting the scholarly focus from scenes of food preparation to the regional and global food routes that shape Morrison's treatment of racial identity, motherhood, diaspora, and empire. My analysis is indebted to the work of scholars such as Elizabeth DeLoughrey and Paul Gilroy who have shown that the dialectic of local rootedness and oceanic migrations structures contemporary Caribbean and Pacific island cultures and the history of the Black Atlantic.[12] I suggest that the mobility of foodstuffs is as important as the migration of communities and cultural practices to an account of how colonialism and postcolonialism together define the ways modernity unfolds in the Caribbean. Although attentive to the social and environmental injustices of the global food system, Morrison's novel eschews the tidy binaries of island and market and of producer and consumer. In *Tar Baby*, every character is a consumer with appetites that imbricate him or her in the Caribbean landscape and global economy. A significant text for the literature of food, the novel speaks forcefully to the field of postcolonial ecocriticism and to the cultural history of African American and Caribbean foodways.[13] Offering a long view of U.S. food power and global food trade, moreover, the novel cultivates a vision of local eating that encompasses disparate practices and politics: from building a hothouse as a microcosm of empire-building to foraging for food as a strategy of anticolonial resistance.

## THE SUPERMARKET MADE STRANGE

*Tar Baby* begins in the 1970s, shortly after Valerian Street has sold Street Brothers Candy Company and has moved himself and his wife, Margaret, to their Isle des Chevaliers estate. Joining them there are Sydney and Ondine Childs, a black Philadelphia couple who have worked for the Street family since the 1940s, and the Childs' niece Jadine, who has taken a hiatus from modeling and attending art school in Paris on the heels of an untimely marriage proposal from her white boyfriend Ryk. In addition to the characters living at "L'Arbe de la Croix," four others play crucial roles in the plot: the Dominique residents Thérèse and Gideon, the Streets' estranged son Michael (who never actually appears in the story proper), and the novel's ostensible protagonist Son. Thérèse and Gideon work on Isle des Chevaliers as day laborers but lose their jobs at L'Arbe de La Croix over a crate of apples imported for the Streets' Christmas dinner. Planned in honor of Michael, this same dinner serves as the novel's climax when conflicts erupt between Valerian and Son over the dismissal of Thérèse and Gideon and between Margaret and Ondine over the former's past physical abuse of Michael. Although the plot culminates in a formal dining room, it begins in the galley of a sailboat. The prologue to *Tar Baby* revolves around an as-yet-unnamed Son, who absconds from the cargo ship employing him, stows away in a boat that Jadine and Margaret happen to be sailing in the Dominique harbor, and makes his way to L'Arbe de la Croix in search of food. Son then disappears for three chapters, leaving only traces in the form of foraged avocados and foods he pilfers from the estate's kitchen – fresh pineapple, leftover chicken wings, bottled water, and wrapped chocolate bars, most notably (*TB* 105–06, 135–38). When Margaret one night discovers Son hiding in her closet, Valerian outrages her and the Childs by not calling the police but, instead, inviting the stranger to stay for dinner and to remain at the estate as a guest. The discovery of Son comes as little surprise to Thérèse, who had been leaving food out for him after detecting, as she tells Gideon, the scent of his hunger on the estate's grounds. It is Thérèse, moreover, who notices Son's "trail of chocolate foil" and so nicknames him "the chocolate eater" (104–05).

Against critics who position Son and Jadine's romantic relationship at "the heart of the novel,"[14] this moniker of the chocolate eater reinforces Son's claim that hunger, rather than attraction, leads him to L'Arbe de la Croix. As a kind of refrain throughout the novel, Son reflects to himself, "[h]e had not followed the women.... He came to get a drink of water, tarried to bite an avocado" (137). Bodily hungers and socially fraught appetites permeate the narrative of *Tar Baby*. However, the often racially coded forms of eating that occur in the novel – from Valerian's "Eurocentric"[15] meals of croissants and canned fruit to Thérèse's, Gideon's, and Son's shared relish of regional dishes and edible tropical plants – constitute just one aspect of what is a multifaceted story of food. Matters alimentary accrue in *Tar Baby*, and they do so to flesh out the legacy of Caribbean plantation agriculture within the modern food system.

The novel's alimentary threads coalesce in Jadine's early recollection of a Parisian supermarket visited shortly before she departs France for Isle des Chevaliers. To understand the importance of this scene, it is useful to consider how Jadine's character has been interpreted to date. Critics often begin from the premise that the young, jet-set model represents the feminized tar baby in the African American folktale of Br'er Fox (a white plantation farmer and slave master figure) and Br'er Rabbit (a trickster slave who gleans vegetables from the master's garden). Several critics have suggested that Jadine, like the sticky tar baby that temporarily traps Br'er Rabbit, mediates between Valerian and Son, while Son, in the novel's conclusion, extricates himself from Jadine and "escap[es] to the briars" of Isle des Chevaliers.[16] More recent accounts rethink these one-to-one correspondences between the novel and the folktale, itself a dynamic narrative that "continues to be told and retold in oral form."[17] Although Warnes sees Jadine as the novel's sole tar baby figure, for example, he notes that Morrison "modernizes the folktale ... for a newly urban, newly cosmopolitan audience" by adapting the tar baby template to a story of "interracial exchange."[18] According to several feminist accounts, Jadine bucks the tar baby tale altogether in challenging the notions of racial authenticity it relies on (or what the novel terms "ancient properties") even as she struggles to negotiate among disparate cultural and filial identities.[19] As Julie Emberley writes, Jadine offers "a limit case in identity politics . . . [as] a transnational first-world black woman."[20]

Her complex identity comes into sharp focus in the supermarket episode. During a night of fitful sleep on Isle des Chevaliers, Jadine has a nightmare that awakens her to "another picture that was not a dream" (44). The memory has a banal quality at first, opening with a drive from central Paris to a "Supra Market" where "[e]verything on her list was sure to be, and no substitutes or compromises were necessary" (44). Jadine makes this trip in preparation for a dinner party she is hosting to celebrate her high marks in art history along with the news that *Elle* magazine will feature her as its next cover model. The omniscient narrator glibly sums up the planned dinner in a manner that recalls, from Chapter 3, M. F. K. Fisher's distaste for the supermarket and all it sells. The shopping list embodies, the narrator reflects, "a rich and tacky menu of dishes Easterners thought up for Westerners in order to indispose them, but which were printed in *Vogue* and *Elle* in a manner impressive to a twenty-five-year-old" (44–45). The foods Jadine purchases signal her cosmopolitan tastes, purchases that range from prepackaged Major Grey's chutney and Bertolli's olive oil to "real brown rice, fresh pimiento, tamarind rinds, coconut and the split breasts of two young lambs" (44). The narrator's ironic tone in cataloguing this eclectic set of imported foods connects the cross-cultural recipes and biracial models in the pages of *Elle* to the foods lining the Supra Market's aisles. Resonant with postcolonial critiques of globalization, the passage suggests that *Elle* trades on the saleable quality of Jadine's mixed ethnicity just as the supermarket trades on the sought-after flavors of Asian and Mediterranean cuisines. As the scene continues, the novel shows up the presumed banality of the supermarket by disrupting the economic procedures and cultural conventions that typically govern grocery shopping – disrupting, to invoke Pierre Bourdieu, the supermarket's habitus.[21] Warren Belasco explains that grocery store chains that first emerged after the First World War came to embody, during the Cold War, "Taylorized 'consumer engineering,' as shoppers entered through a one-way turnstile and then passed through a maze of aisles designed to maximize impulse purchases before reaching the checkout counter."[22] Just as grocery store architects engineered the environment to encourage overconsumption, the supermarket also showcased a cornucopia of fresh produce from around the world.[23] Jessamyn Neuhaus, who has researched mid-century cookbooks, cites a cookbook published to commemorate the supermarket's twenty-fifth anniversary that explicitly correlates this space of food procurement with "America's attainment of a high standard of living."[24]

When a tall African woman in a canary yellow dress enters the Parisian Supra Market, Jadine's distracted meandering through the store's aisles comes to an abrupt end. Critics focus on the African woman as one of the novel's "diaspora mothers," who, as with Ondine and the "pie ladies" of Eloe, call on Jadine to join their maternal and sisterly community. However, the woman merits attention beyond her status as a foil to Jadine. Doris Witt persuasively argues that the image of black women as nourishing and maternal coincides in Cold War American culture with "a paucity of discourses" about what black women actually ate, thus naturalizing their bodies and appetites.[25] Although the African woman's entrance into the scene offers an alternative model of female beauty – a beauty that is "less commodifiable" (in Sianne Ngai's terms) and less "black-identified" (in Malin Walther Pereira's) – it also offers an alternative form of consumption to the one Jadine practices.[26] The African identity of the unnamed woman unsettles not just Jadine's identity as a model of mixed ethnicity but also her habits as an urban consumer of food. Rejecting the supermarket's social and spatial structures, the woman visits only the dairy section, where, having taken neither a basket nor a cart, she removes three eggs from one of the cartons and proceeds to the register, holding the unpackaged food "aloft between her earlobe and shoulder" (45). When the woman flouts store policy by insisting on purchasing the three eggs, the scene traverses the border between quotidian transaction and symbolic event: "the woman reached into the pocket of her yellow dress and put a ten-louis piece on the counter and walked away, away, gold tracking the floor and leaving them all behind" (45–46). The charged elements of this exchange (the woman's stony silence, gold-clad figure, and resounding departure) clash with its banal details (the clerk's explanation of store policy and the woman's exact payment). Morrison here mixes the narrative modes of magical realism and social realism such that the scene defamiliarizes the habitus of the supermarket. More pointedly, the novel draws attention to a food staple that readers might otherwise take for granted (a carton of eggs) and upends Jadine's sense of her own bountiful shopping list. The scene thus makes not the African woman but the supermarket strange – calling attention to the tastes for global imports and fusion cuisines it promotes.

Although Jadine imagines the African woman to be a vision who will simply disappear through the glass doors of the Supra Market, the narrator asserts her embodied physicality. "She did of course" float through the glass, the narrator tongue-in-cheek observes, but only because "the door always opened when you stepped on the mat before it" (46). As the ethereal vision of the African woman runs quite literally into the glass and metal of the grocery store façade, the novel reframes the supermarket as a space of power rather than routine. In *Distinction*, Bourdieu argues that the value of any market inheres in the spatialized "conditions of acquisition" that dictate where and how consumers acquire goods, gain social status, and distinguish themselves from others.[27] The supermarket scene in *Tar Baby* resonates with this definition of habitus by first depicting and then challenging the cultural capital that Jadine acquires from her routine acquisition of branded and exoticized foods. The woman in the yellow dress enters this marketplace as a kind of interloper, who, in rejecting the supermarket's conventions of value and exchange, lays bare the cozy familiarity of grocery shopping and the insensibility of shoppers to the world beyond its doors. The scene concludes with a direct interaction between Jadine, who is fixated on the canary yellow dress, and the African woman, who returns this awestruck yet envious gaze by facing the store window and shooting "an arrow of saliva between her teeth down to the pavement and the hearts below" (46). It is this visceral rebuke that partly motivates Jadine to leave Paris, sparking a longing for this "woman's woman" beauty that haunts her long after she retreats to Isle des Chevaliers. The African woman occasions a re-valuation of Jadine's sense of her professional and social success by calling into question her relationship to food as a symbol of that success. Put differently, *Tar Baby* insists in this provocative scene on the materiality of both the supermarket and the woman who challenges its conventions.

### BODILY HUNGERS AND IMPERIAL HISTORIES

Spaces of food function throughout *Tar Baby* to draw into relief both embodied forms of consumption and social injustices of the global economy. Food, in other words, is not strictly a symbolic register, as Elizabeth House suggests with her claim that culinary imagery is a metaphoric "hook" Morrison employs to contrast "life-giving idyllic values" with "competitive-success dreams" or as Krumholz indicates with her contention that sugar "defines the challenges for black art in how to reveal what is unspeakable."[28] The Supra Market scene contests a metaphorical interpretation of the foods that pervade the scene by making the ingredients in Jadine's cart and the

*Supermarkets and Exotic Foods: Toni Morrison's "Chocolate Eater"* 97

three, sexualized eggs that the African woman purchases strikingly physical. The novel's prologue similarly includes a juxtaposition of Son's bodily hunger with the mass of imported foods available to the Streets and the Childs at L'Arbe de la Croix.

The prologue opens with Son standing on the deck of the ship *H.M.S. Stor Konigsgaarten* and looking out toward Isle des Chevaliers and Queen of France, Dominique (a fictionalized Caribbean harbor that mirrors real-life Fort-de-France, Martinique). Through Son's initial perceptions, we first encounter the islands through allusions to their imperial histories. The "blushing" harbor and "seven girlish white cruisers" recall colonial narratives of the West Indies, while the enchanting quality of these images contrasts with such humdrum possessions on board the ship as postage stamps, razor blades, and keys (3). The figure of speech evokes the rhetoric of the imperial French government, which feminized the people and landscapes of Martinique and Guadeloupe in perpetuating images of France as "la mère-patrie" and the islands as "la petite patrie."[29] In his 1985 story of fictionalized Martinique leader Maurice, Derek Walcott observes that colonists described the Caribbean in this lexicon both to position the islands as imperial possessions and to posit a diminutive version of Europe in the new world.[30] Although the anthropomorphized island in the beginning of *Tar Baby* frames the novel as magical realist, the prologue flouts a tenet of magical realism as the Latin American "boom" novelists first defined it in the 1960s and 1970s. Describing the Americas as a place where the "strange is commonplace," Cuban novelist Alejo Carpentier indirectly aligns the magical realist novelist – who conveys the marvelously hybrid (or *mestizaje*) character of Latin America – with the European colonist who also marvels at the New World.[31] From the first pages of *Tar Baby*, Morrison turns this articulation of magical realism on its head. Rather than represent the Caribbean as an environment abounding in marvelous wonders, the novel grounds the often strange and seemingly magical environment in banal objects. This turn to banality first occurs when Son pulls his gaze away from Queen of France and returns below deck to tidy up his bunk, remove his shoes, and prepare to jump ship. Although Morrison no doubt draws from Latin American magical realism and especially from the work of novelist Gabriel García Márquez, *Tar Baby* tempers the marveling gaze and neo-baroque style that Carpentier advocated. As when the African woman physically triggers the automatic door sensors at the Supra Market, Son's careful act of removing his sneakers before jumping ship arrests the impression of Queen of France harbor as a marvelous space. In these scenes, *Tar Baby* employs what Federick Luis Aldama defines as "magicorealism," a ludic narrative mode that rejects the imperialist stance of marveling at the Americas – whether as a colonist, tourist, or postcolonial novelist.[32] Aldama's term illuminates *Tar Baby*'s opening scene, where the presence of razor blades and sneakers modulates an otherwise dreamlike description of the Caribbean harbor. Just as the physical façade of the Supra Market disturbs Jadine's sense that the African woman is a phantom, the accruing stuff of the prologue offsets Son's (but also the North American or European reader's) "sweet expectations" of Dominique and Isle des Chevaliers (*TB* 3).

The prologue further counters the affect of Caribbean enchantment when Morrison shifts from an alimentary figure of speech ("*sweet* expectation") to a highly kinesthetic description of hunger. After jumping ship and swimming across the harbor, Son comes upon the small *Seabird II* sailboat that Jadine and Margaret have taken out for a sunset dinner sail. Unbeknown to the women, Son hoists himself on board and hides out in a small dark closet, where he drifts into a light sleep and dreams of women from his hometown of Eloe (the "pie ladies"). The hunger-fueled dream ends when a bottle of Bain de Soleil thumps down the hallway to within inches of Son's hideout, prompting Margaret to venture below deck and collect the bottle with her "beautifully shaped ... ivory" hand (7). As with the African woman's purchase in the Supra Market and the quotidian objects aboard the ship, the Bain de Soleil bottle is an ordinary commodity whose appearance interrupts a magical realist section of narrative. It is at this point that the third-person narrator zeroes in on Son's pressing hunger. When Margaret and Jadine disembark, Son turns to examine the closet in which he has been hiding, which turns out to contain "twelve miniature orange trees, all bearing fruit" (7). With a "wide surgical hunger," Son rapidly consumes the oranges and then moves on to the boat's galley, where he finds leftover curry, stale Norwegian flat bread, Dijon mustard, a cut lime, and bottled water (7).[33] The remnants of Jadine and Margaret's meal, which become Son's physical salvation, are a microcosm of the supermarket and the access it affords consumers to foods from around the globe.

As Son eats, the narrator transitions from enumerating the galley's empty food cartons to evoking the three-hundred-year history of Caribbean slavery: "He covered the bread with mustard, ate it and drank all that was left of the bottled water before going back on deck. There he saw the stars and exchanged stares with the moon, but he could see very little of the land, which was just as well because he was gazing at the shore of an island that, three hundred years ago, had struck slaves blind the moment they saw it"

(8). The description alludes to the escaped slaves whose ghosts, according to local legend, inhabit Isle des Chevaliers, thus connecting Son's hunger and the foods that sate it to the historical legacy of Caribbean colonialism. In the very next sentence (the opening of chapter 1), Morrison returns us to the immediate present, in which the "end of the world, as it turned out, was nothing more than a collection of magnificent winter houses on Isle des Chevaliers" (9). Moving from the history of plantation slavery to the immediacy of tourist development, the transition overlays the mythology of Isle des Chevaliers with experiences of hunger and acts of eating that define the present. These experiences supplement, moreover, food metaphors in *Tar Baby* with the material and physical realities of food.

*Tar Baby* thus tells its story of Isle des Chevaliers and Dominique through spaces and experiences of procuring, preparing, and eating "edible matter".[34] Another scene significant to this narrative of the Caribbean occurs during a dinner Son shares with Gideon and Thérèse at their home in Queen of France. As their guest, Son enjoys a meal of local dishes comprising fried goat meat, smoked fish, pepper gravy, sweet cookies, canned milk, thick black coffee, and a bottle of rum (149–50). Over after-dinner drinks, the conversation turns to the daily habits of North Americans, at least as Thérèse extrapolates those habits from TV programs. Thérèse queries Son, in particular, about American proclivities for tropical plants: "they grow food in pots to decorate their houses," she asks, "[a]vocado and banana and potato and limes?" (152). Akin to the miniature orange trees on the *Seabird II*, the fruit trees that Thérèse imagines are decorating homes across the United States represent a food source transformed into an aestheticized commodity. Although none are indigenous to the Caribbean, three of the four edible plants that Thérèse singles out in her conversation with Son (avocado, banana, and lime) have been essential to Caribbean food culture and have become major exports for the region under neoliberal, or free market, trade regimes.[35] As I discuss at more length later, *Tar Baby* shows that the global market for exoticized foods has shaped not only the colonial Caribbean but also contemporary life and work in the region. The free market ideologies of neoliberalism, which the Bretton Woods agreement of 1945 advanced in establishing the International Monetary Fund (IMF) and World Bank and which the World Trade Organization today enforces, in turn offer an important context for the novel.[36]

Just as the African woman's purchase at the Supra Market conjures up the novel's diaspora mothers and Son's foraged meal aboard *Seabird II* evokes slavery, the meal shared in Thérèse and Gideon's kitchen brings to the fore the Caribbean's colonial past. Following Thérèse's query of Son,

Gideon relays the local folktale of African slaves who went blind on first seeing the Dominique harbor, escaped to Isle des Chevaliers when the slave ship sank, and now, as ghosts, roam the densely forested island on the French soldiers' horses:

"They ride those horses all over the hills. They learned to ride through the rain forest avoiding all sorts of trees and things. They race each other, and for sport they sleep with the swamp women in Sein de Veilles. Just before a storm you can hear them screwing way over here. Sounds like thunder," he said, and burst into derisive laughter.
Son laughed too, then asked, "Seriously, did anybody ever see one of them?"
"No, and they can't stand for sighted people to look at them without their permission. No telling what they'll do if they know you saw them."
"We thought you was one," said Thérèse.
"She thought," said Gideon. "Not me. Personally I think the blindness comes from second-degree syphilis." (152–53)

Gideon's sardonic version of this legend culminates in a reference to syphilis that unsettles the very origin myth he sets out to tell Son. Gideon assumes the role of a picaresque storyteller, who is irreverent about sacred mythologies and who approaches the act of storytelling with a demeanor of mischief. Thérèse, by comparison, adopts myth as her narrative mode, insisting, in response to Gideon, on the reality of the marvelous on Isle des Chevaliers. This back-and-forth between the picaresque and the mythical similarly informs Patrick Chamoiseau's Martiniquan novel *Chronique de sept misères* (1986), a work of magicorealism (to use Aldama's term) contemporaneous with *Tar Baby* that chronicles the food markets of Fort-de-France during the Vichy regime of the Second World War. Kindred to Morrison's novel, Chamoiseau structures *Chronique de sept misères* around the voices of female vendors and male "djobbers" (or odd-jobbers).[37] In a preface to the English translation, Édouard Glissant argues that the djobbers enact a gritty yet hypnotic manner of storytelling that develops first out of a subsistence economy and then alongside industrial and consumer society.[38] Themselves odd-jobbers, Gideon and Thérèse use oral narrative similarly – if in opposing tonal registers – to lampoon consumer culture, particularly as it bears down on Caribbean communities.

The melding of myth and banter at dinner intoxicates Son and makes "his head light" (153). However, his intoxication in the scene is also a literal result of imbibing copious amounts of rum, the drink produced from Caribbean sugarcane that was "the most sought after commodity[,] the largest single English import, and the most valuable item in the French overseas trade" during the colonial period.[39] The presence of rum in Thérèse and Gideon's kitchen – and its role in catalyzing stories of the island – counteracts the reification of rum in the global marketplace as a consumer product stripped of colonial violence and geographic origin.[40] Reification is a deliberate marketing strategy for alcohol corporations such as Bacardi, Diageo, and Pernod Ricard, all of which celebrate the island heritage of rum (with drinks like "Malibu" and "Havana") and yet also downplay the social and environmental histories of rum production by promoting their brands' tropical "flavors."[41] Bruce Robbins argues that such popular discourses tend to deploy an allegorical narrative of "commodity democratization" that casts the consumable product in the role of an upstart protagonist who overcomes government regulations and cultural taboos, all to afford consumers unfettered access to pleasure.[42] According to Robbins, these commodity histories (or pseudo-histories) stress the agency of things in creating global markets and satisfying consumer desires, thus occluding the agency of institutions, corporations, communities, and, I would add, ecosystems.

Resonant with the commodity history genre Robbins identifies, a 2005 article in *The Nation* entitled "The Secret History of Rum" opens with an anthropomorphic anecdote about the spirit: "Rum has always tended to favor and flavor rebellion, from the pirates and buccaneers of the seventeenth century to the American Revolution onward."[43] This portrait replaces human and bureaucratic agents of the alcohol trade with the commodity itself, which, the writer continues, "introduced globalization to a waiting world [in] tying together Europe, the Americas, Africa and the Caribbean in a complex alcoholic web of trade and credit." The world's leading rum producers similarly personify rum as a charismatic figure of open markets. Bacardi makes its Carta Blanca line into a humanlike character, who is "the soul of the Bacardi brand – youthful, high-quality, sociable, sensual, and passionate"; while Pernod Ricard describes the metamorphosis of its Havana Club brand from an "elite" spirit of the Spanish crown to a "worldwide" drink for the masses.[44] Most notably, Diageo promotes the Captain Morgan line of rums through a cartoonish icon that skews Henry Morgan's historical role in the British conquest of Panama and Jamaica.[45] By marketing rum through playful characters who singlehandedly create a global alcohol market available to all, such rhetoric short-circuits awareness of what Jane Bennett terms "the assemblages" of human and nonhuman agents comprising material systems in general and food systems in particular.[46] *Tar Baby* also fetishizes some of the commodities that permeate the novel such that underlying social histories and material assemblages disappear from view. The bottle of Major Grey's chutney in the Supra Market and the empty carton of curry in the *Seabird* galley, for example, are oblique traces of the South Asian diaspora in the Caribbean, a community that Morrison's novel does not represent. That said, as compared to global consumer brands like Captain Morgan, scenes of eating in *Tar Baby* (like the dinner in Gideon and Thérèse's kitchen) work to reconnect global commodities to Caribbean foodways, trade routes, and geopolitical histories – connections that the folklore of Isle des Chevaliers deepens.

### CARIBBEAN FOOD ROUTES

The most likely inspiration for Morrison's fictional Caribbean is Martinique, which French colonists first occupied in 1635 by constructing Fort-de-France, clearing forests for sugar plantations, and, by decree of King Louis XIII, enslaving the island's indigenous population. The French army killed or removed by force this Carib population in a subsequent war, in turn fueling the slave trade from Africa and the migration of indentured servants from South Asia.[47] Flash forward to the decades since the Second World War, a period during which Martinique has remained an "overseas department" of France while, at the same time, black leaders such as former Fort-de-France mayor Aimé Césaire have mobilized movements for decolonization. Beginning with Son's swim away from the *H.M.S. Stor Konigsgaarten* and toward the escaped slaves of Isle des Chevaliers, *Tar Baby* takes up these multiple histories of Martinique. Geographer Dennis Conway notes that since the 1823 Monroe Doctrine and especially since the Second World War "European hegemony [has gradually given] way to U.S. hegemony" in the Caribbean partly because the United States has invested massively in the infrastructure that once supported European empires.[48] *Tar Baby* crystallizes this shift of power by transforming the abstract paradigm of free trade into a lived narrative of the routes that cocoa, sugarcane, and other foods have traveled, first to support colonial empires and ultimately to facilitate consumer culture.

It is here that *Tar Baby* takes shape as a significant text for the field of postcolonial ecocriticism. In defining this field, Cara Cilano and DeLoughrey have argued, "[b]ecause the monoculture plantocracy violently altered the natural and social environment of the Caribbean, the region has provided an especially important space for theorizing the vexed relationship between nature and culture."[49] The work of DeLoughrey, George Handley, Graham Huggan, and Elaine Savory affirms this claim by building on Glissant's argument that "the Caribbean's violent 'irruption into modernity' [sic] created a schism between nature and culture in the region that its literature [has] sought to bridge."[50] This body of scholarship suggests the significance of food routes and foodways to postcolonial studies of the environment and environmental justice. DeLoughrey and Handley make this point elegantly: "[t]he new material resources of the colonies literally changed human bodies and national cultures as New World foods such as tomatoes, potatoes, maize, chili peppers, peanuts, cassava, and pineapple were transplanted, naturalized, and creolized all over the globe, while Asian and African crops such as sugarcane and coffee became integral to the plantocracies of the Americas."[51] Food historians echo this analysis. James McWilliams and Frederick Opie, for example, both trace the propagation of sugarcane in the Caribbean back to the early colonial period when Columbus, on his second voyage to the New World in 1494, introduced the plant to the region.[52] As McWilliams stresses, sugarcane is a grass of New Guinea origin that colonial planters were able to cultivate quickly by exploiting the plant's capacity for asexual propagation.[53] These patterns of monoculture production (which favored export commodities over local cuisines and community food security) made hunger a fact of life in the Caribbean. That said, Judith Carney demonstrates that a "shadow world of cultivation" comprising kitchen gardens and provision grounds ensured relative food security for African slave communities.[54] These forms of food production and procurement in turn animated the culinary development of soul food, Opie argues, by enabling the melding of West African, Western Europe, and indigenous American foodstuffs in African Caribbean cooking.[55]

The interrelated histories of commodity monoculture, community agriculture, and multicultural cuisine pervade *Tar Baby*, as evident in Thérèse's remark on the avocado and banana plants that find their way into North American living rooms. Such moments do political work in the novel by stitching the contemporary Caribbean into the *longue durée* of agricultural and botanical empire in the Americas. In a famous 1493 letter to King Ferdinand of Spain, Columbus enumerated the natural resources and fecund soils that his crew found in the West Indies. This act of naming resources no doubt energized Spain's imperial conquest of the Americas. Most notably, Columbus intermingled bucolic descriptions of agricultural and mineral "wonders" in the Caribbean with references to the power of the Spanish military: "Hispaniola is a wonder. The mountains and hills, the plains and meadow lands are both fertile and beautiful. They are most suitable for planting crops and for raising cattle of all kinds, and there are good sites for building towns and villages. The harbours are incredibly fine and there are many great rivers with broad channels and the majority contain gold."[56] Exemplifying what Mary Louise Pratt has termed the "imperial gaze," Columbus interprets the New World to be a landscape teeming with natural marvels that are of great commercial value to European empires.[57] In other words, similar to the classical georgic works of Hesiod and Virgil discussed in Chapter 2, Columbus correlates agricultural resources with imperial power.

Morrison invokes this Columbian rhetoric in an early description of Isle des Chevaliers that reshapes Carpentier's trope of new world wonders to describe not just the island landscape, itself a hodgepodge of indigenous and imported flora, but also built environments:

> The end of the world, as it turned out, was nothing more than a collection of magnificent winter houses on Isle des Chevaliers. When laborers imported from Haiti came to clear the land, clouds and fish were convinced that the world was over, that the sea-green green of the sea and the sky-blue blue of the sky were no longer permanent. Only the champion daisy trees were serene. After all, they were part of a rain forest already two thousand years old and scheduled for eternity, so they ignored the men and continued to rock the diamondbacks that slept in their arms. It took the river to persuade them that indeed the world was altered. (9)

Morrison's language draws on the same topographical markers structuring Columbus's letter: the "salubrious rivers," "champion trees," "sea-green green of the sea," and "safe and wide harbors" (to intermix images from *Tar Baby* and the *Four Voyages*). However, the ecological inventory of Isle des Chevaliers radically alters Columbus's pastoral-cum-imperial rhetoric. In *Tar Baby*, the grounds of L'Arbe de la Croix have become fallow due to overdevelopment; the chief site of botanical cultivation on the island is the enclosed environment of Valerian's greenhouse; and the local economy hinges not on agriculture or natural resource extraction but on a service economy of construction and grounds maintenance. Put differently, Morrison imagines the Cold War-era Caribbean to be confronting post-industrialism (a key term for Chapter 5's inquiry into recent narratives of global meat). The dearth of gardens and plantations in *Tar Baby* reflects the challenges Caribbean nations have faced since the 1960s and 1970s to make diversified forms of food production viable in the face of industries such as tourism and call centers as well as free trade rules that restrict protective subsidies for local farmers while promoting imports from U.S.-owned companies such as Dole and Del Monte.[58]

In place of sugar production and cane fields, Isle des Chevaliers is populated with the "champion daisy trees" and "swamp women" of its forest, on the one hand, and the imported flora of Valerian's greenhouse, on the other. The greenhouse enacts in miniature the "horticultural imperialism" Belasco traces back to the 1893 World's Columbian Exposition, which contrasted a cosmopolitan and cornucopian West to the specialized "monocultural plantations" of Latin America.[59] If his greenhouse is a sealed and controlled space, Valerian's development of vacation homes on Isle des Chevaliers harms the swamp ecosystem, an environmental injustice attributable in part to clear-cutting. As the narrator tells us, the men employed to clear the land for development "folded the earth where there had been no fold and hollowed her where there had been no hollow" (9).[60] The novel reveals that Valerian originally buys Isle des Chevaliers for "almost nothing," contracts an architect to build an impressive vacation home in the hills "away from the mosquitoes," and later subdivides other parcels for sale to "discreet" foreign buyers (53). This description of real estate investment and the expatriate desire fueling it calls to mind Morrison's 1973 novel *Sula*, which opens with a third-person description of Medallion, Ohio. The black residents of Medallion have lived in the hills known as "The Bottom" since white farmers falsely promoted the area to freed slaves as fertile bottom land while retaining for themselves the actual valley and its loamy soil.[61] While the geopolitics of Isle des Chevaliers invert those of Medallion (the island's hills are an enclave of white second-homeowners), *Tar Baby* similarly embeds the landscape with social histories of imperialism and segregation: Anglo-American and French Algerian expatriates occupy the mosquito-free hills of Isle des Chevaliers; a Mexican architect designs L'Arbe de la Croix for the Streets; nonunionized Haitian workers clear the land and build homes; African American servants manage the household and the kitchen; and African Caribbean residents of Queen of France commute by boat daily to perform (in Chamoiseau's sense) odd jobs. Just as Medallion embodies U.S. histories of slavery and Jim Crow, then, both the built and natural environments of Isle des Chevaliers carry the colonial histories of the Caribbean.

If the novel opens with invocations of European empire, it propels this imperial history into the present through the figures of Valerian and the candy giant that acquires Street Brothers Candy Company. The contemporary development of Isle des Chevaliers emerges from Valerian's aspiration, as Morrison has noted in interviews, to establish a modern-day "fiefdom."[62] Valerian's name, to this point, alludes not only to the popular herbal sleep aid *valeriana officinalis* but also to the Roman emperor who ruled from AD 253–60 and whose profile appeared on a silver coin.[63] The layered valence of Valerian's name speaks to his green thumb but also his oblivion to his son's trauma and his accumulation of wealth – suggesting that he acts as a kind of botanical emperor on the island. The development of Isle des Chevaliers into a destination for affluent expatriates produces social inequity along with a kind of ecological entropy as the island stagnates in the wake of construction projects. However, even as Valerian's real estate investment project damages the environment, *Tar Baby* underscores the island's capacity for resilience and resistance.[64] Articulating a postmodern sense of environment, the novel portrays the island to be at once organic and constructed and draws into relief the coexistence of built and wild spaces. My argument here builds on Karla Armbruster and Kathleen R. Wallace's account of *Tar Baby*, which identifies in Morrison's fiction a "nonhuman perspective" that challenges North American wilderness discourse by depicting the environment as including the wild and the artificial, the ancestral and the mediated.[65]

## MULTINATIONAL FOOD ROUTES AND CANDY GIANTS

*Tar Baby* entwines the ecological and socioeconomic lives of Isle des Chevaliers in order to represent what Rob Nixon defines as the "slow violence" of land development and resource extraction in the global South.[66] As one emblem of those legacies, Valerian profits not just from real estate but also from a multinational food trade, while devoting much of the novel's present to tending his greenhouse and dining on light meals of baked potatoes and white wine. Although we could read Valerian as an aging retiree with a food compulsion and a green thumb, he also represents a relic (or remainder) of neoliberalism: the American robber baron whose private company has been absorbed into an evidently publicly traded multinational corporation. When Michael refuses to assume control of Street Brothers Candy Company, Valerian decides to sell the company and move full-time to Isle des Chevaliers. In the wake of this decision, he turns "his attention to refining the house ... measuring French colonial taxes against American residential ones, killing off rats, snakes and other destructive animal life, [and] adjusting the terrain for comfortable living" (53). Here the narrator configures Valerian, whose wealth comes from the sugar-and-cocoa industry, as a descendent of the French planter class. As with Jadine's shopping cart in Paris, furthermore, the catalogues of transplanted flora and fauna on Isle des Chevaliers and in Valerian's greenhouse yoke together the colonial and (post)industrial food economies. When Valerian looks out from his greenhouse to see tamarind and cocoa, he accordingly summons up the botanical trade routes and exoticized foods that partly motivated settler colonialism in the Caribbean.

Although *Tar Baby* traces Valerian's identity as a retired candy executive back to the colonial sugar and cocoa trades, the novel ultimately distinguishes colonialism from late capitalism by depicting late-twentieth-century food markets as structured around financial instruments and value-added goods – structured, that is, around tax credits instead of gold and around wrapped chocolate bars instead of cocoa beans. This distinction comes to light when Valerian waxes romantic about the tropical foods that ornament L'Arbe de la Croix: "he'd had countless discussions with friends and clients about the house he was building in the Caribbean, about land value, tax credit, architects, designers, space, line, color, breeze, tamarind trees, hurricanes, cocoa, banana and *fleur de fuego*" (54, emphasis in original). This inventory implies that colonialism and capitalism both proceed through the cultivation, extraction, and circulation of the very things that Valerian lists. However, while the profits of Street Brothers chocolate bars enable Valerian to retire to Isle des Chevaliers, he perceives the cocoa plant not as the raw material of his wealth but as just one more pleasing feature of the Caribbean landscape. As a food executive whose confection company has been headquartered in Philadelphia (and, hence, far from its tropical food source), Valerian thus imagines his position in the Caribbean to be one not of colonist but of retiree.

His blind spot is arguably an effect of globalization, whose structures and procedures make invisible Valerian's economic interests in the Caribbean, just as Jadine's grocery list blots out the people and places behind the Supra Market's packaged foods. Sophie and Michael Coe, in their popular history of chocolate, evince a view of Hershey's founding CEO (Milton Snavely Hershey) that similarly abstracts the chocolate industry from the places of cocoa cultivation:

In that traditionally "'Pennsylvania Dutch" country there rose a chocolate operation that would be a formidable rival to its European competitors, whether Swiss Calvinists or English Quakers. Here, among these wooded hills, lies the town of Hershey (population 12,000), the main thoroughfares of which are called Chocolate and Cocoa, and with side streets named from the ports from which Hershey's cocoa beans came: Caracas, Granada, Aruba, Trinidad, Java Para, and Ceylon.[67]

Coe and Coe avoid any mention of either historical or current practices of child labor in cocoa fields and similarly elide the plantation system that international chocolate companies like Hershey and Nestlé have supported. In lieu of a truly transnational lens on chocolate, the places of chocolate production appear in the book only via the quaint street names of Hershey,

Pennsylvania. This image of Hershey reverberates in Valerian's self-portrait as an entrepreneur who "never left the neighborhood or forgot the workers" even when his company expanded to acquire "more salesmen and ... machinery" (*TB* 52). As with the Coe chronicle of Hershey, Valerian's interior monologues remember Street Brothers Candy Company as having paternalistically cared for local workers while preserving European traditions of chocolate making. His nostalgia conflicts with subsequent information (relayed by the omniscient narrator) that he has recently sold the family company to a corporation that "could and did triple ... volume in two years" (52). Despite this acquisition, Valerian maintains that Street Brothers Candy is a family business. In some sense, the self-image is accurate. In contrast to the Hershey Bar or Nestlé Kit Kat, the Streets' best-selling candy brand – "Teddy Boys" – is a regional rather than global commodity that grows out of a Street family recipe for a "heavy chocolate concoction."[68] Instead of enjoying an international market, the brand sells primarily in corner stores in the American South. Unlike the Hershey and Nestlé corporations, moreover, Street Brothers Candy Company never diversifies its product line. Perhaps for this very reason, Valerian must sell out to just such a "candy giant" and the wider system of multinational capitalism it represents.

The narrative of late capitalism in *Tar Baby* – which crystallizes in the Parisian Supra Market that Jadine patronizes and the corporate buyout that Valerian authorizes – culminates when Morrison alludes to a 1975 controversy surrounding the baby formula industry.[69] The reference appears just once, when Gideon tells Son that Thérèse worked as a wet nurse to local white mothers until the appearance of infant formula in the Caribbean made her work superfluous. Gideon interrupts Thérèse in mid-sentence, noting that her caricatured view of abusive white mothers stems from how formula made more or less obsolete her work as a wet nurse:

"She was a wet nurse," [Gideon] told Son, "and made her living from white babies. Then formula came and she almost starve to death. Fishing kept her alive."

"Enfamil," said Thérèse, banging her fist on the table. "How can you feed a baby a thing calling itself Enfamil. Sounds like murder and a bad reputation. But my breasts go on giving," she said. "I got milk to this day!" (154)

Moving from the fantastically violent mothers of American talk shows to the "bad reputation" of infant formula, this passage juxtaposes the importation of U.S. media and food products with the decline of Thérèse's livelihood on Dominique. Although Morrison posits the target market for formula as the affluent white families who once employed Thérèse, in fact, consumer product companies promoted formula to poor women of color in Africa and Latin America throughout the 1970s.[70] When the companies advertised "formula drops" as a form of food relief that would alleviate hunger in these same communities, exposés of tainted formula packages provoked international outrage.[71] Anthropologist Penny Van Esterik details the resulting consumer boycott, which originated in North America with breastfeeding advocacy organizations such as the Infant Formula Action Coalition (INFACT) and targeted the marketing practices of corporations like Nestlé and Bristol-Meyers Squibb (the maker of Enfamil). Van Esterik explains the critique of the global formula industry that mobilized the boycott: "in their search for new markets, [corporations] launched massive and unethical campaigns that encouraged mothers in developing countries to abandon breastfeeding for a more expensive, inconvenient, technologically complex, and potentially dangerous method of infant feeding – infant formula from bottles."[72] Although the boycott elicited a backlash from feminist groups who advocated for a broad range of infant feeding choices, groups like INTACT worked not to ban the sale of formula but to reform those marketing practices around breast milk substitutes that increased rather than decreased infant malnutrition and mortality.

The allusion to Enfamil in *Tar Baby* returns us, then, to the persistence of hunger in and the consequences of neoliberal trade for regions like the Caribbean. The allusion clarifies three seemingly disparate concerns in the novel: diaspora, motherhood, and food trade. The largest manufacturer of infant formula in the 1970s was the Swiss-based Nestlé Corporation, which began marketing milk products in the 1860s. Vintage French and American advertisements suggest that Nestlé was the first company to promote dehydrated cow's milk as a "sterile" alternative to breast milk and as an ideal food for infants and children (Figure 8). This material artifact elucidates a long-standing connection between the baby food and candy industries, suggesting that the thematic preoccupations in *Tar Baby* with motherhood and child abuse are coextensive with the novel's correlation of the colonial and postcolonial trade in exoticized foods like chocolate. As a foil to the novel's diaspora mothers (Ondine, Thérèse, the African woman, and the "pie ladies" of Eloe), *Tar Baby* offers not only the abusive mothering of Margaret but also the economic opportunism of food corporations.

Rather than naming U.S. hegemony explicitly as one of its subjects (as we will see Ruth Ozeki's fiction does), *Tar Baby* casts a wide-angle lens on food power that encompasses colonial and neoliberal histories and familial, environmental, and geopolitical forces. Interleaving the literary modes of

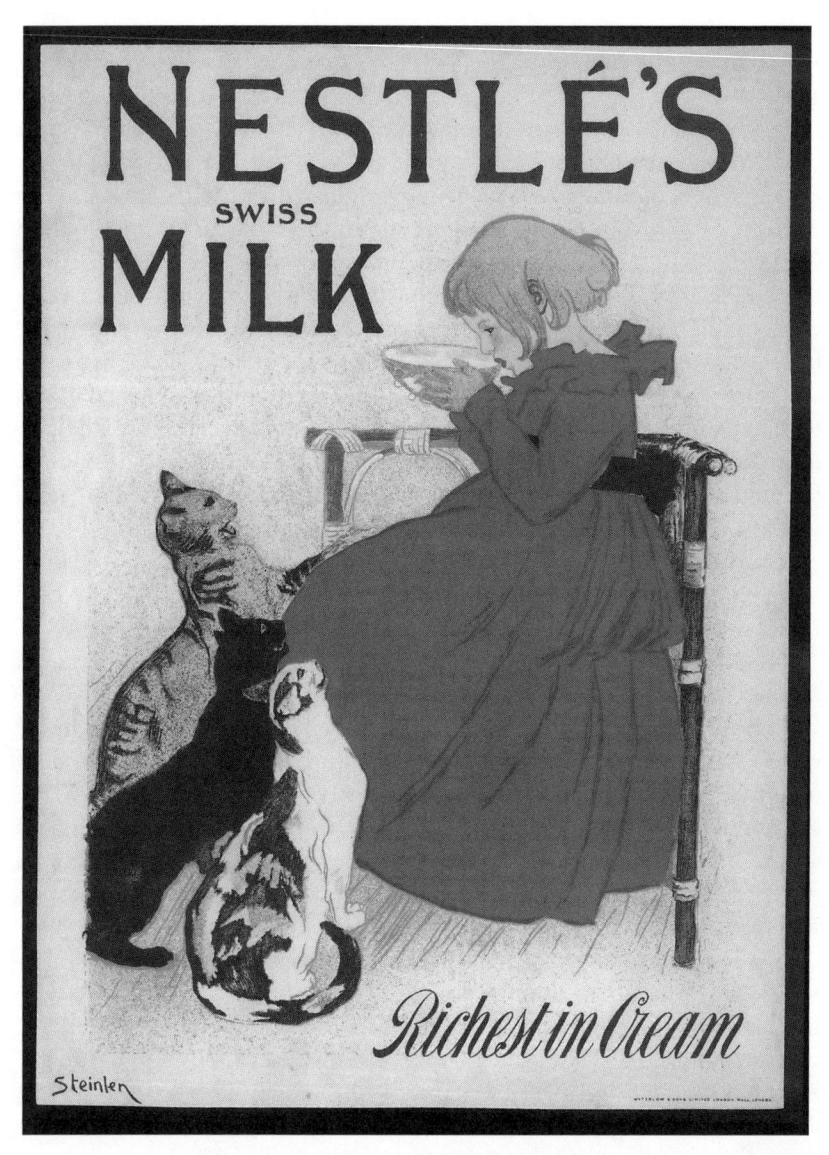

8 "Nestlé's Swiss Milk – Richest in Cream." Théophile Alexandre Steinlen, 1894. Reprinted with the permission of the Mary Evans Picture Library.

magical realism and social realism, *Tar Baby* reformulates ideas of the Caribbean in Europe and North America that depend on making tropical flora like cocoa into exotic yet commodifiable things. The novel presents a dense substratum of objects – chocolate wrappers, foraged fruits, infant formula, bottled spirits, and other consumable goods – that intervenes in this imperialist vision of the Caribbean. Attending to both the symbolic and material life of food in *Tar Baby* thus clarifies the tension in the novel, to cite Goyal, between mythic and realistic modes. With the former, the island appears to be a living, breathing "repository" of diasporic communities that "exist beyond the particulars of time and space," while with the latter, *Tar Baby* "indicates a skepticism about the value of tradition, particularly in its relation to constructions of gender."[73] As the novel's prologue illustrates, everyday acts and ordinary objects shade the mythic narrative of the islands such that three distinct chronotopes take shape in *Tar Baby*: the colonial Caribbean, the black diaspora (stretching from the colonial through the postcolonial eras), and the neoliberal economy.[74] All three chronotopes revolve, we have seen, around food routes and bodily hungers. Engaging with the *longue durée* of the Caribbean, *Tar Baby* draws on postcolonial critiques of globalization and empire while refracting those critiques through a food-centered narrative. As a context for the trope of sweets in *Tar Baby*, Emma Parker mentions the social history of sugar in the West Indies and the violence that the sugar plantation system and the Middle Passage perpetuated in fulfilling European demands for sweetness.[75] Although Parker, like House and Krumholz, foregrounds the symbolic aspects of food, the politics of food are equally central to Morrison's fiction.[76]

The politics of food in *Tar Baby* come to a head during the climactic Christmas Eve dinner, to which Valerian invites the entire household after Michael fails to show up at L'Arbe de la Croix for the holiday. The tone of the conversation at dinner turns from civil to hostile when Ondine reveals Margaret's past abuse of her son and Son simultaneously vocalizes his condemnation of Valerian's wealth. The occasion for the latter is Valerian's decision to terminate Thérèse and Gideon for taking some of the apples he acquired to fulfill Margaret's wish of having apple pie at Christmas. (To obtain the hard-to-get fruit, Valerian must bribe a member of the French consulate.) Warnes observes that it is precisely because North American apples are "contraband" in French-controlled Dominique that they are of such high value to the Streets and, hence, "Valerian's reassertion of ownership over the household's foods ... and his violent response to [Thérèse and Gideon's] theft reinvigorate the hierarchy over which he presides."[77] Incensed by this sequence of events, Son loses himself in a train of thought on Valerian's complicity in what we can think of as neoliberal trade and conspicuous consumption practices:

> Son's mouth went dry as he watched Valerian chewing a piece of ham, his head-of-a-coin profile content, approving even of the flavor in his mouth although he had been able to dismiss with a flutter of his fingers the people whose sugar and cocoa had allowed him to grow old in regal comfort; although he had taken the sugar and cocoa and paid for it as though it had no value, as though the cutting of cane and picking of beans was child's play and had no value; but he turned it into candy, the invention of which really was child's play, and sold it to other children and made a fortune in order to move near, but not in the midst of, the jungle where the sugar came from and build a palace with more of their labor and then hire them to do more of the work he was not capable of and pay them again according to some scale of value that would outrage Satan himself and when those people wanted a little of what he wanted, some apples for *their* Christmas, and took some, he dismissed them with a flutter of the fingers, because they were thieves, and nobody knew thieves and thievery better than he did and he probably thought he was a law-abiding man, they all did, and they always did, because they had not the dignity of wild animals who did not eat where they defecated but they could defecate over a whole people and come there to live and defecate some more by tearing up the land and that is why they loved the property so, because they had killed it soiled it defecated on it and they loved more than anything places where they shit. (202–03, emphasis in original)

As in his foraged meal in the *Seabird II* galley and intoxicated dinner with Thérèse and Gideon, Son's stream-of-consciousness rant against the Streets melds the colonial and neoliberal food trades. According to his critique, Valerian is the "head-of-a-coin" emperor whose fortune derives from the very islands that he has developed into a second-home community, and yet Son also suggests that Valerian is the titular head of a modern economy that assigns the Caribbean "no value" in order to concentrate power and profit in the corporations that turn raw ingredients into manufactured and branded products like chocolate. The colonial plantation and neoliberal export economies cross-pollinate, Son reasons, to allow Valerian to live like a king on Isle des Chevaliers all the while importing foods from home: the apples that, under the logics of both empire and consumer culture, he refuses to gift to Thérèse and Gideon.

This condemnation of Valerian's candy-backed wealth may sound familiar to the point of clichéd in the context of early twenty-first-century critiques of empire, neoliberalism, and globalization. However, if we consider that Morrison wrote *Tar Baby* in the late 1970s, the novel stands as an early account of the late capitalist economy that speaks to the later theoretical work of David Harvey, Arjun Appadurai, Fredric Jameson, Saskia Sassen, and others.[78] In line with the correlation these scholars draw between free trade ideologies and institutions and everyday consumer habits and desires, Son verbalizes his critique of Valerian: "So he said to Valerian, in a clear voice, 'If they had asked, would you have given them some of the apples?'" (205). The subsequent exchange between the two characters stages a moral debate over Valerian's right not only to terminate his employees for gleaning food but also to import food to Isle des Chevaliers in the first place. Both here and in Son's monologue, Morrison invokes the labor theory of value associated with Marx only to reinforce critiques of the theory that argue it fails to account for how capitalism increasingly decouples labor costs from commodity values. Put simply, the labor of Thérèse and Gideon is grossly devalued in the neoliberal economy Son lambasts. While Valerian claims the crate of apples is a commodity he purchases and thus possesses, Son redefines the apples to be a marker of an unequal marketplace in which elite consumers have a world of food at their doorstep, whether at home in Philadelphia or away in the Caribbean, while communities like the one Thérèse and Gideon represent have fewer and fewer food choices. Since the 1960s, the structural adjustment programs that the IMF and World Bank have administered as part of loans to countries in the global South have mandated that loan recipient nations concentrate national investments in a few crops. Island nations like Morrison's fictionalized Dominique have, as a consequence of such structural adjustment programs, seen local food supplies decline and become less diverse. Warnes begins to suggest why chocolate and apples are the two foods at issue in the Christmas Eve dinner scene when he observes that the former illustrates "the continuing dependence of developing countries on the export trade" while the latter shows the gap between "a food's place of production and place of consumption" in the contemporary period.[79] If chocolate emblematizes the colonial and neoliberal world economies, the apple, Michael Pollan argues, has been an affordable source of sweetness (not to mention intoxication) in the United States that has symbolized, ironically in light of the fruit's origins in Western Asia, the American frontier.[80] In the twin contexts of the apple's "all-American" status and chocolate's global horizons, Son's diatribe against Valerian functions to expose the transnational food routes that stretch from seed propagation to food procurement and that govern the globally uneven access to food embodied in *Tar Baby*'s contested crate of apples.

The conflicts between Son and Valerian dovetail with an allusion in the same scene to the island's mythology that connects the Streets' eating habits, once more, to the colonial past of Isle des Chevaliers and Dominique:

> Somewhere in the back of Valerian's mind one hundred French chevaliers were roaming the hills on horses. Their swords were in their scabbards and their epaulets glittered in the sun. Backs straight, shoulders high – alert but restful in the security of the Napoleonic Code.
> Somewhere in the back of Son's mind one hundred black men on one hundred unshod horses rode blind and naked through the hills and had done so for hundreds of years. They knew the rain forest when it was a rain forest, they knew where the river began, where the roots twisted above the ground; they knew all there was to know about the island and had not even seen it. They had floated in strange waters blind, but they were still there racing each other for sport in the hills behind this white man's house. Son folded his hands before his jawline and turned his savanna eyes on those calm head-of-a-coin evening ones. (206)

Another instance of magical realism, the passage transforms the two men into spectral figures: that of the French soldiers in Valerian's case and of the blind slaves in Son's. In the locked gaze of Valerian's "head-of-a-coin-profile" and Son's "savanna eyes" – surreal images that counteract the familiarity of a Christmas dinner table – Morrison provides a touchstone for the project of *Tar Baby*. From the French chevaliers who brought captive African slaves to harvest sugarcane to the white U.S. candy executive who purchased the island for his retirement and from the global chocolate industry to diasporic foodways, this climatic scene makes inextricable the colonial and late modern histories of the Americas. Put differently, the standoff between the two men prevents us from reading Valerian as an aging retiree or Isle des Chevaliers as a generic tropical destination. The scene insists instead that we read both the characters and locales of *Tar Baby* as individuated participants in a global food chain.

In the foreword to the 2004 edition of *Tar Baby*, Morrison explains that the tar baby tale provided the "bones of the narrative," which, "like African masks ... merge[s] the primal and the contemporary, lore and reality."[81] Interweaving mythical tales of the Caribbean's long history with accruing references to the Pan-American present, Morrison's formal method in *Tar Baby* is resonant with the historiography of Walter Benjamin. In his "Theses on the Philosophy of History," Benjamin sketches a historical method that "recites events without distinguishing between major and minor ones" and that establishes "a conception of the present as the 'time of the now' [but] shot through with chips of Messianic time."[82] Ramón Saldívar writes that Benjamin's text thus "proposes an alternative function for the historian: the role of collector of communal wisdom [who] ground[s] the continuity of knowledge in legend and tradition, those deep repositories of historical understanding."[83] Benjamin defines the writing of history, in other words, as a form of narrative that draws a community's past out of the mundane and the ephemeral as well as official "surviving records."[84] Consonant with this idea, I have argued that *Tar Baby* produces a diachronic story of the Americas told from its island microstates rather than from its metropolitan markets. The novel's formal hybridity – its rapid alterations between folklore and material culture and between magical realism and social realism – functions to historicize the U.S. presence in the Caribbean by chronicling the intersections of colonialism and neoliberal free trade. *Tar Baby* tells a story of migration, slavery, intervention, investment, and, finally, consumption that hinges on the cultural practices around and material routes of food in general and of sweet things in particular. By locating *Tar Baby* in the Francophone Antilles rather than in the U.S. Virgin Islands, furthermore, Morrison draws a line from the novel's principal and secondary locales (the Caribbean, on the one hand, and New York, Philadelphia, Paris, and Florida, on the other), making visible both the multiple empires that have garnered food power in the Americas and the diasporic communities for whom access to the means of food production and to community food security have been central to decolonial resistance.

Extending the conceptual and geographic scope of the original tar baby folktale, Morrison's novel squarely engages with post-Columbian discourses that fuel consumer desires for edible plants as a rationale for foreign investment in and control of the tropics. *Tar Baby* vets this (neo)colonial imaginary against both antiglobalization and cosmopolitan views of consumption and trade and, in doing so, fractures long-standing pastoral narratives that imagine the Caribbean to be an Edenic space ripe for the picking.[85] *Tar Baby*'s subtexts of the plantation economy and the Middle Passage are shot through, we have seen, with material markers of the colonial and late modern food economies. Out of these materials, the novel crafts a narrative of the Americas that radiates outward from the Caribbean region to the supermarkets of U.S. and European cities. In this sense, Morrison makes political critiques of U.S. intervention and investment in Latin America since the late nineteenth century and especially since the Second World War vital to the novel's structure, a formal strategy that Ruth Ozeki also employs in crafting her narrative of the U.S.-Japan meat trade from the Cold War into the present. In 2007 (more than twenty-five years after the publication of *Tar Baby*), Argentine President Nestor Kirchner and Venezuelan President Hugo Chávez announced plans to establish a Bank of the South as an intra-hemispheric counterpoint to the

U.S.-led Organization of American States (OAS) and Inter-American Development Bank. Challenging the United States as the hemisphere's cultural and economic center, *Tar Baby* proves germane to such acts of resistance to neoliberal institutions by locating economic globalization at the intersection of corporate opportunism and individual appetites for certain foods. In Son's furtively consumed chocolate bars, Thérèse and Gideon's gleaning of imported apples, the African woman's purchase of three eggs in a Parisian supermarket, and Valerian's windfall from the merger with a candy giant, *Tar Baby* creates a narrative of the Americas anchored to the Caribbean's past, present, and future with respect to global food routes and regional foodways.

The conjunction of child abuse and food disempowerment in *Tar Baby* affirms that the novel should, in the final analysis, be read as an environmental justice text. In recent decades, cocoa and sugar – which remain vital raw materials for the U.S. food industry – have been of grave concern to environmental and human rights organizations because of two practices that in many cases enable their cultivation: clear-cutting and child labor. One response to these practices has been the development of cooperative cocoa farms that commit to not use child labor and in some cases sign on with fair-trade-certifying organizations. Consumer demand for fair-trade and single-origin chocolate has followed suit, translating into exponential growth for gourmet chocolate makers. Artisanal chocolate makers like Askinosie Chocolate – "a small batch bean to bar chocolate manufacturer located in Springfield, Missouri, sourcing 100 percent of their beans directly from the farmers" – identify (and often craft stories about) the communities from whom they source cocoa.[86] Despite this movement, however, chocolate remains a global commodity whose value inheres in the very distance between cocoa beans in Africa and Latin America and chocolate makers in Europe and the United States. *Tar Baby* rejoins the global chocolate economy – whether mass-produced or artisanal – through its stories of supermarkets and bodily hungers, land development and diaspora. A fiction that de-fetishizes foods like chocolate by surfacing lived experiences of slavery, environmental profiteering, and hunger, Morrison's 1981 novel is a crucial text for the food justice movement and its particular resistance to neoliberalism. *Tar Baby* is, in other words, a crucial text for the current configuration – and potential reconfiguration – of fair trade.

CHAPTER 5

# *Postindustrial Pastoral: Ruth Ozeki and the New Muckrakers*

> I wanted to tell the truth, to effect change, to make a difference. And up to a point, I had succeeded: I got a small but critical piece of information about the corruption of meats in America out to the world, and possibly even saved a little girl's life in the process. And maybe that is the most important part of the story, but the truth is so much more complex.
>
> Ruth Ozeki, *My Year of Meats*[1]

In the *Consequences of Modernity,* Anthony Giddens captures a key characteristic of postindustrial society: the political power and material wealth that institutions, firms, and professional innovators accrue through the management of information.[2] By century's end, food power similarly accrues to those who design, license, and oversee complex systems of information. Asian American novelist and documentarian Ruth Ozeki takes up precisely this postindustrial life of food in her novels *My Year of Meats* (1999) and *All Over Creation* (2003). Consider her character Will Quinn, an Idaho potato farmer in *All Over Creation* who, having purchased GPS software to monitor weather patterns and soil conditions, now spends as much time "at the computer ... trying to input data and generate readouts and maps" as farming his 3,000 acres.[3] Although Will has clout within his community from having acquired such information technologies, he is now beholden to a network of companies that license software and capitalize on technical expertise. In his study of realist writers who address industrial agriculture (John Steinbeck, Ernest J. Gains, and Jane Smiley, in particular), William Conlogue contends that the "most insidious irony of industrial agriculture is that it removes a farmer from [the] farm; animals, plants, soils, and people are less living things than they are plotted pieces of information."[4] Months after investing in this information-centric model of what is today termed *precision farming,* Ozeki's character Will admits that he is "still trying to master the basics" of data analysis, suggesting that he must rely on third parties to make sense of the constant stream of information about his farm that software generates (127, 269–70). The novel's conclusion crystallizes this portrait of information-age agriculture with allusions to two recent legal conflicts: (1) the "patent and copyright infringement" suits corporations like Monsanto have filed against farmers who are found to have transgenic seeds (GMOs) in their fields without possessing the requisite "technology use agreements" and (2) those libel "cases against activists" for documenting industrial agriculture practices (326).[5] As this gloss suggests, Ozeki's fiction summons georgic images of rustic farmers and fecund land only to position agriculture within the postindustrial structures of IT networks and intellectual property laws. Against the grain of precision farming, however, *All Over Creation* and *My Year of Meats* give voice to current social movements – from seed saving to bioart – that promote amateurism as a rejoinder to what Alan Liu terms the "ethos of informationalism" driving a postindustrial culture of technical specialization and "knowledge work."[6]

Focusing on *My Year of Meats*, this chapter argues that Ozeki's stories of Jane Takagi-Little's and Akiko Ueno's individual experiences of food compete for our attention with a ludic satire of postindustrialism that centers on the U.S. beef lobby and its marketing campaigns in Japan. The conflict between these two registers – the interpersonal and the systemic – emerges in the relationship between Jane's first-person narrative and the other perspectives and discourses Ozeki weaves into the novel. *My Year of Meats* employs realism, metafiction, and melodrama in equal measure and samples from professional, scientific, and epistolary documents. This formal hybridity functions, often comedically, to connect food with just about everything under the sun, unsettling nostalgic strains in contemporary slow food discourse by showing just how thoroughly enmeshed food is with postindustrial systems of media, marketing, data management, and commerce. *My Year of Meats* thus maps the transpacific routes that American meat travels – a story that involves a massive network of ranchers, feedlots, grain companies, pharmaceutical conglomerates, slaughterhouses, meatpackers, lobbyists, and media outlets.

To date, critics have read *My Year of Meats* persuasively as a "cosmofeminist" narrative in which transnational bonds among women represent a social alternative to the free trade precepts of neoliberalism and economic globalization.[7] By comparison, book reviewers have tended to identify Ozeki with both the international slow food and North American locavore (or local food) movements.[8] These largely opposed takes on Ozeki share in common the sense that her fiction analogizes cultural diversity and biodiversity as a rhetorical tactic for rejecting "global economic exchange networks."[9] From this focus on Ozeki's political allegiances (whether to transnational feminism or slow food), I turn to a consideration of her formal strategies for narrating the postindustrial and networked structure of agriculture at the turn of the millennium. In *My Year of Meats*, we can identify a productive tension between intimate and informational narratives, or between centripetal and centrifugal impulses. Even as the novel lampoons meat and its importance to U.S. political and economic relationships to Japan, Jane's first-person story comes to revolve around a documentary project about the history of toxic hormones used during the Cold War to fatten livestock and prevent miscarriages. In organizing the documentary through the lens of her mother's and her own reproductive histories, Jane deflects attention away from the technologies and networks structuring the modern-day meat system and toward her own life story. *My Year of Meats* exceeds the parameters of its protagonist's perspective on meat, however, by expanding out from the stories of Jane, her mother, and Akiko to chart connections between meat and media in a postindustrial context. The novel offers the reader, I conclude, an information-rich toolkit for debunking the industrialized – and postindustrial – food system, a system that genetically modified seeds in *All Over Creation* and growth hormones in *My Year of Meats* emblematize. This thesis points to a fundamental attribute of the novel after postmodernism, which is invested in mapping systems at all scales and yet remains bound up with liberal ideas of individuality.[10]

## OZEKI AMONG THE LOCAVORES

Since publishing *My Year of Meats*, Ozeki has become a cultural figure within the social movements for local agriculture and slow food. When *All Over Creation* extended the project of *My Year of Meats* by pitting heirloom crops against GMOs, one reviewer suggested that Ozeki had defined a new genre of fiction. "Isolating what must be one of the strangest literary niches ever," Claire Dederer wrote for the *New York Times*, "[Ozeki] has written another novel about the foul nature of what we put in our bodies."[11] Questioning the political upshot of Ozeki's food-centered fiction, Ursula K. Heise argues that *All Over Creation* problematically invites "readers to think of plants as humans and humans as plants," an equation that "lines up the novel's multicultural concerns ... with its environmentalist dimensions so as to suggest a 'natural' affinity between the two types of politics."[12] In *My Year of Meats*, Jane's documentary similarly aligns the uses of synthetic hormones in feedlots and obstetrics. If *All Over Creation* correlates open-pollinated seeds and multiethnic families, the documentary project in Ozeki's earlier novel sees agribusiness and reproductive medicine as analogous. Critics generally have praised Ozeki for crafting fictions in which edible flora and fauna are "filled with drama."[13] There is certainly textual evidence to support this assessment, as when the narrator of *All Over Creation* compares Yumi Fuller (who runs away from her homogenous hometown of Liberty Falls, Idaho) to a "random seedling ... in a field of genetically identical potatoes" (4). Interpreting such analogies as evidence of Ozeki's environmentalism, Karen Cardozo and Banu Subramaniam laud her "insistent attention to the co-constitutive relation of the natural and the cultural."[14]

On this view, Ozeki's fiction exemplifies what philosopher Jane Bennett terms the vibrant materialism of human-nonhuman "assemblages." For Bennett, the slow food movement offers a promising model for "the creation of a collaborative, ecologically-oriented, and virtuous globalization" that recognizes, rather than obliterates, the "agency of food."[15] The approbation in *All Over Creation* of organic farming methods has earned Ozeki the status of a spokeswoman for sustainable agriculture. In 2004, for example, she moderated "The Food and Biodiversity Conference" at the American Museum of Natural History in New York, which had the expressed mission to make agriculture "a tool for conservation."[16] Conference speakers included the creative director of an agriculture education center, a Columbia nutrition professor, and the well-known vegetarian cookbook author Mollie Katzen. Akin to the "Seeds of Resistance" activists in *All Over Creation* who oppose biotechnology corporations and genetically modified organisms (GMOs), the 2004 conference promoted alternatives to technology-intensive agriculture. Selecting Ozeki as a session moderator, the organizers presented her novels as primers for the social movement they sought to galvanize. Ozeki also served as the keynote speaker at a 2008 academic conference on "Women and Food," where she delivered an address on the relationship between the politics of feminism and the local food movement. The program declares Ozeki's affinity with North American "locavores" – adherents to slow food principles who encourage consumers to eat locally produced foods, engage in backyard gardening, patronize small farmers, and revive regional culinary traditions.[17] The program's biographical note traces Ozeki's career path from television producer and documentary filmmaker to "internationally acclaimed" novelist, and then goes on to characterize Ozeki as a locavore who "divides her time" between Manhattan and rural British Columbia and between writing and urban husbandry. To depict Ozeki as a committed locavore, the conference program highlights the Chinese Silkie chickens that she and her husband raise for eggs in their Manhattan kitchen, for fertilizer on their

British Columbia farm, and sometimes to eat.[18] Referring to these chickens as exotic fetishizes the Asian origins of the breed, however, while linking the Japanese-American novelist to predominately Euro-American movements like the Tuscany-based Slow Food International organization and the 100-mile-radius diet that California locavores champion.

Slow food and locavore advocates oppose the privileging in industrial agriculture of a few, commodifiable species and, in response, promote the cultivation of heirloom crops and heritage animal breeds so as to conserve them and attendant culinary traditions (or foodways). Environmental writers such as Novella Carpenter, Barbara Kingsolver, Gary Paul Nabhan, Michael Pollan, and Carlo Petrini have popularized precisely these tenets.[19] Ozeki's fiction certainly resonates with this body of nonfiction, as is most evident in *All Over Creation* with the characters Lloyd and Momoko Fuller, Idaho potato farmers who distribute rare seeds to home gardeners and small farmers, and in *My Year of Meats* with the character Verne Beaudroux, a rural Louisiana chef who incorporates medicinal kudzu into his regional cooking. However, the slow food commitments of Ozeki's novels seem to inhere in analogies of people and plants that her characters draw. Heise demonstrates how these analogies gloss over crucial differences between cultural diversity and botanical diversity; for if invasive plants (along with monoculture farms) can put native flora at risk, to draw a similar conclusion about cultural diversity would reinforce racist and xenophobic discourses. To this point, Julie Sze notes that the kudzu plant is of Japanese origin and, hence, technically "invasive" in the American South. As such, it is in *My Year of Meats* a double-edged symbol of both the "freedom and danger in the flows ... of people, plants, and cultures."[20] Rather than fault Ozeki for crafting analogies that exhibit either an imprecise sense of biodiversity or unwitting complicity with xenophobia, I take up the question of whether her fiction does indeed align so neatly with contemporary sustainable agriculture politics. Concerned at once with global flows and slow food, we can identify in Ozeki's work a generative negotiation between local foodways and cosmopolitan uses of media and networks.

Ozeki's novels mix modes and media to connect a wide range of issues – from multiethnic identity and biodynamic farming to public relations and transnational trade. Cheryl Fish argues that the theme of interconnectedness in *My Year of Meats* serves a moral project in encouraging "coalitional movements for social change" while demarcating the "failure to make connections" as "dangerously naïve."[21] Susan McHugh develops a related point about *All Over Creation*, which she calls a "narrative web of interconnected stories" wherein the rhizomatic structure of the potato symbolizes the "wildly heterozygous" nature of alternative food movements.[22] What these arguments about interconnectedness as a theme tend to neglect is the form of Ozeki's fiction, which remixes discourses (slow food and pro-life in *All Over Creation*, political tracts and TV scripts in *My Year of Meats*) to compound the moral upshot of the novels. Rather than a singular moral purpose, these fictions distribute competing moral and political concerns across characters. As critics, then, we might approach Ozeki's work seeking not her politics (as has been the tendency) but the politics of form. Through this lens, Ozeki's expressed sympathies with locavore and other antiglobalization social formations come under pressure. In *My Year of Meats* and *All Over Creation*, local food cultures are always hyperconnected – plugged into global networks through neoliberal trade and mass media but equally through alternative markets and oppositional uses of information.[23]

### *ALL OVER CREATION* AND THE NETWORKED FARM

The formal complexity of Ozeki's second novel, *All Over Creation*, inheres in its two arguably dueling narratives. The first revolves around protagonist Yumi Fuller's return to Idaho after a twenty-year absence to care for her aging parents, while the second focuses on the formation of an unlikely coalition between Yumi's conservative parents, Lloyd and Momoko, and a motley band of anti-GMO activists, led by the character Geek, who travel under the moniker "Seeds of Resistance." Central to both narratives is the trope of information, which appears more than thirty times in the novel, usually in the context of how either stories or seeds circulate within and across communities. The most noteworthy instances of this keyword include factsheets circulated by the Idaho Potato Promotions Council (153, 179, 183, 229), political actions organized by the Seeds of Resistance (88, 184), and dialogues about the Monsanto-inspired Cynaco corporation and the expensive "business of information" they fund to quell protests of their NuLife potato seed (167, 276). One of the political actions that the Seeds of Resistance stages in an Ohio supermarket comedically highlights the role that networks of information play in alternative food politics as much as in agribusiness marketing: "By 1212 ... information was relayed from Aisle 1: Fresh Produce through to Aisle 7: Cleaning Products & Picnicware, and the operatives headed toward the checkout lanes. A quick reconnoiter revealed a healthy target demographic – mothers with infants, preschool toddlers, and some early-elementary-school children, too" (88). This consciousness-raising exercise has a virtual counterpart in the group's anti-GMO website and soft porn portal (which showcases the eroticism of food and women to raise money for Seeds of Resistance activism) (152, 184).

The importance of information and of IT-based networks to the plot of *All Over Creation* comes to light in an episode that, linking the novel's two threads, suggests how Ozeki interweaves pastoral and postindustrial ideas of food. The fourth chapter opens ambiguously in terms of point of view, as we are initially unsure whether the omniscient narrator or Yumi offers up the following extended analogy about open-pollinated seeds: "Every seed has a story, Geek says, encrypted in a narrative line that stretches back for *thousands* of years.... Seeds tell the story of migrations and drifts, so if you learn to read them, they are very much like books – with one big difference" (171, emphasis in original). "What's that?," Yumi's six-year-old daughter, Ocean, interjects, and we realize we are listening in on a bedtime story, albeit one that swerves from creation myth to postmodern metafiction. Yumi continues, "The difference is this: Book information is relevant only to human beings. It's expendable, really. As someone who has to teach for a living, I shouldn't be saying this, but the planet can do quite well without books. However, the information contained in a seed is a different story, entirely vital, pertaining to life itself" (171). The scene's structure, which initially keeps us guessing as to who speaks and to whom, illustrates Yumi's lesson that storybooks are shifty and unreliable media of information. An adjunct writing instructor in Hawai'i, Yumi ironically goes on to define not the book but the open-pollinated seed as an ideal medium for archiving information and circulating stories about the world.

In both *All Over Creation* and *My Year of Meats*, characters repeatedly explain agriculture through analogies to communication media: from books and libraries to "software programs" and "computer chips" (*AOC* 123–4, 173–4; *YM* 125). With scenes like Yumi's story to Ocean in mind, Cardozo and Subramaniam stress the "co-constitutive relation of the natural and the cultural" in Ozeki's fiction.[24] However, their account does not address the centrality of information technologies and new media to these turn-of-the-millennium narratives of potatoes and meat. The heirloom seeds Momoko and Lloyd Fuller propagate on a tiny plot adjacent to their 3,000-acre potato farm, for example, wind up in "envelopes for dissemination by the U.S. Postal Service to destinations around the world" (113). Afraid the seeds will die out with the Fullers, Geek labors throughout the second half of *All Over Creation* to transform their seed collection from an "ancient, dusty library" to an ordered system with a comprehensive online catalog (161, 281). This archival project becomes central to the narrative, as Geek enlists Momoko (who suffers from Alzheimer's) to identify each seed in what he sees as a "library containing the genetic information of hundreds, maybe thousands" of rare fruits and vegetables (162). "Talk about narrative!," Geek exclaims to Yumi, convincing her of the urgency of migrating the knowledge contained in one person's mind into a public database (162–63). Put differently, the seed archive that Geek engineers – akin to the political happenings he organizes for the Seeds of Resistance – is about information dispersal as well as sustainable agriculture. McHugh comes closest to my argument when she compares the Seeds of Resistance to nonexpert social networks "who have taken it upon themselves to know" about and mobilize against biotechnologies, a description of the current anti-GMO movement that sociologists Rachel Schurman and William Munro echo.[25] McHugh's focus, however, is on the inspiration Ozeki takes from a real-life campaign to thwart Monsanto's New Leaf™ potato, which the company shelved in 2001 when many potato farmers refused to transition from the century-old Burbank potato clone to Monsanto's transgenic seed. Evident in Geek's seed archive and Yumi's bedtime story, however, *All Over Creation* confronts a postindustrial food system in which not just agribusiness but also oppositional movements operate through networks – the "space of flows" that Manuel Castells defines as the organizing structure of the information age.[26] As Geek tells new Seeds of Resistance recruit Frank, the anti-GMO movement is "a network of cells ... [k]eeping information and energy flowing ... like a seed bomb" (257).

The analogies of agriculture and print culture and of biological organisms and communication media that pervade *All Over Creation* are not unique to Ozeki's fiction; they pop up in a number of books about food production in the contemporary period. Considered together, these texts offer a vision of the food system (and the organisms within it) as networked. In her 1998 pamphlet *Porkopolis*, British muckraking artist Sue Coe presents such analogies in graphical form. Overlaying the disturbing image of caged hens pecking one another onto a hand-drawn grid, her print "Battery Cage" lambasts the concentrated animal feeding operation (or feedlot) for turning the bodies of living creatures into expendable components in an agricultural matrix (Figure 9). By comparison, Jonathan Safran Foer's 2009 nonfiction work *Eating Animals* employs images of blank pages and printed type to help readers wrap their minds around the otherwise unimaginable scale of factory farms.[27] The materiality of the book – as a medium for reproducing text – functions in *Eating Animals* to illustrate the consequences of raising animals in a system that is at once industrialized (as in factory-like) and postindustrial (as in information-rich and IT-driven). The chapter "Hiding/Seeking," for example, contains an epigraph in the bottom-right

# Postindustrial Pastoral: Ruth Ozeki and the New Muckrakers 125

9 "Battery Cage." © 1990 Sue Coe. Reprinted with the permission of Galerie St. Etienne, New York.

corner of the first page that reads: "In the typical cage for egg-laying hens, each bird has 67 square inches of space – the size of this rectangle."[28] The subsequent chapter, which provides an account of the causal links between factory farming and new strains of influenza, opens with five pages on which the chapter title is repeated over and over again. This disorienting sequence terminates with the note, "On average, Americans eat the equivalent of 21,000 entire animals in a lifetime – one animal for every letter on the last five pages."[29] Safran Foer returns to this rhetorical tactic several times, subsequently comparing the slaughtering of pigs to peeling open a book and relating the 9.6 square inches that feedlot chickens inhabit to a "piece of printer paper."[30] His method differs from Ozeki's and Coe's in that *Eating Animals* employs communication media – and the physical material of books in particular – less to capture the actual connections between food systems and information systems (or networks) and more to provide a means for the reader to visualize the industrialized raising, slaughtering, and butchering of livestock. In describing the schematic design of feedlots, *Eating Animals* suggests that "the factory farm" is both like a factory and like a computer network: "Find a piece of printer paper and imagine a full-grown bird shaped something like a football with legs standing on it. Imagine 33,000 of these rectangles in a grid.... Now enclose the grid with windowless walls and put a ceiling on top. Run in automated (drug-laced) feed, water, heating, and ventilation systems. This is a farm."[31] The description could, if we substituted "cables" and "electricity" for "feed" and "water," pertain to one of Google's data centers (which have, to my argument, been termed *server farms*). This unsettling consonance between server farms and feedlots calls to mind N. Katherine Hayles's argument in *How We Became Posthuman* that "[i]nformation technologies leave their mark on books in the realization that sooner or later, the body of print will be interfaced with other media."[32] Ozeki's fiction and Safran Foer's and Coe's polemics show us that the bodies of agriculture, like books, increasingly interface with information systems and technologies.

In her 2011 essay "Discomfort Food," Molly Wallace observes that characters in *All Over Creation* use analogies to explain agricultural technologies whose impacts neither they nor experts, as Ulrich Beck would affirm, apprehend.[33] The essay provides a helpful context for *All Over Creation* in Wallace's discussion of the legal doctrine of substantial equivalence. Regulatory agencies and biotech corporations invoke the doctrine to fast-track approvals of GMOs based on the premise that they are more or less equivalent to already approved technologies, such as chemical pesticides.[34] Anne-Lise François offers a theoretical explanation of this practice in suggesting that it emblematizes the belief in "fully expressed knowledge – evident in the proliferating graphic metaphors [of molecular biology] – by which everything and anything could, by the slightest shift in syntax, be realized and at the same moment articulated."[35] According to Wallace, Ozeki's fiction rejects precisely such confidence in the capacity to know, engineer, and manage the organic world. Her novels instead seek "to fill the gap at the center of GM risk with what they *do* 'know' – about morality and reproduction, about multiculturalism and diversity, about God and Nature, about corporations and toxic chemicals – each of which produces a different version of the 'unknown' of GMOs."[36] However, this analysis needs refinement when we catalogue the many analogies in *All Over Creation* and *My Year of Meats* that work to explain not *technologies* but *biological* bodies and processes. The novels in such moments call into question the environmentalist aspiration to realign agriculture with the natural world by contesting the related notion that natural systems are less complex and more comprehensible than synthetic ones.

While Geek compares open-pollinated seeds to open-source software, the narrator of *All Over Creation* compares irrigators that disperse chemical pesticides to the organic world, describing them as "huge aluminum insects":

[T]hey inch across the contours of the land, sucking water into their segmented bodies from underground aquifers to rain back onto the desert. Rainbirds, they're called. Robotic and prehistoric, mechanical yet seeming so alive, they span the fields and stretch to the horizon. Emitters, regularly spaced along the length of their bodies, spray a mix of water and chemicals into the air, which catch the light and create row upon row of prismatic iridescence, like an assembly line of rainbows. (245)

This melding of the analog and digital – or biology and biotech – highlights a defining feature of late modernity: even the most organic of bodies carry informational imprints (think of seed patents and livestock tracking numbers) and circulate, alongside books, within both virtual and material networks. We have seen the metonymic chain in Ozeki's 2003 novel leading from the bodies of seeds through the analog media of print books to the digital cloud. *My Year of Meats* develops a similar chain running from animals in factory farms to film reels and TV networks. In these narratives of food networks and networked agriculture, we can identify the outlines of an emergent mode of American pastoral that at once laments and marvels at postindustrialism.

### *MY YEAR OF MEATS* AND THE FEEDLOT EXPOSÉ

Ozeki's first novel orbits around TV director Jane Takagi-Little, Japanese housewife Akiko Ueno, her abusive husband Joichi (PR liaison in Japan for the U.S. trade organization Beef-EX), and the families who appear on the reality TV show *My American Wife!* that Beef-Ex sponsors. When *My Year of Meats* opens, Jane has just landed the job of directing *My American Wife!*, which is tasked with promoting U.S. beef to Japanese women via weekly spots on "all-American" housewives and their meat-and-potatoes cooking. Jane reflects on the show's debut episode: "I honestly believed I had a mission.... I had spent so many years, in both Japan and America, floundering in a miasma of misinformation about culture and race, [sic] I was determined to use this window into mainstream network television to educate. Perhaps it was naïve, but I believed, honestly, that I could use wives to sell meat in the service of a Larger Truth" (27). At the novel's outset, Jane thus envisions leveraging corporate-sponsored television to support a cosmopolitan and feminist project. Midway through her year of directing *My American Wife!*, however, she grows disillusioned with the show and begins a covert documentary about the synthetic estrogen diethylstilbestrol (DES), administered between 1948 and 1971 to both factory-farmed livestock and 4 to 6 million women.[37] Jane believes that the media of TV and film can foster ties among different communities as well as redress past societal wrongs. While Jane hopes, first, that *My American Wife!* and, later, that her own documentary will achieve these aims, Ozeki (who is both a writer and filmmaker) seems to see the novel as the ideal medium through which to contest, as Don DeLillo describes the capacities of fiction, the "single uninflected voice, the monotone of the state, the corporate entity, the product, the assembly line."[38] In his analysis of *My Year of Meats*, David Palumbo-Liu argues that the novel makes use of sentiment – Jane's sentiments especially – as an affect for protesting the rational-choice discourse of capitalism.[39] This compelling argument does not address, however, the unresolved tension between sentiment and information in *My Year of Meats*, a novel that both provokes readers to feel deeply and arms them with facts in order to demystify the impersonal structures of late capitalism in general and meat capitalism in particular.

In producing *My American Wife!* and the DES documentary, Jane relies on the same research material that Ozeki drew on when drafting the novel; and also like Ozeki, Jane knows almost nothing about U.S. meat production or the international meat trade when the show gets underway. While filming the second episode of *My American Wife!* in Texas and Oklahoma, Jane learns that antibiotic residues in supermarket meat present serious health risks to consumers. This revelation occurs when Oda, one of her crewmembers, suffers anaphylactic shock after eating the episode's featured meal of veal schnitzel. In language reminiscent of Coe's *Porkopolis*, the local emergency room doctor explains to Jane that feedlots are "breeding grounds for all sorts of disease – so cattle are given antibiotics as a preventive measure, which builds up and collects in the meat" (60). This education continues when Jane meets with the African American Dawes family, whom Joichi refuses to feature in *My American Wife!* on the grounds of both their race and the pork chops Helen Dawes plans to prepare for the episode. Echoing the ER physician, Helen informs Jane that the family no longer eats beef due to the expense and has stopped eating chicken because they discovered that hormone residues were altering her husband Purcell's baritone voice (116–17). These various disclosures about growth hormones prompt Jane to research the U.S. meat industry in depth, research that informs a series of "documentary interludes" Jane reports to her implied reader (123–25, 205–06, 218–20, 247–50). After Jane learns that cheap cuts of poultry contain high levels of synthetic hormones, she reflects, "I'd just never given it much thought before. But now I couldn't get the image of Mr. Purcell out of my head. 'Meat is the Message,' or so I'd written, and suddenly I wanted to know more" (123–24).

For Jane, the message that meat carries and encodes proves to be above all about DES. As Jane zooms in on the postwar medical establishment that prescribed DES misguidedly to boost women's fertility, the novel zooms out to a zany narrative about disassembly lines, animal science, food marketing, and the power of U.S. agribusiness in Japan.[40] On one level, the novel is a *bildungsroman* in which Jane gains an education about DES and its serious consequences for women and livestock. On another, the novel is a playful work of metafiction grappling with the problem of information overload. While Jane dwells in her documentary on what Cynthia Laitman Orenberg terms "the daughters of DES," the novel proclaims multiple times, in a striking riff on Marshall McLuhan's mantra "the media is the message," that "meat is the message" (*YM* 119, 123–24).[41] *My Year of Meats* delivers on this message by shifting midstream from a story about television sponsorship to one about the technologies and economics of meat, while also suggesting that the two stories are inextricable. Ozeki thematizes this connection through the role of Beef-EX in *My American Wife!*; but she also embeds the link in the novel's form by saturating *My Year of Meats* with information that draws extensively on the work of a new generation of North American muckrakers and documentarians.

In 1906, Upton Sinclair entered the canon of American literature by exposing the practices of Chicago stockyards in his novel *The Jungle*.[42] Few writers picked up where Sinclair left off by pursuing his story of industrialized slaughter and meatpacking labor; and for much of the twentieth century, *The Jungle* arguably had more influence on public policy than on literature. Despite Sinclair's canonical status as a novelist and journalist, *The Jungle* has few offshoots in the canon of twentieth-century American fiction. Sinclair himself was more interested in the political effect than the literary legacy of *The Jungle*, which he hoped would overhaul working conditions in the meat industry, and in reflecting on the book's impact, he famously complained that *The Jungle* hit the nation's "stomach" rather than its conscience.[43] Although the Pure Food and Drug Act (passed just months after *The Jungle* hit shelves) established federal protocols for meatpacking inspection, Congress left the industry's practices with respect to worker pay and animal welfare largely untouched.[44] In the century since *The Jungle* first made headlines and turned stomachs, the so-called disassembly line has expanded in geographic scope and economic output, making it possible to render billions of live animals each year into crates of packaged meat. Akin to the years after *The Jungle* appeared, the first decades of the twenty-first century have seen a rise in public concern about the now global market for factory-farmed meat.

Activists and scientists contend that the contemporary meat system is both inhumane and ecologically untenable due to a variety of factors: animal cruelty and illness, exploitative labor conditions, the reliance on growth hormones and antibiotics, and the output of methane that feedlots release into the atmosphere.[45] These realities come to life in Barron Bixler's photographs of an industrial dairy at a moment when there are no cows in the enormous "milking parlor," an image that shows both the scale of feedlots and the centrality of technology to their inner workings (Figure 10). Since the

10 "Milking Parlor, California 2007." © Barron Bixler. Reprinted with the permission of the artist.

1990s, a number of artists and writers have worked to expose the unsafe, unsustainable, and unjust nature of feedlots and meatpacking plants – a body of work that revives Sinclair's project of the 1900s.[46] Ozeki takes some of her inspiration for the plot of *My Year of Meats* from these exposés, and the novel also makes use of the melodramatic mode that characterizes most muckraking projects in leaving almost nothing unsaid (to cite Peter Brooks's definition of melodrama).[47] However, Ozeki partly breaks with the conventions of muckraking and a related mode that Cecilia Tichi terms novels of "civic protest." While muckrakers and protest novelists "narro[w] the range of ideas and objects that are brought to public attention" via "powerful one-dimensional images,"[48] *My Year of Meats* moves out from industrialized meat production to explore a postindustrial network of media outlets, political lobbies, and consumer product corporations. The novel expands the horizons of both *The Jungle* and more recent *feedlot exposés* (of which *Eating Animals* is an example) by addressing the Pacific Rim economy and U.S.-Japan relations alongside what Carol Adams termed in 1990 the sexual politics of meat.[49]

In interviews, Ozeki has acknowledged that she originally thought of *My Year of Meats* as a fiction about TV sponsorship, noting that the premise of *My American Wife!* came from her prior career as a TV producer. While working for a New York production company that aired shows in Japan, Ozeki and a group of feminist collaborators pitched a reality show on the lives of unconventional rural women (*Mrs. America*). Picked up by a network, *Mrs. America* featured women in their kitchens and, like *My American Wife!*, had the U.S. beef export lobby as a sponsor.[50] The sponsorship signified an artistic compromise for Ozeki, and like Jane, she staged her protest of the beef lobby's involvement in *Mrs. America* by producing one episode about a vegetarian lesbian couple. Despite this experience, Ozeki claims she "knew almost nothing" after the show concluded about agribusiness generally or the meat industry specifically.[51] It was research for the novel that alerted Ozeki to the history of confined feedlots and to the particular health risks posed by growth hormones. The novel's appended bibliography testifies to this research with its references to Adams's feminist study, Coe's multimedia book *Dead Meat*, Peter Singer and Jim Mason's animal rights treatise *Animal Factories*, Jeremy Rifkin's and Orville Schell's histories of American ranches and feedlots, and, finally, Orenberg's research on growth hormones and reproductive health.[52] These sources construct a kind of knowledge base that undergirds Ozeki's narrative of a food network reaching from industrialized factory farms to global PR machines, a narrative that works to transform a "miasma of misinformation" into public knowledge (27).

132    *Global Appetites: American Power and the Literature of Food*

Ozeki's reference to Coe in the bibliography merits particular note. A British artist and member of the collective Graphic Witness, Coe sees her books *Dead Meat* (1995) and *Porkopolis* (1988) – which feature lithographs, silkscreens, photo etchings, cartoon strips, and modernist montages alongside written commentary – as works of graphic journalism. A *New York Times* review of her recent "Elephants We Must Never Forget" exhibition observes that Coe directs "her graphic ire at the barbaric practices of the meat industry."[53] Critic Cary Wolfe makes this same point by way of animal theory, claiming that her art "relies on a subject from whom *nothing, in principle, is hidden*."[54] The two images entitled "Feed Lot" and "Veal Skinner" illustrate that Coe's muckraking exposes at once the scale of feedlots – the tens of thousands of animals who live in crowded conditions and are slaughtered en masse – and the experience of individual animals (Figures 11–12). The rhetorical appeal of these images is both logical and emotional. Taking in the haunting illustrations, the viewer reckons with a swath of data in the written text about animal mortality, illness, and abuse. At the same time, Coe puts viewers into the bodies of both living and dead animals, an experience of inhabiting others that is nothing short of harrowing. A similar double vision is at work in *My Year of Meats*: on the one hand, a fact-packed, wide-angled narrative of factory farming and global meat and, on the other, a close-in portrait of individual lives – Jane's, Akiko's, the women who appear on *My American Wife!*, and, importantly, the cow whose carcass collides with Jane's pregnant body at the slaughterhouse she films near the novel's end.

The relationship of *My Year of Meats* to muckraking comes into focus through a comparison with Eric Schlosser's 2001 book *Fast Food Nation*, which details the political power of meatpacking corporations as well as patterns of gender and race discrimination that shape working conditions across the meat industry. In *Exposés and Excess*, Tichi claims that Schlosser "widens [*The Jungle*'s] spectrum of dramatic personae" beyond Sinclair's immigrant workers and villainous bosses to include migrant laborers, fast food executives, meatpackers, feed companies, government regulators, and politicians.[55] Whereas Sinclair appeals to the "sensational tradition of nineteenth-century sentimental melodramatic narrative," Tichi argues, Schlosser employs a strategy of "emotional containment" to delineate the structural injustices of industrialized meat production.[56] Schlosser focuses on the U.S. corporations that dominate the global meat industry – from Cargill's meatpacking subsidiary Excel to Archer Daniels Midland's feed business. "Today's unprecedented degree of meatpacking concentration," he writes, has meant that the four largest meatpacking companies have

## Postindustrial Pastoral: Ruth Ozeki and the New Muckrakers 133

11 "Feed Lot." © 1991 Sue Coe. Reprinted with the permission of Galerie St. Etienne, New York.

lobbied successfully for deregulation of animal welfare and worker safety laws.[57] However, reviewers of *Fast Food Nation* have stressed neither its depiction of animal cruelty nor its exposure of the abysmal wages and, in the case especially of women, the sexual abuse that many meat workers endure.

12 "Veal Skinner." © 1991 Sue Coe. Reprinted with the permission of Galerie St. Etienne, New York.

Rather, the book's reception has presented it as a story about the public health risks of fast food. Just as Sinclair lamented that *The Jungle* hit the public's "stomach," then, *Fast Food Nation* seems to have spoken most forcefully to the contemporary discourse on obesity in the United States.

We do well, however, to elucidate the other concerns that inform exposés like Schlosser's. The structure of *Fast Food Nation* contextualizes the health consequences of fast food through sustained descriptions of feedlots and slaughterhouses. The long section entitled "The Most Dangerous Job" contains a series of vignettes on the lives of both animals and meatpacking workers. Consider the section's opening, in which Schlosser offers an eyewitness account of a massive slaughterhouse at night:

> The slaughterhouse is an immense building, gray and square, about three stories high, with no windows on the front and no architectural clues to what's happening inside.... The fab room is cooled to about 40 degrees, and as you head up the line, the feel of the place starts to change. The pieces of meat get bigger. Workers – about half of them women, almost all of them young and Latino – slice meat with long slender knives.... On the kill floor, what I see no longer unfolds in a logical manner. It's one strange image after another. A worker with a power saw slices cattle into halves as though they were two-by-fours, and then the halves swing by me into the cooler. It feels like a slaughterhouse now. Dozens of cattle, stripped of their skins, dangle on chains from their hind legs.... Now the cattle suspended above me look just like the cattle I've seen on ranches for years, but these ones are upside down swinging on hooks. For a moment, the sight seems unreal; there are so many of them, a herd of them, lifeless. And then I see a few hind legs still kicking, a final reflex action, and the reality comes hard and clear. For eight and a half hours, a worker called a 'sticker' does nothing but stand in a river of blood, being drenched in blood, slitting the neck of a steer every ten seconds or so, severing its carotid artery.[58]

The description is bone chilling, and yet the sensation of disgust it stirs does not displace the clear-eyed analysis of the plant's structure: its extreme temperatures and enclosed environment, the ethnicity and gender of workers, and the violent efficiency of the kill floor and disassembly line. One could fault Schlosser for depersonalizing individual workers and animals; however, in this, he eschews prevailing conventions in feedlot exposés of depicting one worker as an archetype (a trope that structures *The Jungle*) and of foregrounding the writer's own traumatic experience of a slaughterhouse (a strategy that Safran Foer utilizes in *Eating Animals* and that, as we will see, Ozeki's protagonist also employs). Schlosser leverages a first-person perspective simultaneously to document the *form* of industrialized slaughter and to provide the *feel* of this particular slaughterhouse. His description provocatively journeys in reverse from processed cuts of meat at the end of the high-speed disassembly line to the whole bodies of cattle at its entrance. By extension, the reader journeys imaginatively from the grocery store meat counter or fast food order line to the tens of thousands of animals that a typical commercial slaughterhouse renders day-and-night.[59] In dialogue with environmental justice activism, if at odds with veganism, *Fast Food Nation* thus makes consumer health concerns associated with the fast food industry inseparable from the welfare of laborers and animals.

### PERSONAL TOXINS AND SYSTEMIC FICTIONS

Like *Fast Food Nation*, *My Year of Meats* culminates in a hallucinatory narrative of an abattoir. The scene occurs during Jane's final episode of *My American Wife!*, filmed just before Beef-EX insists that the production company fire her. The rationale for this termination is a series of episodes that allegedly fail to stimulate U.S. beef sales in Japan because they showcase families who either do not fit an "all-American" stereotype, do not eat beef, or have suffered meat-related illness: a lesbian couple who prepare pasta primavera for their taping, an evangelical mother who cooks a meal of Australian lamb chops, and the choir singer Purcell, who has suffered endocrine disruption from the hormones in poultry. Aware that her job is on the line, Jane decides to go out with a bang by obtaining footage of "Dunn & Son, Custom Cattle Feeders" (a Colorado feedlot) and a nearby slaughterhouse and meat-packing plant while filming an episode for the show set in Bunny Dunn's kitchen. On the final day of shooting, Jane and her crew venture into the slaughterhouse. Akin to Schlosser, Ozeki employs an eyewitness account in the scene to put us – viscerally and visually – inside this industrialized environment: "There was no place to stand, so we kept moving, and it was like some sort of obscene square dance, with us doing the do-si-do around massive swinging animals that had been hoisted into the air by a hind leg, suspended between the incremental stages of life and death and final dismemberment" (*YM* 282). The scene is the apex of Jane's yearlong education in DES and the business of meat. It appears in the tenth of the novel's twelve chapters, each of which chronicles one month in Jane's "year of meats" (1991, to be exact). The year ends with Jane's loss of her job and her pregnancy; but it also ends with the completion of her documentary, which garners the attention of major media outlets and affirms Jane's identity as an independent filmmaker. (The press learns of the film from Bunny Dunn after she and her husband decide to report their son's illegal use of DES in their feedlot to the USDA, an event that prompts national media outlets to inundate Jane with requests for distribution rights.) In contrast to Coe's *Dead Meat* and Schlosser's *Fast Food Nation*, Jane's project does not focus on the working conditions or environmental consequences of industrial meat production, but rather develops out of her interest in synthetic hormones and search for her own reproductive risk factors as, to cite Orenberg, a "daughter of DES."[60]

As she captures and edits the footage, Jane's family medical history and bodily trauma take center stage. At the same time, the omniscient account of the feedlot and meatpacking plant as well as an array of "documentary interludes" in the novel balance the personal sense of injury with an attention to the interconnected systems of meat, medicine, and mass media. The novel thus exhibits characteristics of what Mark McGurl terms the "posthuman sentimental": fictions in which "*systems* and *affects* come intimately together."[61]

As Jane sees it, the abattoir is not a node within the system of "animal capital" (Nicole Shukin's provocative term) but rather a place of personal reckoning about DES – its legacy in her body and its continued illegal use in feedlots.[62] The thousands of cattle slaughtered each day at the abattoir receive limited attention in the footage Jane captures, especially as compared to the narrator's detailed descriptions of "massive swinging animals," "carcasses," and "hooves" (282). Similarly, only two sentences of her first-person narration refer to the many laborers working at the slaughterhouse: "the workers stood on raised platforms, all in identical blood-drenched coats, yellow hard hats, goggles that obscured their faces, and earplugs that shut out sound. They used power tools to perform various operations on the hanging carcasses" (282). Putting the slaughterhouse into a kind of soft focus, Jane's camera zeroes in on a lone worker and single cow:

The worker put his hand on the cow's arched neck to steady her, and I stood behind Oh and turned on the sun gun and aimed the beam at her pulsing throat. The worker was talking to her all the while, saying, 'There now, girl, calm down, it's gonna be all over soon,' and then he did the most amazing thing. He bent down and looked straight into her bugging eye and stroked her forelock, and it seemed to calm her. And when he straightened up again, he used the upward movement of his body to sink the knife deep into her throat, slicing crosswise, then plunging it straight into her heart. (*YM* 283–84)

However graphic, Jane's description of "the kill" drains it of social reference points: the worker has no face, no name, no race, and no class; while the cow is suspended from a fast-moving line of live animals behind Jane and of undifferentiated carcasses before her. At this moment, Jane discovers the aims of her documentary project: to capture the intimate, rather than structural, connections between her body and the body of the cow she confronts. As she turns the "sun gun" on the cattle's throat, the kill floor becomes an interpersonal realm.

There is a conflict, in other words, between this filmic work and the work of *My Year of Meats*. The Dunn & Son footage crystallizes Jane's investments not only in DES but also in the media of film and its capacity to make abstract forces intimate and to bring bodies close. While conducting an interview with two workers at the feedlot earlier in this same chapter, Jane revels in the cinematic medium. The two men express virulent racism in explaining to Jane that the antibiotics Gale Dunn mixes into the animal feed keep the meat "clean" for "unclean" Japanese consumers: "these cows here's goin' straight to Japan. . . . I heard they even eat the assholes and everything" (266). The interview raises the question of how the structure of factory farms perpetuates (or taps into) structural racism. However, Jane concentrates instead on the demeanor of the ranch hand: "It was a great sound bite. Having had his say, Donny settled back into a silent sulk" (267). The scene ends with Jane and Suzuki engrossed in shooting the feedlot pens: "On the far side of the pen was a cluster of heifers, feeding at the bunker. Suzuki ignored them and trained the camera on the ground just below us. In the dust lay a slimy, half-dried puddle containing a misshapen tangle of glistening calf-like parts" (267). When Jane first imagines how the shoot at Dunn & Son will go, she anticipates "one spectacular shot" to capture the feedlot's 20,000 cattle. As she and her crew "train" the camera on a single meat worker, a lone cow, and a "tangle of glistening calf-like parts," the footage brackets the scale and technological nature of such an operation and instead dwells on the close-up shot. In this pivotal section of the novel, Jane thus strives to give coherence to what she calls the "too complex" story of her year of meats. Her solution to this problem of complexity is to zoom in to the point that the proliferating people, animals, institutions, and systems that her research has uncovered slip out of view.

Julie Sze extols Jane's intimate and interpersonal approach to her subject, arguing persuasively that the mother-daughter narrative she pursues makes accessible the otherwise technical dimensions of DES.[63] The filial and gendered lens on DES is certainly central to *My Year of Meats* as a whole, which develops an extended metaphor comparing misogyny and animal cruelty as well as the rationalization of women's bodies and the bodies of domesticated animals. Monica Chiu clarifies this metaphor: the novel, she writes, shows "a figurative consumption of women who battle both men and infertility, the former agents in an international beef-for-capital campaign, the latter the unfortunate result of contaminated meat ingestion."[64] These connections recall the associations in Toni Morrison's *Tar Baby* (examined in Chapter 4) between abusive food corporations and abusive mothers and between the global market for exotic foods and the erosion of local, female-centered modes of food production. In *My Year of Meats*, as in *Tar Baby*, stories of how the world food system impacts communities of women contribute a new line of thinking about globalization. Many theoretical accounts of globalization downplay gender in addressing how multinational corporations enlist free trade ideology to access natural resources and consumer markets in the global South. Although a growing field of scholarship examines the gendered dynamics of globalization, the question of what the food system means for the capacities of women to procure, produce, and market goods has only recently entered globalization theory.[65] Narrating the effects of globalization on women as both producers and consumers of food, *Tar Baby* and *My Year of Meats* rejoin established globalization discourses by representing trade liberalization as a threat to women's food sovereignty.

Ozeki's protagonist blurs, however, the environmental politics of industrial meat (which Beef-EX represents) with the gendered politics of synthetic hormones (which DES inspires Jane to unravel). When read primarily through the first-person narrative and accompanying documentary project, Jane's year of meats becomes the story of DES. Although that story proves telling about the entwined histories of women's health care and animal husbandry in the United States, Ozeki sets up a conflict for Jane – one that is as much artistic as ethical – between telling a story about personal exposure to toxins and telling a story about the meat system. Jane, we have seen, stresses the significance of DES to her family's medical history and her own reproductive risk factors. At one point, for example, she shifts from chronicling the rise of growth hormones in confined feedlots to expressing her desire for revenge against the pharmaceutical companies that manufactured DES during the Cold War and then marketed it to doctors and ranchers: "Using DES and other drugs, like antibiotics, farmers could process animals on an assembly line, like cars or computer chips.... This was an economy of scale. It was happening everywhere, the wave of the future, the marriage of science and big business. If I sound bitter, it's because my grandparents, the Littles, lost the family dairy to hormonally enhanced cows" (125). In explaining "the economy of scale" to which DES contributes via the fate of her paternal grandparents' dairy, Jane calls to mind Terry Tempest Williams's 1992 memoir *Refuge*, which connects her mother's breast cancer origins to nuclear testing and to the environmental precariousness of the Great Salt Lake.[66] Defining this type of environmental writing as "toxic discourse," Lawrence Buell and Stacey Alaimo both suggest that firsthand experience often motivates narratives of environmental illness and endocrine disruption.[67] In the context of nonfiction works like *Refuge*, we can appreciate the rhetorical power of Jane's personal account of U.S. agribusiness and pharmacology as they have impacted the Little family's small dairy as well as her mother's and her own DES exposure.

However, this personal frame seems to turn Jane's attention away from those communities she encounters through *My American Wife!* that have experienced other consequences of the marriage between pharmacology and agribusiness. For example, the Dawes and Martinez families present Jane with occasions to investigate the racial inequities underlying industrialized agriculture in the United States. While Purcell Dawes suggests that exposure to toxins like DES disproportionately impacts poor consumers, the Martinez episode brings social justice issues around migrant farming into our field of vision. Alberto and Catalina Martinez, whom Jane selects for the second episode of *My American Wife!*, are Mexican American farmers living in Texas who worked as migrant farmworkers before saving enough money to buy their own farm. We read their story through the perspective of Ozeki's omniscient third-person narrator. The shift in point of view makes visible the lives of agricultural workers, who deal on a daily basis with pesticides, growth hormones, and genetically modified seeds. Jane does not pursue this line of inquiry, however, interpreting the Martinez story for *My American Wife!* viewers as one of upward social mobility: "They had scraped up the money to buy the little white farmhouse and a few acres of surrounding land, and the way I figured it, Alberto, Catalina, and little Bobby were on their way to becoming a real American success story" (58). In the episode's final frame, as the young Bobby Martinez stands "in a sea of golden grass" and Jane reflects on the "surreal and exquisite motion" of the child and his 4-H prize-winning piglet, Ozeki's protagonist directs the filmic eye onto single and singular bodies (61).

Jane's year of meats from this moment focuses more and more on DES exposure as an experience that bonds middle-class women in Japan and the United States. In her own story of DES, Orenberg writes, "for all their differences, [the daughters of DES] are forged into a sisterhood – unwilling, but undeniable. They are bonded not merely by the common fear that they could develop the dreaded adenocarcinoma (although relatively few have so far), but also by real physical problems."[68] In step with this feminist history of DES, Jane comes to understand DES prescriptions as an indicator for how the medical establishment views women and particularly immigrant women. During a trip home to visit her parents, Jane speculates that her mother's gynecologist likely prescribed DES after the Second World War: "Doc must have subscribed to the *Journal of Obstetrics and Gynecology*, seen the ads. So he gave her a prescription, probably about 125 milligrams of diethylstilbestrol, otherwise know as DES, to take once a day during the first trimester of me"

(156). The speculation highlights sexist and racist biases within the postwar medical community, which defined Japanese women's bodies as frail and in need of pharmaceutical intervention – a paradigm, Nancy Langston shows, that informed mid-century marketing of DES not only to doctors but also to feedlot owners.[69] By the end of *My Year of Meats*, Jane's exposé of Dunn & Son's illegal administering of DES provides an occasion for personal catharsis. While her interviews with Bunny Dunn, Alberto Martinez, the Dawes, and others certainly shape the documentary, the project becomes a means for Jane to understand, importantly, her reproductive health and the miscarriage she suffers when a cattle's carcass slams her to the floor and knocks her unconscious (284).

Ozeki complements Jane's project with parallel plots about the Pacific Rim meat trade and the particular effects of meat consumption on Akiko Ueno. The third-person narrative of Akiko registers throughout *My Year of Meats* the global reach of U.S. beef by crystallizing that power in Joichi's violent insistence that his wife consume the products of his employer, Beef-EX. In chapter 3, we learn that Akiko is anemic and that Joichi believes that a red meat diet modeled on Tex-Mex cuisine will put meat on her bones and make her fertile. To this end, he compels her to watch *My American Wife!* weekly and prepare each episode's featured meal (20). Contra her husband's beliefs, meat makes Akiko sick: "Akiko had a hard time with positive thoughts. After dinner, when the washing up was done, she would go to the bathroom, stand in front of the mirror, and stare at her reflection. Then, after only a moment, she'd start to feel the meat. It began in her stomach, like an animal alive, and would climb its way back up her gullet, until it burst from the back of her throat" (37). Compared to this bodily rejection of beef (which figuratively brings a slaughtered animal back to life), Akiko's eventual return to a diet of vegetables and fish improves her somatic health – a significant transformation in the novel that follows on Joichi's violent rape of her and the resulting pregnancy. Akiko's pescetarian diet stands, along with the lesbian couple Lara and Dyann's vegetarianism, as an alternative to the diet that *My American Wife!* and Beef-EX market globally. The stories and eating habits of these characters thus supplement Jane's documentary, a point evident in both Akiko's encounters with Tokyo supermarkets and Dyann's freelance writing about the influence that pharmaceutical corporations exert on ranchers and feedlot owners (*YM* 87, 205–06).

MEAT MARKETING AND OZEKI'S TRANSPACIFIC PLOT

We should be wary of defining the concerns of *My Year of Meats* strictly in terms of those of its protagonist. David Palumbo-Liu similarly cautions, "we are meant to take [Jane's cinematic perspective] with a dose of skepticism – is Jane merely mimicking the commercial discourse she knows will be effective in allowing her to go forward with her 'subversive' multicultural agenda?"[70] He argues that the novel is a pastiche of perspectives and discourses, while suggesting that it employs modernist techniques of character development to "lend new forms of information an affective and ethical content."[71] His analysis suggests that the postmodern pastiche in *My Year of Meats* is subordinate to the character-centered stories of Jane and Akiko. However, the novel generates a dizzying array of ethical positions on and emotional responses to its leitmotifs of media, meat, and agribusiness. The abundance of perspectives in *My Year of Meats* stems from a postmodern imperative to interweave individual experiences and thoughts with de-individuated discourses, which, in this case, include recipes, news reports, scientific data, TV scripts, and ephemeral correspondence. These discourses ultimately yoke the novel's satire of television sponsorship to its narrative of agribusiness and the transpacific meat marketplace.

Ozeki's choice of Japan as the locale for the U.S. Beef-EX marketing campaign invites exposition along these lines as it addresses both the marketing savvy and military entanglements of American agribusiness. Since the Second World War, the United States and Japan have waged a quiet yet aggressive trade war over beef. This conflict came to a head in the 1990s and 2000s, when the United States petitioned the World Trade Organization (WTO) to compel Japanese imports of American beef against trade restrictions in Japan that grew out of perceived risks to consumer health and food safety with the rise of mad-cow disease.[72] In *My Year of Meats*, a conspiracy plot that speaks to this trade history showcases the novel's postmodern elements. Reframing *The Jungle* by locating the story of industrialized meat in a Pacific Rim context, the novel depicts a collusion of corporations, trade organizations, and mass media and a conflict between global food capitalism and national food sovereignty that is too complex to narrate via first-person realist or modernist narrative alone. As with Jane's stakes in DES, the stories of the Little dairy farm in Quam, Minnesota and of Akiko Ueno in Tokyo tie this otherwise sprawling conspiracy plot into storylines that rearticulate complex structures via simple and ordinary contexts – recalling William Empson's seminal definition of the pastoral.[73] Akiko Ueno's nightly cooking of U.S. beef stands in for the millions of Japanese viewers who watch *My American Wife!*, just as the Little family history embodies the migration of Japanese women to the United States after the Second World War. At the same time, each of these families represents the tip of a narrative iceberg that opens up onto an underexamined history of how American meat entered Japan.

Red meat became prominent in Japanese culture after the Second World War, when the U.S. occupation government of 1945–52 began promoting a grain-and-beef-centered diet in Japan. In this historical context, the main intertext of *My Year of Meats* – Sei Shōnagon's *Pillow Book* – takes on significance. As Chiu observes, Japanese Buddhism prohibited meat eating during the Heian Court period in which Shōnagon lived and wrote. Anthropologist Emiko Ohnuki-Tierney further explains that the Buddhist "doctrine of mercy for all living beings" informed legal strictures against "the consumption of land-dwelling animals" and inspired images of the carnivorous West as barbaric.[74] At the start of *My Year of Meats*, Jane alludes to these social prohibitions and connects them to the *Pillow Book* (14). This long-standing taboo diminished to some extent during the U.S. occupation of Japan, when General Douglas MacArthur oversaw food relief and land reform programs that promised to modernize Japanese agriculture. Historians argue that these reforms paved the way for the United States to become Japan's chief trade partner during the Cold War.[75] During the Second World War, food shortages plagued Japan as well as its occupied colonies, which allowed the United States to become an agricultural trade partner in the region after the war, and by 1992 (one year after *My Year of Meats* takes place), American produce, grain, and meat accounted for nearly half of Japan's total food imports. Katsuro Sakoh summarizes these developments thus: "Before World War II, Japan … produced virtually all of its food needs. Today, Japan is the world's largest net importer of farm products."[76] This postwar history extends to Japan the power of the United States within the global food supply during and after the war, a history Chapter 3 discusses at length.

The Japanese imperial army had, in fact, begun promoting a diet of red meat as early as the 1930s. Katarzyna Cwiertka suggests that the popularity of red meat in Japan in the contemporary period dovetails with the Japanese military's rhetoric during the interwar years: "In 1936, for example, the catering division of the First Guards Infantry Regiment stated that 'Westernized dishes with a high fat content, such as deep-fried dishes, meat dishes and salads' were most enthusiastically welcomed by all 1,800 members of the regiment."[77] In the period between 1926 and 1946, the Japanese military published Western-themed menus in a monthly mass magazine entitled *Ryoyu* (Provisions' Friend), which devoted its pages to "nourishing" a meat-centered diet in Japan by fusing Japanese and Euro-American cuisines.[78] Restaurants and canteens republished the menus, while state-sponsored nutritionists – as in the United States and Europe during the same period – marketed a meat-rich diet as crucial not only to the bodily health of citizens but also to national security and prosperity. These government campaigns built on an established discourse in Japan that "advocated the abandonment of rice agriculture and the adoption of raising animals for meat ... to compete with meat eating Westerners."[79] The postwar occupation of Japan capitalized on the earlier state-sponsored rhetoric, and U.S. agribusiness was arguably the principal benefactor of increased meat and grain consumption. Beginning in 1951, for example, packaged bread increasingly substituted for rice in the traditional Japanese breakfast.[80] This postwar bread and meat "invasion," Ohnuki-Tierney suggests, finds its apotheosis in the late twentieth and early twenty-first centuries with the appearance of McDonald's franchises in Tokyo, Kyoto, and elsewhere.[81] However, it also finds a violent point of departure in the Second World War, when, as the prior chapter notes, U.S. food advertisers combined racist epithets about the Japanese with images of the physical advantage American foods would give to Allied soldiers. The notorious 1944 Bugs Bunny cartoon "Nips the Nips" casts a particularly dark shadow over the postwar entrance of U.S. meat into Japan with its image of the animated character handing out grenades hidden in ice cream bars that explode off-screen in the mouths, one imagines, of Japanese soldiers.[82]

These alimentary histories manifest today in the high stakes of the U.S.-Japanese food trade in general and the beef trade in particular. While beef exports to Japan have been small relative to total trade volume, meat has propelled conflicts between the two nations for decades. Ozeki signals her awareness of these conflicts at several points in the novel, most overtly when Jane acknowledges that the preparation of a lamb dish in the Bukowsky episode of *My American Wife!* is "tantamount to treason" in the eyes of Beef-EX. Jane reasons that "most of the lamb products imported by Japan came from Australia, not the U.S., and that Australia was America's main foreign competitor for the Japanese meat market" (137). This awareness of the Japanese market's importance to the U.S. beef industry proves prescient when Joichi later reprimands Jane for her decision to feature lamb on the show (143, 164). The importance of Japanese meat eating to the U.S. agricultural economy and to trade negotiations finds poignant expression in a scene in *My Year of Meats* that represents the commercial interests of Beef-EX through Joichi's rage at Akiko for preparing that same lamb dish: "'How dare you serve Australian lamb in my house!' [Joichi] hissed, then he lunged forward and knocked the platter from [Akiko's] hands. She raised her arms to ward off a blow. He obliged, boxing her ear with his fist and knocking her into the television" (143). In light of Joichi's position at Beef-EX, this scene correlates his abuse of Akiko with the meat industry's power, suggesting that

Joichi's violence encapsulates the force that the United States has used to promote its food interests in Japan.

In 2003 (five years after the publication of *My Year of Meats*), the two countries came to loggerheads over Japan's intermittent ban of U.S. beef since the first reported case of bovine spongiform encephalopathy (BSE), or mad-cow disease.[83] Although sixty countries participated in the embargo, the United States made Japan a focal point of a complaint to the WTO and of retaliatory trade measures. Two years later, President George W. Bush and Secretary of State Condoleezza Rice selected beef exports as the focus for trade talks with Japanese Prime Minister Junichiro Koizumi.[84] One reporter described the talks in striking terms, observing that Rice, on visiting Japan, "devoted more of her comments to American beef than to North Korean bombs."[85] The talks ended in a stalemate. Congress did not pass legislation requiring universal testing of U.S. cattle for BSE (a practice the Japanese government mandates for all domestic slaughterhouses), and in late 2005, Japan agreed to lift the beef ban with the caveat that only meat from cattle slaughtered before reaching 21 months in age would be imported from the United States. Just one month after lifting the original ban, Japan renewed it when inspectors found spinal column pieces in a U.S. shipment of meat.[86] The net result: U.S. beef exports to Japan plummeted from $3.9 billion in 2003 to $66.4 million in 2006; while worldwide exports fell from a record 2.52 billon pounds in 2003 to 461 million pounds in 2004.[87] These international skirmishes over beef have positioned free trade ideology against the sovereignty of nations to set environmental and agricultural standards and to mitigate consumer health risks related to food. The United States has largely prevailed in this struggle, in the sense that Japan's food sovereignty has rapidly declined since the postwar occupation. In the 1960s, Japan produced 90 percent of the meat its citizens consumed, but by 1988 that ratio had declined to 85 percent for chicken, 80 percent for pork, and 45 percent for beef (no doubt in part because overall meat consumption had also increased). In short, Japan became during the Cold War the "largest net importer of farm products in the world."[88]

The transpacific conflicts over meat are a crucial context for the fictional world of *My Year of Meats*. The 2003–05 standoff between Japan and the United States brings to fruition Ozeki's 1998 story about the U.S. beef export lobby and its fictional television campaign. Beef-EX deploys the principles and tactics of economic globalization by supplementing trade agreements with cultural forms of influence. Lurking still further in the background of *My American Wife!* is the military that has lent the United States authority in postwar and postindustrial Japan. The novel evokes that military through allusions to the U.S. declaration of war against Iraq in January 1991, the month Jane's narrative begins. As news reports from Desert Storm filter through Jane's consciousness, *My Year of Meats* introduces a layered reference to the war in Iraq and the 1945 nuclear attacks on Japan: "It was January 1991," Jane tells us, "the first month of the first year of the last decade of the millennium. President Bush had just launched Desert Storm, the largest air bombardment and land offensive since World War II" (7). Akin to the history of DES in *My Year of Meats*, such allusions to the Second World War are refracted through Jane's family history. In later vignettes about the Little dairy farm, Jane reflects on the significance of the war for her mixed ethnicity (her parents met in Japan in the 1940s) and her agricultural roots (her deceased father was a U.S. army botanist and her mother a Japanese gardener in Hiroshima) (*YM* 147–56, 235). Even more pointedly, she links her father's death from cancer to his military service in Hiroshima and, as we have seen, speculates that doctors prescribed DES to her mother partly out of postwar prejudices about Japanese war brides (156).

A late documentary interlude that Jane relays about wartime weapons production and postwar ranching in the western United States dovetails with this subtext about the legacy of the Second World War. The interlude opens chapter 10, where Jane describes a series of nuclear testing sites and plutonium manufacturing plants: the once "uranium production centers" of Grand Junction, the Colorado Springs Air Force Base, the Rocky Flats plutonium plant outside Denver, and the "atomic city" of Hanford (245–46). The last site brings to the novel's foreground the atomic bombings of Hiroshima and Nagasaki: "Hanford was one of three atomic cities hastily constructed in 1943 to produce plutonium for the Manhattan project" (246). It is here that *My Year of Meats* addresses most explicitly the military-industrial complex and its effects on U.S. agribusiness and agriculture by alluding to the postwar identities of these atomic spaces. We read that the Atomic Energy Commission permitted radioactive tailings at the closed mine in Grand Junction to be used in new housing construction, while the radioactive iodine from nuclear testing in Hanford has long "contaminated local dairy cattle, their milk, and all the children who [have] drank it" (246). These details suggest that the U.S. war plant initially displaces and later contaminates American farms and ranchlands.

In the space of two pages, Jane's research assistant Dave undercuts her dichotomy of agrarian farmland and toxic war industries. Dave reports to the *My American Wife!* crew, "'the impact of countless hooves and mouths over the years has done more to alter the type of vegetation and land forms of the West than all the water projects, strip mines, power plants, freeways and sub-division developments combined" (*YM* 249–50). This scathing critique of ranches and feedlots goes somewhat unremarked, as Jane concludes the documentary interlude on a "triumphant note" by imagining that Dave's battery of facts will draw viewers into the next episode of *My American Wife!* ("The Bunny Dunn Show") (250). However, the accrual of information takes on a life of its own, as Ozeki integrates the scale and impact of U.S. meat production into wider histories of nuclear weapons, suburbanization, and free trade. Behind Jane's nostalgia for a lost American pastoral and lament over the chemical legacy of the Second World War lurks another image of the American West, one that is transnational as well as national in scope and postindustrial as much as pastoral in structure. Similarly to the poetry of Lorine Niedecker (a subject of Chapter 3), *My Year of Meats* traces the coincidence of atomic war and industrialized agriculture. While Niedecker's mid-century poems explore the food rationing regimes of the Second World War, Ozeki's novel shows the transpacific horizons of American agribusiness.

As discussed in Chapter 3, the United States emerged from the Second World War as the world's largest meat consumer, an outcome that *My Year of Meats* addresses when Dave tells Jane, "the average American family of four eats more than two hundred sixty pounds of meat in a year" (*YM* 250). The irony of the postindustrial food system, which *My Year of Meats* illuminates, is its propensity for producing a glut of commodities while simultaneously failing to reduce malnourishment rates. American surpluses of foodstuffs like wheat and beef expanded during the Cold War, and, in response, corporations up and down the American food chain reached beyond the nation's borders for consumers. We can understand *My Year of Meats*, then, as spotlighting the significance of Japan within global food politics of the last half-century.

*My Year of Meats* subjects the neoliberalism of American agribusiness to parody by portraying *My American Wife!* as a form of media subterfuge on the part of Beef-EX. This fictional parody speaks to a political reality. The National Cattleman's Beef Association (NCBA) and the U.S. Meat Export Federation (USMEF) leveraged television and other media throughout the 1990s and 2000s to promote meat eating in Japan, and they did so by targeting Japanese housewives. The organizations' coordinated efforts to expand the Japanese meat market culminated in 2002 with a marketing campaign entitled "Desire Beef." Sponsored by the USMEF, "Desire Beef" bears an uncanny resemblance to the fictional story of *My American Wife!* and especially to the memos that circulate in *My Year of Meats* between Jane's New York production office, the Japanese TV network, and Beef-EX representatives. An advocacy group for U.S. farmers and ranchers known as the Kansas/Asia Community Connection articulates the goals of "Desire Beef" as follows:

> The USMEF launched a campaign in Japan to "deliver messages of safety, taste, and nutrition directly to Japanese consumers," with three American wives and mothers as spokespersons.... The full-scale campaign was to run in newspapers in March and April 2002, in women's magazines from April through June, and on television through September. The targeted group was "moms and children living at home."[89]

With this target group in mind, "Desire Beef" featured celebrity Japanese housewife Yu Hayami as its official spokesperson and included a book tour for her cookbook *American Beef Cooking*, which sold at more than 3,000 bookstores across Japan. If the USMEF's campaign had occurred before Ozeki published *My Year of Meats*, it would arguably be the novel's most important source; instead, the marketing campaign postdates the novel by four years. I would thus explain the parallel as an instance of life imitating art – or rather, of agribusiness imitating the postmodern novel.

Jane's documentary about DES seems at times to eclipse Ozeki's narrative of a food system that is at once industrialized and postindustrial – a system shaped by not only agricultural technologies (like confined feedlots and growth hormones) but also trade instruments and media campaigns. While Jane examines the impact of DES on women like her mother and Bunny Dunn, the novel rejoins this frame through a multi-perspectival narrative that moves outward from DES to represent meat as one node in a network that is at once regional and transnational, technological and cultural. For Nina Cornyetz, the "maze of alternative sources or citations" in *My Year of Meats* "collapses distinctions between creative and critical writing," challenging readers to shift through, compile, organize, and "discer[n] the authentic from the inauthentic."[90] If Willa Cather calls on the realist novel to decouple fiction from reportage (a point I make in Chapter 2), Ozeki reworks, at century's end, the muckraking novel.

*My Year of Meats* no doubt emphasizes Jane's perspective by, for example, making Akiko's healthy pregnancy a foil for both her miscarriage and her identity as a daughter of DES; and in the end, the novel does not fully realize the transpacific story to which its overlapping plots gesture. Ozeki seems to connect the novel's multiple narratives through an endless chain of metonymy that includes domestic violence, confined feedlots, TV programming, corporate advertising, world war, free trade, and ethnic cuisines. Critics have accepted this formal gambit as largely successful. Chiu, for example, maintains that the novel accomplishes a sophisticated critique of "patterns of ingestion for beef and for humans, attendant consumer culture, ... the work of this culture on the American Dream" and the "grisly" violence of both the meat market and the patriarchal culture of Manifest Destiny.[91] However, the novel's metonymic substitutions of domestic violence and confined feedlots should give us pause. Animal rights thinkers have crafted similar analogies between human and nonhuman beings. In *My Year of Meats*, however, analogies of women and cattle and of global meat and television media work quite differently than in animal welfare tracts like *Dead Meat*. At the novel's close, the satire of the U.S. beef industry recedes as *My Year of Meats* zeroes in on Jane's film and its depiction of the meat system as a metaphor for patriarchal structures on the one hand and consumer culture on the other.

This metaphorization of meat comes into sharp focus in the novel's penultimate scene, in which Jane edits the film reels from the Dunn & Son slaughterhouse. Her work on the raw footage is cathartic with respect to the trauma of her miscarriage, the temporary loss of her lover, and the news that the Japanese television network has indeed fired her. The chapter opens with Jane talking to her implied reader from her Manhattan apartment about the trouble she is having editing her "meat video":

First I quote Chris Marker, who is a filmmaker of note and also a fan of Shōnagon. I think about him a lot when I'm editing. Then I tell you that suspended by her leg, the dead cow spins, drained but still dripping from the mouthlike wound that bisects her throat. Then, as though in response to some unearthly cue, the wound gives a muscular throb, and a bright-red geyser springs upward from the floor. The wound opens, wraps its lips around the thick red stream, greedily sucks in the blood. When it's finished and the blood's all gone, the mouth closes and the lips seal – satisfied, seamless. The cow is thrashing, frightened, but whole again.

Alive and kicking. I do it again and again. Twisting the dial, shuttling the tape backward and forward, running my finger across the cusp of life and death, over and over, like there's a trick here, something that if I practice I might get good at. Sucking life back into a body. (325–26)

Jane's effort to edit a film about the "too complex" story of her year of meats finds closure as she makes this final cut of the Dunn & Son footage, which promises, in turn, to make her famous.[92] If Jane's documentary begins as a muckraking project that readers might classify with *The Jungle*, *Dead Meat*, and *Fast Food Nation*, the life of the filmmaker and the space of her editing room have become the main storyline of *My Year of Meats*.

The final pages of the novel linger not just on the body of a single cow but also on the medium of film, whose "miracle" for Jane is to make a dead life whole again – a sentiment kindred to DeLillo's view of fiction as "all about reliving things."[93] "Editing my meat video was hard," Jane tells us, "[it] was not a TV show, which was what I'd become accustomed to. It was a real documentary, the first I'd ever tried to make, about an incredibly disturbing subject. There were no recipes, no sociological surveys, no bright attempts at entertainment. So how to tell the story?" (334). This metafictional question also pervades *All Over Creation*, as characters ask repeatedly, "How do you tell a story?" when the correlations between events are difficult to parse (57, 218). In both novels, Ozeki positions the protagonist's story as just one among many but also recognizes the impulse to give shape to the "too complex" narrative of food in the information age by refracting it through individual bodies and intimate experiences. *My Year of Meats* develops the story that Jane's documentary begins to tell – a story about disassembly lines in confined feedlots, about pharmacology and hormone-contaminated meat, about global appetites for beef, and, finally, about the power of U.S. agribusiness in Japan (335). However, as Jane edits the scene of a dead cow striking her pregnant body to the floor of the slaughterhouse, the role of the meat industry in global power relations fades into the medium of filmmaking.

### ALMANAC FOR THE POSTINDUSTRIAL AGE

We might ask what makes *My Year of Meats* an exemplar of the post-industrial pastoral, to conclude with one of the chapter title's key terms. The novel includes few depictions of either cultivation or husbandry, arguably the twin strands of the pastoral tradition reaching back to classical georgic and idyllic literature. By comparison, *All Over Creation* is much more clearly a narrative of rural life, part of a body of literature that includes Cather, Cherríe Moraga, Steinbeck, Smiley, and others. But in what sense is Ozeki's tale of meat and media a pastoral one? The hybrid form of *My Year of Meats* blends sentimentalism, pastiche, and a mode Bruce Robbins describes as "the sweatshop sublime." Robbins identifies in both contemporary fiction and cultural theory an impulse to apprehend "the outer reaches of a world system of . . . inconceivable magnitude and interdependence," an impulse that no doubt informs the aims of *Global Appetites*.[94] Ozeki seems to aspire with *My Year of Meats* and *All Over Creation* to employ fiction as a form through which to apprehend multiple systems at once – from agribusiness and food countercultures to mass media and documentary film.[95] The assembly of information within the novel takes on a life of its own, even as it is partly "gathered back into" the sentimentalism of Jane's narrative.[96] Here, Kenneth Goldsmith's notion of "uncreative writing" illuminates the cultural significance of *My Year of Meats*. Focusing on a wide range of electronic literature genres, Goldsmith argues that contemporary writers act increasingly as assemblers, catalogers, and, in some cases, hoarders of information.[97] Although it is a work of print fiction, *My Year of Meats* exhibits precisely these traits both in its composition process (the voluminous amount of information Ozeki evidently combed through to draft the novel) and in its structure (the incorporation of "documentary interludes," memoranda, and data into narrative). Readers certainly seem to suffer from information overload, a response evident in the long lists critics generate to bring into focus those metonymic chains leading from meat to media and back again. However, the experience of reading Ozeki's fiction is one in which we simultaneously suffer from and take pleasure in the stream of "incoming information" that defines postindustrial society.[98] We do so, moreover, through the ludic strains in the novel that make abstract, gigantic, and "too complex" systems accessible.

If we understand the novel to be activating characteristics of the georgic almanac, however, the reader's obligation is no longer to parse every connection. Katherine Anderson observes that almanacs are "both simple to define and difficult to categorize"; narrowly defined, an almanac is an agricultural calendar, while capaciously defined, almanacs can contain information on disparate topics such as astrology, cosmology, housekeeping, agriculture, and home remedies.[99] From Hesiod's *Works and Days* to twenty-first-century urban farming blogs, the almanac is no doubt an information-rich form that aims to digest an ocean of data, knowledge, praxis, and technological innovation to help the reader/user put information to use. To quote from the 2012 edition of *The Farmer's Almanac* (first published in 1818), the almanac offers readers a "compendium of knowledge ... [t]hat goes beyond today's experts and enlightens you with generations of perception, expedience, and common sense [sic]."[100] Joni Adamson, writing about *Almanac of the Dead*, describes in similar terms the Mayan and Anglo-American almanacs, which function as "living books" by integrating the calendar form with stories as well as bodies of vernacular knowledge.[101] The term "living books" recalls Yumi Fuller's description of open-pollinated seeds in *All Over Creation* and, in turn, highlights the impetus in Ozeki's fiction to make the contemporary novel a living-breathing instrument of knowledge transfer. Several aspects of *My Year of Meats* call up the almanac explicitly, including its overarching calendar structure (each chapter corresponds to one month in Jane's year of meats) and the use of epigraphs from Shōnagon's eleventh-century *Pillow Book* (itself a kind of ladies almanac). Finally, and as with *All Over Creation*, *My Year of Meats* is a realist narrative that is simultaneously a "compendium" of facts, vignettes, recipes, pamphlets, and everyday practices. In contrast to a novelist like Richard Powers, whose novels are arguably virtuosic in the knowledge they integrate with narrative, Ozeki makes the array of information she assembles user-friendly.[102]

In this instantiation, the postindustrial pastoral (or, more specifically, the information-age almanac) is a deliberate contradiction: a narrative well versed in network society and yet intent to cut its systems of production and consumption down to size by miniaturizing them and making them knowable. We can here understand Ozeki's fiction in relationship to two emergent cultural forms that draw from the DIY spirit of almanacs: a genre of environmental nonfiction I call locavore memoir (the subject of Chapter 6) and the multimedia practice of bioart. Examples of the locavore memoir have been small in number but significant in cultural impact. Exemplified most notably by Pollan's *Second Nature: A Gardener's Education*, ethnobotanist Nabhan's *Coming Home to Eat*, and Kingsolver's *Animal Vegetable Miracle*, the locavore memoir chronicles a year of growing, foraging, preserving, bartering for, cooking, and making food from the author's immediate vicinity.[103] A constraint-based project, the genre imposes a number of rules on its author. (Thus does Nabhan commit to eat only foods from within a 250-miles radius of his Tucson, Arizona home.) More directly relevant to Ozeki's fiction, the locavore memoir aims to disseminate knowledge about farming, husbandry, food preservation, and cooking via a number of almanac-esque devices: recipes, home remedies, and glossaries, to name a few; and in almost every case, the book is organized as a twelve-month chronicle of the author's experiment in sourcing food locally.

Best-selling examples of the genre like *Animal, Vegetable, Miracle* tend, however, to romanticize preindustrial food culture and downplay connections between agriculture and empire. It is precisely this tendency that Ozeki's fiction counters. Instead, her novels sit between the locavore retreat from long-distance food travel and the bioart aspiration to build new food networks. If locavores strive to inspire gardeners and foragers, bioartists aim to turn food consumers into tinkerers, hobbyists, and lay scientists. In line with Ozeki's anti-GMO renegades in *All Over Creation*, the bioart group Critical Art Ensemble sees its projects as ensuring open flows of information and knowledge about the food system. Responding to the rapid adoption of GMOs since the early nineties, the group's 2004 project "Free Range Grain" mixed tactical media with science education in a portable, public lab that tested foods from participants' pantries for GMO traces. Critical

Art Ensemble describes the goals of "Free Range Grain" as follows: "Myths, fantasy, misleading speculation, disinformation, and so on abound in the public sphere.... We want to bring the routinized processes of science to the public – let them see them and act within them."[104] Bioartists thus seek to make sense for a nonexpert public of what *My Year of Meats* calls "the miasma of misinformation," building an alternative to the world of agribusiness by making consumers into users of biotechnology, practitioners of agricultural science, and disruptors of an engineered food system. With an eye toward breaking up the monopoly on information that Monsanto symbolizes for Critical Art Ensemble, as for Ozeki, "Free Range Grain" spurs the creation of a countercultural network in which expertise becomes know-how. If we consider *My Year of Meats* and *All Over Creation* as companion novels, Ozeki's body of fiction manifests a kindred concern with transforming the sheer amount of data about American agribusiness into stories – narrative primers on alternative food movements from seed saving to vegetarianism that readers can digest and perhaps put to use. Attending to "complex stories" of food, Ozeki shuttles between the pastiche and a number of vernacular forms – from seed catalogs to cookbooks – that make sense of an abstract and globalized food system via the interpersonal, the intimate, and the everyday.

CHAPTER 6

# The Locavore Memoir: Food Writing in the Age of Information

> The 100-yard feast (or fast) came to a close. I simultaneously wanted to suck down a cup of coffee and to never let the experiment end. I would miss that slightly hungry, spry feeling. I would miss having my choices limited. I would miss my intimacy with the garden. When I was eating faithfully only from her, I knew all of her secrets. Where the peas were hiding, the best lettuces, the swelling onions. . . . When I went back to shopping at the supermarket, all those choices would open up again. I could choose from forty-seven different kinds of French cheese. On a whim, I could eat pizza. Or gelato. These are the wonderful things about life – and I made them more precious by not partaking for one short month.
> Novella Carpenter, *Farm City: The Education of an Urban Farmer* (2009)[1]

> Every human eater slowly reformulates the planet as they consume it.
> Zack Denfeld and Cathrine Kramer, *Edible: The Taste of Things to Come* (2012)[2]

The word "local" appears 100 times in Gary Paul Nabhan's 2002 book *Coming Home to Eat: The Pleasures and Politics of Local Foods*, more than two times the occurrences of "global" and its derivatives.[3] However unintentionally, this early example of the genre I term *locavore memoir* resists the global reach of American agribusiness in the twenty-first century first and foremost through the weight of its words. *Coming Home to Eat* relays Nabhan's "modest proposal" of making a yearlong commitment to eat only foods grown, raised, or foraged within a 250-mile radius of his Tucson, Arizona home. The occasion for this project is a belief, shared by many American environmentalists, that the industrialized food system produces, above all, environmental problems. Reacting to data that Americans obtain on average nine-tenths of their food from "nonlocal sources," Nabhan aspires that "nine out of every ten kinds of plants and animals [he] would eat over the coming months would be from species that were native to this region when the first desert cultures settled in to farm here several thousand years ago" (38). Defining the Sonoran Desert as a culturally and ecologically coherent *foodshed*, *Coming Home to Eat* gives voice to a countercultural food movement that promotes both eating locally and restoring native – or heritage – foods. Starting with its title, Nabhan's book defines this political resistance to agribusiness as a new form of culinary pleasure, redirecting the gastronomical discourse of fine dining toward a delight in eating right.

To follow through on his experiment in a region that likely has more acreage devoted to golf courses and master-planned communities than farms and gardens requires not just ingenuity and resourcefulness but also rules. Nabhan is admittedly less rule-bound than the locavore writers who have followed in his footsteps: early on, we read that he has only "a few tentative hypotheses about what 'eating locally' and 'coming into the foodshed' might ultimately mean" (34). He nonetheless acknowledges that his experiment makes friends nervous because it seems to make personal restraint a necessary precondition for cultivating an ecologically sustainable and regionally centered food system. If the supermarket comes to represent a space of endless choice during the Cold War, the locavore diet that has become popular since 9/11 advocates a kind of self-imposed rationing. At first glance, then, both the locavore memoir and the year it typically chronicles aim to recuperate the flora, fauna, and foodways that the author understands to be culturally indigenous and ecologically integral to the place he or she calls home. This new genre of environmental nonfiction and activism champions an intense localism. At the same time, the locavore venture develops out of a profoundly global sensibility about food and draws, moreover, on global networks of resources, knowledge, and people.

The period that *Coming Home to Eat* narrates (1999 through 2000) unfolds against a backdrop of global conflicts between free trade institutions and transnational slow food, anti-GMO, and environmental justice coalitions. These conflicts come to a head in a reference Nabhan makes late in the book to protests at the 1999 World Trade Organization (WTO) talks: "the forced closure of the [WTO] meetings in Seattle was something altogether unprecedented. For the first time, it became clear that millions of people were deeply worried about the ways in which globalization trends were wreaking havoc on family farms, migrant farmworkers, fishermen, and consumer food choices" (262). Nabhan is a member of this global movement and participates, specifically, in seed saver networks that connect him to activists around the world, such as Indian sustainable agriculture leader Vandana

Shiva.[4] The definition he offers of a local foodshed also embodies a distinct kind of globalism in that it crosses the U.S. Mexico border and integrates Anglo-American, Chicano, and Native American foodways. Finally, although *Coming Home to Eat* is highly critical of the United States and its food and agriculture policies, Nabhan has scaled up the foodshed concept in a project that re-maps the North American hemisphere along the lines of eleven "place-based food traditions," ranging from "Chile Pepper Nation" in the Southwest to "Salmon Nation" in the Pacific Northwest and Alaska.[5] Put simply, the localism of locavores like Nabhan is far more bound up with hemispheric and planetary affiliations than we might think.

*Coming Home to Eat* can now be grouped with a growing collection of kindred books. Among them are Slow Food International founder Carlo Petrini's 2001 manifesto, L.A. chef Suzanne Goin's 2005 seasonal cookbook, Barbara Kingsolver's 2007 memoir of her family's own yearlong locavore experiment, and Novella Carpenter's 2009 story of farming a vacant lot in West Oakland.[6] This published body of literature joins forces with everyday practices and political actions related to organic agriculture, farmers' markets, community gardens, humane husbandry, and heritage cuisines – a constellation of issues that came into alignment at the 2008 Slow Food Nation event in San Francisco. Animated by the agrarian, back-to-the-land rhetoric of writers like Henry David Thoreau and Wendell Berry[7] and the cosmopolitan, fusion cuisine of places like Northern California, the locavore memoir has proven to be a wildly popular form of nonfiction within the wider literature of food, a fact especially evident in the sales of journalist Michael Pollan's trifecta *Second Nature: A Gardener's Education* (2003), *The Omnivore's Dilemma* (2006), and *In Defense of Food: An Eater's Manifesto* (2008).[8] With increasing popularity has come a cultural ripple effect, as this body of nonfiction has inspired documentary films, infographics, magazine features, and op-eds about the merits (and blind spots) of eating locally and farming organically.[9] The films *Food, Inc.* (an offshoot of Pollan's and Eric Schlosser's respective nonfiction) and *Forks over Knives* (an exposé of the meat industry that dovetails with the muckraking work I discuss in Chapter 5) have made perhaps the biggest splash in terms of both the public conversation and consumer behavior change they have inspired.[10] The current vogue of eating locally has in turn given rise to social satire of the movement – along the lines of the well-known "Is it local?" scene from the series premiere of *Portlandia*.[11]

Defining this trend as something "to watch," the *Oxford New American Dictionary* named "locavore" the 2007 word of the year. That same year, the

Intergovernmental Panel on Climate Change (IPCC) released a report showing that industrial agriculture contributes approximately half of total annual methane emissions, a report locavores routinely cite as evidence for their position that the more consumers cultivate backyard gardens and support local farmers and ranchers the less they contribute directly to greenhouse gas emissions.[12] As the term "locavore" was making headlines in the late 2000s, I was developing the framework for this book around an initial hypothesis that food localism stems from a nostalgia for the preindustrial that draws for its popular appeal on idyllic strains within the Western pastoral tradition. Novelist Barbara Kingsolver's *Animal, Vegetable, Miracle* certainly lends credibility to this claim.[13] In contrast to Nabhan, Kingsolver's family feels they must leave their home in Tucson to embark on a year of local eating because of the perceived austerity of Arizona's desert foodshed. The family relocates to a farm in rural Virginia, where they hope to "find . . . a real American culture of food."[14] Filled with yearning for a Eurocentric and pastoral lifestyle, the story Kingsolver tells in *Animal, Vegetable, Miracle* opens with a lament over Americans' "drift away from [their] agricultural roots."[15] Speaking to my claim that the histories of industrial agriculture and world war in the United States are co-constitutive, Kingsolver goes on to observe, "we got ourselves uprooted entirely by a drastic reconfiguration of U.S. farming, beginning just after World War II. Our munitions plants, challenged to beat their swords into plowshares, retooled to make ammonium nitrate surpluses into chemical fertilizers instead of explosives."[16] In *The Omnivore's Dilemma*, Pollan makes a similar observation in his account of Iowa corn farmer George Naylor. Employing a metaphor resonant with Calvin Coolidge's 1925 speech (with which I open *Global Appetites*), Pollan describes the American Midwest as a landscape "teeming [with] cities of corn" and notes that Naylor defines his primary buyer as the U.S. "military-industrial complex."[17] The U.S. government has certainly supported agricultural production – and overproduction – since the 1940s in an effort to keep corn cheap for multinational grain and meat conglomerates like Archer Daniels Midland (ADM).[18] This policy framework by extension has fueled the development of corn-based processed foods, the export of foodstuffs and food brands, and, finally, the ascension of American food power. Pollan thus observes that American agribusiness has exploited our "predilection to eat a variety of species" by making a monoculture of processed foods that rely on the "protean" corn plant feel like a cornucopia (to refer back to my analysis in the Introduction of the painting "Still Life #30"). In opposition to the institutions, corporations, and consumers who promote what Pollan calls "industrial eating," the locavore memoir imagines an ethical and ecological return to the local.[19]

However, the longing for an agriculture and a cuisine rooted in the local that is evident in works like *Animal, Vegetable, Miracle* seems to require that the locavore live in the postindustrial United States nearly a century after Coolidge celebrated the transformation of food production into a "great industrial enterprise."[20] All of these writers define the project of reconnecting to a local foodshed by way of experiences with the global food marketplace, and even as they seek to exit that marketplace, they reveal their appetites for foods that travel far and wide. If agribusiness produces global markets for just a handful of commodities like corn and beef, the locavore craves a delicate balance between "coming home to eat" and indulging in unique edible goods from elsewhere. In *The Omnivore's Dilemma*, these twin impulses are on display during a meal Pollan prepares for friends while researching Virginia "grass farmer" Joel Salatin of Polyface Farm. The meal features foods from the locale where Pollan has been a guest: two chickens slaughtered on Wednesday, a dozen eggs gathered on Thursday, heirloom sweet corn, a lemony arugula salad, and an expensive Virginia wine. Recalling the depiction of cosmopolitan eaters in Toni Morrison's 1981 novel *Tar Baby* (the subject of Chapter 4), Pollan flouts his own "eat local" creed by acquiring Belgian chocolate for a soufflé. His rationale? Even the strictest locavore, he maintains, is "free" to procure goods that do not grow locally, for such a practice "predates the globalization of our food chain by a few thousand years."[21] In a recent analysis of sustainable food discourse in American literature, Dan Philippon suggests why Pollan is so quick to make allowances for a food like chocolate. Discussing Berry's seminal essay "The Pleasures of Eating," Philippon argues that such figures within the North American and European sustainable food communities have promoted a seductive idea of "extensive pleasure" that "collapses the all-too-common distinction between aesthetics or pleasure on the one hand and politics on the other."[22]

One consequence of this redefinition of culinary pleasure is a tendency to subsume the politics of food – and particularly politics of class and race – in the pleasures of slow food cuisine. In stark contrast to *Tar Baby*, for example, *The Omnivore's Dilemma* includes no reference to the colonial histories or contemporary labor practices of either chocolate or the spices Pollan uses to brine meat. This blind spot leaves him and other locavores wide open to critique. Cultural geographer Julie Guthman, in her analysis of California's "countercuisine"[23] as it developed during the 1970s and 1980s, contends that local food proponents have long used "the industrial eater" as a straw man against whom they can project "the reflexive consumer [who] pays attention to how food is made."[24] Along with sociologists E. Melanie DuPuis, David Goodman, and Michael K. Goodman, Guthman demonstrates that locavores accordingly overlook systemic inequities related to farm and restaurant labor as well as food access, inequities that both agribusiness and organic agriculture perpetuate.[25] These food studies scholars thus question how oppositional locavore praxis has been in the United States, especially given that its eat local rallying cry has been amenable to cooptation by food retailers like Chipotle Mexican Grill and Walmart.

Guthman further claims that the locavore "emphasis on educating people to the provenance of their food" taps into a cultural agenda that recalls xenophobic and even eugenic ideas of "national vigor, purity, [and] home soil" during the Second World War.[26] I would argue that it is no coincidence that locavores have revived WWII movements in the United States such as victory gardening (discussed in Chapter 3). Their endeavors have gained steam during a decade when the United States has again been at war: the post-9/11 period in which counterterrorism in the Middle East and North Africa has dovetailed with nationalist calls for energy independence that argue for increasing the cultivation of biofuels. Locavores have rallied around the idea that the conventional food system is among the most carbon-intensive enterprises on the planet, and their commitment to local food has in turn been appealing to both cultural isolationists and "peak oil" groups. In line with the food rationing propaganda of the Second World War, the U.S. government now holds up the locavore diet, along with backyard gardening, as a means to protect against bioterrorism, while re-scaling "the local" to mean the nation state.[27] The disparate proponents of local foodsheds – from environmental writers and green chefs to fast food retailers and State Department officials – have reduced the enormous carbon footprint of the modern food system to the miles that foods travel from producers to consumers. Both James McWilliams and David Cleveland have shown the limitations of this food-mile construct as the sole indicator of the changes locavores hope to achieve.[28] Despite these inaccuracies, the post-9/11 politics of national security have arguably given the locavore diet some of its social traction.[29] At the same time that we can thus explain the currency of locavore rhetoric, my analysis throughout *Global Appetites* of the tensions between global food markets and regional food cultures speaks to the chief limitation of the locavore memoir, at least in its most reverential form. In short, the locavore desire to restore agricultural and culinary practices elides the histories of empire, territorial war, and slavery that define food in the era before American agribusiness and that, as a narrative like *Tar Baby* shows us, continue to in the era since.

Since Nabhan published *Coming Home to Eat* more than a decade ago, I have come to see the eat local movement as not simply a nostalgic retreat from globalization. In sifting through the literary, artistic, and filmic record of locavores, I have instead found that these re-localization projects on the one hand convey desires for exotic and rare foods that rearticulate colonial histories and on the other depend on what Manuel Castells terms "network society" for developing political coalitions and cultural practices that offer alternatives to the proverbial supermarket.[30] The very call to end long-distance food travel is a late modern one according to Massimo Montanari: "In a world as genuinely fragmented as were the ancient and medieval worlds, the aim was to build a *universal* model of food consumption in which all (at least all ... who could afford to do so) might recognize themselves. In the global village of our own era, in contrast, values of identity, diversity, and local specificity have been established."[31] Although we should not dismiss the charges of elitism directed at Anglo-American locavores, Montanari's analysis illuminates the common ground they do share with environmental justice activists who work to safeguard both cultural and ecological diversity. Whereas the premise that these two kinds of diversity are analogous can both misconstrue ecological science and over-privilege the local,[32] it helps to organize a set of social movements that are *translocal* in structure, even as the actors within those movements oppose the "McDonaldization" of local cultures that globalization accomplishes.[33]

For their part, North American locavores participate in the informational and material networks that globalization affords while staking out new imaginative terrain for the future of food that rejects the seeming imperviousness of both globalization in the abstract and agribusiness in the specific. Developing his account of network society, Castells argues that a "space of flows" has displaced the "space of places" in the information age, suggesting that a cultural formation in the United States like the 100-mile diet can only be nostalgic. However, he observes that the present is also an age in which "*localities* [become] nodes of communication networks" and in which spaces of production and consumption are increasingly interwoven through an ever-expanding metropolis that makes discrete places, like farms and shopping centers, more proximate than in the industrial age.[34] In simultaneously leveraging global networks and positioning food within small-scale, DIY packets (to use a computational image), the locavore project suggests that the politics of eating locally are akin to open-source software: open, that is, to scaling up or down and to hacking for different social ends. My argument here builds on Goodman et al.'s claim that, contra the "mainstreaming" of locavore principles, a "reflexive localism" attentive to power structures and built on "shared knowledge" is also underway in contemporary culture.[35] What appears to be a fantasy of restoring preindustrial farming, hunting, and gathering practices turns out to be a complex pastiche of the local and the global.

The outcome of a social experiment that requires an enormous amount of ingenuity to sustain, both the locavore memoir and slow food movement rely on a geographically dispersed community of foragers, farmers, gardeners, and cooks while often clashing with neighbors and neighboring communities who aspire not to eat locally or to revive heritage foods but to shop and cook with affordability, nutrition, and convenience in mind. As the upstart of the locavore memoir coterie, Carpenter articulates these conflicts near the end of her month-long "100-yard" diet, when she acknowledges that the supermarket is a place of choice and access whose absence in many inner-city communities is hardly a cause for celebration.[36] Part of what makes *Farm City* the most striking addition to the locavore memoir genre is its context: the "GhostTown" neighborhood of inner-city West Oakland. As a white woman living with her boyfriend Bill in this multiethnic community, Carpenter is at times thoughtful about and at times insensible to her socioeconomic position in GhostTown as a self-styled urban farmer. As she navigates the rhetorical and social challenges that this position poses, she breaks nearly every convention of the locavore memoir: her story takes nearly three years to tell rather than the standard calendar year; it is organized not around the four seasons of agriculture but around three of the animal breeds that she ventures to raise for meat on a vacant lot adjacent to her apartment (the turkey, the rabbit, and the pig); and, finally, her locavore experiment proper occupies just a 30-page section of this 300-page nonfiction text. That experiment jettisons, moreover, the 100-mile-radius diet Bay Area locavores have taken as an almost sacred metric of sustainability in favor of a deliberately absurd 100-yard benchmark for eating locally.

If the *San Francisco Chronicle* reviewer calls *Farm City* "a contemporary restaging of [Berry's] agrarian American dream," I follow the *New York Times* reviewer in finding Carpenter's story "anything but bucolic."[37] The book is more about the precarious, open-source future of urban food production than about the imagined past of rural America. Carpenter accordingly divides her political loyalties between the slow food and urban food justice movements. As a result, there is a stronger imperative in *Farm City* for collectivity and mobilization than in other locavore memoirs. By the close of her years farming the vacant lot, Carpenter comes to the realization that urban farming "wasn't about one farm" (269). Rather, as she notes near the outset, urban farming is a necessarily transient, ephemeral, and communal effort to "plant in the cracks in the city" (61). As for her month-long locavore experiment, Carpenter satirizes her own decision to restrict so radically her diet as well as locavore discourse more generally. In Carpenter's case, the seed for her impulse to spend the month of July 2006 eating only what she can harvest and slaughter herself or forage and barter in GhostTown takes root when she is thousands of miles from home visiting her sister in rural France. There, late one night, she has what she describes as "a reckless thought about self-sufficiency" (118). Framing her experiment as one of "bravado," Carpenter calls into question the high-minded tone of books like *The Omnivore's Dilemma* and *Animal, Vegetable, Miracle* (135–36). Unlike her involvement in urban farm organizations that aim to alleviate poverty (like the Oakland-based City Slicker Farms), Carpenter admits that the locavore diet at its most extreme is an act of profound individualism – as particularly evident when she hides fat rendered from one of the ducks she slaughters in the back of the refrigerator so as to safeguard the prized morsel from her boyfriend (159).

In *Coming Home to Eat*, Nabhan imagines that the fifteen months he spends eating only from the Sonoran foodshed will forever bind him to his local context and community, even if the degree of that connection will ebb and flow: "Whenever I have doubts about whether all this effort has been worth it, I go out to the wilds beyond my backyard and taste a fruit or flower freshly plucked from a tree or vine. My mouth, my tongue, and my heart remind me what my mind too often forgets: I love the flavor of where I live, and all the plants and creatures I live with" (304). If Nabhan values local foods for conveying the unique "flavor" of his desert home and the particular sense of wilderness he enjoys outside his back door, Carpenter readily concedes how good both fast food and fusion cuisine taste. Her project is most provocative, then, in questioning whether ideas of the local that are tied to "the wilds" of hunting and gathering – a motif both Nabhan and Pollan indulge – can inform the project of creating sustainable foodsheds in cities. Although she at times idealizes the vegetable and animal products of her GhostTown farm, she also acknowledges that the supermarket and all it conveys can provide a kind of food security and access that is of great value to many urban communities. Before beginning her 100-yard diet (which she labels both a feast and a fast), Carpenter devotes a week to gorging on everything from sushi and falafel to coffee and chocolate (135). Similarly, when the month comes to a close, she waxes ecstatic about the cornucopia that awaits her in the supermarket – however corn-based it may be (183). These moments in the memoir draw into relief the entanglements with globalization that I am arguing makes the locavore project possible. The images that most linger in the reader's mind about the 100-yard diet within *Farm City* are not just those of Carpenter's local honey, but also of her searing caffeine-withdrawal headaches, her austere meals of scrawny game birds and meager potatoes, and the far-from-bucolic bloodiness of urban slaughter. For all of Carpenter's moxie, *Farm City* thus delineates the challenges of adopting the local as the sole yardstick for creating much needed alternatives to agribusiness that are sustainable and community-centric.

As a "crazed, starved, foraging locavore," Carpenter finds even a month too long to sustain her self-imposed constraints and so gives herself permission to re-engage with both local and global food networks (152). In particular, she decides to barter for a home-cooked meal (complete with cake) from her neighbor "Grandma" while also ordering green tea plants via express mail (156, 180). Yet her connections to communities and foods beyond her backyard extend beyond these instances of breaking "the rules." Carpenter also taps into geographically dispersed knowledge networks and communities of practice[38] to hone her skills as a "greenhorn." The book is after all the education of Novella Carpenter. To this final point, and in line with the argument at the end of Chapter 5, the driving force behind *Farm City* is an investment less in reclaiming the local and more in reclaiming DIY know-how as a means to exploit "the cracks" in American agribusiness.[39] The slow attainment of that know-how relies on the social networks that Castells claims redefine locality in the information age. Throughout her years in GhostTown, Carpenter draws on online and offline knowledge communities as well as traditional and vanguard primers: from the McMurray Hatchery website (where she obtains her first "meat bird packages") and the Seed Savers Exchange (where she purchases heirloom Sungold tomato seeds) to *The Encyclopedia of Country Living* and *The Integral Urban House* (guides first produced for the back-to-the-land, homesteading counterculture of the 1970s) (13, 61, 127, 239). Although these networks "capitalize on romantic, old-timey" ideas of food and agriculture, they also look to the future of food as much as to its past (127). In this, *Farm City* resonates with art-science collectives like The Center for Genomic Gastronomy that recontextualize preindustrial practices like seed saving as forms, to cite Cathrine Kramer and Zack Denfeld, of "open source biohacking."[40] As Kramer and Denfeld observe about the interactive exhibition they curated in 2012 (*Edible: A Taste of Things to Come*), twenty-first-century experiments with the local are integrally part of global networks and planetary ecology. By their account, even the most locally situated of eaters shuttle "between the kitchen and the biosphere" in that as they select what to consume (and what to give up) they also "reformate the planet."[41]

*Farm City* certainly exhibits some of the nostalgia found in a book like *Animal, Vegetable, Miracle*. In the end, however, Carpenter's education in urban farming demystifies the locavore vision as she learns how ephemeral, transitory, and vulnerable inner-city agriculture is to gentrification pressures and to social conflicts over whether farms and gardens are indeed the optimal means by which to eradicate poverty and build community. "I had been lucky," she writes in the book's penultimate chapter:

Somehow, all the forces had aligned to make my life full and abundant. I had arrived at a time when an abandoned lot could be taken over, a backyard turned into a place to keep animals, connections between humans made. This time had now passed.

My farm will eventually be bulldozed and condos will be built. Bill and I will move somewhere else. Where, undoubtedly, we will first build the garden. Then set up a beehive. Then the chickens. (267)

Filmmaker Scott Hamilton Kennedy delves into precisely this sense of how fragile urban farms are in his documentary about the largest urban community garden in U.S. history, which was located in South Central Los Angeles but was ultimately bulldozed and returned to its prior state as a vacant lot.[42] Although her own reflections on the tenuousness of urban agriculture end on a triumphant note about the resilience of farming and farmers, Carpenter questions the privileging of the local above all else by describing the work of urban food production as one that necessitates transience, not to mention moxie. Seeing urban agriculture as a process of apprehending the past, present, and future of any one community and of seeing its connections to the wider world, Carpenter activates not a bucolic but a georgic mode. At stake in this information-age georgic (or what I term in Chapter 5 the postindustrial almanac) is not a restoration of the past but an experiment in cultivating possible food futures. By the early twenty-first century, the future of food for those like Carpenter, who oppose the global reach and technological paradigm of agribusiness but are not prepared to retreat entirely from global networks, is a future in which the city, rather than the country, is the locus for food systems that are environmentally sustainable and culturally sustaining. Contra both localist and nationalistic food discourses, writers like Carpenter are thus composing alternatives to the paradigms of industrialization, free trade, and biotechnologies that American agribusiness has advanced since the First World War.

During the years spent writing this book, food became an increasingly prominent area of inquiry within a range of disciplines: from public health, climate science, and environmental law to sociology, anthropology, and cultural history. As evidence of this growing interest, we need only observe the number of universities that have invited Pollan since the 2006 publication of *The Omnivore's Dilemma* to deliver a plenary talk on food, culture, and the environment.[43] The emergence of food studies as an interdisciplinary field over the past decade has linked cultural and environmental questions about the food system, arguably distinguishing it from established fields such as agriculture history and agronomy that concentrate on economics, public policy, and technological innovation.[44] As a contribution to food studies, *Global Appetites* has shown that central to the field's intellectual concerns is the role of literature in variously promoting, documenting, and positing alternatives to a fully industrialized and profoundly interconnected food system. The literature of food I have examined calls into question universal frameworks for the cultivation and consumption of food, such as the idea advanced during the Green Revolution that only industrialized farms can feed the world. As we have seen, the global routes that food travels, and the prominence of U.S. agriculture and American food brands in shaping those routes, may represent a cosmopolitan culture or, alternatively, an unsustainable and unjust system. The work of this book has been twofold. First, it provides a cultural history for contemporary developments related to sustainable agriculture, slow food, and fair trade, on the one hand, and GMOs and convenience foods, on the other – a history that begins in the First World War with the rise of American agribusiness and industrialized agriculture and that shows the persistence of imperial practices of agriculture, eating, and food traffic in the late modern period. Second, it makes the case that literature, alongside other cultural forms, provides a rich and underexplored archive for apprehending this history.

To date, the disciplines of literary history and cultural theory have not, in the main, taken up food studies. With important exceptions, such as Denise Gigante's study of taste in the eighteenth century and Andrew Warnes's examination of hunger and ethnic foodways in African American literature, literature scholars have tended to treat both agriculture and eating in terms of the symbolic meanings they convey about other cultural issues, such as class and gender.[45] Building on the work of critics like Warnes as well as prominent food studies scholars such as Warren Belasco and Guthman, I have argued that food functions in imaginative works of the twentieth and early twenty-first centuries not just as symbol but also as rhetoric and praxis. The literature of food is, in other words, a social field where writers employ different modes to comprehend complex systems of production and consumption while also shaping food and agriculture practices. We have seen that the established account of Willa Cather as a regional and romantic novelist of the American Midwest undergoes revision when we attend to her war-inflected narratives of industrial farms and food technologies. Chapter 2 repositions Cather as a central figure for the history of American agribusiness and the global food trade, a writer whose geopolitical imagination is transnational as well as regional and whose debt to pastoral visions of the American plains expands, particularly after 1918, to include a vision of farmers as consumers, entrepreneurs, and, more darkly, war profiteers.

The other writers I have discussed expand on Cather's sense of food as an intricate system that is irreducible to a single place and that is at once technological, ecological, and cultural. In the period since the First World War, the U.S. repurposing of war technologies for food production has combined with the global marketing of both branded commodities and ethnic cuisines to make bucolic notions of agriculture implausible in the literature of food; and these same historical developments have transformed the meaning of "eating well" in American culture. If M. F. K. Fisher's literary precursor, the nineteenth-century gourmand Jean Anthelme Brillat-Savarin, could compose a primer on the perfect French meal, *How to Cook a Wolf* seems compelled to question its own devotion to French gastronomy (and especially to Brillat-Savarin's ideas of taste) through a political satire of American monoculture and its overproduction of meat in a time of world war and international famine. When defined to include both agriculture and cuisine, we can see that the subject of food prompts writers to interrogate and in some cases upend the anthropocentricism of food writing in particular and literature in general (from lyric poetry to dramatic theater). Lorine Niedecker, Toni Morrison, Ruth Ozeki, and Samuel Beckett all produce works that grapple with the entire food chain, exploring the relationships of farmers, ranchers, and eaters to other organisms – from potato seeds and cacao plants to harvested carrots and slaughtered cattle. In *New Goose*, for example, Niedecker creates unconventional poetic speakers who dispute a discourse of national solidarity through rationing: the collective voices of government regimes and malnourished communities. For his part, Beckett crafts in *Waiting for Godot* an experimental drama of hunger that brings onto stage the fallow landscape of the postwar world, which becomes a kind of character in the play. By comparison, Morrison and Ozeki push antiglobalization politics into new conceptual terrain through food-centered narratives that refract a U.S.-centric story of agriculture (and agricultural pioneers) through the long histories and transnational spaces of empire. These writers imaginatively reconfigure the food system by drawing our attention not only to its global institutions but also to local forms of innovation and resistance, from sharing food with a stranger to planting open-pollinated seeds.

It is in these ways that literature proves germane to contemporary food politics, and my project has been to make the stories writers tell about the past, present, and future of the modern food system speak powerfully to those arenas that have been, to date, the focus of food studies: the history of sustainable agriculture movements, the politics of nutrition science, and the national as well as international impacts of U.S. food policy. In the case of *Waiting for Godot*, Beckett's vision for experimental theater arguably does not include stirring European and American audiences to take political action in response to the persistence of hunger after the Second World War despite the wartime rhetoric that shared sacrifice would translate into shared prosperity after an Allied victory. Other texts I have examined pull back from the political realm by voicing a kind of determinism about industrial agriculture, which at times precludes the potential for either innovation or resistance (both of which have been hallmarks of food culture since ancient times). In the contemporary period it is easy to take for granted industrial agriculture and American food power as foregone conclusions. However, taken together, the writers at the center of *Global Appetites* (who help to define a late modern literature of food) show us that this power is up for grabs both by other nation states and by social movements. Alongside American agribusiness, the staying power of local and regional cuisines and the inventiveness of alternative agricultures shape the history of the twentieth century and, perhaps with particular vigor, the futures of food imagined in our present moment. Even in the era of processed meals and genetically modified seeds, writers prove to be compatriots with farmers, chefs, and activists in thinking about food as profoundly alchemical in its capacity to transform cultures and ecosystems. Thus do we witness the marriage of canned foods and wild truffles in *How to Cook a Wolf*, the metamorphosis of blackened radishes into carrots in *Waiting for Godot*, and the melding of diasporic foodways and supermarkets in *Tar Baby*.

This argument returns us to the dialectical relationship of agriculture and eating that centrally informs the thesis and arc of *Global Appetites*. In the period since the First World War, food is dialectical in two senses. First, during the last century, a material dialectic has formed around the interdependencies of food production and food consumption. We have seen that "production" in this period comprises not only farming and husbandry but also the engineering, manufacturing, processing, and packaging of food; by the same token, "consumption" includes not only cooking and eating but also acts of procuring, unwrapping, preparing, reassembling, digesting, and otherwise assimilating the edible world. Second, a discursive dialectic has developed around emergent narratives and practices. This dialectic, which has unfolded over the decades since the United States began to achieve global food power, works to illuminate the ramifications of food for particular cultures and communities. From Cather's Nebraska novels to Carpenter's urban farming memoir and from Beckett's spare drama of postwar famine to Morrison's sweeping narrative of bodily hunger and cosmopolitan taste, the literature of food conveys the material and discursive structures that have shaped the modern food chain. Contesting absolute commitments to the local while questioning the value of global markets and global appetites, this literature challenges univocal accounts of American agribusiness and its social achievements and thus speaks powerfully to oppositional movements that are today seeking to cultivate sustainable food futures.

# *Notes*

CHAPTER I

1. Calvin Coolidge, "Address before the Annual Convention of the American Farm Bureau Federation, Chicago, Ill., December 7, 1925" (Washington, D.C.: Government Printing Office, 1925), http://memory.loc.gov/ammem/coolhtml/coolbibTitles02.html.
2. The Center for Genomic Gastronomy, *Edible: The Taste of Things to Come*, Exhibition Catalog (Dublin: Science Gallery, 2012), 22.
3. "While we have land to labour," Jefferson argued in 1781, "let us never wish to see our citizens occupied at a workbench, or twirling a distaff." In stark contrast, as Warren Belasco shows, by the time of Coolidge's speech a vision of large-scale agriculture and "rationalized [food] planning" had come to the foreground of American politics. Thomas Jefferson, *Writings: Autobiography, Notes on the State of Virginia, Public and Private Papers, Addresses, Letters*, ed. Merrill D. Peterson (New York: Library of America, 1984), 291; Warren Belasco, *Meals to Come: A History of the Future of Food* (Berkeley: University of California Press, 2006), 36.
4. "Agribusiness, N.," in *Oxford English Dictionary Online* (Oxford and New York: Oxford University Press, 1989, 2012). For detailed histories of industrial agriculture and American agribusiness, see William Conlogue, *Working the Garden: American Writers and the Industrialization of Agriculture* (Chapel Hill: University of North Carolina Press, 2001); Deborah Fitzgerald, *Every Farm a Factory: The Industrial Ideal in American Agriculture* (London and New Haven: Yale University Press, 2003); Andrew Kimbrell, ed., *Fatal Harvest: The Tragedy of Industrial Agriculture* (Washington, D.C. and London: Island Press, 2002); Mark L. Winston, *Nature Wars: People vs. Pests* (Cambridge, MA: Harvard University Press, 1997).
5. The term *agri-food studies*, as used in anthropology and cultural geography, serves to encompass the intricate yet often obfuscated ties between production and consumption within the modern food system. David A. Cleveland et al., "Effect of Localizing Fruit and Vegetable Consumption on Greenhouse Gas Emissions and Nutrition, Santa Barbara County," *Environmental Science and Technology* 45, no. 10 (2011): 4555–62.
6. Belasco, *Meals to Come: A History of the Future of Food*, 156–71, quotation on 171.
7. Ibid., especially 185, 87.

8. Ruth L. Ozeki, *All Over Creation* (New York: Penguin Books, 2003), 127.
9. Monica Davey, "In Farm Belt, Ethanol Plant Hits Resistance," *The New York Times*, November 13, 2007; Laurie Garrett, "Food Failures and Futures" (Washington, D.C.: Maurice R. Greenberg Center for Geoeconomic Studies, 2008); Richard Manning, *Against the Grain: How Agriculture Has Hijacked Civilization*, 1st ed. (New York: North Point Press, 2004).
10. Roland Barthes, "Toward a Psychosociology of Contemporary Food Consumption," in *Food and Culture: A Reader*, ed. Carole Counihan and Penny Van Esterik (New York and London: Routledge, 2008): 28–35, especially 33–34.
11. In 2008, this metric was set at 1,680 kcal/day or fewer for adults in developing nations. As a point of comparison, that same year the average daily calorie consumption in the United States was 2,670 kcal/day. However, Gavin Jones, in his literary study of the problem of poverty in U.S. culture, highlights the fact that malnourishment remains a reality for many communities in the United States living in poverty. FAO Statistics Division, "FAO Methodology for the Measurement of Food Deprivation" (Rome: United Nations, 2008), 8; USDA, "Loss-Adjusted Food Availability," U.S. Department of Agriculture, www.ers.usda.gov/Data/FoodConsumption/FoodGuideIndex.htm-calories; Gavin Jones, *American Hungers: The Problem of Poverty in U.S. Literature, 1840–1945* 20/21 (Princeton: Princeton University Press, 2008).
12. Warren Belasco, *Appetite for Change: How the Counterculture Took on the Food Industry* (London and Ithaca: Cornell University Press, 1989, 2007).
13. *Edible: The Taste of Things to Come*, back inset.
14. Massimo Montanari, *Food Is Culture*, Arts and Traditions of the Table: Perspectives on Culinary History (New York: Columbia University Press, 2006), 99.
15. Ibid., 98, 100–01.
16. Henry Luce, "The American Century," *Life* (1941).
17. Ibid.
18. Hsuan L. Hsu, "Circa 1898: Overseas Empire and Transnational American Studies," *Journal of Transnational American Studies (JTAS)* 3, no. 2 (2011): 1–6.
19. I am here adapting Wallerstein's account of the world system and the importance of capitalist agriculture in its formation. Immanuel Wallerstein, *The Modern World System: Capitalist Agriculture and the Origins of the European World Economy in the Sixteenth Century* (New York: Academic Press, 1974).
20. Anthony Giddens, *The Consequences of Modernity* (Stanford: Stanford University Press, 1990), 21.
21. Ursula K. Heise, *Sense of Place and Sense of Planet: The Environmental Imagination of the Global* (Oxford and New York: Oxford University Press, 2008), 4; Arjun Appadurai, *Modernity at Large: Cultural Dimensions of Globalization* (Minneapolis: University of Minnesota Press, 1996); Ulrich Beck, *Risk Society: Towards a New Modernity*, trans. Mark A. Ritter (1986; repr., London: Sage Publications, 1992); Daniel Bell, *The Coming of Post-Industrial Society: A Venture in Social Forecasting* (1976; repr., New York: Basic Books, 1999); David Harvey, *The New Imperialism* (Oxford and New York:

Oxford University Press, 2003); *Spaces of Global Capitalism: Towards a Theory of Uneven Geographical Development* (London and New York: Verso, 2006); Fredric Jameson, *Postmodernism, or the Cultural Logic of Late Capitalism* (London and Durham: Duke University Press, 1991); Saskia Sassen, *Globalization and Its Discontents: Essays on the New Mobility of People and Money* (New York: New Press, 1998).
22. Harvey, *The New Imperialism*.
23. See especially Lawrence Buell, *The Future of Environmental Criticism: Environmental Crisis and Literary Imagination*, Blackwell Manifestos (Oxford: Blackwell Publishing, 2005); Elizabeth M. DeLoughrey and George B. Handley, *Postcolonial Ecologies: Literatures of the Environment* (Oxford and New York: Oxford University Press, 2011); Greg Garrard, *Ecocriticism*, The New Critical Idiom (New York and London: Routledge, 2004); Ursula K. Heise, "Ecocriticism and the Transnational Turn in American Studies," *American Literary History* 20, no. 1 (2008): 381–404; *Sense of Place and Sense of Planet: The Environmental Imagination of the Global*; Rob Nixon, *Slow Violence and the Environmentalism of the Poor* (Cambridge, MA: Harvard University Press, 2011). The work of bridging environmental studies and globalization theory has also occurred in the fields of sociology, cultural geography, and political theory. On this score, Ramachandra Guha's work merits mention: Ramachandra Guha and Joan Martinez-Alier, *Varieties of Environmentalism: Essays North and South* (London: Earthscan Publications Ltd., 1997).
24. Belasco, *Appetite for Change: How the Counterculture Took on the Food Industry*; *Meals to Come: A History of the Future of Food*; Amy Bentley, *Eating for Victory: Food Rationing and the Politics of Domesticity* (Chicago and Urbana: University of Illinois Press, 1998); Denise Gigante, *Taste: A Literary History* (London and New Haven: Yale University Press, 2005); Harvey A. Levenstein, *Paradox of Plenty: A Social History of Eating in Modern America* (Oxford and New York: Oxford University Press, 1993); Doris Witt, *Black Hunger: Soul Food and America* (London and Minneapolis: University of Minnesota Press, 2004).
25. Barthes, "Toward a Psychosociology of Contemporary Food Consumption"; Mary Douglas, "Deciphering a Meal," in *Food and Culture: A Reader*, ed. Carole Counihan and Penny Van Esterik (New York and London: Routledge, 2008), 44–53; Claude Leví-Strauss, "The Culinary Triangle," in *Food and Culture: A Reader*, ed. Carole Counihan and Penny Van Esterik (New York and London: Routledge, 2008), 36–43.
26. Montanari, *Food Is Culture*, 147.
27. This term signifies the food habits and culinary traditions of a particular culture.
28. Jennifer L. Fleissner, "Henry James's Art of Eating," *ELH* 75, no. 1 (2008): 27–62, quotation on 28; See also Deane W. Curtin and Lisa M. Heldke, *Cooking, Eating, Thinking: Transformative Philosophies of Food* (Bloomington: Indiana University Press, 1992); Carolyn Korsmeyer, *Making Sense of Taste: Philosophy and Food* (London and Ithaca: Cornell University Press, 1999).

29. Terry Gifford, *Pastoral*, The New Critical Idiom (New York and London: Routledge, 1999); Leo Marx, *The Machine in the Garden: Technology and the Pastoral Ideal in America* (Oxford and New York: Oxford University Press, 1964; repr., 2000); Raymond Williams, *The Country and the City* (Oxford and New York: Oxford University Press, 1973).
30. Wendell Berry, "The Pleasures of Eating," in *What Are People For?* (New York: North Point Press, 1990), 145–52.
31. Bruce Gardner explains that U.S. agricultural imports "more than doubled in real value between 1900 and 1930" and continued to expand throughout the 1940s and 1950s. Bruce L. Gardner, *American Agriculture in the Twentieth Century: How It Flourished and What It Cost* (Cambridge, MA: Harvard University Press, 2002), 149; See also Levenstein, *Paradox of Plenty: A Social History of Eating in Modern America*, 100.
32. George Orwell, "The British Crisis, 8 May 1942," in *My Country Left or Right, 1940–1943*, ed. Sonia Orwell and Ian Angus (Boston: Nonpareil Books, 2000): 207–16.
33. I am grateful to my two anonymous readers for clarifying these principles of selection and helping me to articulate them more precisely.
34. Jonathan Safran Foer, *Eating Animals* (New York: Back Bay Books, 2010); Eric Schlosser, *Fast Food Nation: The Dark Side of the All-American Meal* (Boston: Houghton Mifflin, 2001).
35. For extended critiques of the Green Revolution, see: Kimbrell, *Fatal Harvest: The Tragedy of Industrial Agriculture*; Vandana Shiva, *Earth Democracy: Justice, Sustainability, and Peace* (Cambridge, MA: South End Press, 2005); *Stolen Harvest: The Hijacking of the Global Food Supply* (Cambridge, MA: South End Press, 2000); Brian Tokar, "Monsanto: A Checkered History," *The Ecologist* (1998), www.mindfully.org/Industry/Monsanto-Checkered-HistoryOct98.htm.
36. Dwight D. Eisenhower, "Military-Industrial Complex Speech" (Public Papers of the Presidents, 1961).
37. Michael Pollan, *The Omnivore's Dilemma: A Natural History of Four Meals* (New York: Penguin Books, 2006), 42. Extending this analysis, agricultural historian Ron Kroese argues that, by 1944, farm magazines promoting chemicals developed for the Second World War were "coming home" to help farmers. Ron Kroese, "Industrial Agriculture's War against Nature," in *Fatal Harvest: The Tragedy of Industrial Agriculture*, 20–28, quotation on 23.
38. Monsanto is not the only figure one could discuss in this context. Companies that include DuPont and Dow Chemical also claim a large market share of the global agrochemical and seed industries, valued at $120 billion and $32 billion respectively. "Global Agrochemical Market Worth $196 Billion by 2014," *AgroNews* (2009); "Global Seed Market Values Grow by 10 Percent to Nearly $32b," *Seed Today*, May 11, 2010; BCC Research, "Global Markets for Agrochemicals," www.bccresearch.com/report/CHM054A.html.
39. Although better known as GM seeds or GMOs, the term *transgenic* more accurately describes the seeds that Monsanto and other biotech companies have pioneered by splicing genetic material from one species into another.

Daniel Charles, *Lords of the Harvest: Biotech, Big Money, and the Future of Food* (Cambridge, MA: Perseus Publishing, 2001); Peter Pringle, *Food, Inc.: Mendel to Monsanto – the Promises and Perils of the Biotech Harvest* (New York: Simon & Schuster, 2003).

40. Monsanto Inc., *For Happier Picnicking Days ... Luxtrex Styrene (a Monsanto Plastic)* (New York: *Saturday Evening Post*, circa 1950), Advertisement.
41. Rachel Carson, *Silent Spring* (Boston: Houghton Mifflin, 1962; repr., 1994), 15.
42. Monsanto Inc., "The Desolate Year," *Monsanto Magazine* 42, no. 4 (1962): 4–9.
43. Carson, *Silent Spring*, 174–78.
44. Justin Gillis, "Bionic Growth for Biotech Crops: Gene-Altered Agriculture Trending Global," *The Washington Post*, January 12, 2006; Andrew Leonard, "It's Monsanto's World. We Just Live in It," *Salon.com* (2006), www.salon.com/2006/02/09/monsanto/; Peter Whoriskey, "Monsanto's Dominance Draws Antitrust Inquiry," *The Washington Post*, November 29, 2009.
45. Belasco, *Meals to Come: A History of the Future of Food*, 220.
46. Monsanto Inc., "Press Kit," http://monsanto.mediaroom.com/.
47. With the patented line of *Bt* seeds, scientists incorporate genes from the bacteria *Bacillus thuringiensis* into a hybrid corn seed; the so-called gene of interest in the *Bt* bacteria generates a protein deadly to the corn borer pest. Ric Bessin, "Bt-Corn: What It Is and How It Works," University of Kentucky College of Agriculture, www.ca.uky.edu/entomology/entfacts/ef130.asp.
48. Monsanto Inc., *How Can We Squeeze More Food from a Raindrop?* (New York: *The New Yorker*, 2009), Advertisement.
49. Geoffrey Lean, "Ministers Back 'Terminator' GM Crops; Website Reveals Plans to Scrap Prohibition on Seeds That Threaten," *Independent*, March 5, 2006; Jerry Mander, "Machine Logic: Industrializing Nature and Agriculture," in *Fatal Harvest: The Tragedy of Industrial Agriculture*, 16–19.
50. Anne-Lise François, "'O Happy Living Things': Frankenfoods and the Bounds of Wordsworthian Natural Piety," *diacritics* 33, no. 2 (2003): 42–70, quotation on 44.
51. Manuel Castells, *The Rise of the Network Society* (Oxford: Blackwell, 2010), 378.
52. Ibid.
53. In *The Machine in the Garden*, Marx aims "to describe and evaluate the uses of the pastoral ideal in the interpretation of American experience ... under the impact of industrialism" (4). In line with the Myth and Symbol School of American Studies (of which it is an exemplar), the book identifies pastoral symbols as national touchstones while elevating literature as a special field of symbol making. In contrast to "simple" forms of pastoral thought that inform, Marx argues, white flight to the postwar suburb, the "complex" pastoral can be found in nineteenth- and twentieth-century novels that register the presence of industrial machinery in the countryside and, in doing so, subject pastoral tropes of bucolic life, human-nonhuman harmony, peace, and self-sufficiency to "the pressure of change." Marx, *The Machine in the Garden: Technology and the Pastoral Ideal in America*, 4, 24–32.

54. The postindustrial pastoral thus differs from what Terry Gifford terms the "post-pastoral" mode in environmental literature and ecocriticism and from what Michael Bennett labels "anti-pastoral" traditions within African American literature. Michael Bennett, "Anti-Pastoralism, Frederick Douglass, and the Nature of Slavery," in *Beyond Nature Writing: Expanding the Boundaries of Ecocriticism*, ed. Karla Armbruster and Kathleen R. Wallace (London and Charlottesville: University of Virginia Press, 2001), 195–210; Gifford, *Pastoral*.
55. Pollan, *The Omnivore's Dilemma: A Natural History of Four Meals*.
56. Thomas Pynchon, *The Crying of Lot 49*, Perennial Classics ed. (New York: HarperPerennial, 1965; repr., 1999), 2.
57. Gary Paul Nabhan, *Coming Home to Eat: The Pleasures and Politics of Local Foods* (New York and London: W. W. Norton, 2002).
58. Novella Carpenter, *Farm City: The Education of an Urban Farmer* (New York: Penguin Books, 2009).

CHAPTER 2

1. Willa Cather, *O Pioneers!*, ed. Susan J. Rosowski, Charles W. Mignon, and Kathleen A. Danker, Willa Cather Scholarly Edition (Lincoln: University of Nebraska Press, 1992); Louise H. Westling, *The Green Breast of the New World: Landscape, Gender, and American Fiction* (London and Athens, GA: University of Georgia Press, 1996), 58. Page references to *O Pioneers!* are to the 1992 scholarly edition; hereafter cited in text.
2. Walt Whitman, "Pioneers, O Pioneers," in *The Complete Poems*, ed. Francis Murphey (New York: Penguin Books, 1975), 257–61. Whitman's poem first appeared in 1865 and was republished in the 1867, 1871, and 1876 editions of *Leaves of Grass*, where it appeared in the section entitled "Marches Now the War Is Over." Parenthetical citations are to line numbers in the 1975 Penguin edition; hereafter cited in text.
3. Calvin Coolidge, "Address before the Annual Convention of the American Farm Bureau Federation, Chicago, Ill., December 7, 1925" (Washington, D.C.: Government Printing Office, 1925), http://memory.loc.gov/ammem/coolhtml/coolbibTitles02.html.
4. Raymond Williams, *The Country and the City* (Oxford and New York: Oxford University Press, 1973), 24.
5. Thomas Jefferson, *Writings: Autobiography, Notes on the State of Virginia, Public and Private Papers, Addresses, Letters*, ed. Merrill D. Peterson (New York: Library of America, 1984), 291; Leo Marx, *The Machine in the Garden: Technology and the Pastoral Ideal in America* (Oxford and New York: Oxford University Press, 1964, repr., 2000), 15, 24–32.
6. Studies that inform my distinction between the pastoral and georgic modes include: Paul Alpers, *What Is Pastoral?* (Chicago: University of Chicago Press, 1996); Lawrence Buell, *The Future of Environmental Criticism: Environmental Crisis and Literary Imagination*, Blackwell Manifestos (Oxford: Blackwell

Publishing, 2005); William Empson, *Some Versions of Pastoral* (New York: New Directions, 1935; repr., 1974); Greg Garrard, *Ecocriticism*, The New Critical Idiom (New York and London: Routledge, 2004); Terry Gifford, *Pastoral*, The New Critical Idiom (New York and London: Routledge, 1999); Marx, *The Machine in the Garden: Technology and the Pastoral Ideal in America*; Williams, *The Country and the City*.

7. The term *rural modernity* has primarily appeared in sociological case studies on how particular technologies or economic developments associated with modernity impact rural communities in postcolonial contexts. "Rural Modernity and Its Discontents," http://ruralmodernity.wordpress.com; Elizabeth B. Jones, *Gender and Rural Modernity*, Studies in Labour History (Surrey: Ashgate, 2009).

8. See Mary Paniccia Carden, "Creative Fertility and the National Romance in Willa Cather's *O Pioneers!* and *My Ántonia*," *Modern Fiction Studies* 45, no. 2 (1999): 275–302; Mike Fischer, "Pastoralism and Its Discontents: Willa Cather and the Burden of Imperialism," *Mosaic* 23, no. 1 (1990): 31–44; Joseph W. Meeker, "The Plow and the Pen," *Cather Studies* 5 (2003): 77–89; Walter Benn Michaels, *Our America: Nativism, Modernism, and Pluralism* (London and Durham: Duke University Press, 1995); Melissa Ryan, "The Enclosure of America: Civilization and Confinement in Willa Cather's *O Pioneers!*," *American Literature* 75, no. 2 (2003): 275–303; Joseph R. Urgo, *Willa Cather and the Myth of American Migration* (Chicago and Urbana: University of Illinois Press, 1995); Westling, *The Green Breast of the New World: Landscape, Gender, and American Fiction*.

9. Fischer argues that Cather's historical fictions occlude Native American land claims in the plains and American Southwest. He further observes that the frontier wars of the 1860s "made [the Homestead Act's] implementation possible" precisely by displacing native tribes and thus securing tracts of land for the pioneers. Fischer, "Pastoralism and Its Discontents: Willa Cather and the Burden of Imperialism," 37; Westling, *The Green Breast of the New World: Landscape, Gender, and American Fiction*.

10. Willa Cather, *My Ántonia*, ed. Charles Mignon and Kari Ronning, Willa Cather Scholarly Edition (Lincoln: University of Nebraska Press, 1994; repr., 2003); *One of Ours* (New York: Vintage Books, 1991). Page references are to these editions; hereafter cited in text.

11. Frank Norris, *The Octopus: A Story of California* (New York: Penguin Books, 1994); Upton Sinclair, *The Jungle* (New York: Penguin Books, 1985).

12. As Chapter 1 discusses at more length, I define agribusiness to signify the incorporation of industrial, biotechnological, and information systems into agriculture as well as the integration of food production and consumer culture. Sustained studies and critiques of industrialized agriculture include: Wendell Berry, *Citizenship Papers* (Washington, DC: Shoemaker and Hoard, 2003); Andrew Kimbrell, ed., *Fatal Harvest: The Tragedy of Industrial Agriculture* (Washington, DC and London: Island Press, 2002); Jim Mason and Peter Singer, *Animal Factories: What Agribusiness Is Doing to the Family Farm, the*

*Environment, and Your Health* (New York: Harmony Books, 1990); Duff Wilson, *Fateful Harvest: The True Story of a Small Town, a Global Industry, and a Toxic Secret* (New York: Harper Collins Publishers, 2001).
13. Willa Cather, "The Novel Démeublé," in *Stories, Poems and Other Writings* (New York: Library of America, 1992), 835–37, quotation on 836.
14. Cecelia Tichi defines muckraking as a form of nonfiction or fiction that aims to redress the social problems of poverty, corporate monopolies, and environmental pollution. In coining the term as a pejorative moniker, President Theodore Roosevelt adapted "muckrakers" from John Bunyan's character "The man with the Muck-rake" in *Pilgrim's Progress*, who gives up salvation for a life of worldly profit and who always looks down at filth rather than up to the heavens. Chapter 5 takes up the resurgence of muckraking journalism in the late twentieth century as a form through which writers detail the practices of agricultural corporations and, especially, feedlots and meatpackers. Cecelia Tichi, *Exposés and Excess: Muckraking in America, 1900/2000* (Philadelphia: University of Pennsylvania Press, 2003); "Exposés and Excess," review of *Fast Food Nation: The Dark Side of the All-American Meal* by Eric Schlosser, *American Literary History* 15, no. 4 (2003): 822–29.
15. Robert Thacker, "Journalist and Teacher, Writer and Poet, 1895–1912," The Willa Cather Foundation, www.willacather.org/about-willa-cather/.
16. Willa Cather, "Escapism," in *Stories, Poems and Other Writings*, 967–73, quotation on 971–72.
17. Ibid., 972.
18. Mark McGurl, *The Novel Art: Elevations of American Fiction after Henry James* (Princeton: Princeton University Press, 2001), 12–19.
19. For discussions of this latter and crucial dimension of Cather's work, see especially, Jonathan Goldberg, *Willa Cather and Others* (London and Durham: Duke University Press, 2001); Michael North, *Reading 1922: A Return to the Scene of the Modern* (Oxford and New York: Oxford University Press, 1999); Sharon O'Brien, *Willa Cather: The Emerging Voice* (Cambridge, MA: Harvard University Press, 1997); Westling, *The Green Breast of the New World: Landscape, Gender, and American Fiction*.
20. North, *Reading 1922: A Return to the Scene of the Modern*, 173, 92–94.
21 McGurl, *The Novel Art: Elevations of American Fiction after Henry James*, 17; McGurl builds on Veblen's 1899 analysis of the leisure class: Thorstein Veblen, *Theory of the Leisure Class* (New York: Penguin Books, 1994).
22. McGurl, *The Novel Art: Elevations of American Fiction after Henry James*, 5.
23. William Conlogue, *Working the Garden: American Writers and the Industrialization of Agriculture* (Chapel Hill: University of North Carolina Press, 2001), 22, 26–30.
24. Matthew J. C. Cella, "Harmonious Fields and Wild Prairies: Transcendental Pastoralism in Willa Cather's Nebraska Novels," in *Bad Land Pastoralism in Great Plains Fiction* (Iowa City: University of Iowa Press, 2010), 99–134.

25. Cella quotes from Emerson's 1858 address on farming to argue that the transcendentalist "yeoman is part laborer, part artist, and part prophet: he toils against the 'elements' while mastering those same elements . . . to reshape the land so that it reflects the ordered fields of his imagination." Ibid., 105, 10.
26. I am grateful to Claire Bowen for her insight into this aspect of the novel.
27. Pearl James, "The 'Enid Problem': Dangerous Modernity in *One of Ours*," *Cather Studies* 6(2006): 92–128, quotation on 98.
28. Susanne Freidberg, *Fresh: A Perishable History* (Cambridge, MA: Belknap Press of Harvard University Press, 2009).
29. According to the 2007 USDA Agricultural Census, 55 percent of farm operators in the United States do not list farming as their primary occupation. Moreover, while farms with sales of more than $1,000,000 represented less than 5 percent of all farms in the United States as of 2007, they generated nearly 60 percent of total agricultural production. Farmer indebtedness around the world has also been on a sharp incline since the early twentieth century. In the United States, total farmer debt rose from approximately $50 billion in 1970 to an estimated $370 billion in 2012 (in real dollars). USDA, "2007 Census of Agriculture," (Washington, D.C.: U.S. Department of Agriculture, 2007), www.agcensus.usda.gov/index.php; "Farm Sector Income and Costs: Assets, Debt, and Wealth" (Washington, D.C.: U.S. Department of Agriculture, 2011), www.ers.usda.gov/topics/farm-economy/farm-sector-income-finances.aspx.
30. Jefferson, *Writings: Autobiography, Notes on the State of Virginia, Public and Private Papers, Addresses, Letters*, 291.
31. Willa Cather, "Nebraska: The End of the First Cycle," *The Nation*, September 5, 1923. I have in mind here Georg Lukács's analysis of commodity fetishism as those capitalist processes that eclipse complex social relationships among laborers, consumers, and corporations and foreground, instead, our relationship to things. Georg Lukács, *History and Class Consciousness: Studies in Marxist Dialectics*, trans. Rodney Livingstone (Cambridge, MA: MIT Press, 1972).
32. Willa Cather, "The Bohemian Girl," *McClure's Magazine*, August 1912.
33. James Woodress compares the storyline of *My Ántonia!* to Cather's childhood in Red Cloud, Nebraska: "in the spring of 1883 [Cather's father] sold his sheep farm at Back Creek Valley, Virginia, near Winchester, and moved his family to Webster County, Nebraska. They spent their first 22 months on Grandfather Cather's farm some dozen miles north of Red Cloud," before moving into town. James Woodress, "Historical Essay," in Cather, *My Ántonia*, 369–402, quotation on 369.
34. Carden, "Creative Fertility and the National Romance in Willa Cather's *O Pioneers!* and *My Ántonia*."
35. McGurl, *The Novel Art: Elevations of American Fiction after Henry James*, 129–32.
36. Williams, *The Country and the City*, 24.
37. Fischer, "Pastoralism and Its Discontents: Willa Cather and the Burden of Imperialism," 31.
38. Ibid., 33–34.

39. For further analysis of this discourse, see especially David J. Goldberg, *Discontented America: The United States in the 1920s* (London and Baltimore: John Hopkins University Press, 1999); Michaels, *Our America: Nativism, Modernism, and Pluralism*, 7, 31–32.
40. Willa Cather, *The Professor's House* (New York: Vintage Books, 1990).
41. Michaels, *Our America: Nativism, Modernism, and Pluralism*. See also Matthias Schubnell, "The Decline of America: Willa Cather's Spenglerian Vision in *the Professor's House*," *Cather Studies* 2(1993): 92–117.
42. St. John de Crèvecoeur, *Letters from an American Farmer and Sketches of Eighteenth-Century America*, ed. Albert E. Stone (New York: Penguin Books, 1981), 42–43; hereafter cited in text.
43. Williams, *The Country and the City*, 32.
44. Wendell Berry, *The Unsettling of America: Culture and Agriculture* (New York: Avon Books, 1977), 30.
45. Conlogue, *Working the Garden: American Writers and the Industrialization of Agriculture*, 25.
46. Ibid.
47. Westling, *The Green Breast of the New World: Landscape, Gender, and American Fiction*, 72–73.
48. By structure of feeling, I mean Williams's concept from *Marxism and Literature*: "meanings and values as they are actively lived and felt" in a particular social moment and context. Raymond Williams, *Marxism and Literature* (Oxford and New York: Oxford University Press, 1978), 132.
49. Westling argues that Cather rejects conventional ideas of femininity in drawing heroines who are isolated from the domestic sphere and who identify with the masculine epic tradition. At the same time, she observes, the depiction of wilderness and "the wild" in her fiction is deeply ambivalent. Westling, *The Green Breast of the New World: Landscape, Gender, and American Fiction*, 61–66.
50. Carden, "Creative Fertility and the National Romance in Willa Cather's *O Pioneers!* and *My Ántonia*," 279.
51. Richard C. Harris, "Getting Claude 'Over There': Sources for Book Four of Cather's *One of Ours*," *Journal of Narrative Theory* 35, no. 2 (2005): 248–56; "The Newly Discovered Cather–Alfred A. Knopf Correspondence and *One of Ours*," *Willa Cather Newsletter and Review* 54, no. 3 (2011): 101–07; Janis P. Stout, "The Making of Willa Cather's *One of Ours*: The Role of Dorothy Canfield Fisher," *War, Literature and the Arts* 11, no. 2 (1999): 48–59; "Response to Richard C. Harris's 'Getting Claude "Over There": Sources for Book Four of Cather's *One of Ours*,'" *Journal of Narrative Theory* 35, no. 2 (2005): 259–62; Steven Trout, *Memorial Fictions: Willa Cather and the First World War* (Lincoln: University of Nebraska Press, 2002).
52. North, *Reading 1922: A Return to the Scene of the Modern*, 178, 86; Mary Ryder, "'As Green as Their Money': The Doughboy Naïf in *One of Ours*," *Cather Studies* 6 (2006): 145–59; Steven Trout, "From 'The Namesake' to *One of Ours*: Willa Cather on War," *American Literary Realism* 37, no. 2 (2005): 117–40.

53. Richard C. Harris, "'Pershing's Crusaders': G.P. Cather, Claude Wheeler, and the AEF Soldier in France," *Cather Studies* 8 (2010): 74–90, quotation on 75.
54. We read twice in the novel that both his neighbors and Enid pronounce Claude's name, much to his irritation, as "clod."
55. Sally Mara Sturman and Susan Mitchell, "Cover Design," in *One of Ours* (New York: Vintage Books, 1991).
56. Frederick Jackson Turner, *The Frontier in American History* (New York: H. Holt and Company, 1920).
57. Ryder, "'As Green as Their Money': The Doughboy Naïf in *One of Ours*," 147–48.
58. Ibid., 156. See also, Merrill M. Skaggs, "Cather's War and Faulkner's Peace: A Comparison of Two Novels, and More," in *Faulkner and His Contemporaries*, ed. Ann Abadie and Joseph R. Urgo (Oxford, MS: University of Mississippi Press, 2004), 40–53.
59. Paul Fussell, *The Great War and Modern Memory* (Oxford and New York: Oxford University Press, 1975; repr., 2000), 9.
60. Ibid., 192.
61. Ibid., 29–35.
62. "President Calls for War Declaration, Stronger Navy, New Army of 500,000 Men, Full Co-Operation with Germany's Foes," *The New York Times*, April 2, 1917.
63. Ibid.
64. James, "The 'Enid Problem': Dangerous Modernity in *One of Ours*," 93, 102–03, 11, 17.
65. Ibid., 102.
66. Anthony Giddens, *The Consequences of Modernity* (Stanford: Stanford University Press, 1990), 21, 83.
67. Fussell, *The Great War and Modern Memory*, 24, emphasis in original.
68. Hesiod, *Works of Hesiod and the Homeric Hymns*, trans. Daryl Hine (Chicago: University of Chicago Press, 2005).
69. Fussell, *The Great War and Modern Memory*, 235. Fussell also notes that irony pervades this device in British writing about the First World War: "A nation of gardeners was not likely to miss the opportunities for irony in pretending that 'thickets' of barbed wire were something like the natural hedges of the English countryside." Ibid, 237.
70. The war's direction turned in 1918 when, due to multiple fronts against and economic blockades of Germany, the Allied powers defeated the Central Army.
71. North, *Reading 1922: A Return to the Scene of the Modern*, 192.
72. Ibid, 187; Susan Meyer, "Sanitary Piggeries and Chaste Hens: Willa Cather and the Pure Food Movement," *Willa Cather Newsletter and Review* 54, no. 2 (2010): 38–47, especially 44–45.
73. Jewell notes that Cather viewed cooking as an art form and believed that the standardization of diets was, in her words, "a crime against art." His essay builds on Guy Reynolds' analysis of Cather's work in the context of Americanization debates. Andrew Jewell, "'A Crime against Art': *My Ántonia*, Food, and Cather's Anti-Americanization Argument," *Willa Cather Newsletter and*

*Review* 54, no. 2 (2010): 72–76, especially 72, 74; Guy Reynolds, *Willa Cather in Context: Progress, Race, Empire* (Basingstoke: Macmillan, 1996).

74. Warren Belasco, *Meals to Come: A History of the Future of Food* (Berkeley: University of California Press, 2006); Warren Belasco "Dietary Modernization," review of *Revolution at the Table: The Transformation of the American Diet* by Harvey Levenstein, *Reviews in American History* 18, no. 2 (1990): 262–66; Harvey Levenstein, *Paradox of Plenty: A Social History of Eating in Modern America* (Oxford and New York: Oxford University Press, 1993). See also Jill Lepore, *The Mansion of Happiness: A History of Life and Death* (New York: Alfred A. Knopf, 2012), 31. About *One of Ours*, Pearl James argues that Enid's housekeeping, cooking, and vegetarianism come to stand for her New Woman identity. In response to this "mechanized and rationalized" approach, Claude conflates his "nostalgia for 'natural' preindustrial frontier life with a nostalgia for a traditional heterosexual union and division of labor." James, "The 'Enid Problem': Dangerous Modernity in *One of Ours*," 103, 06, 08.

75. Marx, *The Machine in the Garden: Technology and the Pastoral Ideal in America*.

76. "Agribusiness, N," in *Oxford English Dictionary Online* (Oxford and New York: Oxford University Press, 1989, 2012).

77. See Bruce L. Gardner, *American Agriculture in the Twentieth Century: How It Flourished and What It Cost* (Cambridge, MA: Harvard University Press, 2002); Richard Manning, *Against the Grain: How Agriculture Has Hijacked Civilization* (New York: North Point Press, 2004); Kimbrell, *Fatal Harvest: The Tragedy of Industrial Agriculture*.

78. See Thomas Bender, *A Nation Among Nations: America's Place in World History* (New York: Hill and Wang, 2006); Arturo Warman, *Corn and Capitalism: How a Botanical Bastard Grew to Global Dominance* (Chapel Hill: University of North Carolina Press, 2003).

79. Gardner, *American Agriculture in the Twentieth Century: How It Flourished and What It Cost*.

80. Stout, "The Making of Willa Cather's *One of Ours*: The Role of Dorothy Canfield Fisher."

81. Gardner, *American Agriculture in the Twentieth Century: How It Flourished and What It Cost*.

82. Virgil, *Georgics*, trans. Janet Lembke (London and New Haven: Yale University Press, 2005). Janet Lembke writes in the preface to her new translation of the *Georgics* that Virgil's text is about "what happens to the land when smallholders are displaced" during and after the Roman Civil War (xvi). In foregrounding Virgil's attention to manual labor, however, Lembke understates the conception of agriculture in the *Georgics* as a technological, commercial, and even martial enterprise. To cite in translation, Virgil writes in Book I, "I must speak of militant farmers' weapons, / without which the crops could not be sown nor sprouted: / first, the plow and the curved share's heavy hardwood frame / The grain carts of Ceres rolling slowly on the farms, /sledges and drags to smooth the soil, the hoes of unkind heft; / Greek wickerware, as well, and plain farming tools, arbutus – wood hurtles and the window used in Bacchus's secret rites"

(I.160–166). However, Virgil also composes an ethic of environmental stewardship for agriculture, as when the poem encourages farmers to rotate crops, let fields go fallow after harvests, and replenish the soil's nutrients (I.71–99).
83. The organization is called Archi's Acres. Archie's Acres, "Veterans Sustainable Agriculture Training (VSAT) Program," www.archisacres.com/page/vsat-program.
84. Dwight D. Eisenhower, "Military-Industrial Complex Speech" (Public Papers of the Presidents, 1961).

CHAPTER 3

1. Elmer Davis, "Food Rationing and the War: An Address by Mr. Elmer Davis on December 27, 1942," ed. U.S. Office of War Information, 1942, 1.
2. Lorine Niedecker, *Lorine Niedecker: Collected Works*, ed. Jenny Penberthy (Berkeley: University of California Press, 2002), 121. Page references to Niedecker's poems in this chapter are to the 2002 *Collected Works* unless otherwise specified.
3. Alice L. McLean, *Aesthetic Pleasure in Twentieth-Century Women's Food Writing: The Innovative Appetites of M. F. K. Fisher, Alice B. Toklas, and Elizabeth David*, Studies in Twentieth-Century Literature (New York and London: Routledge, 2011), 3.
4. Per Jenny Penberthy's notes on the unpublished "Mother Goose" and "Mother Geese" manuscripts from 1936 (the latter of which appeared in *New Directions*), it appears that Niedecker was unsuccessful in having this poem published in *Poetry* as part of her 13-poem "Mother Goose" manuscript. Niedecker, *Lorine Niedecker: Collected Works*, 86, 372.
5. Jo Ellen Green Kaiser, "Feeding the Hungry Heart: Gender, Food, and War in the Poetry of Edna St. Vincent Millay," *Food and Foodways* 6, no. 2 (1996): 81–92, especially on 87; Edna St. Vincent Millay, *The Murder of Lidice* (New York: Harper Brothers, 1942); *Make Bright the Arrows* (New York and London: Harper Brothers, 1940).
6. George Orwell, *Animal Farm* (New York: Harcourt Brace, 1946).
7. George Orwell, "The British Crisis, 8 May 1942," in *My Country Left or Right, 1940–1943*, ed. Sonia Orwell and Ian Angus (Boston: Nonpareil Books, 2000), 207–16.
8. Fredric Jameson, *A Singular Modernity: Essay on the Ontology of the Present* (London and New York: Verso, 2002); Tyrus Miller, *Late Modernism: Politics, Fiction, and the Arts between the World Wars* (Berkeley: University of California Press, 1999).
9. By examining literature from this period in the context of government documents, I am building on Michael Szalay's thesis that after the Great Depression literary modernism cannot be understood apart from governmental institutions and ideologies related to social welfare and national security. Michael Szalay, *New Deal Modernism: American Literature and the Invention of the Welfare State* (London and Durham: Duke University Press, 2000), 8.

10. This analysis starts from Jameson's contention that the evident aversion to politics in late modernism "requires a good deal of footwork to sustain." Jameson, *A Singular Modernity: Essay on the Ontology of the Present*, 164.
11. I am grateful to one of my anonymous readers for pointing me to this insight about the chapter's principles of selection.
12. Niedecker, *Lorine Niedecker: Collected Works*, 89, 92.
13. Ibid., 109, 125.
14. Ibid., 113.
15. Ibid.
16. Rachel Blau DuPlessis and Peter Quartermain, "Introduction," in *The Objectivist Nexus: Essays in Cultural Poetics*, ed. Rachel Blau DuPlessis and Peter Quartermain (Tuscaloosa and London: The University of Alabama Press, 1999), 1–22, quotation on 3.
17. Ibid., 11.
18. Michael Davidson, "Life by Water: Lorine Niedecker and Critical Regionalism," in *Radical Vernacular: Lorine Niedecker and the Poetics of Place*, ed. Elizabeth Willis, Contemporary North American Poetry Series (Iowa City: University of Iowa Press, 2008), 3–20, quotation on 8.
19. Davidson, "Life by Water: Lorine Niedecker and Critical Regionalism," quotation on 14. Several essays in *Radical Vernacular* show the complexity of Niedecker's sense of place and of rural Wisconsin in particular: Glenna Breslin, "Lorine Niedecker: The Poet in Her Homeplace," in Willis, *Radical Vernacular*, 189–206; Jonathan Skinner, "Particular Attention: Lorine Niedecker's Natural Histories," in Willis, *Radical Vernacular*, 41–59.
20. Ruth Jennison, "Scrambling Narrative: Niedecker and the White Dome of Logic," *JNT: Journal of Narrative Theory* 41, no. 1 (2011): 53–81, quotations on 55–56, 71.
21. In the context of the "global spread of English," Ramazani defines transnational poetics to include "disjunctive" forms that "emphasize the intercultural discontinuities and conflicts between the materials they force together," "organic" forms that "integrate these materials," and diasporic forms that tend to organize around "long, shared racial or ethnic history." We might see Niedecker's poetry as shuttling between the disjunctive and organic frameworks, in Ramazani's terms. Jahan Ramazani, *A Transnational Poetics* (Chicago: University of Chicago Press, 2009), 20.
22. Niedecker, *Lorine Niedecker: Collected Works*, 383; Jenny Penberthy, "Life and Writing," in *Lorine Niedecker: Collected Works*, 1–11, especially on 6; Marjorie Perloff, *Poetic License: Essays on Modernist and Postmodernist Lyric* (Evanston: Northwestern University Press, 1990), 41–42, 83.
23. The manuscript for this unpublished poem was dated December 30, 1950. Niedecker, *Lorine Niedecker: Collected Works*, 142–43, 386; *New Goose*, ed. Jenny Penberthy (Berkeley: Rumor Books, 2002).
24. Davidson, "Life by Water: Lorine Niedecker and Critical Regionalism," 11–12; Peter Middleton, "Folk Poetry and the American Avant-Garde: Placing Lorine Niedecker," *Journal of American Studies* 31, no. 2 (1997): 203–18, quotation on 204

25. Middleton, "Folk Poetry and the American Avant-Garde: Placing Lorine Niedecker," quotation on 212; Elizabeth Willis, "Possessing Possession: Lorine Niedecker, Folk, and the Allegory of Making," *XCP: Cross-Cultural Poetics* 9 (2001), http://wings.buffalo.edu/epc/authors/niedecker/willi.html, n.p. Becky Peterson similarly argues, "[f]or Niedecker, poetry is at the crux of debates about use and uselessness, work and leisure." Becky Peterson, "Lorine Niedecker and the Matter of Life and Death," *Arizona Quarterly* 66, no. 4 (2010): 115–34, quotation on 117.
26. Niedecker's letters often included regional linguistic variants and markers of her own poverty so as "to remind her cosmopolitan friends [often with a light touch] that she was one of the 'folk,' not just a folk poet." Elizabeth Savage, "'Bleach[Ed] Brotherhood': Race, Consumer Advertising, and Lorine Niedecker's Lyric," *Tulsa Studies in Women's Literature* 28, no. 2 (2009): 291–313, quotation on 295.
27. Penberthy, "Life and Writing," 6.
28. Elizabeth Willis, "The Poetics of Affinity: Lorine Niedecker, William Morris, and the Art of Work," *Contemporary Literature* 46, no. 4 (2005): 579–603, quotations on 579, 584.
29. "Hoard's History: Generations of Leadership," *Hoard's Dairyman*, www.hoards.com/biographies; Kendra Smith-Howard, "Antibiotics and Agricultural Change: Purifying Milk and Protecting Health in the Postwar Era," *Agricultural History Society* 84, no. 3 (2010): 327–51, especially on 331, 347. Warren Belasco notes, "farmers grew twenty percent more wheat and seventy-five percent more potatoes per acre" in 1950 as compared to 1925. Warren Belasco, *Meals to Come: A History of the Future of Food* (Berkeley: University of California Press, 2006), 194.
30. Willis, "The Poetics of Affinity: Lorine Niedecker, William Morris, and the Art of Work," 580. Davidson notes that Niedecker's 1937 short story "Uncle" tells the story of a resort on Black Hawk Island, based loosely on her maternal grandparents' lives; the proprietors' nephew works to organize a dairy cooperative. Davidson, "Life by Water: Lorine Niedecker and Critical Regionalism," 9.
31. I am grateful to Harris Feinsod for guiding me to this and several other insights about the poem.
32. Connected to her through Zukofsky, Pound read Niedecker's work and was among her advocates on the modernist literary scene. Penberthy, "Life and Writing," 4; Savage, "'Bleach[Ed] Brotherhood': Race, Consumer Advertising, and Lorine Niedecker's Lyric," 294.
33. Belasco, *Meals to Come: A History of the Future of Food*, 11; "Dietary Modernization," review of *Revolution at the Table: The Transformation of the American Diet* by Harvey Levenstein, *Reviews in American History* 18, no. 2 (1990): 262–66.; Harvey Levenstein, *Paradox of Plenty: A Social History of Eating in Modern America* (Oxford and New York: Oxford University Press, 1993), especially on 46, 147, 200.
34. Florida Citrus Commission, *Canned Florida Grapefruit Juice Advertisement* (1943), Print advertisement; Gerd Horten, *Radio Goes to War: The Cultural*

*Politics of Propaganda During World War II* (Berkeley: University of California Press, 2003), 97–98.
35. Horten, *Radio Goes to War: The Cultural Politics of Propaganda During World War II*, 97.
36. Tracey Deutsch, *Building a Housewife's Paradise: Gender, Politics and American Grocery Stores in the Twentieth Century* (Chapel Hill: University of North Carolina Press, 2010), 164.
37. Belasco, *Meals to Come: A History of the Future of Food*, 17.
38. Brook Houglum, "'Speech without Practical Locale': Radio and Lorine Niedecker's Aurality," in *Broadcasting Modernism*, ed. Debra Rae Cohen, Michael Coyle, and Jane Lewty (Gainesville: University of Florida Press, 2009), 221–237, especially on 222, 25, 28.
39. Elizabeth Savage, "'A Few Cool Years after These': Midlife at Midcentury in Niedecker's Lyrics," *Journal of Modern Literature* 33, no. 3 (2010): 20–37, quotation on 34; see also "'Bleach[Ed] Brotherhood': Race, Consumer Advertising, and Lorine Niedecker's Lyric."
40. Niedecker, *Lorine Niedecker: Collected Works*, 113; *New Goose*, 57.
41. *Lorine Niedecker: Collected Works*, 112; *New Goose*, 55.
42. *Lorine Niedecker: Collected Works*, 121; *New Goose*, 75.
43. *Lorine Niedecker: Collected Works*, 118–19.
44. Timothy Carmody, "Modernism's Objects," review of *The Objectivist Nexus: Essays in Cultural Poetics*, ed. Rachel Blau DuPlessis and Peter Quartermain, *Journal of Modern Literature* 27, no. 1 (2003): 207–10, quotation on 210. Michael Golston offers a similar account of Objectivism with his discussion of Zukofsky's poetics. Michael Golston, "Petalbent Devils: Louis Zukofsky, Lorine Niedecker, and the Surrealist Praying Mantis," *Modernism/Modernity* 13, no. 2 (2006): 325–47.
45. During the Second World War, Paul K. Conkin writes, American farmers enjoyed productivity gains of 2 percent on average, while skyrocketing demand "used up all the surpluses helped by the Commodity Credit Corporation," thus boosting prices. Paul K. Conkin, *A Revolution Down on the Farm: The Transformation of American Agriculture since 1929* (Louisville: University Press of Kentucky, 2008), 77, 80. For additional studies of this period in U.S. farm policy and economics, see Bruce L. Gardner, *American Agriculture in the Twentieth Century: How It Flourished and What It Cost* (Cambridge, MA: Harvard University Press, 2002), especially on 171, 265, 297; Karen A. J. Miller, "Agricultural Policy," in *The American Economy: A Historical Encyclopedia* ed. Cynthia Clark Northrup (Santa Barbara: ABC-CLIO, 2003), 6.
46. Quoted in Gardner, *American Agriculture in the Twentieth Century: How It Flourished and What It Cost*, 175.
47. Ron Kroese, "Industrial Agriculture's War against Nature," in Andrew Kimbrell, ed., *Fatal Harvest: The Tragedy of Industrial Agriculture* (Washington, D.C. and London: Island Press, 2002), 20–28, quotation on 23–24. See also Mark L. Winston, *Nature Wars: People vs. Pests* (Cambridge, MA: Harvard University Press, 1997).

48. Kroese, "Industrial Agriculture's War against Nature," 26.
49. Quoted in Amy Bentley, *Eating for Victory: Food Rationing and the Politics of Domesticity* (Chicago and Urbana: University of Illinois Press, 1998), 3.
50. Szalay writes, "[t]he Depression was occasioned, many believed, ... because the American public either did not or could not purchase the goods churned out by American industry." Szalay, *New Deal Modernism: American Literature and the Invention of the Welfare State*, 5.
51. Ibid., 9.
52. Ibid., 23, 64.
53. The Victory program authorized President Roosevelt to reorganize government bureaucracies in order to provide full support to the war. Davis, "Food Rationing and the War: An Address by Mr. Elmer Davis on December 27, 1942."
54. Rationing of sugar, coffee, tires, steel, and gasoline began early in 1942. Levenstein, *Paradox of Plenty: A Social History of Eating in Modern America*, 80–81.
55. Deutsch, *Building a Housewife's Paradise: Gender, Politics and American Grocery Stores in the Twentieth Century*, 177.
56. Davis, "Food Rationing and the War: An Address by Mr. Elmer Davis on December 27, 1942."
57. Ibid.
58. Franklin D. Roosevelt, "Address to the Congress of the United States: Four Freedoms," ed. Office of the President, January 6, 1941.
59. Ramón Saldívar, *The Borderlands of Culture: Américo Paredes and the Transnational Imaginary* (London and Durham: Duke University Press, 2006), 204.
60. Ibid., 211.
61. "Radio Background Material: Rationing," ed. U.S. Office of War Information, July 1, 1942, 3.
62. Ibid., 2, emphasis mine.
63. Artists for Victory, "Artists for Victory, Inc. Records," Research Information System (SIRIS) (Washington, DC: Smithsonian Institution, 1942–1946); Ellen G. Landau, "Artists for Victory: An Exhibition Catalog," (Washington, D.C.: U.S. Government Printing Office, 1983).
64. MOMA, "The Museum and the War Effort: Artistic Freedom and Reporting for 'the Cause,'" Museum of Modern Art, www.moma.org/interactives/exhibitions/2008/wareffort/.
65. For a longer discussion of the "produce and conserve" campaign, see Bentley, *Eating for Victory: Food Rationing and the Politics of Domesticity*, 37; Barbara McLean Ward, ed. *Produce and Conserve, Share and Play Square: The Grocer and the Consumer on the Home-Front Battlefield During World War II*, Strawbery Banke Museum (London and Hanover, NH: University Press of New England, 1994).
66. NOAA History, "Women in the Weather Bureau During World War II," National Oceanic & Atmospheric Administration (NOAA), www.history.noaa.gov/stories_tales/women5.html.

67. Deutsch, *Building a Housewife's Paradise: Gender, Politics and American Grocery Stores in the Twentieth Century*, 162.
68. Levenstein, *Paradox of Plenty: A Social History of Eating in Modern America*, 96, 100.
69. Gavin Jones argues that attempts to comprehend the persistence of poverty in the United States have been "remarkably controversial aspects of American intellectual and social history, just as they continue to unsettle national ideologies and to disrupt conventional ways in which we think of class and cultural identity." Gavin Jones, *American Hungers: The Problem of Poverty in U.S. Literature, 1840–1945* (Princeton: Princeton University Press, 2008), xiv.
70. John Burnett, *England Eats Out: A Social History of Eating out in England from 1830 to the Present* (London and New York: Pearson Longman, 2004).
71. Orwell, "The British Crisis, 8 May 1942," 208.
72. James Hinton, "Militant Housewives: The British Housewives' League and the Attlee Government," *History Workshop* 38 (1994): 128–56, quotation on 138.
73. Belasco, *Meals to Come: A History of the Future of Food*, 162.
74. David Kamp, *The United States of Arugula: The Sun-Dried, Cold-Pressed, Dark-Roasted, Extra Virgin Story of the American Food Revolution* (New York: Broadway Books, 2006), 33.
75. Edward Ragg devotes an entire chapter of his 2010 book-length study of Stevens to the poet's concern with eating and gastronomy: "Numerous Stevens poems refer to bread and wine, where such staples imply imaginative and domestic well-being, whether present or disturbingly absent. Following Santayana, Stevens gave the word 'poverty' a particular resonance; sensing economic and imaginative hardships frequently conjoin. Domestic comforts thus take on aesthetic significance in the poetry, not least through gastronomy." Edward Ragg, "Abstract Appetites: Food, Wine and the Idealist 'I,'" in *Wallace Stevens and the Aesthetics of Abstraction* (Cambridge and New York: Cambridge University Press, 2010), 136–65, quotation on 136.
76. Wallace Stevens, *The Collected Poems of Wallace Stevens* (New York: Vintage, 1990), 401.
77. Jean Anthelme Brillat-Savarin, *The Physiology of Taste: Or, Meditations on Transcendental Gastronomy*, trans. M. F. K. Fisher (New York: Counterpoint, 1949), 5.
78. M. F. K. Fisher, *The Gastronomical Me* (New York: Duell, Sloan and Pearce, 1943, 1954; repr., North Point Press, 1989). Page references are to the 1989 edition, hereafter cited in text.
79. For an authoritative account of these geographic migrations, see Joan Reardon's biographies: Joan Reardon, *M. F. K. Fisher among the Pots and Pans: Celebrating Her Kitchens*, California Studies in Food and Culture (Berkeley: University of California Press, 2008), especially on 77–98; *Poet of the Appetites: The Lives and Loves of M. F. K. Fisher* (New York: North Point Press, 2004), especially on 96–120.
80. Parrish committed suicide in response to an acute and debilitating circulatory illness that caused him to lose his leg. Reardon, *M. F. K. Fisher among the Pots*

*and Pans: Celebrating Her Kitchens*, 81; *Poet of the Appetites: The Lives and Loves of M. F. K. Fisher*, 118.
81. Susan Derwin, "The Poetics of M. F. K. Fisher," *Style* 37, no. 3 (2003): 266–78, quotation on 266; McLean, *Aesthetic Pleasure in Twentieth-Century Women's Food Writing: The Innovative Appetites of M. F. K. Fisher, Alice B. Toklas, and Elizabeth David*, 90.
82. Elaborating on his concept of the habitus as those social structures, practices, and spaces that define an individual's "disposition" for certain things and experiences over others, Bourdieu suggests that taste does not belong strictly to the upper class or the practiced gourmand, but to everyone. Pierre Bourdieu, *Distinction: A Social Critique of the Judgement of Taste*, trans. Richard Nice (Cambridge, MA: Harvard University Press, 1984), 175.
83. Ibid., 197.
84. The editors of the 1988 edition explain the publication history of the book as follows: "*How to Cook a Wolf* was first published in 1942, when wartime shortages were at their worst. It was revised by the author in 1951, by the addition of copious marginal notes and footnotes and a special section of additional recipes. These have now been incorporated in their proper places in the text, and are enclosed in brackets." Joan Reardon notes that the book had its origins in essays about food rationing that Fisher wrote in the early forties for the regional newspaper *Whittier News*. M. F. K. Fisher, *How to Cook a Wolf* (New York: World Publishing, 1942, 1954; repr., New York: North Point Press, 1988), ix; Reardon, *M. F. K. Fisher among the Pots and Pans: Celebrating Her Kitchens*, 82. Page references are to 1988 edition; hereafter cited in text as *HW*.
85. Max Rudin, "M. F. K. Fisher and the Consolations of Food," *Raritan* 21, no. 2 (2002): 127–38; quotation on 131. David Lazar seconds Rudin that Fisher is a modernist writer who took food as her principal subject. David Lazar, "The Usable Past of M. F .K. Fisher," *Southwest Review* 77, no. 4 (1992): 515–31.
86. Bentley, *Eating for Victory: Food Rationing and the Politics of Domesticity*; Burnett, *England Eats Out: A Social History of Eating out in England from 1830 to the Present*, 256; Michael Pollan, *In Defense of Food: An Eater's Manifesto* (New York: Penguin Books, 2008), 47.
87. In the United States, wartime cookbooks offered recipes to help readers comply with rationing and with the government's new "Basic Seven" chart, the precursor to the Food Pyramid, developed in the early 1940s by the U.S. Food Nutrition Board. During the war, the Nutrition Board also developed the first set of Recommended Daily Allowances (RDAs) for vitamin and mineral intake. The government's rationing program cited the Basic Seven chart and the RDAs to bolster the argument that a rationed diet would be nutritionally complete. Bentley, *Eating for Victory: Food Rationing and the Politics of Domesticity*, 69; Levenstein, *Paradox of Plenty: A Social History of Eating in Modern America*, 66–67. See also McLean Ward, *Produce and Conserve, Share and Play Square: The Grocer and the Consumer on the Home-Front Battlefield During World War II*.
88. Anne Zimmerman, *An Extravagant Hunger: The Passionate Years of M. F. K. Fisher* (Berkeley: Counterpoint, 2011), 214.

89. McLean, *Aesthetic Pleasure in Twentieth-Century Women's Food Writing: The Innovative Appetites of M. F. K. Fisher, Alice B. Toklas, and Elizabeth David*, 78.
90. Zimmerman, *An Extravagant Hunger: The Passionate Years of M. F. K. Fisher*, 212–14.
91. Claude Leví-Strauss, *The Savage Mind* (Chicago: University of Chicago Press, 1966, 1967), 19–21.
92. During the Second World War, Parr argues, Keynesian economic theory fueled the ideology of "the highly capitalized kitchen," which affirmed "the affluence and thus superiority" of Western states. At the same time, modernist designers from Europe and the United States "gloried in the kitchen" as a space for design experiments. Joy Parr, "Issue Introduction: Modern Kitchen, Good Home, Strong Nation," *Technology and Culture* 43, no. 4 (2002): 657–67, quotations on 659–61.
93. Julian Holder, "The Nation State or the United States?: The Irresistible Kitchen of the British Ministry of Works, 1944–1951," in *Cold War Kitchen: Americanization, Technology, and European Users*, ed. Ruth Oldenziel and Karin Zachmann (Cambridge, MA and London: MIT Press, 2009), 235–58, quotation on 246.
94. Ruth Oldenziel and Karin Zachmann, "Kitchens as Technology and Politics: An Introduction," in Oldenziel and Zachmann, *Cold War Kitchen*, 1–29, quotations on 2–4.
95. Ibid., 6.
96. Belasco, *Meals to Come: A History of the Future of Food*, 192.
97. Reardon, *M. F. K. Fisher among the Pots and Pans: Celebrating Her Kitchens*, 79.
98. Jessamyn Neuhaus, "The Way to a Man's Heart: Gender Roles, Domestic Ideology, and Cookbooks in the 1950s," *Journal of Social History* 32, no. 3 (1999): 529–55, quotation on 535.
99. I am indebted to Harris Feinsod for this observation.
100. Paul Alpers, *What Is Pastoral?* (Chicago: University of Chicago Press, 1996), 6; Primo Levi, *Survival in Auschwitz; and the Reawakening: Two Memoirs*, trans. Stuart Woolf (New York: Summit Books, 1986).
101. Neuhaus, "The Way to a Man's Heart: Gender Roles, Domestic Ideology, and Cookbooks in the 1950s," 535.
102. The Hershey Company produced the Field Ration D and Tropical bars throughout the Second World War, manufacturing over 140,000 per hour (or around 24 million per week) by 1945. Both bars were designed to be distasteful so that soldiers would eat them only in emergencies; in addition, the Tropical Chocolate bar was produced to withstand high temperatures. Hershey Community Archives, "Ration D Bars," www.hersheyarchives.org/essay/details.aspx?EssayId=26.
103. Levenstein, *Paradox of Plenty: A Social History of Eating in Modern America*, 83–84. Both media coverage and government documents attest to the gap between U.S. and British rationing programs: Jackson S. Elliott, "Meat Rationing Likely to Start in Few Days," *The Washington Post*, August 15, 1942; John Lindberg, "Food, Relief and Famine," ed. Transit Department (Geneva:

League of Nations, 1946); "How Britain Was Fed in War Time: Food Control 1939–1945," ed. London Ministry of Food (London: H. M. Stationery Office, 1946).
104. Niedecker, *Lorine Niedecker: Collected Works*, 119.
105. Rachel Blau DuPlessis explains the form surrealism tends to take in Niedecker's poetry: "What Niedecker meant by 'surrealist' might be a phenomenology of consciousness (and unconsciousness) and the desire to render the movements of mind. A shorthand summary of Niedecker's long-standing interests under this rubric would include automatic writing, trance states, an interest in dreams, a sense of the absurdity of associations, consciousness and its movements, 'subliminal' formations, possibly even the weirdness of everyday life." Rachel Blau DuPlessis, "Lorine Niedecker's 'Paean to Place' and Its Fusion Poetics," *Contemporary Literature* 46, no. 3 (2005): 393–421, quotation on 395.
106. Other poems that address disparities of affluence and food access both within the United States and internationally include: "I doubt I'll get silk stockings out / of my asparagus," "Motor cars / like China," and "Poet Percival said: I struck a lode," which ends with the ironic line, "This is truly a rich and beautiful country." (Percival was a nineteenth-century poet and self-trained scientist who served as Wisconsin's state geologist.) Lorine Niedecker, *Lorine Niedecker: Collected Works*, 103, 113, 119.
107. Levenstein, *Paradox of Plenty: A Social History of Eating in Modern America*, 80–81.
108. When Truman imposed a price ceiling on meat in 1946, ranchers responded by refusing to bring their livestock to market. The media warned of the looming "meat crisis" and "meat famine," and consumers rallied to demand that the administration lift price caps. Ibid., 83.
109. See especially Gardner, *American Agriculture in the Twentieth Century: How It Flourished and What It Cost*; John C. Hudson, *Making the Corn Belt: A Geographical History of Middle-Western Agriculture*, Midwestern History and Culture (Bloomington: Indiana University Press, 1994); Richard Manning, *Against the Grain: How Agriculture Has Hijacked Civilization* (New York: North Point Press, 2004).
110. "How Britain Was Fed in War Time: Food Control 1939–1945." Rations of sweets and other so-called personal foods ended in April 1949; bread, potato and preserve rations were lessened in 1948, milk in 1950, and tea in 1952. Between the autumn of 1953 and the spring of 1954, sugar, eggs, bacon, ham, cheese, fats, and meats were de-rationed entirely, and the British government then abolished the Ministry of Food. Lindberg, "Food, Relief and Famine"; Paul Reynaud, "Rationing: A War Weapon," ed. Minister of Finance (Paris: Centre D'Informations Documentaires, 1940); Ina Zweiniger-Bargielowska, *Austerity in Britain: Rationing, Controls, and Consumption, 1939–1955* (Oxford and New York: Oxford University Press, 2000).
111. George Orwell, *Nineteen Eighty-Four* (New York: Harcourt Brace, 1949; repr., New York: Penguin Books, 1983), especially on 5, 60–61. Ina Zweiniger-

Bargielowska shows that food rations and shortages profoundly damaged civilian morale after the war, arguing, "[t]he continuation of austerity after the war contrasted sharply with immediate post-war expectations." Moreover, there were tremendous class divisions with respect to experiences of and attitudes toward government austerity measures. Although 54 percent of the nation overall approved of rationing as of 1943, only 37 percent of workers in factories approved; and nearly half of male factory workers believed that they did not have enough food to "keep fit." Zweiniger-Bargielowska, *Austerity in Britain: Rationing, Controls, and Consumption, 1939–1955*, 29–31, 66–68, 75.

112. Tony Judt, *Postwar: A History of Europe since 1945* (New York: Penguin Books, 2005), 162.
113. Bentley explains, "Whereas the Marshall Plan . . . succeeded in providing food to select European countries while rebuilding their economies, earlier attempts to relieve immediate postwar famine conditions through voluntary rationing failed." Bentley, *Eating for Victory: Food Rationing and the Politics of Domesticity*, 170.
114. Lindberg, "Food, Relief and Famine." Levenstein, *Paradox of Plenty: A Social History of Eating in Modern America*, 84.
115. George Orwell, "London Letter, 17 August 1941," in *My Country Left or Right*, 145–54, quotation on 154.
116. Zweiniger-Bargielowska, *Austerity in Britain: Rationing, Controls, and Consumption, 1939–1955*, 66–67.
117. Judt, *Postwar: A History of Europe since 1945*, 162.
118. Burnett, *England Eats Out: A Social History of Eating out in England from 1830 to the Present*, 258.
119. Elizabeth David, *A Book of Mediterranean Food* (New York: John Lehmann, 1950; repr., New York: New York Review of Books, 2002), 11, 17. Hereafter cited in text as *MF*.
120. Elizabeth David, *South Wind through the Kitchen: The Best of Elizabeth David* (New York: North Point Press, 1998), 245.
121. Lisa Chaney, *Elizabeth David: A Biography* (London: Macmillan, 1998), 215.
122. Ibid., 158–61, 179, 193.
123. McLean, *Aesthetic Pleasure in Twentieth-Century Women's Food Writing: The Innovative Appetites of M. F. K. Fisher, Alice B. Toklas, and Elizabeth David*, 139.
124. Fredric Jameson, *Modernism and Imperialism* (Lawrence Hill, Derry: Field Day Theater Company Limited, 1988), 11.
125. Ibid.
126. *Waiting for Godot* was first produced in French at the Théâtre de Babylone, Paris in 1952. Samuel Beckett, *Waiting for Godot*, trans. Samuel Beckett (New York: Grove Press, 1954; originally published as *En attendant Godot*), 104–5. Page references are to the Grove edition; hereafter cited in text.
127. This paradox rewrites Camus's "Myth of Sisyphus" in which Sisyphus faces the choice of rolling a rock up a hill each day or leaving it, the only certainty being that the rock will always be there. In the case of *Waiting for Godot*, Gordon argues, the characters lack "defiance" about their lot and thus exist in a state of despair about their need to get by and go on in the face of both stasis

and absurdity. Lois Gordon, *Reading Godot* (London and New Haven: Yale University Press, 2002), 57–58.
128. Hugh Kenner contends that the existential themes of the play inhere in a "note of uncertainty," which "plagues the whole Beckett cosmos such that the reliability of a witness is always open to question." Hugh Kenner, *Flaubert, Joyce and Beckett: The Stoic Comedians* (Boston: Beacon Press, 1962; repr. London: Dalkey Archive Press, 2002), 67.
129. Fredric Jameson, *A Singular Modernity: Essay on the Ontology of the Present* (London and New York: Verso, 2002), quotations on 200–01, 05.
130. Joseph Roach, "'All the Dead Voices': The Landscape of Famine in *Waiting for Godot*," in *Land/Scape/Theater*, ed. Elinor Fuchs and Una Chaudhuri (Ann Arbor: University of Michigan Press, 2002), 84–93.
131. Gordon, *Reading Godot*, 63; Jameson, *A Singular Modernity: Essay on the Ontology of the Present*, 200–01.
132. According to Daniel Stempel, the manuscript for *En attendant Godot* suggests that the couple, who have known one another for fifty years, first met in the mid-1890s. Although Stempel concludes that Act I takes place in the "first years of the war," one could argue either that it takes place in the mid-1940s, near the war's end, or that it eschews such chronology altogether. The invocations of the Holocaust and the character of the landscape further suggest that the characters inhabit an interminable state of wartime (or postwar) rubble. Daniel Stempel, "History Electrified into Analogy: A Reading of *Waiting for Godot*," *Contemporary Literature* 17, no. 2 (1976): 263–78, quotation on 273.
133. Theodor W. Adorno, *Aesthetic Theory*, trans. Robert Hullot-Kentor (Minneapolis: University of Minnesota Press, 1998), 108, emphasis in original.
134. Ibid.
135. When Vladimir compares the landscape of the road to this remembered landscape of their past – that of "Macon country" – Estragon denies any memory of such a place, claiming that he has spent his entire life in the place of the play, which he calls "Cackon country."
136. Fortunately for them, Pozzo suggests, the land is now subdivided by the public road on which they and the lone tree stand.
137. Samuel Beckett, *Endgame and Act without Words*, trans. Samuel Beckett (New York: Grove Press, 1958; originally published as *Fin de partie suivi de acte sans parole*); *Happy Days* (New York: Grove Press, 1961).
138. In response to Nagg's final demand in the play for a sugar-plum, Hamm exclaims, "There are no more sugar-plums!" Beckett, *Endgame and Act without Words*, 10, 49, 54–55. I am grateful to Brendan O'Kelly for drawing my attention to this resonance between *Godot* and *Endgame* and for a subsequent insight into the idea that the principal trace of a market in Beckett's plays is hunger.
139. Quoted in Gardner, *American Agriculture in the Twentieth Century: How It Flourished and What It Cost*, 175. See also Kroese, "Industrial Agriculture's War against Nature," 24.

CHAPTER 4

1. In 2008, this metric was set at 1,680 kcal/day for adults in developing nations. As a point of comparison, that same year the average daily calorie consumption in the United States was 2,670 kcal/day. United Nations, "Millennium Project," www.unmillenniumproject.org/goals/gti.htm;"The Millennium Development Goals Report" (New York: United Nations, 2010), www.un.org/millenniumgoals/pdf/MDG%20Report%202010%20En%20r15%20-low%20res%2020100615%20-.pdf; FAO Statistics Division, "FAO Methodology for the Measurement of Food Deprivation," 8; USDA, "Loss-Adjusted Food Availability," U.S. Department of Agriculture, www.ers.usda.gov/Data/FoodConsumption/FoodGuideIndex.htm#calories.
2. While some definitions of food security/insecurity emphasize the availability and quantity of food, others focus on a community's access to foods that provide nourishment while also supporting cultural traditions and ethnic identities. FAO Statistics Division, "FAO Methodology for the Measurement of Food Deprivation"; Alison Hope Alkon and Kari Marie Norgaard,"Breaking the Food Chains: An Investigation of Food Justice Activism," *Sociological Inquiry* 79, no. 3 (2009): 289–305; Alexandra Spieldoch, *A Row to Hoe: The Gender Impact of Trade Liberalization on Our Food System, Agricultural Markets and Women's Human Rights*, ed. International Gender and Trade Network (Geneva: Friedrich-Ebert-Stiftung, 2007).
3. The Caribbean witnessed a nearly 8 percent increase in the number of undernourished people between 1990 and 2008. Food and Agriculture Organization, "High Food Prices and Food Security: Threats and Opportunities," in *State of Food Insecurity in the World* (Rome: United Nations, 2008), www.fao.org/docrep/011/i0291e/i0291e00.pdf; "How Does International Price Volatility Affect Domestic Economies and Food Security?," in *State of Food Insecurity in the World* (Rome: United Nations, 2011), www.fao.org/docrep/014/i2330e/i2330e00.htm.
4. Food and Agriculture Organization, "Climate Change and Food Security: A Framework Document," in *High-Level Conference on World Food Security: The Challenges of Climate Change and Bioenergy* (Rome: United Nations, 2008), www.fao.org/forestry/15538-079b31d45081fe9c3dbc6ff34de4807e4.pdf;
Laurie Garrett, "Food Failures and Futures," Maurice R. Greenberg Center for Geoeconomic Studies (Washington D.C.: Council on Foreign Relations, 2008); P. J. Gregory, et al., "Climate Change and Food Security," *Philosophical Transactions of the Royal Society* 360 (2005): 2139–48.
5. For the first book-length study to address food justice movements in the United States, see Robert Gottlieb and Anupama Joshi, *Food Justice* (Cambridge, MA: MIT Press, 2010).
6. Morrison's 2008 historical novel, *A Mercy*, arguably builds on this dimension of *Tar Baby* in chronicling the multiple racial and linguistic communities of seventeenth-century North America before the formation of the United States and the rise of the slave trade and plantation economy. Toni Morrison, *A Mercy* (New York: Alfred A. Knopf, 2008).

7. I use the term *longue durée* in historian Fernand Braudel's sense as "a history to be measured in centuries" rather than through the conventional scale of dates and decades. Fernand Braudel, *On History*, trans. Sarah Matthews (Chicago: University of Chicago Press, 1982), 27; For an application of this concept to literary history, see Wai Chee Dimock, *Through Other Continents: American Literature across Deep Time* (Princeton: Princeton University Press, 2006), 4.
8. Toni Morrison, *Tar Baby* (New York: Vintage International, 1981; repr., 2004), 53. Hereafter cited in text as *TB*.
9. Yogita Goyal, "The Gender of Diaspora in Toni Morrison's *Tar Baby*," *Modern Fiction Studies* 52, no. 2 (2006): 393–414, quotation on 393.
10. Linda Krumholz, "Blackness and Art in Toni Morrison's *Tar Baby*," *Contemporary Literature* 49, no. 2 (2008): 263–92, quotation on 276–77.
11. Andrew Warnes, *Hunger Overcome?: Food and Resistance in Twentieth-Century African American Literature* (London and Athens, GA: University of Georgia Press, 2004), see especially 125–26, 49, 58, 63.
12. Elizabeth M. DeLoughrey, *Routes and Roots: Navigating Caribbean and Pacific Island Literatures* (Honolulu: University of Hawai'i Press, 2007); Paul Gilroy, *The Black Atlantic: Modernity and Double Consciousness* (Cambridge, MA: Harvard University Press, 1995). DeLoughrey offers a postcolonial theory and history of rooted migration that engages with anthropologist James Clifford's analysis of mobility as a defining feature of modernity. James Clifford, *Routes: Travel and Translation in the Late Twentieth Century* (Cambridge, MA: Harvard University Press, 1997)
13. As I explain in Chapter 1, this term signifies the food habits and culinary traditions of a particular culture.
14. Goyal, "The Gender of Diaspora in Toni Morrison's *Tar Baby*," 396.
15. Warnes, *Hunger Overcome?: Food and Resistance in Twentieth-Century African American Literature*, 142.
16. John Duvall interprets the relationship of Jadine and Son as inherently violent; while Sandra Paquet, Ann Rayson, and Judylyn Ryan all highlight Jadine's ambivalent relationship to folklore. Jennifer Heinert more recently has read Jadine as the only tar baby figure in Morrison's novel, although she acknowledges that Jadine implicitly rejects this role. John N. Duvall, "Descent in the 'House of Chloe': Race, Rape, and Identity in Toni Morrison's *Tar Baby*," *Contemporary Literature* 38, no. 2 (1997): 325–49, quotation on 347; Sandra Pouchet Paquet, "The Ancestor as Foundation in *Their Eyes Were Watching God* and *Tar Baby*," *Callaloo* 13, no. 3 (1990): 499–515; Ann Rayson, "Foreign Exotic or Domestic Drudge?: The African American Women in *Quicksand* and *Tar Baby*," *MELUS* 23, no. 2 (1998): 87–100, especially 99; Judylyn S. Ryan, "Contested Visions / Double-Vision in *Tar Baby*," *Modern Fiction Studies* 39, nos. 3 & 4 (1993): 597–621, especially 619; Jennifer Lee Jordan Heinert, "(Re)Defining Race: Folktale and Stereotypes in *Tar Baby*," in *Narrative Conventions and Race in the Novels of Toni Morrison* (New York and London: Routledge, 2009), 36–55.
17. Heinert, "(Re)Defining Race: Folktale and Stereotypes in *Tar Baby*," 39.

18. Warnes, *Hunger Overcome?: Food and Resistance in Twentieth-Century African American Literature*, 136, 40.
19. Evelyn Jaffee Schreiber connects this negotiation to a narrative of racial trauma, while critics such as Goyal and Linden Peach stress an equally central narrative of feminist cosmopolitanism. Evelyn Jaffe Schreiber, "Race, Trauma, and Home in the Novels of Toni Morrison," *Southern Literary Studies* (Baton Rouge: Louisiana State University Press, 2010), 119; Goyal, "The Gender of Diaspora in Toni Morrison's *Tar Baby*": Linden Peach, "Toni Morrison," in *The Cambridge Companion to American Fiction after 1945* (Cambridge: Cambridge University Press, 2012), 233–43.
20. Julia V. Emberley, "A Historical Transposition: Toni Morrison's *Tar Baby* and Frantz Fanon's Post Enlightenment Phantasms," *Modern Fiction Studies* 45, no. 2 (1999): 403–31, quotation on 427–28.
21. Pierre Bourdieu, *Distinction: A Social Critique of the Judgement of Taste*, trans by Richard Nice (Cambridge, MA: Harvard University Press, 1984), originally published as *La Distinction: Critique sociale du jugement* (Paris: Les Éditions de Minuit, 1979).
22. Warren Belasco, *Meals to Come: A History of the Future of Food* (Berkeley: University of California Press, 2006), 174. Tracey Deutsch makes a related point in showing that during the Cold War grocery stores became sites for "operations of... the state... and its dependence on top-down, standardized, and predictable consumption." Tracey Deutsch, *Building a Housewife's Paradise: Gender, Politics and American Grocery Stores in the Twentieth Century* (Chapel Hill: University of North Carolina Press, 2010), 3.
23. Shane Hamilton, "The Economies and Conveniences of Modern-Day Living: Frozen Foods and Mass Marketing, 1945–1965," *Business History Review* 77, no. 1 (2003): 33–60, especially 45.
24. Jessamyn Neuhaus, "The Way to a Man's Heart: Gender Roles, Domestic Ideology, and Cookbooks in the 1950s," *Journal of Social History* 32, no. 3 (1999): 529–55, quotation on 532.
25. Doris Witt, *Black Hunger: Soul Food and America* (London and Minneapolis: University of Minnesota Press, 2004), 185–87.
26. Sianne Ngai, "Competitiveness: From *Sula* to *Tyra*," *Women's Studies Quarterly* 34, nos. 3/4 (2006): 107–39, quotation on 114; Malin Walther Pereira, "Periodizing Toni Morrison's Work from *The Bluest Eye* to *Jazz*: The Importance of *Tar Baby*," *MELUS* 22, no. 3 (1997): 71–82, quotation on 75.
27. Bourdieu, *Distinction: A Social Critique of the Judgement of Taste*, 65–66.
28. Elizabeth B. House, "The 'Sweet Life' in Toni Morrison's Fiction," *American Literature* 56, no. 2 (1984): 181–202, quotations on 182, 202; Krumholz, "Blackness and Art in Toni Morrison's *Tar Baby*," 289.
29. Richard D. E. Burton, "'Maman-France Doudou': Family Images in French West Indian Colonial Discourse," *Diacritics* 23, no. 3 (1993): 69–90, quotation on 69.
30. Derek Walcott, "Café Martinique: A Story," in *What the Twilight Says: Essays* (New York: Farrar, Straus and Giroux, 1998), 234–45, especially 236–37.

31. Alejo Carpentier, "The Baroque and the Marvelous Real," trans. Lois Parkinson Zamora and Tanya Huntington in *Magical Realism: Theory, History, Community*, ed. Lois Parkinson Zamora and Wendy B. Faris (Durham and London: Duke University Press, 1995), 89–108, quotation on 104.
32. Frederick Luis Aldama, *Postethnic Narrative Criticism: Magicorealism in Oscar "Zeta" Acosta, Ana Castillo, Julie Dash, Hanif Kureishi, and Salman Rushdie* (Austin: University of Texas Press, 2003).
33. According to Warnes, Son's feast summons up the specter of capitalism through the physical tastes of food from Europe and Asia, while the miniature orange trees invoke a tradition of African American narrative – from *The Interesting Narrative* of Olaudah Equiano (1789) to Morrison's *Beloved* (1987) – that realigns an imperialist fruit with "utopian freedom." Warnes, *Hunger Overcome?: Food and Resistance in Twentieth-Century African American Literature*, 48–49.
34. In *Vibrant Matter*, political theorist Jane Bennett devotes a chapter to a strand within the philosophy and science of food reaching from Thoreau to twenty-first-century research on fats, which, she claims, "discern[s] a productive power intrinsic to foodstuffs" and shows eating to be an "encounter" of nonhuman and human bodies that act on and transform one another. She calls this chapter "Edible Matter." Jane Bennett, *Vibrant Matter: A Political Ecology of Things* (London and Durham: Duke University Press, 2009), 49.
35. The avocado originated in southern Mexico and was imported to the West Indies and other tropical climes in the seventeenth century; the lime is native to Indonesia and Malaysia and was introduced into the Caribbean by the Spanish in the sixteenth century; the banana also originated in Malaysia. Center for New Crops and Plant Products, "The New Crop Resource Online Program," Purdue University, www.hort.purdue.edu/newcrop/.
36. Building on the analysis of free trade and U.S. food power in Chapter 1, I draw in this chapter on the work especially of David Harvey, Thomas Klak, and Kurt Weyland. David Harvey, *The New Imperialism* (Oxford and New York: Oxford University Press, 2003); Thomas Klak, "Introduction: Thirteen Theses on Globalization and Neoliberalism," in *Globalization and Neoliberalism: The Caribbean Context*, ed. Thomas Klak (New York and Oxford: Rowman and Littlefield Publishers, 1998), 3–23; Library of Congress, "Bretton Woods System," http://lcweb2.loc.gov/frd/cs/japan/jp_glos.html; Kurt Weyland, "Neoliberalism and Democracy in Latin America: A Mixed Record" *Latin American Politics and Society* 46, no. 1 (2004): 135–57.
37. Patrick Chamoiseau, *Chronicle of the Seven Sorrows*, trans. Linda Coverdale (Lincoln: University of Nebraska Press, 1999).
38. Édouard Glissant, "A Word Scratcher," in *Chronicle of the Seven Sorrows* (Lincoln: University of Nebraska Press, 1999), vii.
39. Anissa Turner, "Rum Trade: From Slavery to the Present (Case Number 384)," *The TED Case Studies* (1997), www1.american.edu/ted/rum.htm.
40. Following the work of Georg Lukács and other Marxist critics, I use the term *reification* to signify the process under capitalism by which the social (and, I

would add, ecological) histories of goods are obscured in the circulation and marketing of commodities, which in turn become fetishized things. Georg Lukács, *History and Class Consciousness: Studies in Marxist Dialectics*, trans. Rodney Livingstone (Cambridge, MA: The MIT Press, 1972), especially 91, 184.
41. At the time of this writing, London-based Diageo owned Jamaican-distilled Captain Morgan's Rum, while French-based Pernod Ricard owned both Barbados-distilled Malibu Rum and Cuban-aged Havana Club.
42. Bruce Robbins, "Commodity Histories," *PMLA* 120, no. 2 (2005): 454–63, quotation on 456.
43. Ian Williams, "The Secret History of Rum," *The Nation*, December 5, 2005, par. 1.
44. "Homepage," Bacardi, http://www.bacardi.com/us/lda; "Homepage," Pernod Ricard, www.havana-club.com.
45. Geraldine Barnes and Adrian Mitchell, "Measuring the Marvelous: Science and the Exotic in William Dampier," *Eighteenth-Century Life* 26, no. 3 (2002): 45–57, especially 46.
46. Bennett, *Vibrant Matter: A Political Ecology of Things*, 24.
47. During the period of independence movements in the Caribbean, France made French Guiana, Martinique, and Guadeloupe overseas departments of the French government. By comparison, Dominica, which was a French colony through the late eighteenth century, achieved political independence from England in 1978. Burton, "'Maman-France Doudou': Family Images in French West Indian Colonial Discourse"; Gad Heuman, *The Caribbean*, Brief Histories (London: Hodder Education of Oxford University Press, 2006), especially 67–77, 115–16, 61–63; James Wiley, "Dominica's Economic Diversification: Microstates in a Neoliberal Era?," in Klak, *Globalization and Neoliberalism*, 155–77.
48. Dennis Conway, "Misguided Directions, Mismanaged Models or Missed Paths?," in Klak, *Globalization and Neoliberalism*, 29–50, quotation on 30. For a transnational analysis of the 1823 Monroe Doctrine, see Thomas Bender, *A Nation among Nations: America's Place in World History* (New York: Hill and Wang, 2006).
49. Cara Cilano and Elizabeth M. DeLoughrey, "Against Authenticity: Global Knowledges and Postcolonial Ecocriticism," *Interdisciplinary Studies in Literature and Environment (ISLE)* 14, no. 1 (2007): 71–87, quotation on 78.
50. DeLoughrey and Handley here cite Glissant's *Le Discours Antillais*, where he argues, most notably, "history is spread out beneath [the] surface" of the Caribbean islands. Elizabeth M. DeLoughrey and George Handley, eds., *Postcolonial Ecologies: Literatures of the Environment* (Oxford and New York: Oxford University Press, 2011), 27; Édouard Glissant, *Caribbean Discourse: Selected Essays*, trans. J. Michael Dash (London and Charlottesville: University of Virginia Press, 1989), 11. For other studies of Caribbean literature, post-coloniality, and the environment see DeLoughrey, *Routes and Roots: Navigating Caribbean and Pacific Island Literatures*; George Handley, "Derek

Walcott's Poetics of the Environment in *The Bounty,*" *Callaloo* 28, no. 1 (2005): 201–15; Graham Huggan, "'Greening' Postcolonialism: Ecocritical Perspectives," *Modern Fiction Studies* 50, no. 3 (2004): 701–33; Elaine Savory, "Toward a Caribbean Ecopoetics: Derek Walcott's Language of Plants," in DeLoughrey and Handley, *Postcolonial Ecologies,* 80–96.

51. DeLoughrey and Handley, *Postcolonial Ecologies: Literatures of the Environment,* 13.
52. James McWilliams, *Revolution in Eating: How the Quest for Food Shaped America* (New York: Columbia University Press, 2005), 20; Frederick Douglass Opie, *Hog and Hominy: Soul Food from Africa to America,* Arts and Traditions of the Table (New York: Columbia University Press, 2008), 3.
53. McWilliams, 20. Sidney Mintz makes a similar point in his seminal history of sugar. Sidney W. Mintz, *Sweetness and Power: The Place of Sugar in Modern History* (New York: Viking, 1985), xviii, 36.
54. McWilliams develops a related account in detailing the garden plots and fallow land that enslaved communities had access to in the New World for the purposes of independent food production and, in some cases, to sell food surpluses to white colonists at Sunday markets. These markets, he claims, served as "carnivalesque" spaces. Calling these spaces of food production "the botanical gardens of the dispossessed," Carney further identifies African slaves "as pioneers of crops entirely novel to their masters." Judith Carney, *In the Shadow of Slavery: Africa's Botanical Legacy in the Atlantic World* (Berkeley: University of California Press, 2010), especially 123, 25, 27, 30–31; McWilliams, 39, 50–51.
55. Opie, *Hog and Hominy: Soul Food from Africa to America,* especially 1, 10–13.
56. Christopher Columbus, "Letter of Columbus to Various Persons Describing the Results of His First Voyage and Written on the Return Journey," in *The Four Voyages of Christopher Columbus,* ed. J. M. Cohen (London: Penguin Books, 1969), 115.
57. Mary Louise Pratt, *Imperial Eyes: Travel Writing and Transculturation* (New York and London: Routledge, 1992).
58. Such rules have prevented Martinique from taking advantage of trade agreements with France designed to help the island's farmers to compete with Del Monte and Dole. Janet Henshall Momsen, "Caribbean Tourism and Agriculture: New Linkages in the Global Era?" in Klak, *Globalization and Neoliberalism,* 115–30; Klak, "Introduction: Thirteen Theses on Globalization and Neoliberalism."
59. Belasco, *Meals to Come: A History of the Future of Food,* 152, 56.
60. Glissant emphasizes a similar ecological and social transformation of Martinique: "In the Center, the literal undulations of the cane fields. The mountains are subdued and become hills. . . . The delta has been chewed up by make-believe enterprises, by an airstrip. Falling away before us, tiers of banana trees, a curtain of dense green foam between us and the land." Glissant, *Caribbean Discourse: Selected Essays,* 10–11.
61. Toni Morrison, *Sula* (New York: Penguin Books, 1973, 1982), 5.
62. Nellie McKay, "An Interview with Toni Morrison," *Contemporary Literature* 24, no. 4 (1983): 413–29, quotation on 417.

63. Dr. Peter J. Llewellyn, "*Valerian Herb*" (Washington, D.C.: National Institutes of Health, 2007); Richard D. Weigel, "Valerian (A.D. 253–60) and Gaillienus (A.D. 253–268)," *De Imperatoribus Romanis: An Online Encyclopedia of Roman Emperors*, www.roman-emperors.org/gallval.htm.
64. Anissa Wardi devotes a chapter of her 2011 book to the importance of swamps and bayous as "bodies of postcolonial resistance" in *Tar Baby*, reinforcing the identification of Jadine with cosmopolitanism and Son with Black Nationalism. Anissa Janine Wardi, "Wetlands, Swamps, and Bayous: Bodies of Resistance in Kasi Lemmons's *Eve's Bayou* and Toni Morrison's *Tar Baby*," in *Water and African American Memory: An Ecocritical Perspective* (Gainesville: University Press of Florida, 2011).
65. Karla Armbruster and Kathleen R. Wallace, "The Novels of Toni Morrison: 'Wild Wilderness Where There Was None,'" in *Beyond Nature Writing: Expanding the Boundaries of Ecocriticism*, ed. Karla Armbruster and Kathleen R. Wallace (London and Charlottesville: University of Virginia Press, 2001), 211–230, especially 212, 23.
66. Rob Nixon, *Slow Violence and the Environmentalism of the Poor* (Cambridge, MA: Harvard University Press, 2011).
67. Sophie D. Coe and Michael D. Coe, *The True History of Chocolate* (London: Thames and Hudson, 1996), 252.
68. Susan Neal Mayberry, *Can't I Love What I Criticize?: The Masculine and Morrison* (London and Athens, GA: University of Georgia Press, 2007), 127.
69. Evelyn Hawthorne's article first alerted me to this reference with her observation that the scene relates to *Tar Baby*'s themes of motherhood and child abuse. Evelyn Hawthorne, "On Gaining the Double-Vision: *Tar Baby* as Diasporean Novel," *Black American Literature Forum* 22, no. 1 (1988): 97–107, especially 102.
70. Syed H. Akhter, "Review of *Multinational Corporations and the Impact of Public Advocacy of Corporate Strategy: Nestle and the Infant Formula Controversy* by S. Prakash Sethi," *Journal of International Business Studies* Q3 (1994): 658–60; New York Times News Service, "U.N. Baby Formula Vote Unlikely to Hamper Firms," *Chicago Tribune*, May 27, 1981.
71. Ann Crittenden, "Baby Formula Sales in Third World Criticized: Some Producers Accused of Excessive Promotion," *The New York Times*, September 11, 1975, 56.
72. Penny Van Esterik, "The Politics of Breastfeeding: An Advocacy Update," in *Food and Culture: A Reader*, ed. Carole Counihan and Penny Van Esterik (New York and London: Routledge, 1997, 2008), 467–81, quotation on 471.
73. Goyal, "The Gender of Diaspora in Toni Morrison's *Tar Baby*," 394.
74. I follow Bakhtin's definition of the chronotope as a temporal period bounded in a particular time-in-space that enables meaning making: "whatever these meanings turn out to be, in order to enter our experience (which is social experience) they must take on the *form of a sign* that is audible and visible for us.... Without such temporal-spatial expression, even abstract thought is impossible. Consequently, every entry into the sphere of meanings is accomplished only through the gates of the chronotope." Mikhail Bakhtin, *The*

*Dialogic Imagination: Four Essays*, trans. Caryl Emerson and Michael Holquist (Austin: University of Texas Press, 1982), 258.
75. Emma Parker, "'Apple Pie' Ideology and the Politics of Appetite in the Novels of Toni Morrison," *Contemporary Literature* 39, no. 4 (1998): 614–43, especially 618–19, 34.
76. Ibid., 624.
77. Warnes, *Hunger Overcome?: Food and Resistance in Twentieth-Century African American Literature*, 152–53.
78. David Harvey, *Spaces of Global Capitalism: Towards a Theory of Uneven Geographical Development* (London and New York: Verso, 2006); Arjun Appadurai, *Modernity at Large: Cultural Dimensions of Globalization* (Minneapolis: University of Minnesota Press, 1996); Fredric Jameson, *Postmodernism, or the Cultural Logic of Late Capitalism* (London and Durham: Duke University Press, 1991); Saskia Sassen, *Globalization and Its Discontents: Essays on the New Mobility of People and Money* (New York: New Press, 1998).
79. Warnes, *Hunger Overcome?: Food and Resistance in Twentieth-Century African American Literature*, 154.
80. Michael Pollan, *The Botany of Desire: A Plant's-Eye View of the World* (New York: Random House, 2002), especially 1–58.
81. Toni Morrison, "Foreword," in *Tar Baby* (New York: Vintage Books, 2004), xiii.
82. Walter Benjamin, "Theses on the Philosophy of History," in *Illuminations*, ed. Hannah Arendt (New York: Schocken Books, 1968), 253–64, quotations on 254, 263.
83. Ramón Saldívar, *The Borderlands of Culture: Américo Paredes and the Transnational Imaginary* (London and Durham: Duke University Press, 2006), 8.
84. Ibid., 9.
85. For an intertextual interpretation of the novel's setting as at once Edenic and satanic, see Lauren Lepow, "Paradise Lost and Found: Dualism and Edenic Myth in Toni Morrison's *Tar Baby*," *Contemporary Literature* 28, no. 3 (1987): 363–77.
86. Askinosie Chocolate, "Our Story," www.askinosie.com/.

CHAPTER 5

1. Ruth L. Ozeki, *My Year of Meats* (New York: Penguin Books, 1998), 360. Hereafter cited in text as *YM*.
2. Anthony Giddens, *The Consequences of Modernity* (Stanford: Stanford University Press, 1990), 38.
3. Ruth L. Ozeki, *All Over Creation* (New York: Penguin Books, 2003), 127. Hereafter cited in text as *AOC*.
4. William Conlogue, *Working the Garden: American Writers and the Industrialization of Agriculture* (Chapel Hill: University of North Carolina Press, 2001), 25.

5. The former issue invokes the now well-known legal case of Percy Schmeiser, a Canadian rapeseed farmer sued by Monsanto for allegedly planting unlicensed transgenic canola; while the latter recalls the U.S. "veggie libel laws," which prohibit writing about, documenting, or, in some cases, protesting fields and feedlots. As for the first of these, although Schmeiser countered that the seeds had been carried by wind into his fields, the Canadian federal court sided with Monsanto. Pringle, *Food, Inc.: Mendel to Monsanto – the Promises and Perils of the Biotech Harvest* (New York: Simon & Schuster, 2003), 178.
6. Alan Liu, *The Laws of Cool: Knowledge Work and the Culture of Information* (Chicago and London: University of Chicago Press, 2004), 71.
7. See especially Shameem Black, "Fertile Cosmofeminism: Ruth L. Ozeki and Transnational Reproduction," *Meridians: feminism, race, transnationalism* 5, no. 1 (2004): 226–56; Monica Chiu, "Postnational Globalization and (En)Gendered Meat Production in Ruth L. Ozeki's *My Year of Meats*," *LIT: Literature Interpretation Theory* 12, no. 1 (2001): 99–128; Nina Cornyetz, "The Meat Manifesto: Ruth Ozeki's Performative Poetics," *Women and Performance: A Journal of Feminist Theory* 12, no. 1 (2001): 207–24; David Palumbo-Liu, "Rational and Irrational Choices: Form, Affect, and Ethics," in *Minor Transnationalism*, ed. Shu-mei Shih and Francoise Lionnet (London and Durham: Duke University Press, 2005), 41–72; Julie Sze, "Boundaries and Border Wars: DES, Technology, and Environmental Justice," *American Quarterly* 58, no. 3 (2006): 791–814.
8. Susan Squier, who led a conversation with Ozeki at the 2012 MLA Convention, supports this framing of the novelist in intimating that her fiction gives narrative structure to cultural movements that aim to "[r]ediscove[r] the [l]ocal." Susan Squier, "Chicken Auguries," *Configurations* 14, nos. 1–2 (2008): 69–86, quotation on 83.
9. Ursula K. Heise, "Ecocriticism and the Transnational Turn in American Studies," *American Literary History* 20, no. 1 (2008): 381–404, quotation on 399.
10. In a 2011 essay, Bruce Robbins shows the preponderance of post-9/11 novels that depict social "superstructures, or infrastructures" while simultaneously retreating into private, filial life (as in Jonathan Franzen's novels *The Corrections* and *Freedom* and Don DeLillo's *Falling Man*). For his part, Mark McGurl observes that as closed systems come to signify "chaotic conformism" in the context of a Cold War containment regime and cybernetics, novelists emphasize open systems, however open they may be to "the incursions of commercial or ideological competitors." In *The Program Era*, McGurl traces the influence not of large-scale systems (like global financial markets) but of smaller-scale ones (such as the academic R&D lab and creative writing workshop) on the post-1945 American novel. Bruce Robbins, "The Worlding of the American Novel," in *The Cambridge History of the American Novel*, ed. Leonard Cassuto, Clare Virginia Eby, and Benjamin Reiss, Cambridge Histories Online (Cambridge and New York: Cambridge University Press, 2011), 1096–1106, quotation on 1096; Mark McGurl, *The Program Era: Postwar Fiction and the Rise of Creative Writing* (Cambridge, MA: Harvard University Press, 2009), 193.

11. Claire Dederer, "All Over Creation," review of *All Over Creation* by Ruth L. Ozeki, *The New York Times*, March 16, 2003. Other reviewers echo Dederer's account of Ozeki's fiction and its literary and social significance. See especially Lisa Funderburg, "Books in Brief: My Year of Meats," review of *My Year of Meats* by Ruth L. Ozeki, *The New York Times*, July 26, 1998; Catherine Clyne, "Creating Novel Life Forms – Literally: The Satya Interview with Ruth Ozeki," *Satya Magazine* (2003), www.ruthozeki.com/about/profiles-reviews/satya-magazine-interview.
12. Heise goes on to argue that *All Over Creation* glosses over the ecological problems that attend certain kinds of biodiversity (such as non-native species) while casting as uniformly villainous all instances of monoculture and genetic engineering: "the trope of bio-cultural diversity allows Ozeki not only to reject global economic exchange networks, obvious in the indictments of transnational agribusiness corporations in both of her novels, but at the same time to safeguard cultural globalization and the web of encounters and literal and metaphorical cross-breeding it enables. By rejecting the (allegedly economic) logic of genetic engineering and embracing the (implicitly racial and cultural) logic of non-native species introduction, Ozeki manages to occlude any consideration of how transnational cultural encounters might be related to and, in quite a few cases, causally dependent on economic globalization." Heise, "Ecocriticism and the Transnational Turn in American Studies," 398–400.
13. Malena Watrous, "Interview with Ruth Ozeki: 'Vegetables Are Filled with Drama. Even the Pea,'" *The Believer* 5, no. 2 (2007): 80–86.
14. Karen Cardozo and Banu Subramaniam, "Genes, Genera, and Genres: The Natureculture of Biofiction in Ruth Ozeki's *All Over Creation*," in *Tactical Biopolitics: Art, Activism, and Technoscience*, ed. Beatriz da Costa and Kavita Philip (Cambridge, MA and London: MIT Press, 2008), 269–98, quotation on 270–71.
15. Jane Bennett, *Vibrant Matter: A Political Ecology of Things* (London and Durham: Duke University Press, 2009), 50–51.
16. Ruth L. Ozeki, "Healthy Eating for You and the Planet, a Celebration of Food and Biodiversity," in *Living with Nature* (New York: American Museum of Natural History & Center for Biodiversity and Conservation, 2004).
17. Ruth L. Ozeki, "You Are What You Eat: Food, Fiction, and Feminist Identity," in *Consuming Women: An Undergraduate Conference* (Canadian Women's Studies Conference, University of British Columbia, 2008).
18. Watrous, "Interview with Ruth Ozeki: 'Vegetables Are Filled with Drama. Even the Pea.'"
19. Novella Carpenter, *Farm City: The Education of an Urban Farmer* (New York: Penguin Books, 2009); Barbara Kingsolver, *Animal, Vegetable, Miracle: A Year of Food Life* (New York: HarperCollins, 2007); Gary Paul Nabhan, *Coming Home to Eat: The Pleasures and Politics of Local Foods* (New York and London: W. W. Norton, 2002); Carlo Petrini, *Slow Food: The Case for Taste*, Arts and Traditions of the Table: Perspectives on Culinary History (New York: Columbia University Press, 2001); Michael Pollan, *The*

Omnivore's Dilemma: A Natural History of Four Meals (New York: Penguin Books, 2006).
20. Sze, "Boundaries and Border Wars: DES, Technology, and Environmental Justice," 801.
21. Cheryl J. Fish, "The Toxic Body Politic: Ethnicity, Gender, and Corrective Eco-Justice in Ruth Ozeki's *My Year of Meats* and Judith Helfand and Daniel Gold's *Blue Vinyl*," *MELUS* 34, no. 2 (2009): 43–62, quotations on 43, 58.
22. Susan McHugh, "Flora, Not Fauna: GM Culture and Agriculture," *Literature and Medicine* 26, no. 1 (2007): 25–54, quotations on 28, 33.
23. In *All Over Creation*, for example, the Seeds of Resistance are a microcosm of what sociologists term "alternative food networks." David Goodman, E. Melanie DuPuis and Michael K. Goodman, *Alternative Food Networks: Knowledge, Practice and Politics* (New York and London: Routledge, 2012).
24. Cardozo and Subramaniam, "Genes, Genera, and Genres: The Natureculture of Biofiction in Ruth Ozeki's *All Over Creation*," 270.
25. McHugh, "Flora, Not Fauna: GM Culture and Agriculture," 28; Rachel Schurman and William Munro, "Ideas, Thinkers, and Social Networks: The Process of Grievance Construction in the Anti-Genetic Engineering Movement," *Theory and Society* 35 (2006): 1–38.
26. According to his argument, "the space of flows" displaces "the space of places" as the chief structure through which people, institutions, firms, and communities interact. However, many scholars of globalization and postindustrialism have critiqued this notion in suggesting that this "disembedding" of people from places has been an uneven and unequal process. Manuel Castells, *The Rise of the Network Society*, 2nd ed. (Oxford: Blackwell, 2010).
27. Jonathan Safran Foer, *Eating Animals* (New York: Back Bay Books, 2010).
28. Ibid., 78–79.
29. Ibid., 117–21.
30. Ibid., 126, 51.
31. Ibid., 130.
32. N. Katherine Hayles, *How We Became Posthuman: Virtual Bodies in Cybernetics, Literature, and Informatics* (Chicago: University of Chicago Press, 1999), 43.
33. Wallace cites Beck's theory of the "world risk society," in which, Beck contends, that the risks of emerging technologies are often unknown even to experts. For Wallace, "discomfort – rather than fear – is ... the emotion that best characterizes" late modernity. Molly Wallace, "Discomfort Food: Analogy, Biotechnology, and Risk in Ruth Ozeki's *All Over Creation*," *Arizona Quarterly* 67, no. 4 (2011): 155–81, quotation on 156.
34. Ibid., 160.
35. Anne-Lise François, "'O Happy Living Things': Frankenfoods and the Bounds of Wordsworthian Natural Piety," *diacritics* 33, no. 2 (2003): 42–70, quotation on 45.
36. Wallace, "Discomfort Food: Analogy, Biotechnology, and Risk in Ruth Ozeki's *All Over Creation*," 161.

37. Sze, "Boundaries and Border Wars: DES, Technology, and Environmental Justice," 791, 97.
38. Don DeLillo, "The Power of History," *The New York Times*, September 7, 1997.
39. Palumbo-Liu, "Rational and Irrational Choices: Form, Affect, and Ethics," 66, 68.
40. I mean "zany" in Sianne Ngai's sense of this aesthetic and affective category: "While the cute is ... about commodities and consumption, the zany is about performing.... You could say that zaniness is essentially the experience of an agent confronted by – even endangered by – too many things coming at her quickly and at once.... This explains why this ludic aesthetic has a noticeably unfun or stressed-out layer to it." Sianne Ngai and Adam Jasper, "Our Aesthetic Categories: An Interview with Sianne Ngai," *Cabinet*, no. 43 (2011), www.cabinetmagazine.org/issues/43/jasper_ngai.php. In a 2011 *PMLA* article, Ngai goes on to align the cute (the second of her three aesthetic categories: the interesting, the cute, and the zany) with the pastoral: "The zany, for instance, is a subspecies of comedy, while cuteness, as a style that speaks to our desire for a simpler relation to commodities, is arguably a kind of pastoral." Sianne Ngai, "Our Aesthetic Categories," *PMLA* 125, no. 4 (2011): 948–58, quotation on 952.
41. In her account of reproductive illnesses associated with DES, Orenberg writes of the disparate identities of women who have suffered from DES exposure: "The daughters of DES are legion. They number in the millions and they have many faces. They range from grade-school age to middle age; from poor to rich; from the very naïve to the hip sophisticate. They have been born in every state in the union, in big cities as well as in small towns." Cynthia Laitman Orenberg, *DES: The Complete Story* (New York: St. Martin's Press, 1981), 54. McLuhan first coined this famous phrase in *Understanding Media*. My thanks to Brendan O'Kelly for noting this resonance. Marshall McLuhan, *Understanding Media: The Extensions of Man* (Cambridge, MA: MIT Press, 1994).
42. Upton Sinclair, *The Jungle* (New York: Penguin Books, 1985).
43. Anthony Arthur, *Radical Innocent: Upton Sinclair* (New York: Random House, 2006); Ann Bausum, *Muckrakers: How Ida Tarbell, Upton Sinclair, and Lincoln Steffens Helped Expose Scandal, Inspire Reform, and Invent Investigative Journalism* (Washington, D.C.: National Geographic, 2007); Cecilia Tichi, *Exposés and Excess: Muckraking in America, 1900/2000* (Philadelphia: University of Pennsylvania Press, 2003); Cecilia Tichi, "Exposés and Excess," Review of *Fast Food Nation: The Dark Side of the All-American Meal* by Eric Schlosser, *American Literary History* 15, no. 4 (2003): 822–29.
44. Jeffory A. Clymer, "Panic! Markets, Crises, and Crows in American Fiction" (review), *Modern Fiction Studies* 54, no. 2 (2008): 425–28; Michael Ryan, "Prospects of the Meat Packing Industry," *Annals of the American Academy of Political and Social Science* 34 (1909): 33–38; James Harvey Young, *Pure Food: Securing the Federal Food and Drugs Act of 1906* (Princeton: Princeton University Press, 1989).
45. In feedlots, where thousands of animals live in crowded conditions, manure accumulates rather than breaks down, and this release of methane into the

atmosphere has become a significant contributor to climate change. B. Metz et al., eds., *Fourth Assessment Report of the Intergovernmental Panel on Climate Change* (Cambridge and New York: Cambridge University Press, 2007); P. Smith et al., "Agriculture," in *Climate Change 2007: Mitigation, Contribution of Working Group III*, ed. Intergovernmental Panel on Climate Change (Cambridge and New York: Cambridge University Press, 2007).

46. See especially Sue Coe, *Dead Meat* (New York and London: Four Walls Eight Windows, 1996); Pollan, *The Omnivore's Dilemma: A Natural History of Four Meals*; Safran Foer, *Eating Animals*; Geoff Tansey and Joyce D'Silva, eds., *The Meat Business: Devouring a Hungry Planet* (London: Earthscan Publications, 1999). These writers are extending a scholarly body of work from the 1970s and 1980s: Carol Adams, *The Sexual Politics of Meat: A Feminist-Vegetarian Critical Theory* (New York: Continuum, 1990, 2000); Jim Mason and Peter Singer, *Animal Factories: What Agribusiness Is Doing to the Family Farm, the Environment, and Your Health* (New York: Harmony Books, 1990); Jeremy Rifkin, *Beyond Beef: The Rise and Fall of the Cattle Culture* (New York: Dutton, 1992); Orville Schell, *Modern Meat: Antibiotics, Hormones, and the Pharmaceutical Farm* (New York: Random House, 1984); Peter Singer, "Animal Liberation," review of *Animals, Men and Morals*, edited by Stanley Godlovitch, Roslind Godlovitch, and John Harris, *New York Review of Books*, April 5, 1973.

47. Quoted in Cecelia Tichi, "Novels of Civic Protest," in *The Cambridge History of the American Novel*, ed. Leonard Cassuto, Clare Virginia Eby, and Benjamin Reiss, Cambridge Histories Online (Cambridge and New York: Cambridge University Press, 2011), 393–408, quotation on 402.

48. Ibid., 399.

49. Adams, *The Sexual Politics of Meat: A Feminist-Vegetarian Critical Theory*. Monica Chiu briefly compares *The Jungle* to *My Year of Meats*, noting that both novels tie meat production to social injustice via exploitation of slaughterhouse workers in Sinclair's case and via the disproportionate health impact of growth hormones on women in Ozeki's. Chiu, "Postnational Globalization and (En)Gendered Meat Production in Ruth L. Ozeki's *My Year of Meats*."

50. Watrous, "Interview with Ruth Ozeki: 'Vegetables Are Filled with Drama. Even the Pea.'"

51. Ibid.

52. Adams, *The Sexual Politics of Meat: A Feminist-Vegetarian Critical Theory*; Coe, *Dead Meat*; Orenberg, *DES: The Complete Story*; Rifkin, *Beyond Beef: The Rise and Fall of the Cattle Culture*; Schell, *Modern Meat: Antibiotics, Hormones, and the Pharmaceutical Farm*.

53. Roberta Smith, "Art in Review: Elephants We Must Never Forget," *The New York Times*, November 21, 2008.

54. Cary Wolfe, *What Is Posthumanism?*. Posthumanities (Minneapolis: University of Minnesota Press, 2010), 167, emphasis in original.

55. Tichi, *Exposés and Excess: Muckraking in America, 1900/2000*, 15.

56. Ibid.

57. Meatpacking companies control the supply and price of beef via "captive" ranches as well as contracts with the largest ranches and feedlot operations, which, in turn, lease their cattle from the meatpacking conglomerates and agree to sell them on demand at set prices. Eric Schlosser, *Cogs in the Great Machine* (London: Penguin Books, 2005), 9.
58. Eric Schlosser, *Fast Food Nation: The Dark Side of the All-American Meal* (Boston: Houghton Mifflin, 2001), 169–71.
59. For discussions of the scale of feedlots, see Janice Castro, "Why the Beef over Hormones?," *Time*, January 16, 1989; Mason and Singer, *Animal Factories: What Agribusiness Is Doing to the Family Farm, the Environment, and Your Health*; Pollan, *The Omnivore's Dilemma: A Natural History of Four Meals*; Schlosser, *Fast Food Nation: The Dark Side of the All-American Meal*; *Cogs in the Great Machine*.
60. Orenberg, *DES: The Complete Story*.
61. Mark McGurl, "The Novel, Mass Culture, Mass Media," in *The Cambridge History of the American Novel*, ed. Leonard Cassuto, Clare Virginia Eby, and Benjamin Reiss, *Cambridge Histories Online* (Cambridge and New York: Cambridge University Press, 2011), 686–99, quotation on 696, emphasis mine.
62. Nicole Shukin, *Animal Capital: Rendering Life in Biopolitical Times* (Minneapolis: University of Minnesota Press, 2009).
63. Sze argues that the history of DES reveals how fully hormones have defined female identity: "What made DES's use in chickens unpalatable (literally), was the way in which it visibly made men 'women,' and made children sexually mature. The 'unnatural' sexual and bodily developments that DES triggered were visible, embodied, and therefore grotesque. When these categories of gender and sexual development were made manifest, DES was banned." Sze, "Boundaries and Border Wars: DES, Technology, and Environmental Justice," 797, 99.
64. Chiu, "Postnational Globalization and (En)Gendered Meat Production in Ruth L. Ozeki's *My Year of Meats*," 100.
65. See especially Alison Hope Alkon and Kari Marie Norgaard, "Breaking the Food Chains: An Investigation of Food Justice Activism," *Sociological Inquiry* 79, no. 3 (2009): 289–305; Vandana Shiva, *Earth Democracy: Justice, Sustainability, and Peace* (Cambridge, MA: South End Press, 2005); Alexandra Spieldoch, *A Row to Hoe: The Gender Impact of Trade Liberalization on Our Food System, Agricultural Markets and Women's Human Rights*, ed. International Gender and Trade Network (Geneva: Friedrich-Ebert-Stiftung, 2007).
66. Terry Tempest Williams, *Refuge: An Unnatural History of Family and Place* (New York: Vintage, 1992).
67. Stacey Alaimo, "Discomforting Creatures: Monstrous Natures in Recent Films," in *Beyond Nature Writing: Expanding the Boundaries of Ecocriticism*, ed. Karla Armbruster and Kathleen R. Wallace (London and Charlottesville: University of Virginia Press, 2001), 279–96, especially on 291–92; Lawrence Buell, "Toxic Discourse," *Critical Inquiry* 24, no. 3 (1998): 639–65, especially on 658–62.

68. The framing of a known toxin as a problem primarily for reproductive health underlies Orenberg's history: "In fact, pregnancy and fertility problems are proving to be the real misfortunes for DES daughters." Orenberg, akin to Jane, thus gives short shrift to other health consequences of DES exposure, such as women's increased cancer risk. Orenberg, *DES: The Complete Story*, 54.
69. Nancy Langston, *Toxic Bodies: Hormone Disruptors and the Legacy of DES* (London and New Haven: Yale University Press, 2010), 28–82.
70. Palumbo-Liu, "Rational and Irrational Choices: Form, Affect, and Ethics," 56.
71. Ibid., 63, 66.
72. Alexei Barrionuevo, "Japan Partially Lifts 2-Year Ban on U.S. Beef, Defusing Trade Dispute," *The New York Times*, December 13, 2005; James Brooke, "Japan Still Bans U.S. Beef, Chafing American Officials," *The New York Times*, April 21, 2005; Katarzyna J. Cwiertka, "Popularizing a Military Diet in Wartime and Postwar Japan," *Asian Anthropology* 1 (2002) 1–30; John Dyck, "U.S.-Japan Agreements on Beef Imports: A Case of Successful Bilateral Negotiations," ed. U.S. Department of Agriculture, 1998, 99–107; Clyde H. Farnsworth, "GATT to Act on Beef in U.S.-Japan Impasse," *The New York Times*, May 5, 1988; Milt Freudenheim, "Beef Dispute: Stakes High in Trade War," *The New York Times*, January 1, 1989; Katsuro Sakoh, "Food Exports and the U.S.-Japan Trade Deficit," *Asian Studies Backgrounder* (1984).
73. About the early modern pastoral in general and Shakespeare's comedies in particular, Empson writes, the "simple man becomes a clumsy fool who yet has better 'sense' than his betters and can say things more fundamentally true; he is 'in contact with nature,' which the complex man needs to be." William Empson, *Some Versions of Pastoral* (New York: New Directions, 1974), 13.
74. Emiko Ohnuki-Tierney, "McDonald's in Japan: Changing Manners and Etiquette," in *Golden Arches East: McDonald's in East Asia*, ed. James L. Watson (Stanford: Stanford University Press, 1997), 161–82, quotation on 166.
75. See Cwiertka, "Popularizing a Military Diet in Wartime and Postwar Japan"; Dyck, "U.S.-Japan Agreements on Beef Imports: A Case of Successful Bilateral Negotiations"; Sakoh, "Food Exports and the U.S.-Japan Trade Deficit"; U.S. Meat Export Federation, "International Markets: Japan" (2008), www.usmef.org/; Thomas I. Wahl, Dermot J. Hayes, and Gary W. Williams, "Dynamic Adjustment in Japanese Livestock Industry under Beef Import Liberalization," *American Journal of Agricultural Economics* 73, no. 1 (1991): 118–32.
76. Sakoh notes that for "the past 20 years, agricultural imports [to Japan] have increased more than 30 times in dollar value, from $550 million in 1960 to $16 billion in 1982." Sakoh, "Food Exports and the U.S.-Japan Trade Deficit," 3, 10.
77. Cwiertka, "Popularizing a Military Diet in Wartime and Postwar Japan," 13.
78. Ibid., 17.
79. Ohnuki-Tierney, "McDonald's in Japan: Changing Manners and Etiquette," 167.
80. Ibid., 168.
81. "McDonald's was introduced in Japan in 1971 by Den Fujita, then a University of Tokyo student. He began with five restaurants and a $1.3 million investment

during an economic boom in Japan.... By 1994, ... McDonald's Japan had expanded to 1,048 outlets." Ibid., 162, 73.
82. Friz Freleng, "Bugs Bunny Nips the Nips" (Warner Brothers Pictures and the Vitaphone Corporation, 1994).
83. "Japan's Beef Scandal," *Nature* 413 (2001); Vikas Bajaj, "Japan Again Suspends Shipments of Beef from U.S.," *The New York Times*, January 21, 2006; Barrionuevo, "Japan Partially Lifts 2-Year Ban on U.S. Beef, Defusing Trade Dispute"; Brooke, "Japan Still Bans U.S. Beef, Chafing American Officials"; Martin Fackler, "In Japan, American Beef Is Once Again on the Menu," *The New York Times*, January 7, 2006.
84. Bajaj, "Japan Again Suspends Shipments of Beef from U.S."; Barrionuevo, "Japan Partially Lifts 2-Year Ban on U.S. Beef, Defusing Trade Dispute."
85. Brooke, "Japan Still Bans U.S. Beef, Chafing American Officials."
86. The risk of BSE has been linked directly to the age of cattle at the time of slaughter. Bajaj, "Japan Again Suspends Shipments of Beef from U.S."; Taro Karasaki, "Tokyo: Ban on U.S. Stays until Safety Ensured," *Asahi Shimbun*, January 23, 2006.
87. Barrionuevo, "Japan Partially Lifts 2-Year Ban on U.S. Beef, Defusing Trade Dispute"; National Cattlemen's Beef Association, "Export Markets," www.beefusa.org/jan-june2012usbeefexports.aspx; U.S. Meat Export Federation, "International Markets: Japan."
88. With respect to beef, Japanese imports represent over 60 percent of the total U.S. export. Sakoh, "Food Exports and the U.S.-Japan Trade Deficit"; Wahl, Hayes, and Williams, "Dynamic Adjustment in Japanese Livestock Industry under Beef Import Liberalization," 119.
89. Kansas/Asia Community Connection, "Beef Trade with Japan," University of Kansas (2008), http://web.archive.org/web/20080202031300/http://www.asiakan.org/trade/beef_trade_japan.shtml.
90. Cornyetz, "The Meat Manifesto: Ruth Ozeki's Performative Poetics," 212, 16.
91. Chiu, "Postnational Globalization and (En)Gendered Meat Production in Ruth L. Ozeki's *My Year of Meats*," 120.
92. The press learns of the video from Bunny Dunn after she and her husband decided to report their son's illegal use of DES in the feedlot to the USDA, an event that prompts national media outlets to barrage Jane with requests for distribution rights.
93. DeLillo, "The Power of History."
94. Bruce Robbins, "The Sweatshop Sublime," *PMLA* 117, no. 1 (2002): 84–97, quotation on 85.
95. It is this aspiration to be "an analyst of systems" that James Wood disparages in his now notorious 2001 *Guardian* essay on what he calls the "great American social novel." James Wood, "Tell Me How Does It Feel?," *The Guardian UK*, October 5, 2001.
96. Palumbo-Liu, "Rational and Irrational Choices: Form, Affect, and Ethics," 64.
97. Kenneth Goldsmith, *Uncreative Writing* (New York: Columbia University Press, 2011), 28.

98. Giddens, *The Consequences of Modernity*, 38.
99. Quoted in Julie Taylor, "'The Voice of the Prophet': From Astrological Quackery to Sexological Authority in Djuna Barnes's *Ladies Almanack*," *Modern Fiction Studies* 55, no. 4 (2009): 716–38, quotation on 719.
100. North American Farmers' Alamanc (Lewiston, ME: Almanac Publishing Company, 2012), www.farmersalmanac.com.
101. Joni Adamson, *American Indian Literature, Environmental Justice, and Ecocriticism: The Middle Place* (Tucson: University of Arizona Press, 2001), 140, 52.
102. I am thinking especially of *Gain*, *The Echo Maker*, and *The Goldbug Variations*. Richard Powers, *Gain* (New York: Picador USA, 1998); *The Echo Maker* (New York: Farrar, Straus and Giroux, 2006); *The Gold Bug Variations* (New York: Harper Perennial, 1991).
103. Kingsolver, *Animal, Vegetable, Miracle: A Year of Food Life*; Nabhan, *Coming Home to Eat: The Pleasures and Politics of Local Foods*; Michael Pollan, *Second Nature: A Gardener's Education* (New York: Grove Press, 2003).
104. Critical Art Ensemble, Beatriz da Costa, and Shyh-shiun Shyu, "Free Range Grain," http://critical-art.net/Original/free/.

CHAPTER 6

1. Novella Carpenter, *Farm City: The Education of an Urban Farmer* (New York: Penguin Books, 2009), 183. Hereafter cited in text.
2. Center for Genomic Gastronomy, Cathrine Kramer, and Zack Denfeld, *Edible: The Taste of Things to Come*, Exhibition Catalog (Dublin: Science Gallery, 2012), 8.
3. Gary Paul Nabhan, *Coming Home to Eat: The Pleasures and Politics of Local Foods* (New York and London: W. W. Norton, 2002). Hereafter cited in text.
4. Vandana Shiva, *Earth Democracy: Justice, Sustainability, and Peace* (Cambridge, MA: South End Press, 2005); *Stolen Harvest: The Hijacking of the Global Food Supply* (Cambridge, MA: South End Press, 2000).
5. "Regional Map of North America's Place-Based Food Traditions," in *Renewing America's Food Traditions: Bringing Cultural and Culinary Mainstays from the Past into the New Millennium*, ed. Gary Paul Nabhan (Flagstaff: Center for Sustainable Environments at Northern Arizona University, 2007).
6. Carlo Petrini, *Slow Food: The Case for Taste,* Arts and Traditions of the Table: Perspectives on Culinary History (New York: Columbia University Press, 2001); Suzanne Goin, *Sunday Suppers at Lucques* (New York: Alfred A. Knopf, 2005); Barbara Kingsolver, *Animal, Vegetable, Miracle: A Year of Food Life* (New York: HarperCollins, 2007).
7. Berry is an important forerunner to the locavore writers, who frequently cite his books and essays dating from the 1970s, in which he called for ethical eating and made a case for the environmental impacts of agriculture and food consumption patterns. See especially Wendell Berry, *Citizenship Papers* (Washington, DC: Shoemaker and Hoard, 2003); "The Pleasures of Eating," in *What Are People*

*For?* (New York: North Point Press, 1990), 145–52; *The Unsettling of America: Culture and Agriculture* (New York: Avon Books, 1977).
8. Michael Pollan, *Second Nature: A Gardener's Education* (New York: Grove Press, 2003); *The Omnivore's Dilemma: A Natural History of Four Meals* (New York: Penguin Books, 2006); *In Defense of Food: An Eater's Manifesto* (New York: Penguin Books, 2008).
9. As for documentary films, see especially Lee Fulkerson, "Forks over Knives" (Monica Beach Media, 2011); Scott Hamilton Kennedy, "The Garden" (Black Valley Films, 2008); Robert Kenner, "Food, Inc." (Magnolia Pictures, 2008); Deborah Koons Garcia, "Symphony of the Soil" (2011); Aaron Woolf, "King Corn" (ITVS and Mosaic Films, 2007).
10. Fulkerson, "Forks over Knives"; Kenner, "Food, Inc."
11. "Is It Local?," in *Portlandia* (IFC, 2010).
12. *New Oxford American Dictionary*, "Oxford Word of the Year: Locavore," *OUP Blog* (2007), http://blog.oup.com/2007/11/locavore/. Today, agriculture contributes over 50 percent of the greenhouse gas methane. B. Metz et al., eds., *Fourth Assessment Report of the Intergovernmental Panel on Climate Change* (Cambridge and New York: Cambridge University Press, 2007); P. Smith et al., "Agriculture," in *Climate Change 2007: Mitigation, Contribution of Working Group III*, ed. Intergovernmental Panel on Climate Change (Cambridge and New York: Cambridge University Press, 2007).
13. Kingsolver, *Animal, Vegetable, Miracle: A Year of Food Life*.
14. Ibid, 20.
15. Ibid., 13.
16. Ibid.
17. Calvin Coolidge, "Address before the Annual Convention of the American Farm Bureau Federation, Chicago, Ill., December 7, 1925," (Washington, D.C.: Government Printing Office, 1925) http://memory.loc.gov/ammem/coolhtml/coolbibTitles02.html; Pollan, *The Omnivore's Dilemma: A Natural History of Four Meals*, 41, 61.
18. Referring specifically to the 1973 U.S. farm bill that then Agriculture Secretary Earl Butz developed under the Nixon administration, Pollan suggests that a New Deal system of supporting farmers with loans and land idling schemes was replaced with a system of direct subsidies that encouraged farmers to sell crops at any price, since direct payments from the government would make up the difference, and hence encouraged farmers to plant monocultures of corn and other commodities. Companies like ADM and Cargill shaped farm bills in this period precisely so that the government would subsidize every bushel of corn, in turn making corn very cheap. Ibid, 53.
19. For this term, Pollan seems to have in mind Wendell Berry's 1989 essay "The Pleasures of Eating," in which he observes that "the industrial eater is, in fact, one who does not know that eating is an agricultural act" and calls for an ethical, agricultural relationship to eating. Berry, "The Pleasures of Eating," 146; Pollan, *The Omnivore's Dilemma: A Natural History of Four Meals*, 98–99.

20. Coolidge, "Address before the Annual Convention of the American Farm Bureau Federation, Chicago, Ill., December 7, 1925."
21. Pollan, *The Omnivore's Dilemma: A Natural History of Four Meals*, 263.
22. Daniel J. Philippon, "Sustainability and the Humanities: An Extensive Pleasure," *American Literary History* 24, no. 1 (2012): 163–79, quotation on 172.
23. Warren Belasco, *Appetite for Change: How the Counterculture Took on the Food Industry* (London and Ithaca: Cornell University Press, 1989, 2007).
24. Julie Guthman, "Fast Food / Organic Food: Reflexive Tastes and the Making of 'Yuppie Chow,'" *Social and Cultural Geography* 4, no. 1 (2003): 45–58, quotation on 46.
25. David Goodman, E. Melanie DuPuis and Michael K. Goodman, *Alternative Food Networks: Knowledge, Practice and Politics* (New York and London: Routledge, 2012); Julie Guthman, "Bringing Good Food to Others: Investigating the Subjects of Alternative Food Practice," *Cultural Geographies* 15, no. 4 (2008): 431–45; "Fast Food / Organic Food: Reflexive Tastes and the Making of 'Yuppie Chow.'" See also James McWilliams, *Just Food: Where Locavores Get It Wrong and How We Can Truly Eat Responsibly* (New York: Little, Brown and Company, 2009), especially on 34, 38–40.
26. Guthman, "Bringing Good Food to Others: Investigating the Subjects of Alternative Food Practice," 431, 35. See also *Weighing In: Obesity, Food Justice, and the Limits of Capitalism*, California Studies in Food and Culture (Berkeley: University of California Press, 2011).
27. For further evidence of this trend, refer to Jennifer Wilkins, "Think Globally, Eat Locally," *The New York Times*, December 18, 2004.
28. For his part, McWilliams credits the food-miles construct for its simplicity as an indicator of "environmental consciousness" but then draws on life-cycle assessment (LCA) analyses to show that the miles food travels across the country and around the world is "only a minor link in the complex chain of food production," and goes on to posit an alternative "hub-and-spoke" model for the future of food in which centers of sustainable agriculture and aquaculture would connect to other communities via a green transportation system. McWilliams, *Just Food: Where Locavores Get It Wrong and How We Can Truly Eat Responsibly*, 17–18, 23–29. For a nuanced analysis of the strengths and shortcomings of the food-miles indicator of food system sustainability, see David Cleveland et al., "Effect of Localizing Fruit and Vegetable Consumption on Greenhouse Gas Emissions and Nutrition, Santa Barbara County," *Environmental Science and Technology* 45, no. 10 (2011): 4555–62
29. Leslye Miller Fraser, "The U.S. Food Supply and Bioterrorism," ed. Center for Food Safety and Applied Nutrition (CFSAN) (Washington, DC: The State Department, 2004); Life begins at 30, "Buying Locally Grown Foods Protects Us from Bioterrorism," http://fogcity.blogs.com/jen/2005/06.
30. Manuel Castells, *The Rise of the Network Society*, 2nd ed. (Oxford: Blackwell, 2010).

31. Massimo Montanari, *Food Is Culture*, trans. Albert Sonnenfeld, Arts and Traditions of the Table: Perspectives on Culinary History (New York: Columbia University Press, 2006), 83.
32. Ursula K. Heise makes this express point about Kingsolver. Ursula K. Heise, "Ecocriticism and the Transnational Turn in American Studies" *American Literary History* 20, no. 1 (2008): 381–404, especially on 392–94.
33. George Ritzer, ed., *Mcdonaldization: The Reader* (Thousand Oaks, CA: Pine Forge Press of Sage Publications, 2002).
34. Castells, *The Rise of the Network Society*, xxxii–xxxiii.
35. Goodman, et al, *Alternative Food Networks: Knowledge, Practice and Politics*, quotations on 8, 29–30, 246–47.
36. Guthman reinforces this idea, arguing that the current call to replenish inner-city "food deserts" through farmers' markets and community gardens fails to credit the value that some minority communities place on the "anonymity, convenience, and normality" of supermarkets. Guthman, "Bringing Good Food to Others: Investigating the Subjects of Alternative Food Practice," 55–56.
37. Peter A. Smith, "'Farm City,' by Novella Carpenter," *San Francisco Chronicle*, June 14, 2009; Dwight Garner, "Living Off the Land, Surrounded by Asphalt," *The New York Times*, June 11, 2009.
38. I adapt this term from Clay Shirky's use of it to describe online communities in the Web 2.0 era. Clay Shirky, *Here Comes Everybody: The Power of Organizing without Organizations* (New York: Penguin Press, 2008).
39. We can see this same impulse in a number of recent urban farm catalogues and how-to manuals. Novella Carpenter and Willow Rosenthal, *The Essential Urban Farmer* (New York: Penguin Books, 2011); Annette Cottrell and Joshua McNichols, *Urban Farm Handbook: City Slicker Resources for Growing, Raising, Sourcing, Trading, and Preparing What You Eat* (Seattle: Mountaineers Books, 2011); Amy Franceschini and Daniel Tucker, *Farm Together Now* (San Francisco: Chronicle Books, 2010); David Hanson and Edwin Marty, *Breaking through Concrete: Building an Urban Farm Revival* (Berkeley: University of California Press, 2012); Sarah C. Rich and Matthew Benson, *Urban Farms* (New York: Abrams, 2012).
40. Center for Genomic Gastronomy, Cathrine Kramer, and Zack Denfeld, "Planetary Sculpture Supper Club" (Bangalore, 2011).
41. *Edible: The Taste of Things to Come*.
42. Kennedy, *The Garden*.
43. A selection of those schools includes: University of Northern Carolina, October 2006; Colorado College, February 2007; Sweet Briar College, September 2007; Williams College, October 2007; University of California–Santa Barbara, January 2008 and February 2011; Brown University, February 2008; Butler College, February 2008; Stanford University, March 2008; Yale University, April 2008; University of Vermont, June 2008; University of Wisconsin–Madison, September 2009; Indiana University, February 2010; Denison University, April 2010; University of Southern California, February

2011; Texas Tech University, October 2011; Southern Methodist University, March 2012.
44. Two series on food and culture at major university presses since 2000 supports this claim. See especially Darra Goldstein, ed., *Series: California Studies in Food and Culture* (Berkeley: University of California Press, 2001–12); Albert Sonnenfeld, ed., *Series: Arts and Traditions of the Table: Perspectives on Culinary History* (New York: Columbia University Press, 2001–12).
45. Denise Gigante, *Taste: A Literary History* (London and New Haven: Yale University Press, 2005); Andrew Warnes, *Hunger Overcome?: Food and Resistance in Twentieth-Century African American Literature* (London and Athens, GA: University of Georgia Press, 2004). See also Ken Albala, *Eating Right in the Renaissance* (Berkeley: University of California Press, 2002). At the time of publication of *Global Appetites*, there were only 250 titles (including dissertations) listed in the World Catalog under the main Library of Congress subject heading "food habits in literature."

# *Bibliography*

Adams, Carol. *The Sexual Politics of Meat: A Feminist-Vegetarian Critical Theory.* New York: Continuum, 1990, 2000.
Adamson, Joni. *American Indian Literature, Environmental Justice, and Ecocriticism: The Middle Place.* Tucson: University of Arizona Press, 2001.
Adorno, Theodor W. *Aesthetic Theory.* Translated by Robert Hullot-Kentor. Minneapolis: University of Minnesota Press, 1998.
"Agribusiness, N." In *Oxford English Dictionary Online.* Oxford and New York: Oxford University Press, 1989, 2012.
Akhter, Syed H. "Review of *Multinational Corporations and the Impact of Public Advocacy on Corporate Strategy: Nestle and the Infant Formula Controversy* by S. Prakash Sethi." *Journal of International Business Studies* Q3 (1994): 658–60.
Alaimo, Stacey. "Discomforting Creatures: Monstrous Natures in Recent Films." In Armbruster and Wallace, *Beyond Nature Writing*, 279–96.
Albala, Ken. *Eating Right in the Renaissance.* Berkeley: University of California Press, 2002.
Aldama, Frederick Luis. *Postethnic Narrative Criticism: Magicorealism in Oscar "Zeta" Acosta, Ana Castillo, Julie Dash, Hanif Kureishi, and Salman Rushdie.* Austin: University of Texas Press, 2003.
Alkon, Alison Hope, and Kari Marie Norgaard. "Breaking the Food Chains: An Investigation of Food Justice Activism." *Sociological Inquiry* 79, no. 3 (2009): 289–305.
Alpers, Paul. *What Is Pastoral?* Chicago: University of Chicago Press, 1996.
Appadurai, Arjun. *Modernity at Large: Cultural Dimensions of Globalization.* Minneapolis: University of Minnesota Press, 1996.
Archie's Acres. "Veterans Sustainable Agriculture Training (VSAT) Program." www.archisacres.com/page/vsat-program.
Armbruster, Karla and Kathleen R. Wallace, eds. *Beyond Nature Writing: Expanding the Boundaries of Ecocriticism.* London and Charlottesville: University of Virginia Press, 2001.
Armbruster, Karla, and Kathleen R. Wallace. "The Novels of Toni Morrison: 'Wild Wilderness Where There Was None.'" In Armbruster and Wallace, *Beyond Nature Writing*, 211–30.
Arthur, Anthony. *Radical Innocent: Upton Sinclair.* New York: Random House, 2006.

Artists for Victory. "Artists for Victory, Inc. Records." Washington, D.C.: Smithsonian Institution, 1942–1946.

Askinosie Chocolate. "Our Story." www.askinosie.com/.

Bajaj, Vikas. "Japan Again Suspends Shipments of Beef from U.S." *The New York Times*, January 21, 2006.

Bakhtin, Mikhail. *The Dialogic Imagination: Four Essays. 1930*. Translated by Caryl Emerson and Michael Holquist. Austin: University of Texas Press, 1982.

Barnes, Geraldine, and Adrian Mitchell. "Measuring the Marvelous: Science and the Exotic in William Dampier." *Eighteenth-Century Life* 26, no. 3 (2002): 45–57.

Barrionuevo, Alexei. "Japan Partially Lifts 2-Year Ban on U.S. Beef, Defusing Trade Dispute." *The New York Times*, December 13, 2005.

Barthes, Roland. "Toward a Psychosociology of Contemporary Food Consumption." In Counihan and Van Esterik, *Food and Culture*, 28–35.

Bausum, Ann. *Muckrakers: How Ida Tarbell, Upton Sinclair, and Lincoln Steffens Helped Expose Scandal, Inspire Reform, and Invent Investigative Journalism*. Washington, D.C.: National Geographic, 2007.

BCC Research. "Global Markets for Agrochemicals." www.bccresearch.com/report/CHM054A.html.

Beck, Ulrich. *Risk Society: Towards a New Modernity*. Translated by Mark A. Ritter. 1986. London: Sage Publications, 1992.

Beckett, Samuel. *Endgame and Act without Words*. Translated by Samuel Beckett. New York: Grove Press, 1958. Originally published as *Fin de partie suivi de acte sans parole* (Paris: Les Editions de Minuit, 1957).

———. *Happy Days*. New York: Grove Press, 1961.

———. *Waiting for Godot*. Translated by Samuel Beckett. New York: Grove Press, 1954. Originally published as *En attendant Godot* (Paris: Théâtre de Babylone, 1952).

Belasco, Warren. *Appetite for Change: How the Counterculture Took on the Food Industry*. London and Ithaca: Cornell University Press, 1989, 2007.

———. "Dietary Modernization." Review of *Revolution at the Table: The Transformation of the American Diet* by Harvey Levenstein. *Reviews in American History* 18, no. 2 (1990): 262–66.

———. *Meals to Come: A History of the Future of Food*. Berkeley: University of California Press, 2006.

Bell, Daniel. *The Coming of Post-Industrial Society: A Venture in Social Forecasting*. 1976. New York: Basic Books, 1999.

Bender, Thomas. *A Nation Among Nations: America's Place in World History*. New York: Hill and Wang, 2006.

Benjamin, Walter. "Theses on the Philosophy of History." Translated by Harry Zohn. In *Illuminations*, edited by Hannah Arendt, 253–64. New York: Schocken Books, 1968.

Bennett, Jane. *Vibrant Matter: A Political Ecology of Things*. London and Durham: Duke University Press, 2009.

Bennett, Michael. "Anti-Pastoralism, Frederick Douglass, and the Nature of Slavery." In Armbruster and Wallace, *Beyond Nature Writing*, 195–210.
Bentley, Amy. *Eating for Victory: Food Rationing and the Politics of Domesticity*. Chicago and Urbana: University of Illinois Press, 1998.
Berry, Wendell. *Citizenship Papers*. Washington, D.C.: Shoemaker and Hoard, 2003.
——— "The Pleasures of Eating." In *What Are People For?*, 145–52. New York: North Point Press, 1990.
——— *The Unsettling of America: Culture and Agriculture*. New York: Avon Books, 1977.
Bessin, Ric. "Bt-Corn: What It Is and How It Works." University of Kentucky College of Agriculture, www.ca.uky.edu/entomology/entfacts/ef130.asp.
Black, Shameem. "Fertile Cosmofeminism: Ruth L. Ozeki and Transnational Reproduction." *Meridians: feminism, race, transnationalism* 5, no. 1 (2004): 226–56.
Bourdieu, Pierre. *Distinction: A Social Critique of the Judgement of Taste*. Translated by Richard Nice. Cambridge, MA: Harvard University Press, 1984. Originally published as *La Distinction: Critique sociale du jugement* (Paris: Les Éditions de Minuit, 1979).
Braudel, Fernand. *On History*. Translated by Sarah Matthews. Chicago: University of Chicago Press, 1982. Originally published as *Écrits sur l'Histoire* (Paris: Flammarion, 1969).
Breslin, Glenna. "Lorine Niedecker: The Poet in Her Homeplace." In Willis, *Radical Vernacular*, 189–206.
Brillat-Savarin, Jean Anthelme. *The Physiology of Taste: Or, Meditations on Transcendental Gastronomy*. Translated by M. F. K. Fisher. New York: Counterpoint, 1949.
Brooke, James. "Japan Still Bans U.S. Beef, Chafing American Officials." *The New York Times*, April 21, 2005.
Buell, Lawrence. *The Future of Environmental Criticism: Environmental Crisis and Literary Imagination*. Blackwell Manifestos. Oxford: Blackwell Publishing, 2005.
——— "Toxic Discourse." *Critical Inquiry* 24, no. 3 (1998): 639–65.
Burnett, John. *England Eats Out: A Social History of Eating out in England from 1830 to the Present*. London and New York: Pearson Longman, 2004.
Burton, Richard D. E. "'Maman-France Doudou': Family Images in French West Indian Colonial Discourse." *Diacritics* 23, no. 3 (1993): 69–90.
Carden, Mary Paniccia. "Creative Fertility and the National Romance in Willa Cather's *O Pioneers!* and *My Ántonia*." *Modern Fiction Studies* 45, no. 2 (1999): 275–302.
Cardozo, Karen, and Banu Subramaniam. "Genes, Genera, and Genres: The Natureculture of Biofiction in Ruth Ozeki's *All Over Creation*." In *Tactical Biopolitics: Art, Activism, and Technoscience*, edited by Beatriz da Costa and Kavita Philip, 269–88. Cambridge, MA and London: MIT Press, 2008.
Carmody, Timothy. "Modernism's Objects." Review of *The Objectivist Nexus: Essays in Cultural Poetics*, edited by Rachel Blau DuPlessis and Peter Quartermain. *Journal of Modern Literature* 27, no. 1 (2003): 207–10.

Carney, Judith. *In the Shadow of Slavery: Africa's Botanical Legacy in the Atlantic World.* Berkeley: University of California Press, 2010.
Carpenter, Novella. *Farm City: The Education of an Urban Farmer.* New York: Penguin Books, 2009.
Carpenter, Novella, and Willow Rosenthal. *The Essential Urban Farmer.* New York: Penguin Books, 2011.
Carpentier, Alejo. "The Baroque and the Marvelous Real." Translated by Lois Parkinson Zamora and Tanya Huntington. In *Magical Realism: Theory, History, Community,* edited by Lois Parkinson Zamora and Wendy B. Faris, 89–108. London and Durham: Duke University Press, 1995.
Carson, Rachel. *Silent Spring.* Boston: Houghton Mifflin, 1962. 1994.
Cassuto, Leonard, Clare Virginia Eby, and Benjamin Reiss, eds. *The Cambridge History of the American Novel.* Cambridge Histories Online. Cambridge and New York: Cambridge University Press, 2011.
Castells, Manuel. *The Rise of the Network Society.* 2nd ed. Oxford: Blackwell, 2010.
Castro, Janice. "Why the Beef over Hormones?" *Time,* January 16, 1989.
Cather, Willa. "The Bohemian Girl." *McClure's Magazine,* August 1912, 420–43.
"Escapism." In *Stories, Poems and Other Writings,* 968–73. New York: Library of America, 1992.
*My Ántonia. 1918. Willa Cather Scholarly Edition,* edited by Charles Mignon and Kari Ronning. Lincoln: University of Nebraska Press, 1994.
"Nebraska: The End of the First Cycle." *The Nation,* September 5, 1923, 236–38.
"The Novel Démeublé." In *Stories, Poems, and Other Writings,* 835–37.
*O Pioneers! 1913.* Willa Cather Scholarly Edition, edited by Susan J. Rosowski, Charles W. Mignon, and Kathleen A. Danker. Lincoln: University of Nebraska Press, 1992.
*One of Ours. 1922.* New York: Vintage Books, 1991.
*The Professor's House. Vintage Classics. 1925.* New York: Vintage Books, 1990.
Cella, Matthew J. C. "Harmonious Fields and Wild Prairies: Transcendental Pastoralism in Willa Cather's Nebraska Novels." In *Bad Land Pastoralism in Great Plains Fiction,* 99–134. Iowa City: University of Iowa Press, 2010.
Center for Genomic Gastronomy, Cathrine Kramer, and Zack Denfeld. *Edible: The Taste of Things to Come, Exhibition Catalog.* Dublin: Science Gallery, 2012.
"Planetary Sculpture Supper Club." Bangalore, India, 2011.
Center for New Crops and Plant Products. "The New Crop Resource Online Program." Purdue University, www.hort.purdue.edu/newcrop/.
Chamoiseau, Patrick. *Chronicle of the Seven Sorrows.* Translated by Linda Coverdale. Lincoln: University of Nebraska Press, 1999. Originally published as *Chronique de sept misères* (Paris: Gallimard, 1986).
Chaney, Lisa. *Elizabeth David: A Biography.* London: Macmillan, 1998.
Charles, Daniel. *Lords of the Harvest: Biotech, Big Money, and the Future of Food.* Cambridge, MA: Perseus Publishing, 2001.
Chiu, Monica. "Postnational Globalization and (En)Gendered Meat Production in Ruth L. Ozeki's *My Year of Meats.*" *LIT: Literature Interpretation Theory* 12, no. 1 (2001): 99–128.

Cilano, Cara, and Elizabeth M. DeLoughrey. "Against Authenticity: Global Knowledges and Postcolonial Ecocriticism." *Interdisciplinary Studies in Literature and Environment (ISLE)* 14, no. 1 (2007): 71–87.
Cleveland, David A., Corie N. Radka, Nora M. Müller, Tyler D. Watson, and Nicole J. Rekestein. "Effect of Localizing Fruit and Vegetable Consumption on Greenhouse Gas Emissions and Nutrition, Santa Barbara County." *Environmental Science and Technology* 45, no. 10 (2011): 4555–62.
Clifford, James. *Routes: Travel and Translation in the Late Twentieth Century*. Cambridge, MA: Harvard University Press, 1997.
Clymer, Jeffory A. "Panic! Markets, Crises, and Crows in American Fiction" (review). *Modern Fiction Studies* 54, no. 2 (2008): 425–28
Clyne, Catherine. "Creating Novel Life Forms – Literally: The Satya Interview with Ruth Ozeki." *Satya Magazine* (2003). www.ruthozeki.com/about/profiles-reviews/satya-magazine-interview.
Coe, Sophie D., and Michael D. Coe. *The True History of Chocolate*. London: Thames and Hudson, 1996.
Coe, Sue. *Dead Meat*. New York and London: Four Walls Eight Windows, 1996.
Columbus, Christopher. "Letter of Columbus to Various Persons Describing the Results of His First Voyage and Written on the Return Journey." Translated by J. M. Cohen. In *The Four Voyages of Christopher Columbus*, edited by J. M. Cohen, 115–26. London: Penguin Books, 1969.
Conkin, Paul K. *A Revolution Down on the Farm: The Transformation of American Agriculture since 1929*. Louisville: University Press of Kentucky, 2008.
Conlogue, William. *Working the Garden: American Writers and the Industrialization of Agriculture*. Chapel Hill: University of North Carolina Press, 2001.
Conway, Dennis. "Misguided Directions, Mismanaged Models or Missed Paths?" In Klak, *Globalization and Neoliberalism*, 29–50.
Coolidge, Calvin. "Address before the Annual Convention of the American Farm Bureau Federation, Chicago, Ill., December 7, 1925." Washington, D.C.: Government Printing Office, 1925. http://memory.loc.gov/ammem/coolhtml/coolbibTitles02.html.
Cornyetz, Nina. "The Meat Manifesto: Ruth Ozeki's Performative Poetics." *Women and Performance: A Journal of Feminist Theory* 12, no. 1 (2001): 207–24.
Cottrell, Annette, and Joshua McNichols. *Urban Farm Handbook: City Slicker Resources for Growing, Raising, Sourcing, Trading, and Preparing What You Eat*. Seattle: Mountaineers Books, 2011.
Counihan, Carole, and Penny Van Esterik, eds. *Food and Culture: A Reader*. New York and London: Routledge, 2007.
Crèvecoeur, St. John de. *Letters from an American Farmer and Sketches of Eighteenth-Century America*, edited by Albert E. Stone. New York: Penguin Books, 1981. 1782.
Critical Art Ensemble, Beatriz da Costa, and Shyh-shiun Shyu. "Free Range Grain." http://critical-art.net/Original/free/.

Crittenden, Ann. "Baby Formula Sales in Third World Criticized: Some Producers Accused of Excessive Promotion." *The New York Times*, September 11, 1975.

Curtin, Deane W., and Lisa M. Heldke. *Cooking, Eating, Thinking: Transformative Philosophies of Food*. Bloomington: Indiana University Press, 1992.

Cwiertka, Katarzyna J. "Popularizing a Military Diet in Wartime and Postwar Japan." *Asian Anthropology* 1 (2002): 1–30.

Davey, Monica. "In Farm Belt, Ethanol Plant Hits Resistance." *The New York Times*, November 13, 2007.

David, Elizabeth. *A Book of Mediterranean Food*. New York: John Lehmann, 1950. New York: New York Review of Books, 2002.

*South Wind through the Kitchen: The Best of Elizabeth David*. New York: North Point Press, 1998.

Davidson, Michael. "Life by Water: Lorine Niedecker and Critical Regionalism." In Willis, *Radical Vernacular*, 3–20.

Davis, Elmer. "Food Rationing and the War: An Address by Mr. Elmer Davis on December 27, 1942," ed. U.S. Office of War Information. 1942.

Dederer, Claire. "All Over Creation." Review of *All Over Creation* by Ruth L. Ozeki. *The New York Times*, March 16, 2003.

DeLillo, Don. "The Power of History." *The New York Times*, September 7, 1997.

DeLoughrey, Elizabeth M. *Routes and Roots: Navigating Caribbean and Pacific Island Literatures*. Honolulu: University of Hawai'i Press, 2007.

DeLoughrey, Elizabeth M., and George B. Handley, eds. *Postcolonial Ecologies: Literatures of the Environment*. Oxford and New York: Oxford University Press, 2011.

Derwin, Susan. "The Poetics of M. F. K. Fisher." *Style* 37, no. 3 (2003): 266–78.

Deutsch, Tracey. *Building a Housewife's Paradise: Gender, Politics and American Grocery Stores in the Twentieth Century*. Chapel Hill: University of North Carolina Press, 2010.

Dimock, Wai Chee. *Through Other Continents: American Literature across Deep Time*. Princeton: Princeton University Press, 2006.

Douglas, Mary. "Deciphering a Meal." In Counihan and Van Esterik, *Food and Culture*, 44–53.

DuPlessis, Rachel Blau. "Lorine Niedecker's 'Paean to Place' and Its Fusion Poetics." *Contemporary Literature* 46, no. 3 (2005): 393–421.

DuPlessis, Rachel Blau, and Peter Quartermain. "Introduction." In *The Objectivist Nexus: Essays in Cultural Poetics*, edited by Rachel Blau DuPlessis and Peter Quartermain, 1–22. Tuscaloosa and London: University of Alabama Press, 1999.

Duvall, John N. "Descent in the 'House of Chloe': Race, Rape, and Identity in Toni Morrison's *Tar Baby*." *Contemporary Literature* 38, no. 2 (1997): 325–49.

Dyck, John. "U.S.-Japan Agreements on Beef Imports: A Case of Successful Bilateral Negotiations," ed. U.S. Department of Agriculture. 1998, 99–107.

Eisenhower, Dwight D. "Military-Industrial Complex Speech." Public Papers of the Presidents, 1961.

Elliott, Jackson S. "Meat Rationing Likely to Start in Few Days." *The Washington Post*, August 15, 1942.

Emberley, Julia V. "A Historical Transposition: Toni Morrison's *Tar Baby* and Frantz Fanon's Post Enlightenment Phantasms." *Modern Fiction Studies* 45, no. 2 (1999): 403–31.

Empson, William. *Some Versions of Pastoral. 1935*. New York: New Directions, 1974.

Fackler, Martin. "In Japan, American Beef Is Once Again on the Menu." *The New York Times*, January 7, 2006.

FAO Statistics Division. "FAO Methodology for the Measurement of Food Deprivation." Rome: United Nations, 2008.

Farnsworth, Clyde H. "GATT to Act on Beef in U.S.-Japan Impasse." *The New York Times*, May 5, 1988.

Fischer, Mike. "Pastoralism and Its Discontents: Willa Cather and the Burden of Imperialism." *Mosaic* 23, no. 1 (1990): 31–44.

Fish, Cheryl J. "The Toxic Body Politic: Ethnicity, Gender, and Corrective Eco-Justice in Ruth Ozeki's *My Year of Meats* and Judith Helfand and Daniel Gold's *Blue Vinyl*." *MELUS* 34, no. 2 (2009): 43–62.

Fisher, M. F. K. *The Gastronomical Me*. New York: Duell, Sloan and Pearce, 1943, 1954. North Point Press, 1989.

*How to Cook a Wolf*. New York: World Publishing, 1942, 1954. New York: North Point Press, 1988.

Fitzgerald, Deborah. *Every Farm a Factory: The Industrial Ideal in American Agriculture*. London and New Haven: Yale University Press, 2003.

Fleissner, Jennifer L. "Henry James's Art of Eating." *ELH* 75, no. 1 (2008): 27–62.

Florida Citrus Commission. *Canned Florida Grapefruit Juice Advertisement*. 1943. Print advertisement.

Food and Agriculture Organization. "Climate Change and Food Security: A Framework Document." In *High-Level Conference on World Food Security: The Challenges of Climate Change and Bioenergy*. Rome: United Nations, 2008. www.fao.org/forestry/15538-079b31d45081fe9c3dbc6ff34de4807e4.pdf.

"High Food Prices and Food Security: Threats and Opportunities." In *State of Food Insecurity in the World*. Rome: United Nations, 2008. www.fao.org/docrep/011/i0291e/i0291e00.pdf.

"How Does International Price Volatility Affect Domestic Economies and Food Security?" In *State of Food Insecurity in the World*. Rome: United Nations, 2011. www.fao.org/docrep/014/i2330e/i2330e00.htm.

Franceschini, Amy, and Daniel Tucker. *Farm Together Now*. San Francisco: Chronicle Books, 2010.

François, Anne-Lise. "'O Happy Living Things': Frankenfoods and the Bounds of Wordsworthian Natural Piety." *diacritics* 33, no. 2 (2003): 42–70.

Fraser, Leslye Miller. "The U.S. Food Supply and Bioterrorism," ed. Center for Food Safety and Applied Nutrition (CFSAN). Washington, D.C.: The State Department, 2004.

Freidberg, Susanne. *Fresh: A Perishable History*. Cambridge, MA: Belknap Press of Harvard University Press, 2009.

Freleng, Friz. "Bugs Bunny Nips the Nips." 8:11 min.: Warner Brothers Pictures and the Vitaphone Corporation, 1994.

Freudenheim, Milt. "Beef Dispute: Stakes High in Trade War." *The New York Times*, January 1, 1989.

Fulkerson, Lee. "Forks over Knives." 90 min.: Monica Beach Media, 2011.

Funderburg, Lisa. "Books in Brief: My Year of Meats." Review of *My Year of Meats* by Ruth L. Ozeki. *The New York Times*, July 26, 1998.

Fussell, Paul. *The Great War and Modern Memory*. Oxford and New York: Oxford University Press, 1975. 2000.

Gardner, Bruce L. *American Agriculture in the Twentieth Century: How It Flourished and What It Cost*. Cambridge, MA: Harvard University Press, 2002.

Garner, Dwight. "Living Off the Land, Surrounded by Asphalt." *The New York Times*, June 11, 2009.

Garrard, Greg. *Ecocriticism*. The New Critical Idiom. New York and London: Routledge, 2004.

Garrett, Laurie. "Food Failures and Futures." Washington, D.C.: Maurice R. Greenberg Center for Geoeconomic Studies, 2008.

Giddens, Anthony. *The Consequences of Modernity*. Stanford: Stanford University Press, 1990.

Gifford, Terry. *Pastoral*. The New Critical Idiom. New York and London: Routledge, 1999.

Gigante, Denise. *Taste: A Literary History*. London and New Haven: Yale University Press, 2005.

Gillis, Justin. "Bionic Growth for Biotech Crops: Gene-Altered Agriculture Trending Global." *The Washington Post*, January 12, 2006, D01.

Gilroy, Paul. *The Black Atlantic: Modernity and Double Consciousness*. Cambridge, MA: Harvard University Press, 1995.

Glissant, Édouard. *Caribbean Discourse: Selected Essays*. Translated by J. Michael Dash. London and Charlottesville: University of Virginia Press, 1989. Originally published as *Les Discours Antillais* (Paris: Gallimard, 1981).

——— "A Word Scratcher." Translated by Linda Coverdale. In Chamoiseau, *Chronicle of the Seven Sorrows*, vii–ix.

"Global Agrochemical Market Worth $196 Billion by 2014." *AgroNews* 2009.

"Global Seed Market Values Grow by 10 Percent to Nearly $32b." *Seed Today*, May 11, 2010.

Goin, Suzanne. *Sunday Suppers at Lucques*. New York: Alfred A. Knopf, 2005.

Goldberg, David J. *Discontented America: The United States in the 1920s*. London and Baltimore: John Hopkins University Press, 1999.

Goldberg, Jonathan. *Willa Cather and Others*. London and Durham: Duke University Press, 2001.

Goldsmith, Kenneth. *Uncreative Writing*. New York: Columbia University Press, 2011.

Goldstein, Darra, ed. *Series: California Studies in Food and Culture*. Berkeley: University of California Press, 2001–12.

Golston, Michael. "Petalbent Devils: Louis Zukofsky, Lorine Niedecker, and the Surrealist Praying Mantis." *Modernism/Modernity* 13, no. 2 (2006): 325–47.

Goodman, David, E. Melanie DuPuis and Michael K. Goodman. *Alternative Food Networks: Knowledge, Practice and Politics.* New York and London: Routledge, 2012.
Gordon, Lois. *Reading Godot.* London and New Haven: Yale University Press, 2002.
Gottlieb, Robert and Anupama Joshi. *Food Justice.* Cambridge, MA: MIT Press, 2010.
Goyal, Yogita. "The Gender of Diaspora in Toni Morrison's *Tar Baby.*" *Modern Fiction Studies* 52, no. 2 (2006): 393–414.
Gregory, P.J. et al., "Climate Change and Food Security," *Philosophical Transactions of the Royal Society* 360 (2005): 2139–48.
Guha, Ramachandra, and Joan Martinez-Alier. *Varieties of Environmentalism: Essays North and South* London: Earthscan Publications Ltd., 1997.
Guthman, Julie. "Bringing Good Food to Others: Investigating the Subjects of Alternative Food Practice." *Cultural Geographies* 15, no. 4 (2008): 431–47.
"Fast Food / Organic Food: Reflexive Tastes and the Making of 'Yuppie Chow.'" *Social and Cultural Geography* 4, no. 1 (2003): 45–58.
*Weighing In: Obesity, Food Justice, and the Limits of Capitalism.* California Studies in Food and Culture. Berkeley: University of California Press, 2011.
Hamilton, Shane. "The Economies and Conveniences of Modern-Day Living: Frozen Foods and Mass Marketing, 1945–1965." *The Business History Review* 77, no. 1 (2003): 33–60.
Handley, George. "Derek Walcott's Poetics of the Environment in *The Bounty.*" *Callaloo* 28, no. 1 (2005): 201–15.
Hanson, David, and Edwin Marty. *Breaking through Concrete: Building an Urban Farm Revival.* Berkeley: University of California Press, 2012.
Harris, Richard C. "Getting Claude 'Over There': Sources for Book Four of Cather's *One of Ours.*" *Journal of Narrative Theory* 35, no. 2 (2005): 248–56.
"The Newly Discovered Cather–Alfred A. Knopf Correspondence and *One of Ours.*" *Willa Cather Newsletter and Review* 54, no. 3 (2011): 101–07.
"'Pershing's Crusaders': G.P. Cather, Claude Wheeler and the AEF Soldier in France." *Cather Studies* 8 (2010): 74–90.
Harvey, David. *The New Imperialism.* Oxford and New York: Oxford University Press, 2003.
*Spaces of Global Capitalism: Towards a Theory of Uneven Geographical Development.* London and New York: Verso, 2006.
Hawthorne, Evelyn. "On Gaining the Double-Vision: *Tar Baby* as Diasporean Novel." *Black American Literature Forum* 22, no. 1 (1988): 97–107.
Hayles, N. Katherine. *How We Became Posthuman: Virtual Bodies in Cybernetics, Literature, and Informatics.* Chicago: University of Chicago Press, 1999.
Heinert, Jennifer Lee Jordan. "(Re)Defining Race: Folktale and Stereotypes in Tar Baby." In *Narrative Conventions and Race in the Novels of Toni Morrison*, 36–55. New York and London: Routledge, 2009.
Heise, Ursula K. "Ecocriticism and the Transnational Turn in American Studies." *American Literary History* 20, no. 1 (2008): 381–404.
*Sense of Place and Sense of Planet: The Environmental Imagination of the Global.* Oxford and New York: Oxford University Press, 2008.

Hershey Community Archives. "Ration D Bars." www.hersheyarchives.org/essay/details.aspx?EssayId=26
Hesiod. *Works of Hesiod and the Homeric Hymns*. Translated by Daryl Hine. Chicago: University of Chicago Press, 2005.
Heuman, Gad. *The Caribbean*. Brief Histories. London: Hodder Education of Oxford University Press, 2006.
Hinton, James. "Militant Housewives: The British Housewives' League and the Attlee Government." *History Workshop* 38 (1994): 128–56.
Hoard's Dairyman. "Hoard's History: Generations of Leadership." www.hoards.com/biographies.
Holder, Julian. "The Nation State or the United States?: The Irresistible Kitchen of the British Ministry of Works, 1944–1951." In Oldenziel and Zachmann, *Cold War Kitchen*, 235–58.
"Homepage." Bacardi. http://www.bacardi.com/us/lda.
"Homepage." Pernod Ricard. www.havana-club.com.
Horten, Gerd. *Radio Goes to War: The Cultural Politics of Propaganda During World War II*. Berkeley: University of California Press, 2003.
Houglum, Brook. "'Speech without Practical Locale': Radio and Lorine Niedecker's Aurality." In *Broadcasting Modernism*, edited by Debra Rae Cohen, Michael Coyle, and Jane Lewty, 221–37. Gainesville: University of Florida Press, 2009.
House, Elizabeth B. "The 'Sweet Life' in Toni Morrison's Fiction." *American Literature* 56, no. 2 (1984): 181–202.
"How Britain Was Fed in War Time: Food Control 1939–1945," ed. London Ministry of Food. London: H.M. Stationery Office, 1946.
Hsu, Hsuan L. "Circa 1898: Overseas Empire and Transnational American Studies." *Journal of Transnational American Studies (JTAS)* 3, no. 2 (2011): 1–6.
Hudson, John C. *Making the Corn Belt: A Geographical History of Middle-Western Agriculture*. Midwestern History and Culture. Bloomington: Indiana University Press, 1994.
Huggan, Graham. "'Greening' Postcolonialism: Ecocritical Perspectives." *Modern Fiction Studies* 50, no. 3 (2004): 701–33.
"Is It Local?" In *Portlandia*, 22:37 min: IFC, 2010.
James, Pearl. "The 'Enid Problem': Dangerous Modernity in *One of Ours*." *Cather Studies* 6 (2006): 92–128.
Jameson, Fredric. *Modernism and Imperialism*. Lawrence Hill, Derry: Field Day Theater Company Limited, 1988.
— *Postmodernism, or the Cultural Logic of Late Capitalism*. London and Durham: Duke University Press, 1991.
— *A Singular Modernity: Essay on the Ontology of the Present*. London and New York: Verso, 2002.
"Japan's Beef Scandal." *Nature* 413 (September 27, 2001).
Jefferson, Thomas. *Writings: Autobiography, Notes on the State of Virginia, Public and Private Papers, Addresses, Letters*, edited by Merrill D. Peterson. New York: Library of America, 1984.

Jennison, Ruth. "Scrambling Narrative: Niedecker and the White Dome of Logic." *JNT: Journal of Narrative Theory* 41, no. 1 (2011): 53–81.
Jewell, Andrew. "'A Crime against Art': *My Ántonia*, Food and Cather's Anti-Americanization Argument." *Willa Cather Newsletter and Review* 54, no. 2 (2010): 72–76.
Jones, Elizabeth B. *Gender and Rural Modernity*. Studies in Labour History. Surrey: Ashgate, 2009.
Jones, Gavin. *American Hungers: The Problem of Poverty in U.S. Literature, 1840–1945*. Princeton: Princeton University Press, 2008.
Judt, Tony. *Postwar: A History of Europe since 1945*. New York: Penguin Books, 2005.
Kaiser, Jo Ellen Green. "Feeding the Hungry Heart: Gender, Food, and War in the Poetry of Edna St. Vincent Millay." *Food and Foodways* 6, no. 2 (1996): 81–92.
Kamp, David. *The United States of Arugula: The Sun-Dried, Cold-Pressed, Dark-Roasted, Extra Virgin Story of the American Food Revolution*. New York: Broadway Books, 2006.
Kansas/Asia Community Connection. "Beef Trade with Japan." University of Kansas (2008). http://web.archive.org/web/20080202031300/ http://www.asiakan.org/trade/beef_trade_japan.shtml.
Karasaki, Taro. "Tokyo: Ban on U.S. Stays until Safety Ensured." *Asahi Shimbun*, January 23, 2006.
Kennedy, Scott Hamilton. "The Garden." 80 min.: Black Valley Films, 2008.
Kenner, Hugh. *Flaubert, Joyce and Beckett: The Stoic Comedians. 1962*. London: Dalkey Archive Press, 2002.
Kenner, Robert. "Food, Inc." 94 min.: Magnolia Pictures, 2008.
Kimbrell, Andrew, ed. *Fatal Harvest: The Tragedy of Industrial Agriculture*. Washington, D.C. and London: Island Press, 2002.
Kingsolver, Barbara. *Animal, Vegetable, Miracle: A Year of Food Life*. New York: HarperCollins, 2007.
Klak, Thomas, ed. *Globalization and Neoliberalism: The Caribbean Context*. New York and Oxford: Rowman and Littlefield Publishers, 1998.
"Introduction: Thirteen Theses on Globalization and Neoliberalism." In Klak, *Globalization and Neoliberalism*, 3–23.
Koons Garcia, Deborah. "Symphony of the Soil." 103 min.: Lily Films, 2012.
Korsmeyer, Carolyn. *Making Sense of Taste: Philosophy and Food*. London and Ithaca: Cornell University Press, 1999.
Kroese, Ron. "Industrial Agriculture's War against Nature." In Kimbrell, *Fatal Harvest*, 20–28.
Krumholz, Linda. "Blackness and Art in Toni Morrison's *Tar Baby*." *Contemporary Literature* 49, no. 2 (2008): 263–92.
Landau, Ellen G. "*Artists for Victory: An Exhibition Catalog.*" Washington, D.C.: U.S. Government Printing Office, 1983.
Langston, Nancy. *Toxic Bodies: Hormone Disruptors and the Legacy of DES*. London and New Haven: Yale University Press, 2010.
Lazar, David. "The Usable Past of M. F. K. Fisher." *Southwest Review* 77, no. 4 (1992): 515–31.

Lean, Geoffrey. "Ministers Back 'Terminator' GM Crops; Website Reveals Plans to Scrap Prohibition on Seeds That Threaten." *Independent*, March 5, 2006.
Leonard, Andrew. "It's Monsanto's World. We Just Live in It." *Salon.com* (2006). www.salon.com/2006/02/09/monsanto/.
Lepore, Jill. *The Mansion of Happiness: A History of Life and Death*. New York: Alfred A. Knopf, 2012.
Lepow, Lauren. "Paradise Lost and Found: Dualism and Edenic Myth in Toni Morrison's *Tar Baby*." *Contemporary Literature* 28, no. 3 (1987): 363–77.
Levenstein, Harvey A. *Paradox of Plenty: A Social History of Eating in Modern America*. Oxford and New York: Oxford University Press, 1993.
Levi, Primo. *Survival in Auschwitz; and the Reawakening: Two Memoirs*. Translated by Stuart Woolf. New York: Summit Books, 1986.
Lévi-Strauss, Claude. "The Culinary Triangle." In Counihan and Van Esterik, *Food and Culture*, 36–43.
——. *The Savage Mind*. Chicago: University of Chicago Press, 1966, 1967.
Library of Congress. "Bretton Woods System." http://lcweb2.loc.gov/frd/cs/japan/jp_glos.html.
Life begins at 30. "Buying Locally Grown Foods Protects Us from Bioterrorism." http://fogcity.blogs.com/jen/2005/06.
Lindberg, John. "Food, Relief and Famine," ed. Transit Department. Geneva: League of Nations, 1946.
Liu, Alan. *The Laws of Cool: Knowledge Work and the Culture of Information*. Chicago and London: University of Chicago Press, 2004.
Llewellyn, Dr. Peter J. "Valerian Herb." Washington, D.C.: National Institutes of Health, 2007.
Luce, Henry. "The American Century." *Life*, 1941.
Lukács, Georg. *History and Class Consciousness: Studies in Marxist Dialectics*. Translated by Rodney Livingstone. Cambridge, MA: The MIT Press, 1972.
Mander, Jerry. "Machine Logic: Industrializing Nature and Agriculture." In Kimbrell, *Fatal Harvest*, 16–19.
Manning, Richard. *Against the Grain: How Agriculture Has Hijacked Civilization*. New York: North Point Press, 2004.
Marx, Leo. *The Machine in the Garden: Technology and the Pastoral Ideal in America*. Oxford and New York: Oxford University Press, 1964. 2000.
Mason, Jim, and Peter Singer. *Animal Factories: What Agribusiness Is Doing to the Family Farm, the Environment, and Your Health*. New York: Harmony Books, 1990.
Mayberry, Susan Neal. *Can't I Love What I Criticize?: The Masculine and Morrison*. London and Athens, GA: University of Georgia Press, 2007.
McGurl, Mark. *The Novel Art: Elevations of American Fiction after Henry James*. Princeton: Princeton University Press, 2001.
——. "The Novel, Mass Culture, Mass Media." In Cassuto et al., *The Cambridge History of the American Novel*, 686–99.
——. *The Program Era: Postwar Fiction and the Rise of Creative Writing*. Cambridge, MA: Harvard University Press, 2009.

McHugh, Susan. "Flora, Not Fauna: GM Culture and Agriculture." *Literature and Medicine* 26, no. 1 (2007): 25–54.
McKay, Nellie. "An Interview with Toni Morrison." *Contemporary Literature* 24, no. 4 (1983): 413–29.
McLean, Alice L. *Aesthetic Pleasure in Twentieth-Century Women's Food Writing: The Innovative Appetites of M. F. K. Fisher, Alice B. Toklas, and Elizabeth David.* Studies in Twentieth-Century Literature. New York and London: Routledge, 2011.
McLean Ward, Barbara, ed. *Produce and Conserve, Share and Play Square: The Grocer and the Consumer on the Home-Front Battlefield During World War II. Strawbery Banke Museum.* London and Hanover, NH: University Press of New England, 1994.
McLuhan, Marshall. *Understanding Media: The Extensions of Man. 1964.* Cambridge, MA: MIT Press, 1994.
McWilliams, James. *Revolution in Eating: How the Quest for Food Shaped America.* New York: Columbia University Press, 2005.
  *Just Food: Where Locavores Get It Wrong and How We Can Truly Eat Responsibly.* New York: Little, Brown and Company, 2009.
Meeker, Joseph W. "The Plow and the Pen." *Cather Studies* 5 (2003): 77–89.
Metz, B., O. R. Davidson, P. R. Bosch, R. Dave, and L. A. Meyer, eds. *Fourth Assessment Report of the Intergovernmental Panel on Climate Change.* Cambridge and New York: Cambridge University Press, 2007.
Meyer, Susan. "Sanitary Piggeries and Chaste Hens: Willa Cather and the Pure Food Movement." *Willa Cather Newsletter and Review* 54, no. 2 (2010): 38–47.
Michaels, Walter Benn. *Our America: Nativism, Modernism, and Pluralism.* London and Durham: Duke University Press, 1995.
Middleton, Peter. "Folk Poetry and the American Avant-Garde: Placing Lorine Niedecker." *Journal of American Studies* 31, no. 2 (1997): 203–18.
Millay, Edna St. Vincent. *Make Bright the Arrows.* New York and London: Harper Brothers, 1940.
  *The Murder of Lidice.* New York: Harper Brothers, 1942.
Miller, Karen A. J. "Agricultural Policy." In *The American Economy: A Historical Encyclopedia* edited by Cynthia Clark Northrup. Santa Barbara: ABC-CLIO, 2003.
Miller, Tyrus. *Late Modernism: Politics, Fiction, and the Arts between the World Wars.* Berkeley: University of California Press, 1999.
Mintz, Sidney W. *Sweetness and Power: The Place of Sugar in Modern History.* New York: Viking, 1985.
MOMA. "The Museum and the War Effort: Artistic Freedom and Reporting for 'the Cause.'" www.moma.org/interactives/exhibitions/2008/wareffort/.
Momsen, Janet Henshall. "Caribbean Tourism and Agriculture: New Linkages in the Global Era?" In Klak, *Globalization and Neoliberalism*, 115–33.
Monsanto Inc. "The Desolate Year." *Monsanto Magazine* 42, no. 4 (1962): 4–9.
  *For Happier Picnicking Days . . . Luxtrex Styrene (a Monsanto Plastic).* New York: *Saturday Evening Post*, circa 1950. Advertisement.

*How Can We Squeeze More Food from a Raindrop?* New York: *The New Yorker*, 2009. Advertisement.

"Press Kit." http://monsanto.mediaroom.com/.

Montanari, Massimo. *Food Is Culture*. Translated by Albert Sonnenfeld. Arts and Traditions of the Table: Perspectives on Culinary History. New York: Columbia University Press, 2006.

Morrison, Toni. "Foreword." In *Tar Baby*, xi–xiv. New York: Vintage International, 2004.

——— *A Mercy*. New York: Alfred A. Knopf, 2008.

——— *Sula*. New York: Penguin Books, 1973, 1982.

——— *Tar Baby*. New York: Vintage International, 1981. 2004.

Nabhan, Gary Paul. *Coming Home to Eat: The Pleasures and Politics of Local Foods*. New York and London: W. W. Norton, 2002.

National Cattlemen's Beef Association. "Export Markets." www.beefusa.org/goveExportMarket.aspx.

National Oceanic and Atmospheric Administration (NOAA). "Women in the Weather Bureau During World War II." www.history.noaa.gov/stories_tales/women5.html.

Neuhaus, Jessamyn. "The Way to a Man's Heart: Gender Roles, Domestic Ideology, and Cookbooks in the 1950s." *Journal of Social History* 32, no. 3 (1999): 529–55.

New Oxford American Dictionary. "Oxford Word of the Year: Locavore." *OUP Blog* (2007). http://blog.oup.com/2007/11/locavore/.

New York Times News Service. "U.N. Baby Formula Vote Unlikely to Hamper Firms." *Chicago Tribune*, May 27, 1981.

Ngai, Sianne. "Competitiveness: From *Sula* to *Tyra*." *Women's Studies Quarterly* 34, no. 3/4 (2006): 107–39.

——— "Our Aesthetic Categories." *PMLA* 125, no. 4 (2011): 948–58.

Ngai, Sianne, and Adam Jasper. "Our Aesthetic Categories: An Interview with Sianne Ngai." *Cabinet* no. 43 (2011). www.cabinetmagazine.org/issues/43/jasper_ngai.php.

Niedecker, Lorine. *Lorine Niedecker: Collected Works*, edited by Jenny Penberthy. Berkeley: University of California Press, 2002.

——— *New Goose*, edited by Jenny Penberthy. Berkeley: Rumor Books, 2002. "Mother Geese," *New Directions* 1 (1936).

Nixon, Rob. *Slow Violence and the Environmentalism of the Poor*. Cambridge, MA: Harvard University Press, 2011.

Norris, Frank. *The Octopus: A Story of California*. New York: Penguin Books, 1994.

*North American Farmers' Alamanc*. Lewiston, ME: Almanac Publishing Company, 2012. www.farmersalmanac.com.

North, Michael. *Reading 1922: A Return to the Scene of the Modern*. Oxford and New York: Oxford University Press, 1999.

O'Brien, Sharon. *Willa Cather: The Emerging Voice*. Cambridge, MA: Harvard University Press, 1997.

Ohnuki-Tierney, Emiko. "McDonald's in Japan: Changing Manners and Etiquette." In *Golden Arches East: McDonald's in East Asia*, edited by James L. Watson, 161–82. Stanford: Stanford University Press, 1997.

Oldenziel, Ruth, and Karin Zachmann, eds. *Cold War Kitchen: Americanization, Technology, and European Users*. Cambridge, MA and London: The MIT Press, 2009.

——. "Kitchens as Technology and Politics: An Introduction." In Oldenziel and Zachmann, *Cold War Kitchen*, 1–29.

Opie, Frederick Douglass. *Hog and Hominy: Soul Food from Africa to America*. Arts and Traditions of the Table. New York: Columbia University Press, 2008.

Orenberg, Cynthia Laitman. *DES: The Complete Story*. New York: St. Martin's Press, 1981.

Orwell, George. *Animal Farm*. New York: Harcourt Brace, 1946.

——. "The British Crisis, 8 May 1942." In *My Country Left or Right, 1940–1943*, edited by Sonia Orwell and Ian Angus, 207–16. Boston: Nonpareil Books, 2000.

——. "London Letter, 17 August 1941." In *My Country Left or Right, 1940–1943*, 145–54.

——. *Nineteen Eighty-Four. New York: Harcourt Brace, 1949*. New York: Penguin Books, 1983.

Ozeki, Ruth L. *All Over Creation*. New York: Penguin Books, 2003.

——. "Healthy Eating for You and the Planet, a Celebration of Food and Biodiversity." In *Living with Nature*. New York: American Museum of Natural History & Center for Biodiversity and Conservation, 2004.

——. *My Year of Meats*. New York: Penguin Books, 1998.

——. "You Are What You Eat: Food, Fiction, and Feminist Identity." In *Consuming Women: An Undergraduate Conference*. Canadian Women's Studies Conference, University of British Columbia, 2008.

Palumbo-Liu, David. "Rational and Irrational Choices: Form, Affect, and Ethics." In *Minor Transnationalism*, edited by Shu-mei Shih and Francoise Lionnet, 41–72. London and Durham: Duke University Press, 2005.

Paquet, Sandra Pouchet. "The Ancestor as Foundation in *Their Eyes Were Watching God* and *Tar Baby*." *Callaloo* 13, no. 3 (1990): 499–515.

Parker, Emma. "'Apple Pie' Ideology and the Politics of Appetite in the Novels of Toni Morrison." *Contemporary Literature* 39, no. 4 (1998): 614–43.

Parr, Joy. "Issue Introduction: Modern Kitchen, Good Home, Strong Nation." *Technology and Culture* 43, no. 4 (2002): 657–67.

Peach, Linden. "Toni Morrison." In *The Cambridge Companion to American Fiction after 1945*, 233–43. Cambridge: Cambridge University Press, 2012.

Penberthy, Jenny. "Life and Writing." In Niedecker, *Lorine Niedecker: Collected Works*, 1–11.

Pereira, Malin Walther. "Periodizing Toni Morrison's Work from *The Bluest Eye* to *Jazz*: The Importance of *Tar Baby*." *MELUS* 22, no. 3 (1997): 71–82.

Perloff, Marjorie. *Poetic License: Essays on Modernist and Postmodernist Lyric*. Evanston: Northwestern University Press, 1990.

Peterson, Becky. "Lorine Niedecker and the Matter of Life and Death." *Arizona Quarterly* 66, no. 4 (2010): 115–34.

Petrini, Carlo. *Slow Food: The Case for Taste.* Arts and Traditions of the Table: Perspectives on Culinary History. New York: Columbia University Press, 2001.
Philippon, Daniel J. "Sustainability and the Humanities: An Extensive Pleasure." *American Literary History* **24**, no. 1 (2012): 163–79.
Pollan, Michael. *The Botany of Desire: A Plant's-Eye View of the World.* New York: Random House, 2002.
  In *Defense of Food: An Eater's Manifesto.* New York: Penguin Books, 2008.
  *The Omnivore's Dilemma: A Natural History of Four Meals.* New York: Penguin Books, 2006.
  *Second Nature: A Gardener's Education.* New York: Grove Press, 2003.
Powers, Richard. *The Echo Maker.* New York: Farrar, Straus and Giroux, 2006.
  *Gain.* New York: Picador USA, 1998.
  *The Gold Bug Variations.* New York: Harper Perennial, 1991.
Pratt, Mary Louise. *Imperial Eyes: Travel Writing and Transculturation.* New York and London: Routledge, 1992.
"President Calls for War Declaration, Stronger Navy, New Army of 500,000 Men, Full Co-Operation with Germany's Foes." *The New York Times*, April 2, 1917.
Pringle, Peter. *Food, Inc.: Mendel to Monsanto – the Promises and Perils of the Biotech Harvest.* New York: Simon & Schuster, 2003.
Pynchon, Thomas. *The Crying of Lot 49*, ed. Perennial Classics. New York: Harper Perennial, 1965, 1999.
"Radio Background Material: Rationing," ed. U.S. Office of War Information. July 1, 1942.
Ragg, Edward. "Abstract Appetites: Food, Wine and the Idealist 'I.'" In *Wallace Stevens and the Aesthetics of Abstraction*, 136–65. Cambridge and New York: Cambridge University Press, 2010.
Ramazani, Jahan. *A Transnational Poetics.* Chicago: University of Chicago Press, 2009.
Rayson, Ann. "Foreign Exotic or Domestic Drudge?: The African American Women in *Quicksand* and *Tar Baby*." *MELUS* **23**, no. 2 (1998): 87–100.
Reardon, Joan. *M. F. K. Fisher among the Pots and Pans: Celebrating Her Kitchens.* California Studies in Food and Culture. Berkeley: University of California Press, 2008.
  *Poet of the Appetites: The Lives and Loves of M. F. K. Fisher.* New York: North Point Press, 2004.
"Regional Map of North America's Place-Based Food Traditions." In *Renewing America's Food Traditions: Bringing Cultural and Culinary Mainstays from the Past into the New Millennium*, edited by Gary Paul Nabhan, Map. Flagstaff: Center for Sustainable Environments at Northern Arizona University, 2007.
Reynaud, Paul. "Rationing: A War Weapon," ed. Minister of Finance. Paris: Centre D'Informations Documentaires, 1940.
Reynolds, Guy. *Willa Cather in Context: Progress, Race, Empire.* Basingstoke: Macmillan, 1996.
Rich, Sarah C., and Matthew Benson. *Urban Farms.* New York: Abrams, 2012.

Rifkin, Jeremy. *Beyond Beef: The Rise and Fall of the Cattle Culture.* New York: Dutton, 1992.
Ritzer, George, ed. *Mcdonaldization: The Reader.* Thousand Oaks: Pine Forge Press of Sage Publications, 2002.
Roach, Joseph. "'All the Dead Voices': The Landscape of Famine in *Waiting for Godot.*" In *Land/Scape/Theater*, edited by Elinor Fuchs and Una Chaudhuri, 84–93. Ann Arbor: University of Michigan Press, 2002.
Robbins, Bruce. "Commodity Histories." *PMLA* 120, no. 2 (2005): 454–63.
——— "The Sweatshop Sublime." *PMLA* 117, no. 1 (2002): 84–97.
——— "The Worlding of the American Novel." In Cassuto, et al., *The Cambridge History of the American Novel*, 1096–1106.
Roosevelt, Franklin D. "Address to the Congress of the United States: Four Freedoms," ed. Office of the President. January 6, 1941.
Rudin, Max. "M. F. K. Fisher and the Consolations of Food." *Raritan* 21, no. 2 (2002): 127–38.
"Rural Modernity and Its Discontents." http://ruralmodernity.wordpress.com.
Ryan, Judylyn S. "Contested Visions/Double-Vision in *Tar Baby.*" *Modern Fiction Studies* 39, nos. 3 & 4 (1993): 597–621.
Ryan, Melissa. "The Enclosure of America: Civilization and Confinement in Willa Cather's *O Pioneers!*" *American Literature* 75, no. 2 (2003): 275–303.
Ryan, Michael. "Prospects of the Meat Packing Industry." *Annals of the American Academy of Political and Social Science* 34 (1909): 33–38
Ryder, Mary. "'As Green as Their Money': The Doughboy Naïf in *One of Ours.*" *Cather Studies* 6 (2006): 145–59.
Safran Foer, Jonathan. *Eating Animals.* New York: Back Bay Books, 2010.
Sakoh, Katsuro. "Food Exports and the U.S.-Japan Trade Deficit." *Asian Studies Backgrounder*, July 26, 1984.
Saldívar, Ramón. *The Borderlands of Culture: Américo Paredes and the Transnational Imaginary.* London and Durham: Duke University Press, 2006.
Sassen, Saskia. *Globalization and Its Discontents: Essays on the New Mobility of People and Money.* New York: New Press, 1998.
Savage, Elizabeth. "'Bleach[Ed] Brotherhood': Race, Consumer Advertising, and Lorine Niedecker's Lyric." *Tulsa Studies in Women's Literature* 28, no. 2 (2009): 291–313.
——— "'A Few Cool Years after These': Midlife at Midcentury in Niedecker's Lyrics." *Journal of Modern Literature* 33, no. 3 (2010): 20–37.
Savory, Elaine. "Toward a Caribbean Ecopoetics: Derek Walcott's Language of Plants." In DeLoughrey and Handley, *Postcolonial Ecologies: Literatures of the Environment*, 80–96.
Schell, Orville. *Modern Meat: Antibiotics, Hormones, and the Pharmaceutical Farm.* New York: Random House, 1984.
Schlosser, Eric. *Cogs in the Great Machine.* London: Penguin Books, 2005.
——— *Fast Food Nation: The Dark Side of the All-American Meal.* Boston: Houghton Mifflin, 2001.

Schreiber, Evelyn Jaffe. *Race, Trauma, and Home in the Novels of Toni Morrison*. Southern Literary Studies. Baton Rouge: Lousiana State University Press, 2010.

Schubnell, Matthias. "The Decline of America: Willa Cather's Spenglerian Vision in *the Professor's House*." *Cather Studies* 2 (1993): 92–117.

Schurman, Rachel, and William Munro. "Ideas, Thinkers, and Social Networks: The Process of Grievance Construction in the Anti-Genetic Engineering Movement." *Theory and Society* 35 (2006): 1–38.

Shirky, Clay. *Here Comes Everybody: The Power of Organizing without Organizations*. New York: Penguin Press, 2008.

Shiva, Vandana. *Earth Democracy: Justice, Sustainability, and Peace*. Cambridge, MA: South End Press, 2005.

——. *Stolen Harvest: The Hijacking of the Global Food Supply*. Cambridge, MA: South End Press, 2000.

Shukin, Nicole. *Animal Capital: Rendering Life in Biopolitical Times*. Minneapolis: University of Minnesota Press, 2009.

Sinclair, Upton. *The Jungle. 1906*. New York: Penguin Books, 1985.

Singer, Peter. "Animal Liberation." Review of *Animals, Men and Morals*, edited by Stanley Godlovitch, Roslind Godlovitch, and John Harris. *New York Review of Books*, April 5, 1973.

Skaggs, Merrill M. "Cather's War and Faulkner's Peace: A Comparison of Two Novels, and More." In *Faulkner and His Contemporaries*, edited by Ann Abadie and Joseph R. Urgo, 40–53. Oxford: University of Mississippi Press, 2004.

Skinner, Jonathan. "Particular Attention: Lorine Niedecker's Natural Histories." In Willis, *Radical Vernacular*, 41–59.

Smith, P., D. Martino, Z. Cai, D. Gwary, H. Janzen, P. Kumar, B. McCarl, et al. "Agriculture." In *Climate Change 2007: Mitigation, Contribution of Working Group III*, ed. Intergovernmental Panel on Climate Change. Cambridge and New York: Cambridge University Press, 2007.

Smith, Peter A. "'Farm City,' by Novella Carpenter." *San Francisco Chronicle*, June 14, 2009.

Smith, Roberta. "Art in Review: Elephants We Must Never Forget." *New York Times*, November 21, 2008.

Smith-Howard, Kendra. "Antibiotics and Agricultural Change: Purifying Milk and Protecting Health in the Postwar Era." *Agricultural History Society* 84, no. 3 (2010): 327–51.

Sonnenfeld, Albert, ed. *Series: Arts and Traditions of the Table: Perspectives on Culinary History*. New York: Columbia University Press, 2001–12.

Spieldoch, Alexandra. *A Row to Hoe: The Gender Impact of Trade Liberalization on Our Food System, Agricultural Markets and Women's Human Rights*, ed. International Gender and Trade Network. Geneva: Friedrich-Ebert-Stiftung, 2007.

Squier, Susan. "Chicken Auguries." *Configurations* 14, nos. 1–2 (2008): 69–86.

Stempel, Daniel. "History Electrified into Analogy: A Reading of *Waiting for Godot*." *Contemporary Literature* 17, no. 2 (1976): 263–78.
Stevens, Wallace. *The Collected Poems of Wallace Stevens*. New York: Vintage, 1990.
Stout, Janis P. "The Making of Willa Cather's *One of Ours*: The Role of Dorothy Canfield Fisher." *War, Literature and the Arts* 11, no. 2 (1999): 48–59.
——— "Response to Richard C. Harris's 'Getting Claude "Over There": Sources for Book Four of Cather's *One of Ours*.'" *Journal of Narrative Theory* 35, no. 2 (2005): 259–62.
Sturman, Sally Mara, and Susan Mitchell. "Cover Design." In *One of Ours*, Dust jacket. New York: Vintage Books, 1991.
Szalay, Michael. *New Deal Modernism: American Literature and the Invention of the Welfare State*. London and Durham: Duke University Press, 2000.
Sze, Julie. "Boundaries and Border Wars: DES, Technology, and Environmental Justice." *American Quarterly* 58, no. 3 (2006): 791–814.
Tansey, Geoff, and Joyce D'Silva, eds. *The Meat Business: Devouring a Hungry Planet*. London: Earthscan Publications, 1999.
Taylor, Julie. "'The Voice of the Prophet': From Astrological Quackery to Sexological Authority in Djuna Barnes's *Ladies Almanack*." *Modern Fiction Studies* 55, no. 4 (2009): 716–38.
Thacker, Robert. "Journalist and Teacher, Writer and Poet, 1895–1912." The Willa Cather Foundation, www.willacather.org/about-willa-cather/.
Tichi, Cecelia. "Exposés and Excess." Review of *Fast Food Nation: The Dark Side of the All-American Meal* by Eric Schlosser. *American Literary History* 15, no. 4 (2003): 822–29.
——— *Exposés and Excess: Muckraking in America, 1900/2000*. Philadelphia: University of Pennsylvania Press, 2003.
——— "Novels of Civic Protest." In Cassuto et al., *The Cambridge History of the American Novel*, 393–408.
Tokar, Brian. "Monsanto: A Checkered History." *The Ecologist* (1998). www.mindfully.org/Industry/Monsanto-Checkered-HistoryOct98.htm.
Trout, Steven. "From 'The Namesake' to *One of Ours*: Willa Cather on War." *American Literary Realism* 37, no. 2 (2005): 117–40.
——— *Memorial Fictions: Willa Cather and the First World War*. Lincoln: University of Nebraska Press, 2002.
Turner, Anissa. "Rum Trade: From Slavery to the Present (Case Number 384)." *The TED Case Studies* (1997). www1.american.edu/ted/rum.htm.
Turner, Frederick Jackson. *The Frontier in American History*. New York: H. Holt and Company, 1920.
United Nations. "The Millennium Development Goals Report." New York: United Nations, 2010. www.un.org/millenniumgoals/pdf/MDG%20Report%202010%20En%20r15%20-low%20res%2020100615%20-.pdf.
——— "Millennium Project." www.unmillenniumproject.org/goals/gti.htm.
Urgo, Joseph R. *Willa Cather and the Myth of American Migration*. Chicago and Urbana: University of Illinois Press, 1995.

USDA. "Farm Income and Costs: Assets, Debt, and Wealth." Washington, D.C.: U.S. Department of Agriculture, 2011. www.ers.usda.gov/topics/farm-economy/farm-sector-income-finances.aspx.

"Loss-Adjusted Food Availability." Washington, D.C.: U.S. Department of Agriculture. www.ers.usda.gov/Data/FoodConsumption/FoodGuideIndex.htm-calories.

"2007 Census of Agriculture." 1–4. Washington, D.C.: U.S. Department of Agriculture, www.agcensus.usda.gov/index.php.

U.S. Meat Export Federation. "International Markets: Japan." 2008. www.usmef.org/.

Van Esterik, Penny. "The Politics of Breastfeeding: An Advocacy Update." In Counihan and Van Esterik, *Food and Culture*, 467–81.

Veblen, Thorstein. *Theory of the Leisure Class*. New York: Penguin Books, 1994. 1899.

Virgil. *Georgics*. Translated by Janet Lembke. London and New Haven: Yale University Press, 2005.

Wahl, Thomas I., Dermot J. Hayes, and Gary W. Williams. "Dynamic Adjustment in Japanese Livestock Industry under Beef Import Liberalization." *American Journal of Agricultural Economics* 73, no. 1 (1991): 118–32.

Walcott, Derek. "Café Martinique: A Story." In *What the Twilight Says: Essays*, 234–45. New York: Farrar, Straus and Giroux, 1998.

Wallace, Molly. "Discomfort Food: Analogy, Biotechnology, and Risk in Ruth Ozeki's *All Over Creation*." *Arizona Quarterly* 67, no. 4 (2011): 155–81.

Wallerstein, Immanuel. *The Modern World System: Capitalist Agriculture and the Origins of the European World Economy in the Sixteenth Century*. New York: Academic Press, 1974.

Wardi, Anissa Janine. "Wetlands, Swamps, and Bayous: Bodies of Resistance in Kasi Lemmons's Eve's Bayou and Toni Morrison's Tar Baby." In *Water and African American Memory: An Ecocritical Perspective*, 83–114. Gainesville: University Press of Florida, 2011.

Warman, Arturo. *Corn and Capitalism: How a Botanical Bastard Grew to Global Dominance*. Chapel Hill: University of North Carolina Press, 2003.

Warnes, Andrew. *Hunger Overcome?: Food and Resistance in Twentieth-Century African American Literature*. London and Athens, GA: University of Georgia Press, 2004.

Watrous, Malena. "Interview with Ruth Ozeki: 'Vegetables Are Filled with Drama. Even the Pea.'" *The Believer* 5, no. 2 (2007): 80–86.

Weigel, Richard D. "Valerian (A.D. 253–60) and Gaillienus (A.D. 253–268)." *De Imperatoribus Romanis: An Online Encyclopedia of Roman Emperors*, www.roman-emperors.org/gallval.htm.

Westling, Louise H. *The Green Breast of the New World: Landscape, Gender, and American Fiction*. London and Athens, GA: University of Georgia Press, 1996.

Weyland, Kurt. "Neoliberalism and Democracy in Latin America: A Mixed Record." *Latin American Politics and Society* 46, no. 1 (2004): 135–57.

Whitman, Walt. "Pioneers, O Pioneers." In *The Complete Poems*, edited by Francis Murphey, 257–61. New York: Penguin Books, 1975.

Whoriskey, Peter. "Monsanto's Dominance Draws Antitrust Inquiry." *The Washington Post*, November 29, 2009.

Wiley, James. "Dominica's Economic Diversification: Microstates in a Neoliberal Era?" In Klak, *Globalization and Neoliberalism*, 155–77.

Wilkins, Jennifer. "Think Globally, Eat Locally." *The New York Times*, December 18, 2004.

Williams, Ian. "The Secret History of Rum." *The Nation*, December 5, 2005.

Williams, Raymond. *The Country and the City*. Oxford and New York: Oxford University Press, 1973.

—— *Marxism and Literature*. Oxford and New York: Oxford University Press, 1978.

Williams, Terry Tempest. *Refuge: An Unnatural History of Family and Place*. New York: Vintage, 1992.

Willis, Elizabeth. "The Poetics of Affinity: Lorine Niedecker, William Morris, and the Art of Work." *Contemporary Literature* 46, no. 4 (2005): 579–603.

—— "Possessing Possession: Lorine Niedecker, Folk, and the Allegory of Making." *XCP: Cross-Cultural Poetics* 9 (2001). http://wings.buffalo.edu/epc/authors/niedecker/willi.html.

—— ed. *Radical Vernacular: Lorine Niedecker and the Poetics of Place*. Contemporary North American Poetry Series. Iowa City: University of Iowa Press, 2008.

Wilson, Duff. *Fateful Harvest: The True Story of a Small Town, a Global Industry, and a Toxic Secret*. New York: Harper Collins Publishers, 2001.

Winston, Mark L. *Nature Wars: People vs. Pests*. Cambridge, MA: Harvard University Press, 1997.

Witt, Doris. *Black Hunger: Soul Food and America*. London and Minneapolis: University of Minnesota Press, 2004.

Wolfe, Cary. *What Is Posthumanism? Posthumanities*. Minneapolis: University of Minnesota Press, 2010.

Wood, James. "Tell Me How Does It Feel?" *The Guardian UK*, October 5, 2001.

Woodress, James. "Historical Essay." In Cather, *My Ántonia*, 369–402.

Woolf, Aaron. "King Corn." 88 min.: ITVS and Mosaic Films, 2007.

Young, James Harvey. *Pure Food: Securing the Federal Food and Drugs Act of 1906*. Princeton: Princeton University Press, 1989.

Zimmerman, Anne. *An Extravagant Hunger: The Passionate Years of M. F. K. Fisher*. Berkeley: Counterpoint, 2011.

Zweiniger-Bargielowska, Ina. *Austerity in Britain: Rationing, Controls, and Consumption, 1939–1955*. Oxford and New York: Oxford University Press, 2000.

# *Index*

Page numbers in *italics* indicate illustrations; page numbers with 'n' refer to notes in the text.

abundance rhetoric: juxtaposed with hunger by Niedecker, 10, 54–59; satirized in "Still Life #30," *2*, *3*; and U.S. rationing program, 61, 64
Adamson, Joni, 151
Adorno, Theodor, 84–85
advertising, *see* marketing discourse
agribusiness: and capitalism, 18, 56, 158; and Cather's fiction, 9–10, 20–21, 44–46, 166, 175n12; compared to reproductive medicine in *My Year of Meats*, 119–20, 139–41; historical emergence of, 1, 44–45; and intellectual property, 15, 118, 127, 173n47; locavore resistance to, 154–55; marketing rhetoric, 13–16; and militarized food systems, 12–13; and modernity, 1, 157, 165; and Ozeki's fiction, 120, 129, 139–40, 146–47, 153, 201n12; relationship to weapons production, 12–13; reliance on information networks, 124; term origin, 1, 44; war as profit center for, 56; and World War II propaganda, 10; *see also* industrial agriculture
agricultural production: promoted by World War I propaganda, 46; U.S. government support of, 157, 209n18; World War II gains in, 10, 59, 184n45; *see also* food production
agricultural settlement: correlated with military conquest, 19; and nativist ideology, 28
agriculture: community supported (CSA), 4; compared to communication media, 123–27; and information technology in *All Over Creation*, 117–18; military technology repurposed for, 12–13, 32, 40–43, 46, 157; in postindustrial society, 1, 48, 117, 148; technology as vital to, 2; U.S. government support of, 157, 209n18; war allied with, 35, 36, 59
Alaimo, Stacy, 139

Alexandra Bergson (*O Pioneers* character): attachment to place, 23, 28–29, 32; as capitalist-farmer, 22–25; and gender roles, 22, 23–25, 32; *see also O Pioneers*
*All Over Creation* (Ruth Ozeki): as almanac, 151–52; analogies of agriculture and communication media, 123–27; analogies of people and plants, 119–21, 201n12; and computerized farming, 2, 117–18; hybrid form of, 150, 152; information trope in, 122–24, 151–52; as muckraking novel, 11; *see also My Year of Meats*; Ozeki, Ruth
almanacs: and bioart, 152; concept of, 151; and locavore memoir, 152; and Ozeki's fiction, 151–53; and realist narratives, 9, 152
*Alternative Food Networks* (Goodman et al.), 161
Ambruster, Karla, 106
*American Beef Cooking* (Yu Hayami), 148
"The American Century," 6, 12
Anderson, Katherine, 151
*An Extravagant Hunger* (Anne Zimmerman), 68
*Animal Factories* (Peter Singer and Jim Mason), 131
*Animal Farm* (George Orwell), 50
*Animal, Vegetable, Miracle* (Barbara Kingsolver): and agriculture/military connection, 157; nostalgia for the preindustrial, 152, 157
Ántonia Shimerda (*My Ántonia* character): as anti-modernization symbol, 26; as earth mother figure, 32; *see also My Ántonia*
Appadurai, Arjun, 7, 113
Artists for Victory, 62

balanced diet, *see* standardized diet
Barthes, Roland, 4, 8–9
Beckett, Samuel: and food power, 12; and politicized form of modernism, 10; *Waiting for Godot*, 82–89

Beck, Ulrich, 7, 126
beef trade, *see* meat industry
Belasco, Warren: as food studies scholar, 8; on future of agriculture, 2; on futuristic kitchens, 71; on government nutrition rhetoric, 55; on New Nutrition, 43; "recombinant culture," 15; on the supermarket, 94–95
Bell, Daniel, 7
Benjamin, Walter, 114–15
Bennett, Jane, 101, 120
Bentley, Amy, 8, 62
Berry, Wendell: and ethical eating, 208n7, 209n19; and pastoral tradition, 8; "The Pleasures of Eating," 9, 209n19; *The Unsettling of America*, 30
bioart, 152–53
biotechnology: and DES, 128, 136–41; and GMOs, 15–16, 124; *see also* GMOs; technology
Bixler, Barron, photographs, *13*, *130*
*A Book of Mediterranean Food* (Elizabeth David): luxury feeding vs. hunger in, 50, 89; as response to British austerity policy, 79–82; transnational gastronomy in, 80–81
Borlaug, Norman, 12
Bourdieu, Pierre: concept of habitus, 94–96, 187n82; concept of taste and M.F.K. Fisher, 66–67; and supermarket scene in *Tar Baby*, 94, 96
bovine spongiform encephalopathy (BSE), and Japan's beef ban, 142, 145
Braudel, Fernand, 193n7
Brillat-Savarin, Jean Anthelme, *The Physiology of Taste*, 65, 166
Buell, Lawrence, 139

capitalism, *see* late capitalism
capitalized farm: in "Nebraska: The End of a Cycle," 26; in *One of Ours*, 45, 48, 56; in *O Pioneers*, 22–25
"capitalized kitchen," 70–71, 188n92
Carney, Judith, 103
Carpenter, Novella: on her locavore experiment, 154; *see also Farm City: The Education of an Urban Farmer*
Carpentier, Alejo, 97
Carson, Rachel, 14
Castells, Manuel, 16, 124, 160
Cather, Willa: agribusiness anticipated by, 30, 166; and attachment to place, 23, 28–29, 177n25; concern about commodity crops, 44; concern with standardization of dietary practices, 43, 179n73; critical appraisal of, 8, 20, 22; critique of muckraking writers, 21–22, 148; and gender roles, 22, 23–25, 32, 43, 178n49; and industrialization of family farms, 9–10, 20–21, 22–25, 30–31, 43–46; as journalist/editor, 21–22; and nativism, 20, 23, 28, 30, 175n9; "Nebraska: The End of a Cycle," 26; "The Novel Démeublé," 21; and postindustrial pastoral, 48; *The Professor's House*, 28; and rural modernity, 9–10, 20, 22–23; "The Bohemian Girl," 27; and U.S. expansionism, 10; and yeoman farmer trope, 30–31; *see also My Ántonia; One of Ours; O Pioneers*
Cella, Matthew, 23, 28, 177n25
Center for Genomic Gastronomy: "Edible: The Taste of Things to Come" exhibit, 1, 4–5, 154, 164; redefinition of preindustrial agriculture, 163–64
Césaire, Aimé, 102
Chamoiseau, Patrick, *Chronique de sept misères*, 100
Chiu, Monica: on Buddhism and meat eating, 142, 143; comparison of *The Jungle* to *My Year of Meats*, 204n49; on use of metaphor in *My Year of Meats*, 138, 148–49
chocolate: and child labor, 107, 116; as emblem of childhood, 47; as exoticized food, 7, 116, 158; as global commodity, 112; and Hershey, 73–74, 188n102; and locavores, 158, 163; in *One of Ours*, 47; in *Tar Baby*, 106–8, 112, 116
chronotope: of Caribbean in *Tar Baby*, 111; concept of, 198n74; of rubble in *One of Ours*, 39
Cilano, Cara, 102
Claude Wheeler (*One of Ours* character): attitude toward women's work, 32; aversion to mechanization, 42–44; critique of industrial agriculture, 45; pastoral vision, 32–34, 37–39; pastoral vision disrupted, 46–47; significance of barbed wire accident, 41–44; and war as heroic adventure, 33–36; and war as refuge from rural modernity, 32, 33, 38, 44; *see also One of Ours*
climate change: and factory farms, 11, 157; and methane emissions associated with agriculture, 11, 157, 203n45, 209n112
cocoa, *see* chocolate
Coe, Sophie and Michael, 107–8
Coe, Sue: "Battery Cage," 124, *125*; *Dead Meat*, 131; "Elephants We Must Never Forget" exhibition, 132; "Feed Lot," 132, *133*; *Porkopolis*, 124, *125*, 128, 132; "Veal Skinner," 132, *134*
Cold War: abundance rhetoric, 2; and global food market, 6, 64, 145, 147; "Kitchen Debate" and GE demonstration kitchen, 71; and

Cold War (cont.)
militarized food systems, 11–13, 89, 119, 139; and supermarket, 94, 155, 194n22; and *Tar Baby*'s narrative of the Caribbean, 104, 115
colonialism, *see* imperialism
Columbus: power correlated with agricultural resources by, 103–4; sugarcane introduced to Caribbean by, 103; *Voyages*, 12
*Coming Home to Eat* (Gary Paul Nabhan): foodshed concept in, 155–56; as locavore memoir, 18; as protest of agribusiness, 18, 121, 154–55
commodity crops: Cather's concern about, 44; impact on food access in *Tar Baby*, 113; linked with food shortages in *How to Cook a Wolf*, 77; and war profiteering, 48; and World War I, 44–45; *see also* monoculture
commodity fetishism: as marketing strategy, 101–2; and Marx, Karl, 7
community supported agriculture (CSA), 4
computerized farming, *see* information technology
concentrated animal feeding operation (CAFO), *see* feedlots
Conlogue, William: on Alexandra Bergson (Cather character), 23; on industrial agriculture, 30, 117
consumerism: and farmers in Cather's fiction, 26, 42–43, 45; juxtaposed with war-related famine in *How to Cook a Wolf*, 73–75; and kitchen technology, 70–72; meat system as emblematic in *My Year of Meats*, 149; and neoliberalism in *Tar Baby*, 102, 111–13, 115; and New Deal policy, 60, 185n50; and "rummaging" in *Waiting for Godot*, 87; and rural modernity, 20
convenience foods, *see* processed foods
cookbooks: *American Beef Cooking* (Yu Hayami), 148; *A Book of Mediterranean Cooking* (Elizabeth David), 10, 50, 79–82; *How to Cook a Wolf* (M.F.K. Fisher), 50, 68–78; and literature of food, 6; mid-century cookbooks, 72, 95, 187n87
Coolidge, Calvin, "Address to Farm Bureau Federation" (1925), 1, 4, 5, 10, 18, 19, 158
countercuisine, 4, 158
"creative economy" (M.F.K. Fisher), 69–71
de Crèvecoeur, St. John, *Letters from an American Farmer*, 29–30
Critical Art Ensemble, 152–53
*The Crying of Lot* (Thomas Pynchon), 17–18
culinary cosmopolitanism: and "Edible: The Taste of Things to Come," 1, 4–5, 164; and globalization, 5; and imperialism, 65; and locavore movement, 158; Massimo Montanari on, 6, 160; and supermarket scene in *Tar Baby*, 94–96, 158; and *The Omnivore's Dilemma*, 158
Cwiertka, Katarzyna, 143

David, Elizabeth: *A Book of Mediterranean Cooking*, 10, 50, 79–82; use of modernist modes, 50, 80–81
Davis, Elmer, 49, 60–61
DDT, 59
*Dead Meat* (Sue Coe), 131
DeLillo, Don, 128, 149–50
DeLoughrey, Elizabeth, 91–92, 102–3
Denfeld, Zack, 154, 164
DES (diethylstilbestrol): effects of, 205n63, 206n68; and *My Year of Meats*, 128–29, 136–41
Deutsch, Tracey, 55–56
diaspora, as *Tar Baby* theme, 11, 91, 95, 99, 109, 116
*Distinction* (Pierre Bourdieu), 67
diversity: biodiversity and cultural diversity in Ozeki's fiction, 118, 120–21, 127, 201n12; and culinary traditions, 12, 43; and monoculture farming, 5, 77, 160
Douglass, Mary, 8–9
DuPlessis, Rachel Blau, 51
DuPuis, E. Melanie, *see* Goodman et al.
Durrell, Lawrence, 80

*Eating Animals* (Jonathan Safran Foer), 124–26
eating out, 64–65, 70, 143
"Edible; The Taste of Things to Come" (Center for Genomic Gastronomy 2012 exhibit), 1, 4–5, 154, 164
Eisenhower, Dwight D., 13, 50
"Electrified Farm" (New York World's Fair exhibit), 2, *3*
"Elephants We Must Never Forget" exhibition (Sue Coe), 132
empire, *see* imperialism
Empson, William, 142, 203n73
environmental criticism, 7, 92, 102, 171n23, 174n54
environmental justice: activism, 136, 155, 160; and postcolonialism, 103
environmental nonfiction, 152, 155
environmental organizations: critique of industrial agriculture, 4, 11; opposition to GMOs, 4, 16, 124
ethical eating, 158, 208n7, 209n19
ethnic cuisine: soul food, 91, 103; stereotypes about, 95

factory farms: and climate change, 11; correlated with obstetrics in *My Year of Meats*, 119–20, 139–40; and *Eating Animals* (Jonathan

factory farms (cont.)
  Safran Foer), 124–26; and *Fast Food Nation* (Eric Schlosser), 132–36; feedlot exposés, 131–36; methane emissions, 11, 157, 203n45, 209n12; and "Milking Parlor, California 2007" (Barron Bixler), *130*; and *Porkopolis* (Sue Coe), 124, *125*, 128, 132; *see also* feedlots
fair trade, 116, 165
famine: Bengali famine, 79; and Green Revolution, 12; in M.F.K. Fisher's works, 65, 73, 77–78, 166; in Niedecker's poetry, 58, 89; in *Waiting for Godot*, 83, 88; and World War II, 45, 75, 79, 189n108, 190n113; *see also* Irish Potato Famine
*Farm City: The Education of an Urban Farmer* (Novella Carpenter): challenges of urban farming in, 160–61, 164; foodshed concept in, 162; georgic mode in, 164; reliance on networks in, 18, 163–64; supermarket valued in, 154, 162–63; as unconventional locavore memoir, 161
*The Farmer's Almanac*, 151
farming: as an enterprise in food system, 1, 48; industrialization of in Cather's fiction, 9–10, 20–21, 22–25, 30–31, 41–46; reliance on information technology, 2, 16–17, 117–19, 122–26, 151–52; *see also* agriculture; factory farms; food production; industrial agriculture; urban farming
*Fast Food Nation* (Eric Schlosser): consumer health concerns in reception of, 133–34; critique of factory farms, 132–36; narrative structure, 135–36; slaughterhouse in, 135
Faulkner, William, 21
feedlot exposés, *124*, 130–39, *130*, *133*, *134*, 149–50
feedlots, 75, 124, 128, 130, 141; *see also* factory farms
feminism: and Ozeki's fiction, 11, 119–20; *see also* gender; women
fine dining, *see* luxury feeding
Fischer, Mike: on Cather's nativism, 20, 175n9; on pioneers and U.S. imperialism, 28
Fisher, Dorothy Canfield, 45
Fisher, M.F.K.: ambivalence toward gourmet eating, 65–66; *The Gastronomical Me*, 65–68; integration of eating practices with geopolitics, 10; modernist modes applied to cookbooks by, 50; *see also How to Cook a Wolf*
Fleissner, Jennifer, and food studies, 9
Foer, Jonathan Safran: *Eating Animals*, 124–26; and georgic mode, 12
food: and biotechnology, 16; as complex chain of activities, 9; and cultural capital, 66, 96; as dialectical, 167–68; equated with weaponry in World War I propaganda, 46; linked with national security, 49, 50, 159; as multivalent concept, 4; networked structure of, 16–17; politicization of in mid-century literature, 50–51; structuralist theories of, 8–9; war allied with, 13
food access: as focus of food justice movement, 90; impact of commodity crops on in *Tar Baby*, 113; impact of supermarket on, 25; and social class in M.F.K. Fisher's works, 66–67, 72, 76–77; and social class in Niedecker's poetry, 49, 50, 56–59, 85; and social class in postwar U.K., 78–79; and social class in *Waiting for Godot*, 85–88; and the supermarket in *Farm City*, 162–63
food aid programs: and Marshall Plan, 78; and postwar British austerity policy, 78; U.S. export market expanded by, 44–45, 64
food consumption: interdependencies with food production, 9, 168; separated from production through globalization processes, 7; *see also* cookbooks; counter-cuisine; culinary cosmopolitanism; eating out; ethnic cuisine; luxury feeding; supermarket
*Food, Inc.* (film), 156
food insecurity: documented by OWI, 62; and reliance on agricultural imports, 90, 192nn2, 3; *see also* famine; hunger
food justice movements: and child labor, 116; food access as focus of, 90; and globalization theory, 7–8; and locavore movement, 160; and *Tar Baby*, 10, 116
food-mile construct, 159, 210n28; *see also* locavore memoir; slow food/locavore movement
food power: as indicator of global power, 4, 10; linked with imperialism in *Tar Baby*, 11, 109, 111, 115–16; origins in U.S. agricultural discourse, 6; role of information management in, 117–18; symbolized in *Waiting for Godot*, 12; transnational social movements as response to, 4; and U.S./Japanese conflicts over meat, 143–45; *see also* U.S. food power
food production: and feedlot exposés, 130–36; and GMOs, 15–16, 124; interdependencies with food consumption, 9, 168; military technology repurposed for, 32, 40–43, 46, 157; and postindustrial pastoral, 17; separated from consumption through globalization processes, 7; *see also* agricultural production; agriculture; factory farms; farming; industrial agriculture; urban farming
food routes: and imperialism/neoliberalism link in *Tar Baby*, 90, 102, 111–15; and nature/culture schism in Caribbean postcolonial literature, 102–3; significance in postcolonial

food routes (cont.)
  environmental criticism, 103; transpacific mapping of in *My Year of Meats*, 118; and transplantation of New World foods, 103
food security: and Caribbean kitchen gardens, 103, 197n54; price shocks (2006–2008), 90, 192n3; and the supermarket in *Farm City*, 162–63; and "victory gardens," 4, 159
foodshed: concept of in *Coming Home to Eat*, 155–56; concept of in *Farm City*, 162
food shortages: influence on Elizabeth David, 80; linked with commodity crops in *How to Cook a Wolf*, 77; and M.F.K. Fisher, 65, 68; uneven impacts of during World War II, 78–79; and *Waiting for Godot*, 86–88; *see also* famine; food insecurity; hunger
food studies: cuisine/agriculture division in, 2, 8–9, 169n5; as interdisciplinary field, 165; literature as germane to, 9, 166–67; scholarship trends in, 8–9, 165–66
food system: and Coolidge's rhetoric, 1–2; farming as an enterprise in, 1, 48; and late capitalism, 21; and literature as analytic tool, 5–8; militarization of, 12–13, *13*; and modernity, 4, 9, 92; in national imaginary, 1–2, 5; as networked, 16–17, 124–26; and power, 4; surplus/hunger paradox in, 4, 170n11
foodways: in *Coming Home to Eat*, 156; concept of, 9, 121; in *Tar Baby*, 92, 102, 114, 116
food writing, *see* literature of food
*Forks over Knives* (film), 156
*For Paul and Other Poems* (Lorine Niedecker), 51–52
François, Anne-Lise, 16, 126
"Free Range Grain" (Critical Art Ensemble), 152–53
free trade: critique of in *Tar Baby*, 10–11, 102, 113, 115; and gender, 118–19, 139; and globalization, 6–7, 104, 139; and meat industry, 145; *see also* globalization; late capitalism; neoliberalism
Fussell, Paul, on war narratives, 34, 38, 179n69

Galbraith, John Kenneth, 60
*The Gastronomical Me* (M.F.K. Fisher), 65–68
Gaud, William, 12
gender: and factory farms, 135; and food writing, 8; and globalization theory, 138–39; *see also* feminism; women
gender roles: and Cather's fiction, 22, 32, 43, 178n49; in *One of Ours*, 43; in *O Pioneers*, 22, 23–25, 32; and World War I propaganda, 35, 37
genetically modified organisms (GMOs), *see* GMOs (genetically modified organisms)
georgic mode: in Cather's fiction, 20–21; in contemporary food rhetoric, 12, 20; in *Farm City*, 164; in feedlot exposés, 12; and Monsanto marketing rhetoric, 13–16; in *One of Ours*, 46–47; and realist narratives, 9
*Georgics* (Virgil), 15, 27, 28, 46, 180n82
Giddens, Anthony, 6, 37, 117
Gifford, Terry, 9
Gigante, Denise, 8, 165
Gilroy, Paul, 91–92
Ginsberg, Allen, "A Supermarket in California," 17
Glissant, Édouard, 12, 102–3, 197n60
globalization: and 1999 WTO Seattle protests, 155–56; concept of, 6–8, 16–17, 202n26; and culinary cosmopolitanism, 5; as enabling connections, 7–8, 16–17; and environmental criticism, 7–8, 171n23; and food aid programs, 44–45; and food system, 5–6, 8–9, 24–25, 145, 167; and gender, 138–39; impact on women in *Tar Baby* and *My Year of Meats*, 138–39; linked with hunger in *How to Cook a Wolf*, 77; and localism, 7–8, 18, 160, 201n12; and locavore movement, 122, 152, 154, 158, 160, 163; and networks, 8, 16–18, 160; as separating places of production and consumption, 7; and slow food movement, 120; *Tar Baby* as critique of, 94, 107–8, 115–16; *see also* free trade; late capitalism; neoliberalism
GMOs (genetically modified organisms): and "Free Range Grain" (Critical Art Ensemble), 152–53; and Monsanto, 15–16, 124, 172n39; and U.S. food power, 4
Goldsmith, Kenneth, 150–51
Goodman et al., *Alternative Food Networks*, 159, 161, 202n23
gourmet dining, *see* luxury feeding
Goyal, Yogita, 91
Great Depression, 60, 181n9
Green Revolution, 12–13, 14, 89
grocery stores, *see* supermarket
Guthman, Julie: on "industrial eating," 158–59; on the supermarket, 211n36

Handley, George, 102–3
Harris, Richard C., 32–33
*Harvard Business Review*, 1, 44
Harvey, David, 7, 113
haute cuisine, *see* luxury feeding
Hawthorne, Nathaniel, 17
Hayami, Yu, *American Beef Cooking*, 148
Hayles, N. Katherine, 126
heirloom crops, 121
Heise, Ursula K.: on globalization, 7; on Ozeki's use of analogies, 119, 121, 201n12
Hemingway, Ernest, criticism of *One of Ours*, 32, 43

heritage animal breeds, 121
Hershey Company, 73–74, 74, 107–8, 188n102
*Hoard's Dairyman*: agricultural technology promoted by, 54, 75, 183n29; Niedecker as copyeditor for, 52, 54
home economics, and New Nutrition, 43
"Home Front Pledge," 62–63
Homestead Act (1862), 19, 23
*How to Cook a Wolf* (M.F.K. Fisher): "capitalized kitchen" criticized in, 70–71; consumerism juxtaposed with war and famine in, 73–75, 89; "creative economy," 69–71; critique of standardized diet in, 69–72, 76–77; integration of eating practices with geopolitics, 68–78; loss of regional cuisine in, 76–77; luxury feeding vs. hunger in, 50, 72–73; meanings of hunger in, 76; as modernist cookbook, 68, 71–72, 77–78; processed foods satirized in, 73–75, 77
*How We Became Human* (N. Katherine Hayles), 126
Hsu, Hsuan, 6
Huggan, Graham, 102
hunger: and food rhetoric, 10; juxtaposed with consumerism in *How to Cook a Wolf*, 73–75, 89; meanings of in M.F.K. Fisher's works, 66–67, 76; as outcome of Caribbean monoculture farming, 103; as theme in *Tar Baby*, 93; as theme in *Waiting for Godot*, 10, 83–84, 86–89; *see also* famine; food access; food insecurity; food justice; food shortages
*Hunger Overcome?* (Andrew Warnes), 91

idyllic mode: in *Letters from an American Farmer* (St. John de Crèvecoeur), 30; in pastoral tradition, 20
imperialism: and Columbus, 103–4; and culinary cosmopolitanism, 65; embedded in *Tar Baby* landscape, 105; and food writing, 10; neoliberalism linked to in *Tar Baby*, 10–11, 90, 102, 106–8, 111–15; pioneer, 20, 175n9; and U.S. power, 6
imperialism, British: and *A Book of Mediterranean Food*, 80–81; food control and rationing as vital to, 79
*In Defense of Food* (Michael Pollan), 156
industrial agriculture: Calvin Coolidge on, 1, 4, 5, 10, 18, 19, 158; depicted in *How to Cook a Wolf*, 75; and early muckrakers, 6; environmentalist critique of, 4; family farms shift to in Cather's fiction, 9–10, 20–21, 22–25, 30–31; immigrant farmers decoupled from in *My Ántonia*, 27–28; and information technology, 117–18; and methane emissions, 11, 157, 203n45, 209n12; and migrant workers in *My Year of Meats*, 140; modernist veneration of, 12–13; World War I impact on, 32, 47; *see also* agribusiness; agriculture; factory farms; farming; feedlots; food production; monoculture
"industrial eating," 157–58, 158–59, 209n19
information management, *see* information technology
information networks, *see* information technology
information technology: and almanacs, 151; and bioart, 152–53; Carpenter's reliance on in *Farm City*, 163–64; and food system, 16–17, 124–26; and Ozeki's fiction, 2, 117–19, 122–24, 150–53; and postindustrial society, 117–18; concern in contemporary food literature, 124–26, 150–51
Intergovernmental Panel on Climate Change (IPCC), 157
International Monetary Fund (IMF), 99, 113
"In the great snowfall before the bomb" (Lorine Niedecker), 52–56
Irish Potato Famine, 77, 83

James, Henry, 21
Jameson, Fredric: on modernism, 80–81, 113; on *Waiting for Godot*, 82, 84
Japan: conflicts with U.S. over meat, 142, 144–45; decline of food power, 145; as food importer, 143–45; meat consumption in, 143–45; as target of "Desire Beef" campaign, 147–48; U.S. postwar occupation of, 143–45
Jefferson, Thomas, and pastoral tradition, 1, 20, 25–26, 169n3
Jim Burden (*My Ántonia* character): image of American Midwest social structure, 28–29; implicated in modernization, 30–31; response to the prairie landscape, 29, 32, *see also My Ántonia*
Judt, Tony, 78, 79
*The Jungle* (Upton Sinclair), 11, 21, 41, 129–30, 132, 134

Kennedy, Scott Hamilton, documentary on urban farming, 164
Kingsolver, Barbara: *Animal, Vegetable, Miracle*, 152, 157; and slow food, 121
kitchen gardens, and food security, 103, 197n54
kitchen technologies, and the "capitalized kitchen," 70–71, 188n92
Koerner, Henry, 62
Kramer, Cathrine, 154, 164
Krumholz, Linda, 91, 96, 111

Langston, Nancy, 141
late capitalism: concept of, 7, 113; critique of in *Tar Baby*, 107–8, 113; depiction of in Ozeki's fiction, 11, 128, 142; and food system, 21; and modernism, 88; *see also* free trade; globalization; neoliberalism
*Letters from an American Farmer* (St. John de Crèvecoeur), 29–30
Levenstein, Harvey: as food studies scholar, 8; on New Nutrition and interwar nutrition rhetoric, 43, 55; on wartime meat consumption, 74
Levi, Primo, 73
Lévi-Strauss, Claude: and bricolage, 70; structuralist theories of food, 8–9
Lewis, Sinclair, on *One of Ours*, 32
literature of food: cuisine/agriculture division in, 9; and food writing, 8, 68, 166; genres included in, 6, 8; and globalization theory, 6–8, 18; importance of, 166–68; new cultural templates in, 9; transnational contexts for, 11–12; vision of networked postindustrial society, 8, 16
Liu, Alan, 118
locavore memoir: and *Animal, Vegetable, Miracle*, 121, 152, 157; and *Coming Home to Eat*, 18, 121, 154–56; concept of foodshed in, 155–56, 158, 162; as contemporary genre, 18, 156–58; and *Farm City*, 18, 154, 161–65; and nostalgia for the preindustrial, 152, 157; and *The Omnivore's Dilemma*, 17, 156, 157–58; preindustrial food histories neglected in, 159–60; systemic inequities overlooked in, 158–59; *see also* slow food/locavore movement
locavore movement, *see* slow food/locavore movement
Luce, Henry, 6
luxury feeding: as a theme in *Waiting for Godot*, 50, 86–89; during World War II, 64–65; George Orwell on, 50, 64–65; M.F.K. Fisher's ambivalence toward, 65–66; and the supermarket in *Tar Baby*, 10, 17, 94–96; vs. hunger in *A Book of Mediterranean Food*, 50, 89; vs. hunger in *How to Cook a Wolf*, 50, 72–73

MacArthur, Douglas, 143
mad-cow disease, and Japan's beef ban, 142, 145
magical realism: and Alejo Carpentier, 97; and *Chronique de sept misères* (Patrick Chamoiseau), 100; mixed with social realism in *Tar Baby*, 95–98, 104–5, 111, 113–15
"magicorealism," 98

*Make Bright the Arrow* (Edna St. Vincent Millay), 50
malnourishment, *see* hunger
marketing discourse: aligned with government propaganda, 56, 58; commodity fetishism in, 101–2; consumer goods as instruments of strength in, 55–56, 58; image of women in, 56, 58
Márquez, Gabriel García, 97
Marshall Plan, 78
Marx, Karl: and commodity fetishism, 7; labor theory of value, 113
Marx, Leo: and food studies, 9; on pastoral tradition, 16–17, 20, 44, 173n53
McGurl, Mark: on modernist novelists, 21, 22; on the new managerial class, 22, 27; on "pastoral intellection," 27; on "posthuman sentimental" fictions, 137
McHugh, Susan, 121–22, 124
McLean, Alice: on Elizabeth David, 80; on M.F.K. Fisher, 66, 68; on World War II food rhetoric, 49
McLuhan, Marshall, 129
McWilliams, James: on Caribbean kitchen gardens, 197n54; on food-mile construct, 159, 210n28; on sugarcane transplantation in Caribbean, 103
meat-and-grain diet: satirized in *My Year of Meats*, 11; U.S. government promotion of in Japan, 142, 144
meat consumption: in Japan, 143–45; in U.S., 74–75, 147, 189n108; in U.S. vs. U.K., 78
meat industry: and early muckrakers, 11, 21, 41, 129–30; and feedlot exposés, 130–36; and Japanese market, 207n88; and meatpacking companies, 205n57; *see also* feedlots; meat consumption; *My Year of Meats*
Mencken, H.L., criticism of *One of Ours*, 32
Meyer, Susan, 43
Michaels, Walter Benn, 28
military-industrial complex: articulated in *One of Ours*, 46–48; and Eisenhower, 13, 50; and literature of food, 50; and meat consumption, 75; *My Year of Meats* allusions to, 146–47; and World War I propaganda, 46
military technology, repurposed for agriculture, 32, 40–43, 46, 157
Millay, Edna St. Vincent, 49–50
modernism: and Artists for Victory, 62; and *A Book of Mediterranean Food*, 50, 80–81; Fredric Jameson on, 80–81, 113; and historical referents, 82–83; and *How to Cook a Wolf*, 68, 71–72, 77–78; and imperialism,

modernism (cont.)
   80–81; and *My Year of Meats*, 142; politicized in mid-century literature, 10, 50
modernity: Anthony Giddens on, 37, 117; concept of late modernity, 7, 127, 202n33; and food system, 4, 9, 92; *see also* rural modernity
monoculture: and corn, 157–58, 209n18; hunger as result of, 103; *see also* commodity crops; factory farms; industrial agriculture
Monsanto: marketing rhetoric, 13–16; New Leaf potato, 124; and Rachel Carson, 14
Montanari, Massimo, 6, 160
Morrison, Toni: *A Mercy*, 192n6; critical appraisals of food tropes, 91–92; *Sula*, 105; *see also Tar Baby*
muckraking writers: Cather's critique of, 21–22; Cecilia Tichi on, 176n14; "civic protest" fiction, 131; and *The Jungle*, 11, 21, 41, 129–30; and *My Year of Meats*, 11, 129, 131–32; and *The Octopus*, 21
Munro, William, 124
*The Murder of Lidice* (Edna St. Vincent Millay), 50
Museum of Modern Art (MOMA), war poster exhibition, 62
*My Ántonia* (Willa Cather): anti-modernization rhetoric in, 26, 27; immigrant farmers decoupled from industrialization in, 27–28; nativism in, 28; pastoral tradition in, 25–26, 27–31; *see also* Cather, Willa; Jim Burden; *One of Ours*; *O Pioneers*
*My Year of Meats* (Ruth Ozeki): agribusiness and obstetrics analogized in, 119–20, 139–41; agribusiness/slow food conflicts in, 11; and *All Over Creation*, 150; allusions to military-industrial complex, 146–47; as almanac, 151–52; compared to *The Jungle*, 204n49; critical appraisal of, 118–19; DES as topic of Jane's documentary, 128–29, 136–41, 148; and documentary mode, 119–20, 128–29, 136–37, 141, 147–50; feedlot exposés as source material for, 131–36; as feminist narrative, 11, 118, 140–41; and globalization's impact on women, 138–39; hybrid narrative strategy, 118–19, 129, 137; information management in, 150–53; mapping of transpacific food routes, 118; meat-and-grain diet satirized in, 11; metaphorization of meat in, 148–50; as muckraking novel, 11, 129, 131–32, 148–50; as narrative of postindustrial food network, 131, 148; as parody of agribusiness marketing campaigns, 147–48; pastiche in, 11, 142, 148, 150, 153; personal vs. systemic registers in, 118–19, 128, 129, 132, 137, 139–42, 148; as postindustrial pastoral, 150–53; postmodern elements in, 142; slaughterhouse in, 136–38; as slow food/locavore narrative, 118; source material for, 128; and *Tar Baby*, 138–39; U.S./Japanese conflicts over meat as context for, 144–46; *see also All Over Creation*; Ozeki, Ruth

Nabhan, Gary Paul, *Coming Home to Eat*, 18, 121, 154–56
National Cattleman's Beef Association (NCBA), "Desire Beef" campaign, 147–48
nativism: in Cather's fiction, 20, 23, 28, 30; in U.S. national imaginary, 28
"Nebraska: The End of a Cycle" (Willa Cather), 26
neoliberalism: and consumerism linked in *Tar Baby*, 111–13, 115; and imperialism linked in *Tar Baby*, 10–11, 90, 102, 106–8, 111–15; and labor theory of value, 113; vs. national sovereignty in trade conflicts, 145; and World Trade Organization (WTO), 99; *see also* free trade; globalization; late capitalism
Nestlé Corporation, 109, *110*
networks: and food system, 8, 16–17, 124–26; and globalization, 8, 16–18, 160; local places as nodes in, 160; slow food/locavore movement reliance on, 18, 122, 124, 155, 158, 160–61, 163–64; and the supermarket, 17, 94–96
Neuhaus, Jessamyn: on M.F.K. fisher, 72; on processed foods, 73; on the supermarket, 95
*New Goose* (Lorine Niedecker): critique of food propaganda in, 55–56, 58, 61; impact of war on rural communities in, 49, 52–54, 56–59; luxury feeding vs. hunger in, 50; *see also* Niedecker, Lorine
New Nutrition, and home economics, 43
New Woman: and Cather's fiction, 22, 180n74; and *One of Ours*, 43; and World War I propaganda, 37
Niedecker, Lorine: abundance juxtaposed with hunger by, 10, 54–59; "Bombings," 51; concern with food access and social class, 49, 50, 56–59, 85; contradictions in U.S. food politics highlighted by, 49, 58–59; *For Paul and Other Poems*, 51–52; and impact of war on rural communities, 52–54, 56–59, 183n26; and impoverishment of rural workers, 56–59, 89; "In the great snowfall before the bomb," 52–56; on meat consumption, 74; modernism politicized by, 10; as Objectivist poet, 51–52, 59; as regional poet with global perspective, 51–54; on U.S. vs. European rations, 74; *see also New Goose*
*Nineteen Eighty Four* (George Orwell), 78
Nixon, Rob, 106

Norris, Frank: food production allegorized by, 21; and industrial agriculture, 6, 8; *The Octopus*, 21
North, Michael, 22, 43
*Notes on the State of Virginia* (Thomas Jefferson), 20
"Notes Toward a Supreme Fiction" (Wallace Stevens), 65, 186n75
*The Novel Art* (Mark McGurl), 21, 22, 27
nutrition rhetoric: and standardized diet, 43, 77; and World War II propaganda, 55–56

Objectivism, 51–52, 59
*The Octopus* (Frank Norris), 21
Office of Price Administration (OPA), 59–60
Office of War Information (OWI). *see* OWI (Office of War Information)
Ohnuki-Tierney, Emiko, 143–44
*The Omnivore's Dilemma* (Michael Pollan), 17, 158; and agriculture/military link, 157; contrasted with *Tar Baby*, 158; and corn-based monoculture, 157–58, 209n18; and culinary cosmopolitanism, 158; as locavore memoir, 17, 156, 157–58
*One of Ours* (Willa Cather): capitalist-farmer in, 44–45, 48; critical appraisal of, 32–33; and emergence of agribusiness, 44–46; Enid Royce as rural modernity symbol, 37, 43, 180n74; and gender roles, 43; georgic mode in, 46–47; indictment of industrialized food systems, 43–46; irony in, 33–34, 45; military-industrial complex articulated in, 12, 32, 40–43, 46–48; as narrative of rural war mobilization, 37, 54; omniscient narrator in, 33, 38, 39–41; pastoral tradition in, 32, 37–39; romanticism countered by realism in, 39–41, 46–47; rural modernity as theme in, 32, 37–38, 42–45; and slow food politics, 45; sources for, 33; war as boon for American farmers in, 44–45, 48, 56; *see also* Cather, Willa; Claude Wheeler; *My Ántonia*; *O Pioneers*
OPA (Office of Price Administration), food propaganda, 59–60
open-pollinated seeds, *see* seeds, open-pollinated
Opie, Frederick, 103
*O Pioneers* (Willa Cather): allusion to Whitman's poem, 19; capitalized farm in, 22–25; food globalization in, 24–25; and gender roles, 22, 23–24, 32; nativism in, 28; and pastoral tradition, 25–26; rural modernity in, 22–25; shift to industrial agriculture in, 22–25; U.S. expansionism as frame for, 19; *see also* Alexandra Bergson; Cather, Willa; *My Ántonia*; *One of Ours*

Orenberg, Cynthia Laitman, 129, 136, 140, 203n41, 206n68
organic agriculture, *see* sustainable agriculture
Orwell, George: *Animal Farm*, 50; food writing politicized by, 50; on inequities in food access, 78; and luxury feeding, 50, 64–65; *Nineteen Eighty-Four*, 78
Oulipo, and constraint-based food writing, 72
OWI (Office of War Information): food insecurity documented by, 61; and military/ agriculture alliance, 55; rationing promoted as egalitarian by, 61–62, *63*; war poster campaign, 62
Ozeki, Ruth L.; analogies of agriculture and communication media, 123–24, 126–27; analogies of people and plants, 118–20, 121, 201n12; hybrid narrative form, 119, 121–22, 150–53; interconnectedness as theme, 121–22; on *My Year of Meats*, 117; and postindustrial pastoral, 150–53; and slow food/locavore movement, 11, 118–22, 152; *see also All Over Creation*; *My Year of Meats*

Palumbo-Liu, David, 128, 142
Parrish, Dillwyn, 65, 67
*Partisan Review*, 64, 65
pastiche, in *My Year of Meats*, 11, 142, 148, 150, 153
pastoral tradition: in agribusiness discourse, 12–16; and Cather's fiction, 19–21, 25–26, 27–31, 32, 37–39, 166; georgic mode in, 9, 12, 20; idyllic mode in, 20; and locavore memoir, 18, 152, 157; and male writers, 8; Mark McGurl on, 27; as masking technology, 15–16; and networked society, 17; Raymond Williams on, 20, 28, 30, 32; scholarly treatment of, 8; and St. John de Crèvecoeur, 29–30; in war narratives, 38, 179n69; and Wendell Berry, 30; William Empson on, 142, 203n73; yeoman farmer in, 20, 25–26, 29–30; *see also* georgic mode; idyllic mode; postindustrial pastoral
patriarchy, meat system as metaphor for in *My Year of Meats*, 149
Penberthy, Jenny, 53–54
pesticides, 14, 44, 89, 127, 140
Petrini, Carlo, 121, 156
Philippon, Dan, 158
*The Physiology of Taste* (Jean Anthelme Brillat-Savarin), 65
"Pioneers, O Pioneers" (Walt Whitman), 19, 30
Pollan, Michael: on food system militarization, 13; *In Defense of Food*, 156; on "industrial

Pollan, Michael (cont.)
eating," 157–58, 209n19; *Second Nature: A Gardner's Education*, 156; and slow food, 121; *The Omnivore's Dilemma*, 17, 156–58
*Porkopolis* (Sue Coe), 124, *125*, 128, 132
postindustrial pastoral: and Cather's fiction, 48; concept of, 15–18, 48, 174n54; and Monsanto's marketing rhetoric, 15; and Ozeki's fiction, 150–53; and the supermarket, 17–18
postindustrial society: agriculture in, 1, 48, 117, 148; concept of, 7, 117, 202n26; and information management, 117–18; and networks, 8, 16–18, 124; and service industries, 48
postmodernism: aspects of in Ozeki's fiction, 119, 123, 142; and globalization, 7; and nature, 106
Pound, Ezra, 55
Pratt, Mary Louise, on the "imperial gaze," 104
precision farming, 117–18
processed foods: and corn-based monoculture in *The Omnivore's Dilemma*, 157–58; linked with war effort in World War II propaganda, 55–56; satirized in *How to Cook a Wolf*, 73–75, *74*, 77; and "Still Life #30," 2, *3*
propaganda, *see* World War I propaganda; World War II propaganda
Pynchon, Thomas, *The Crying of Lot*, 17–18

Quartermain, Peter, on Objectivism, 51

radio, as propaganda medium, 55
Ramazani, Jahan, 52, 182n21
rationing, *see* U.K. rationing program; U.S. rationing program
realism: countered by romanticism in *One of Ours*, 39–41, 46–47; social and magical mixed in *Tar Baby*, 95–98, 104–5, 111, 113–15
Reardon, Joan, 71
*Refuge* (Terry Tempest Williams), 139
reification of commodities, 101–2, 195n40
restaurants, *see* eating out
Roach, Joseph, 83
Robbins, Bruce: on contemporary fiction, 150; and reification of commodities, 101
Rockwell, Norman, "Four Freedoms" covers, 61
romanticism, countered by realism in *One of Ours*, 39–41, 46–47
Roosevelt, Franklin D.: "Four Freedoms" speech, 61; on U.S. government's role in democracy, 60
rum, imperial history of production, 99–101

rural communities: impact of war on explored by Niedecker, 49, 52–54, 56–59; as target of World War I propaganda, 33–36, 56; *see also All Over Creation*; Cather, Willa; *My Ántonia*; *One of Ours*; rural modernity
rural consumerism vs. agricultural productivity: in "Nebraska: The End of a Cycle," 26; in *One of Ours*, 42–43, 45
rural modernity: Alexandra Bergson as signifying, 22–25; and Cather's fiction, 9–10, 20, 22–23; concept of, 20, 175n7; and consumerism in "Nebraska: The End of a Cycle," 26; Enid Royce as signifying, 37, 43, 180n74; as theme in *One of Ours*, 32, 37–38, 42–45; *see also* modernity

Sakoh, Katsuro, 143
Saldívar, Ramón, 61
Sassen, Saskia, 7, 113
Savage, Elizabeth, 57–58
Schlosser, Eric: *Cogs in the Great Machine*, 205n57; *Fast Food Nation*, 132–36; and georgic mode, 12
*Second Nature: A Gardner's Education* (Michael Pollan), 156
seed patents, 15, 118, 127, 173n47
seed saving: as "open source biohacking," 163–64; and terminator gene, 16
seeds, open-pollinated: analogized to multiethnic families in *All Over Creation*, 119; compared to open-source software in *All Over Creation*, 127; as information archives, 123–24
*Sense of Place, Sense of Planet* (Ursula K. Heise), 7
Shukin, Nicole, 137
*Silent Spring* (Rachel Carson), 14
Sinclair, Upton: critique of meat industry, 11; food production allegorized by, 21; and industrial agriculture, 6; *The Jungle*, 11, 21, 41, 129–30, 132, 134
slaughterhouses, *see* feedlot exposés; feedlots; meat industry
Slow Food International, 156
slow food/locavore movement: and Carlo Petrini, 56; and culinary cosmopolitanism, 158; and "eating locally," 155, 158–59; and ethical eating, 158, 208n7, 209n19; and food-mile construct, 159, 210n28; and *How to Cook a Wolf*, 71; ideology coopted by others, 159; and Michael Pollan, 121; as nostalgic retreat from globalization, 160; and *One of Ours*, 45; published literature, 156; reliance on networks, 18, 122, 124, 155, 158, 160–61, 163–64; and Ruth Ozeki, 11, 118–22, 152; tenets and practices, 121, 156; and "victory gardens," 159

Smiley, Jane, 11, 117
social class: and food access in M.F.K. Fisher's works, 66–67, 72, 76–77; and food access in Niedecker's poetry, 49, 50, 56–59, 85; and food access in *Waiting for Godot*, 85–88
social realism, mixed with magical realism in *Tar Baby*, 95–98, 104–5, 111, 113–15
standardized diet: Cather's concern with, 43, 179n73; critiqued in *How to Cook a Wolf*, 69–72, 76–77; promoted by WFA, 77
Steinbeck, John, 11, 117
Stevens, Wallace, 65, 186n75
"Still Life #30" (Tom Wesselmann), 2, *3*
"Stopping by Woods on a Snowy Evening" (Robert Frost), 53
Stout, Janis P., 32
structuralist theories of food, 8–9
supermarket: as globally networked in *Tar Baby*, 17, 94–96; impact on food procurement habits, 36; and the postindustrial pastoral, 17–18; valued in *Farm City*, 162–63, 211n36
"A Supermarket in California" (Allen Ginsberg), 17
"supermarket pastoral," 17–18
sustainable agriculture: and Ozeki, 120–21; and urban farming, 162–65; and Wendell Berry, 9
Szalay, Michael, 60, 185n50
Sze, Julie: on Ozeki's analogies, 121; on Ozeki's treatment of DES, 138

*Tar Baby* (Toni Morrison); allusion to Enfamil controversy, 108–9; black diaspora as theme in, 91–92, 95–96, 109, 111; candy industry in, 91, 105, 106–9, 112; characters as consumers in global food chain, 92, 114; chocolate consumption/trade in, 93, 106–9, 113–14, 116; compared to Columbian rhetoric of Caribbean landscape, 104–5; contrasted with *The Omnivore's Dilemma*, 158; correspondences with tar baby folktale, 93–94, 114–15; critical appraisal of, 91–92; as critique of U.S. food power, 11, 109, 111, 115–16; as environmental justice text, 10, 116; function of food in, 96–99, 111; globalization as separating places of production and consumption in, 107–8; globalization's impact on women in, 116, 138–39; globally networked supermarket in, 17, 94–96; hunger as theme in, 93, 97–99; imperialism and neoliberalism linked in, 10–11, 90, 102, 106–8, 111–15; magical and social realism mixed in, 95–98, 104–5, 111, 113–15; Martinique as inspiration for, 102, 196n47, 197n60; and *My Year of Meats*, 138–39; as narrative of late capitalism, 107–8, 112–13; nature/culture schism in, 104–6; as postcolonial environmental narrative, 92, 94, 102–3, 111; setting of, 90–91; treatment of slavery in, 98–99; *see also* Morrison, Toni
technology: consumer goods as form of, 71; downplayed by world War I propaganda, 34, 37; impact on food transport, 24; modernist valuation of, 12–14; and Monsanto marketing rhetoric, repurposing of, 46, 166; as vital to agriculture, 2; *see also* biotechnology; GMOs; information technology; postindustrial society
Tichi, Cecilia: "civic protest" fiction, 131; on Eric Schlosser, 132; on muckraking, 176n14
transgenic crops, *see* GMOs (genetically modified organisms)
transnational: approach to literature of food, 12, 78, 166–67; and feminism in Ozeki's fiction, 118–19; food coalitions, 4, 155; framework for food power, 11, 90, 147, 166–67; and poetics, 52; *see also* culinary cosmopolitanism; globalization
Trout, Steven, 32
Turner, Frederick Jackson, 33

U.K. rationing program: and *A Book of Mediterranean Food*, 79–82; postwar continuation of, 78–79, 189nn110, 111; and *Waiting for Godot*, 83–85
United Nations, Millennium Development Goals (MFG), 90
*The Unsettling of America* (Wendell Berry), 30
urban farming: and *Farm City*, 161–65; and food production, 17; *see also* farming
U.S. Department of Agriculture (USDA), 50, 59
U.S. expansionism, and Cather's fiction, 10, 19
U.S. food power: dimensions of, 4, 10; domestic violence correlated with in *My Year of Meats*, 141, 144–45; and government support of agricultural production, 157, 209n18; historical precedents, 5; and late modernist literature, 88; likened to abusive motherhood in *Tar Baby*, 109, 116, 138; and World War I, 6, 44; and World War II, 10, 59, 184n45; *see also* food power
U.S. government: promotion of meat-and-grain diet in Japan, 142, 144; support of agricultural production, 157, 209n18
U.S./Japanese beef trade, conflicts over, 142, 144–45

U.S. Meat Export Federation (USMEF), 147–48
U.S. rationing program: and abundance rhetoric, 61, 64; conflicting mandates in, 56–57, *57*; and expansion of food exports, 64; food-waste-to-weapons campaign, 56, *57*, 60, 75; and "Home Front Pledge," 62–63; and *How to Cook a Wolf*, 69–70, 73–74, 76–77; ideology of hoarding in, 62, 64; points-based program, 60; promoted as egalitarian, 49, 61–62, *63*

victory gardens: and food security, 4; and locavore movement, 159; as patriotic, 60
Virgil, *Georgics*, 15, 27, 28, 46, 180n82
vitamins, in nutrition rhetoric, 55

*Waiting for Godot* (Samuel Beckett): food power symbolized by characters, 12; historical referents in, 82–85; and Irish Potato Famine, 83; luxury feeding vs. hunger in, 50, 86–89
Walcott, Derek, 97
Wallace, Kathleen R., 106
Wallace, Molly, 126–27
war: allied with agriculture, 13, 59; framed as adventure, 34–36; as new frontier, 33, 35; as profit center for agribusiness, 56; *see also* military-industrial complex; World War I; World War II
War Food Administration (WFA), *see* WFA
Warnes, Andrew: as food studies scholar, 165; on *Tar Baby*, 91, 93, 111–12
war posters: and Artists for Victory, 62; white housewife image in, 62–64
Wesselmann, Tom, "Still Life #30, 2, *3*
Westling, Louise, 20, 32
WFA (War Food Administration), 50
Williams, Raymond: and food studies, 9; on pastoral tradition, 20, 28, 30, 32
Williams, Terry Tempest, *Refuge*, 139
Willis, Elizabeth, 53, 54
Wilson, Woodrow, 35
Witt, Doris, 8, 95
Wolfe, Cary, 132
women: and globalization in *Tar Baby*, 116, 138–39; image of in war propaganda, 56, 58; and property rights, in *O Pioneers*, 23–25; and reproductive health in *My Year of Meats*, 128, 136–41; as target of war propaganda, 10, 56, 62–63; *see also* feminism; gender
World Bank, 99, 113
World's Fairs, and food futurism, 2, *3*, 71
World Trade Organization (WTO): 1999 Seattle protests referenced by Nabhan, 155; and neoliberalism, 99; and U.S./Japanese conflict over beef, 142, 145
World War I: amalgamation of weapons production and agribusiness, 13; and development of agribusiness, 44–45; impact on industrial agriculture, 32, 47; and U.S. food power, 6, 44
World War I propaganda: agriculture and industry linked in, 35, *36*; food equated to weaponry in, 46; and gender roles, 37; heroic fantasy promoted by, 33–36; and military-industrial complex, 46; and New Woman, 37; rural youth targeted by, 33–36, *36*; weapons technology downplayed by, 34, 37
World War II: atomic bomb, 51–54, 146; and culture of luxury feeding, 64–65, 186n75; references to in *Waiting for Godot*, 83–84; and U.S. food power, 10, 59, 184n45
World War II propaganda: contradictory food rhetoric, 49, 58–59, 64; countered by literature of food, 50–51, 181n9; critique of in Niedecker's poetry, 55–56, 58, 61; democracy equated with abundance in, 61; food linked with national security in, 49–50; image of women in, 56, 58; kitchen as target of, 10, 56; marketing discourse aligned with, 56, 58; nutrition rhetoric, 55–56; and OPA, 59–60; processed foods linked with war effort in, 55–56; role of radio in, 55; war posters, 62–64

yeoman farmer: in *Letters from an American Farmer* (St. John de Crèvecoeur), 29–30; in *Notes on the State of Virginia* (Thomas Jefferson), 20, 25–26, 30; as pastoral trope in *My Ántonia*, 30–31

Zimmerman, Anne, 68
Zukofsky, Louis, 51